TRUE TALES OF TWA FLIGHT ATTENDANTS
Memoirs and Memories
From the Golden Age of Flying

Stories compiled by:

Kathy Kompare
Stephanie Johnson

TELEMACHUS PRESS

This book is a work of non-fiction. The basic facts of the events and characters are reportedly true. The details presented here have been filtered through our memories or the memories of our co-workers. Some of the names have been changed, or not used, to protect personal identities.

TRUE TALES OF TWA FLIGHT ATTENDANTS;
Memoirs and Memories From the Golden Age of Flying
Copyright © 2022 Crew Kit Productions, LTD. All rights reserved, including the right to reproduce this book, or portions thereof, in any form. No part of this text may be reproduced, transmitted, downloaded, decompiled, reverse engineered, or stored in or introduced into any information storage and retrieval system, in any form or by any means, whether electronic or mechanical without the express written permission of the author. The scanning, uploading, and distribution of this book via the Internet or via any other means without the permission of the publisher is illegal and punishable by law. Please purchase only authorized electronic editions and do not participate in or encourage electronic piracy of copyrighted materials.

The publisher does not have any control over and does not assume any responsibility for author or third-party websites or their content.

Cover designed by Telemachus Press, LLC

Front cover art Copyright © iStock/108270315/AK2

Scene separator Copyright© iStock/1367839752/SpicyTruffe

Interior photographs used with permission as noted below each image.

Visit https://truetalestwa.com for more information, reviews and photos

Publishing Services by Telemachus Press, LLC
7652 Sawmill Road
Suite 304
Dublin, Ohio 43016
http://www.telemachuspress.com

ISBN: 978-1-951744-88-5 (eBook)
ISBN: 978-1-951744-88-5 (paperback)
ISBN: 978-1-956867-32-9 (hard cover)

Version 2022.10.11

Acknowledgments

We would like to thank all of the former Trans World Airlines flight attendants, their family members and company employees who took the time to share their memories and adventures with us. Wow, what a ride it was! As they say, "Truth is always better than fiction." You can't make this stuff up!

Table of Contents

Introduction	i
You Were Told Three Times	1
Nice Gams	3
Your Mind Is Where	4
Natural Blonde, Don't Tell	7
Who are you Jerry … You Own What	8
Crew Advice	10
I Can't Understand	10
And Who Is He Traveling With Today	11
Hijacked	12
My Biography	17
Baignade dans la Seine à Paris	21
100 K … Where	22
July 30, 1992, The Great Escape … From the Crash of Flight 843	25
TWA's Emergency Response Team	34
Cats On the Catwalk	35
The Yellow Rubber Ducky Pants	36
Don't Let Them Stop You	39
It Is a What	40
Good Morning Mr. Hughes	41
Princess Diana	43
What Is the Passenger Count	44
The Truth Hurts	45
Baby's Daddy	45
Still Gives Me Nightmares	46
Dining With The Rich and Famous	50
Pigs In a Blanket and We're Not Talking Appetizers	52
Escapades In the Desert	54
It Was a Long Hot Summer	56
#MeToo	57

The Gipper	59
Fashion 101	61
Simply Works	62
You Can't Make This Stuff Up …Tales From a TWA First Officer	63
All It Took Was a Dime	64
I'm Going to Die in Entebbe	66
POSTSCRIPT The G O A T	69
This Is the Last Straw	70
TWA Wants to Know My Hair Products	71
TWA Crew Hijacks Airplane	72
Voulez-vous un café	78
Time Change … Can Lead to Troubles	79
Howard Hughes and the Mechanics	82
Captain Who	83
Que Sera, Sera	84
TWA Application in the '60s	88
The Nightmares of Training	90
Perks of the Job	93
Oink	95
Dallas Cowboys	96
From Tragedy	98
The "Royals" or the Royals	98
Tienen Inodor Viajara or a Well-Traveled Toilet	100
Still Makes Me Sad Today	101
Rookie Mistakes … Learning the Ropes	102
The Vietnam Years 1965 to 1968	105
My Encounter with John F. Kennedy, Jr.	108
Maybe I Missed My Calling, Just Call Me Renee Fleming	110
Five Foot Nine, Three Inch Heels and a Bottle of Jack Daniels	111
To Be or Not To Be	113
You Brought a What on Board	114
Patsy and The Pope	115
The Golden Globes	117
Sparks On My First Flight	118

Red Carpet Treatment 119
Plunk Your Magic Twanger, Froggy 120
Terror on Takeoff 121
Make My Day 123
Just Another Flight Until… 124
We Had It All 126
I Lived the High Life 127
Why 130
Damien, Yes that Damien 130
A Sad Holiday 131
Ex-Boyfriend, All Male Crews Were My Saviors 132
Marine Style … OOH-RAH 136
They'll Get the Trucker First 138
George Hamilton 140
Boys Will Be Boys 141
I Am Only Worth How Much 141
I Always Wanted Wings 142
No You Don't … Get Out of My Way 145
Georgia On My Mind or Maybe It Is Just the Bumps 146
Christmas Eve … Bah Humbug 146
For All Flight Attendants Who Were Ever on Weight Check 149
From Subway to Burgers 150
The Rules Are the Rules 151
A Handful 152
Runner and We Aren't Talking Nike Here 152
The Flight Gods 154
New Yorkers Are Awesome 156
Best Forgotten 157
She Won't Remember You 158
Encanto 159
It's Vegas Baby 162
The Eyes of Warriors 165
Thank You to My GI Joe Hero 166
The Decision Was Made For Me 168

I Can See Clearly Now	170
Flying Miss Daisy	171
My Hiring Adventure	171
Tidy Whities Not So Tidy	175
Coins	177
The Most Beautiful Blue Eyes	177
Silhouettes	179
You Want to Live Where … You Want to be a Mother	180
Sonny	183
Angels Do Indeed Fly	184
Pope John Paul II	185
From the First Flight to the Last	189
World's Best Flight Attendant	190
Mission Instructions Received	191
Do You Know What She is Driving	192
Bang Bang	194
Third Hand	195
Blind As a Bat … Then Maybe Not	196
Everyone Needs a Big Brother and the Kindness of Strangers	197
It Was the Fifties … with Silver Tip Roast, Sleeping Berths and Movie Stars	200
Baby in an Umbrella Stroller … Remember Those	204
How Not to Celebrate Your Wedding Anniversary	205
My Mother Always Said It Is a Small World	206
What Is That Little Spot of Yellow	209
Fire … My Match Collection	211
In Sickness and In Health	212
Michelangelo in Cairo	213
Hermés … No Not Necessary	214
O Dark Hundred	216
She Was Past Cheeky	216
Poor Little Rich Girl	218
She Needed Some Tender Extra Care	220
Moon Over LA-LA Land	221

Bite Off a Nose or an Ear 223
Ralph Lauren Uniform..225
Don't Call Me Peter Pan...225
I Can Hardly Wait to Get to the Pub Tonight 227
Scuse Me..228
How it Began and Ended ... 1954–1959 229
Nine Carats and We Aren't Talking Carrots..232
From the World Famous to the Infamous 233
Should Have Waited..234
Thanks For the Memories 236
Four Levels of Anxiety...237
Jokester or Not..239
Just a Little Help From a Friend...239
My Father Is My Hero...241
Tipping and We Aren't Talking Restaurants 243
It Is True ... She Did Have Violet Eyes 244
Open Mouth and Insert Foot 245
You Light Up My Life ... Or Maybe Not! 246
It Was the '50s ... Fate ... One Inch to Tall...248
JFK-FCO-CDG-ORD-JFK or Twilight Zone 251
Just Another Day At the Office...252
A World-Famous Clown Doing His Thing 253
Once You Have Tasted Flight..254
The City of Angeles, TWA's First Boeing 747..259
The Perfectly Trained Little Pooch...263
Necessity Is the Mother of Invention...264
My First Flight ... A Night to Remember 266
Making New Friends 267
All Hail Our Pilots 269
Felix Unger Strikes...270
Monkey Lamp Blues..271
Remember Karma..276
Is This a Short Order Kitchen 278
It Might Be Very Expensive..279

Hey Little Mama	280
X Rated	280
Do I Want to What	282
Doodah Inspection … As Only the British Can Do	283
Take My Nose Please … Facelift and Nose	284
Fire They Shouted	285
How Sweet It Is to Out Fox Them	286
Welcome Home	286
Captain Bob, Do It Again	287
Paul Newman	289
Bomb Number Two	289
Here's Hoping You're Having a Wonderful Life	293
The Magical Mystery Tour	295
The Parisian Way	296
You Met Whom When You Were Getting a Massage	297
Justifiable Hamicide	297
Where Are My Sunglasses and Cane	299
The Music of the Night	300
What Happens In the Galley Stays In the Galley	301
So, You Want To Go Where	303
Going the Extra Mile	304
April 8, 1937, HOSTESS INSTRUCTION LETTER NO. 177	306
He Who Laughs Last	307
Thursday, May 25th, 1979	308
Where Has All the Glamour Gone	311
From Russia With Love	313
007	315
Unlimited Salad and Breadsticks	317
Coffee, Tea or	318
Only Socks	318
That Wonderful Feeling of Safety	319
Whore De Ovaries … Delicious	321
Yo Ho Ho and a Bottle of Rum	322
Club Soda	324

Is It a Bat, Is It a Squirrel, No It's What?..325
I Go to Rio ... No ... You've Got a Friend 327
Napolis..327
Sticky Notes Left Out Something 329
Mrs. Brisson 331
Greetings 332
Give Me Your Cash 333
Galley Disaster Turns to Buffet Style 334
Be Still My Heart..335
Plop, Plop ... Fizz, Fizz and We Aren't Talking Alka Seltzer 336
Batshit Crazy...337
Close Call..339
Wig or No Wig 340
1956 Grand Canyon Crash a Game Changer 341
Charade ... I Heard That Voice 342
Welcome Aboard 343
How Many Dead Bodies Can One Flight Attendant Have On Flights 344
Did I Really Hear Him Correctly..345
I Can't Get This to Work 348
Feeding the Multitude 348
Bobble Head 349
Fire In Pants..351
One Stormy Flight 352
Removal of a Violent Passenger 353
Sir Richard Starkey...356
Barf Bags Can Be Used For All Kinds of Reasons...357
Buh-bye...358
Lotus Position...359
We Didn't Like It 360
Lunch or What 361
Plenary Indulgences..362
From Pinball to Trashing..363
Put It Where 366
Remembrances 367

We All Need a Hug..372
July 17, 1996, A TWA Jetliner Bound for Paris EXPLODES 373
That Fateful Day 374
Was It Fate..378
Flight 800 and Her Lessons of Love...380
Sunglasses for the Sea..388
Remembering TWA's employees, family members and passengers
    who perished in the crash of Flight 800, July 17, 1996 391
In Conclusion 395
Up, Up and Away, TWA 399

Introduction

Did you ever wonder what would be in a flight attendant's diary? This is a "diary" like none other!

Photo of TWA 747 courtesy of the TWA Museum.

AS YOU WILL read in the hundreds of true stories we have collected, this was a rarefied position of being a Trans World Airlines (TWA) flight attendant who the company referred to as "hostesses." They had been selected literally from hundreds of thousands of applicants who applied each year for a very few positions. As the cream of the crop, so to speak, TWA would mold all in training to have every hair in place, nails perfectly polished, makeup done professionally and uniforms that showed off legs in high heels.

Those who were lucky enough to be chosen flew around the world, wearing designer uniforms from the likes of Don Loper, Pierre Balmain, Oleg Cassini, Stan Herman, Valentino, and Ralph Lauren, plus the benefits of staying in some fabulous hotels in Europe and the Orient.

Yes, the glamour years of the '50s, '60s, '70s and early '80s when being introduced as a TWA flight attendant "stopped" current conversation, and people wanted to know where you were flying, what celebrities you had on flight, and were the pilots and flight attendants as cozy as reported? We'll let you know.

With white gloves and hats, to paper dresses with themes, "no we do not kid here," Valentino hot pants showing off leather boots or maybe it was the other way around, and lastly Ralph Lauren's timeless classic uniform which was surpassed by no other airline, we became known as the "epitome of sophistication" in the airline industry.

This was in the day and age when we walked through an airport or a hotel lobby in our uniform and people would stare at us, "really," as if you were a celebrity. Probably most men secretly dreamt of dating a flight attendant and most women wish they had been lucky enough to have flown as one too. It was the day and age of, if you couldn't marry a movie star then your next best choice was a TWA flight attendant.

We actually became foreign correspondents. Want to know about a hotel or a great restaurant in a particular city, where you can find a deal on a designer purse (never did know if they were stolen, but that is a tale for another day), and what you need to tour in a foreign country or here in the states. Just ask one of us, if we didn't know there would be someone on the crew who would. Sorry we couldn't help you with this perk in Las Vegas, just tell them you were a TWA flight attendant and viola you had seats to the casino shows by the stage, gratis of course. Shopping, touring and lots of eating out were all part of the job experience. So many things to see and do and so little time!

Now, let us describe to you how traveling was in the glamour age. Imagine seats with lots of legroom and sleeping berths in the '50s. In the '60s the seats were wider and guess what? You could recline them without starting a fist fight with the passenger behind you. In the '70s lumbar supports were added to the seats. Sound like what you have now in a luxury car? Ah and something you would never see today, pillows and blankets, in first class and coach.

In 1965, TWA hostesses distributed chewing gum and candy prior to takeoff. They handed out 1.5 million pieces of gum and 81,000 pounds of hard candy! Would you believe that a bassinet was available on flight for infants and baby food? Plus, they even had cartons of milk with sterilized nipples for the little ones.

TWA provided magazines, writing paper and postcards for their passengers. Another little perk, if you returned the addressed postcard or letter to the hostess, they would give it to the agent who met the flight for him/her to mail gratis for you. Junior hostess and pilot wings were always passed out to the children and books to read.

Then there was the food. Not only was your cabin crew groomed and looking like movie stars, but they also knew how to prepare and serve some of the best food in the airline business. From Beluga caviar and pâté, chateaubriand sliced on a serving cart, to filet mignon and rack of lamb cooked to order in convection ovens. Yes, we were the only airline who cooked our steaks and lamb in first class to order. Think au gratin potatoes swimming in cheese and cream! Followed by ice cream sundaes, strawberry trifle and imported cheeses.

For the TWA flight attendants and their passengers these years were truly the glamour years of the jet age. TWA was the airline of choice for Hollywood jet setters and the rich and famous. Why? Because Howard Hughes the provocative businessman, aviator, and motion picture producer and director promoted his airline with the movie and entertaining industry. Then why wouldn't he when he made movies that were box office smashes.

It was not unusual to have famous movie stars, TV personalities, sports legends and teams, Princesses and Princes, rock stars and politicians on flight. In fact, you became rather blasé about having them on board. Not that we didn't enjoy meeting them, talking with them and in some cases even going out with them. But we quickly learned that they liked to talk with us, hang out in the galley and have fun too.

Just asking, how many of you have played cards with President Harry Truman, had President Ronald Reagan do his Jimmy Stewart imitation for you, or chatted with President Richard Nixon? And yes, even Popes flew on chartered TWA planes which were given the nickname of Traveling With Angels. Have you ever prayed with a Pope and had him bless you? Some of us have.

But it wasn't always peaches and cream! We were putting hundreds of thousands of people in metal containers at 33,000 feet in the air. What could wrong? We'll tell you! These are true stories that will make you laugh out loud, and some will bring you to tears. Others you'll find yourself shaking your head in disbelief. From crazy layovers, sex on the plane, galley disasters, sexual harassment, death in flight, terrible crashes and frightening evacuations, great passengers to yes, the rude, the drunks and the truly crazies. And guess what? Even one about how a crew hijacks their own plane! Lastly, we can't forget some tales about Howard Hughes. We told you these were crazy times.

To say that this was not another day at the office with the same faces and possible humdrum would be putting it mildly.

Our flying careers were the "best education" that money could "never" buy! From the Midwest to the Middle East, TWA flight attendants enjoyed a life that few will ever know. Now sit back, relax and no we're not going to say, "Fasten your seat belt," but you might want to when you read these amazing rides.

Welcome aboard …

P.S. You thought we might be exaggerating about the rich and famous we had on board. This just barely scratches the surface.

How would you like to meet and rub shoulders, so to speak, with some of these people that we did? Get ready here we go … Jane Russell, Marilyn Monroe, Elizabeth Taylor and Richard Burton (they didn't have to go through international customs at JFK with the commoners, they were escorted by our PR people), Ginger Rogers, Katherine Hepburn, Jimmy

Stewart, Henry Fonda and Gene Kelly (three of the nicest gentlemen you would ever want to meet!). Michael Jackson and the Jackson Five putting on a performance in the galley for us (yes really happened), John F. Kennedy Jr., Warren Beatty, Jane Fonda, Sean Connery, Roger Moore and George Hamilton. Do we have to say this—all gorgeous. Have you ever met Madonna, Paul McCartney, Ringo Starr and Duran Duran? We did!

Dallas Cowboys quarterback "Dandy Don" Meredith, charismatic Muhammad Ali, Jerry Buss owner of the Lakers, Leonard Tose owner of the Philadelphia Eagles and his coach Dick Vermeil, football legend Jim Brown, Wimbledon tennis stars Bjorn Borg, Martina Navratilova and Jimmy Connors (what a doll and a great Dad too), Indy 500 winners, Bobby Unser and Al Unser Jr. (both super nice, must run in the family.)

Yul Brenner (complete gentleman), Danny Kaye (really blue eyes and loved to chat), Joan Crawford (played cards with on the plane and left the lav cleaner than when she first went in), Bob Hope, Milton Berle, Mickey Rooney, Ann Miller, Vincent Price and Julia Childs who always said she loved our food!

Christopher Reeve (Superman and he was if you get our drift), Susan Lucci (All my Children), Omar Sharif (gorgeous brown eyes, liquid pools), Paul Newman (blue eyes that mesmerize you), Barbara Streisand, Chris Kristofferson, Donna Summers, Arnold Schwarzenegger, Maria Shriver, David Letterman, Michael Keaton (Batman!), Henry Mancini, Charlton Heston and Liam Neeson.

Meg Ryan, Kelly McGillis, Little Richard (he did wear makeup), Reba McEntire (as nice as she appears to be on talk shows), Rudolph Nureyev (always ordered his usual, "one cube of ice in my champagne darling"), Naomi Campbell and Lauren Hutton (both totally glam), Hugh Hefner on a TWA charter aircraft full of bunnies, of course!

Farah Fawcett (totally true, had gorgeous hair), Ryan O'Neal, Chuck Berry (Maybellene), Bette Midler, Ann Margaret, Lily Tomlin, Joan Rivers and her beloved dog Spike. Ton Loc, Van Halen, Vince Gill, Cher (just what you would think, sophisticated) and Axel Rose (Guns and Roses, rock on).

Burt Lancaster and Steve McQueen (what movie stars should look like). Then we have the famous "Rat Pack" of Dean Martin (great kidder), Sammy

Davis Jr., Joey Bishop and Peter Lawford (all so much fun), Liberace (just how you would picture him), Diana Ross (such a lady).

How about New Kids on the Block, The Temptations, Dick Clark, Gloria Gaynor, Alice Cooper, Gladys Knight, Toni Braxton, Broadway and movie stars Julie Andrews and Carol Channing. And we don't want to forget Keith Richards of the Rolling Stones who likes Jack and coke.

Some mundane people (just kidding) as in Princess Grace of Monaco (stunning and gracious), and her children Prince Albert, Princess Caroline and Princess Stephanie who all had exemplary manners.

Patti LaBelle (one of the most down to earth people you would want to meet and fabulous jewelry), Neil Armstrong and John Glenn (both gentlemen), Dan Rather, Paul Anka, Burt Bachrach, Michael Douglas (doesn't get any better) except for Cary Grant!

Billy Dee Williams (very handsome), Roy Rogers and Dale Evans (Giddy up), Red Skelton (loved to talk with us), Sophia Loren (stunning woman), Peter Townsend (The Who), Howard Cosell (I'm telling it like it is), 1978 NY METS team (LAAARRRYYY, Mets fan will get it), Geraldo Rivera, Dixie Carter and Hal Holbrook and one of the cutest and sweetest Dolly Parton.

Jack Lemon and Tony Randall (they were the Odd Couple), James Brown, Mac Davis, Peggy Fleming (Olympic Gold figure skater), Nancy Lopez (American golfer who won 48 events and three majors), Rosie Grier (Rams, Fearsome Foursome and yes did do needlepoint), Dan Rowan and Dick Martin (Laugh-In), Chicago Bulls, Three Dog Night, Harry Bellefonte, Tony Bennett, David Hasselhoff, Loni Anderson, Andy Williams, Minnesota Fats and Henry Winkler (The Fonz).

Andre the Giant, Helen Mirren, Al Pacino, Betty White (we all loved her), Tommy Lasorda and Hall of Famer Dave Debusher, Jesse Owens (Four-time Olympic Gold Medalist at the Berlin games in 1936), Jack Nicklas, a no name golfer, just kidding, he was the greatest and a really nice man too.

Antonio Banderas, Steve Jobs, Steve Wozniak, Bobby Kennedy Jr., Hank Arron (Hammerin' Hank, a gentleman), Meadowlark Lemon, Mia Farrow (always sweet), Andre Previn, Wayne Newton, Ray Charles (great sense of humor), Patty Duke, Polly Bergen, Phyllis Diller, Zsa Zsa Gabor and Rosalind Russell.

Ester Williams, John Stamos, Ed McMann (Here's Johnny, brings three-pound box of chocolates for the hostesses), William Shatner (Doesn't care when you spill wine on him), Gloria Vanderbilt (high society at its best), Marlow Thomas (That Girl), Phil Donahue (talk show host extraordinaire).

And more: Eli Wallach, La Toya Jackson, Dyan Cannon, Diahann Carroll, Arthur Godfrey, Dick Cavett and the beloved Carol Burnett. We'll stop now! Really just too many to list.

We only have one question: So, who did you meet at work?

Now enjoy our diary!

TRUE TALES OF TWA FLIGHT ATTENDANTS

You just can't make this stuff up!

You Were Told Three Times

I WAS WORKING a flight from Los Angeles to New York and we had a full load of passengers. It was customary before the flight for the flight attendants to go up to the cockpit and introduce themselves to the captain and tell him where you were working on the plane.

On this particular day, I was working the first class cabin position, and the captain told me that he wanted to know if there were any problems on the plane concerning commissary items or inflight, after we were airborne. I was thinking to myself, "Where have you been on a number of my flights," but didn't say that, thanked him and said I would definitely tell him if we had any problems.

I have to admit here I had a name for the really senior captains. I called them, "ballbusters." They just didn't let the public get away with too much and they were great to fly with. You knew they had your back. Note: The inelegant expression of ballbusters here is meant as a total compliment.

Everything was going along very nicely in flight, no problems in the front or the back of the plane. We're happy the passengers are happy. And then ... a passenger in the last row of first class lights up a cigar. I know you are all staring at this page now. A CIGAR! Yes, we let people smoke pipes and cigars on the plane along with cigarettes then, but there was a caveat to the pipes and cigars. If anyone complained about the odor the smoker would have to put it out. This was even specified in the *TWA Ambassador Magazine* that was in every seat pocket on the plane. I had the page number memorized.

Within minutes a call light comes on in first class. I went back to answer it and it was a female passenger, who asked that the cigar be put out. I acknowledged her request and went back to the cigar smoker. "Sir, I'm sorry but someone has complained about the smell of your cigar and I'm going to have to ask you to put it out." I immediately turned around and left because I knew that our male passengers were much more agreeable to complying with a request if you didn't stand over them like their mother or the school principal.

How is my request going? Not well. I go back to the cigar smoker about five minutes later and say, "Sir, I know you must be enjoying your cigar, but I'm going to have to ask you again to please put it out because someone has complained about the odor. Thank you." And again, I leave.

Another five minutes goes by and the cigar smoke is still wafting through the cabin. I have to admit here that I was getting ticked now. I walked back and said, "Sir, you have to put out the cigar now." I take out the *TWA Ambassador Magazine* from his seat pocket, flip to page twenty-nine, hand him the magazine and run my finger under the rules where it says, "you have to put out your cigar or pipe if someone complains."

I then said, "Please put out the cigar now." He looks at me and says, "No." At which point I said to him, "Do I understand you correctly that after you have been asked three times to put out your cigar you are not going to put it out?" He says, "Yes, I'm not putting it out."

Without skipping a beat I'm off to the cockpit. I explained to the captain what I just told you and he said, "I'll be out in a minute." Finally, I have my back up!

A few minutes later the captain appears in the cabin with his jacket and hat on which always means they mean business. It was very easy to find the offending passenger because you could just follow the smell and the smoke.

The captain stops at the passenger's seat and introduces himself and then he says, "My lead flight attendant told me that she has asked you three times to put out your cigar. Is that right?" The passenger is just staring at him now and then says, "Yes." The captain says, "I'm the captain and I'm only going to ask you once. Now put out the cigar." To which the man replies, "No."

The captain then says, "You were asked three times nicely by the flight attendant to put out your cigar and now I have asked you once and you still don't want to put out your cigar. Is that right?" This idiot obviously doesn't realize that he is now dealing with one of our ballbusters! He looks at the captain and says, "I'm not putting it out."

The captain turns around, goes back into the cockpit, and gets the CO2 fire extinguisher that is located there. He comes back out, walks down the aisle to the arrogant idiot who won't put out his cigar. Breaks the seal on the canister, pulls up the nozzle, presses the release button and fires off a stream of CO2 at the cigar in the man's hand. The cigar is now covered in white residue from the CO2 and it is out! The captain takes the cigar out of his hand and says, "We won't be smoking any more cigars, will we." Turns around and leaves. As he walks by the galley, he hands me the cigar and says, "Would you please throw this away."

I admit it, I had a really big grin on my face and was trying not to laugh out loud! That was the best thing I had ever seen happen to a jerk on the plane. Trust me I didn't go back out into the cabin for at least ten minutes. That passenger never said another word to me. He knew he was dealing with a ballbuster who would probably have him arrested in New York if he created any more problems. Thank you, captain!

Note: CO2 residue does not hurt the skin, clothing etc. It easily brushes off. But it sure puts out cigars!

Nice Gams

I WAS USING one of my company passes for personal travel and was seated in first class. A man sat down next to me, and I just smiled and acknowledged him with a slight nod of the head and a hello. Then I went back to my book.

After we were airborne, I figured out that he was a pilot from his conversation with one of the flight attendants, who was working the flight. I wasn't in the mood to be chatting up another company employee, and kept my nose in my book and sipped my cocktail.

Then the salad course started and I could no longer keep silent, so I started some light chit chat with him, "Oh, you're a pilot for TWA. Where are you based? I'm based in Chicago." He looks at me and immediately says,

"Do you know flight attendant so and so?" I'm deliberately not divulging her real name here, but will just refer to her now as Sue. I said, "Yes, most everyone knows Sue. Why do you ask?"

"Well, I just flew with her and she is quite the woman." I'm thinking to myself, yes she is. Now picture tall, statuesque, always every hair in place and she wore three-inch heels with her uniform skirt. To say the male passengers were putty in her hands would be putting it mildly.

But it only gets better from here. The pilot says, "She comes up to the cockpit on the ground and walks in to introduce herself. The captain turns around and looks her up and down and says, 'Nice gams.' She looks at him and doesn't even flinch and says, 'I'll talk with you later' and leaves."

He then continues, "After we were airborne for about two hours, there is a knock on the cockpit door, and the engineer opens it and who walks in but Sue. She sits down in the ACM's seat (additional crew member seat which is directly behind the captain's), hikes up her skirt, takes her legs and proceeds to wrap them around the captain's neck. And then she says, 'I thought you might want to get a closer look?'" I KNOW, I was trying not to spit out my food now.

Then he says, "The captain looks over at me and says, 'In our next contract we are getting swivel seats.'" I thought I was going to lose it! I must have laughed for two minutes straight.

A few weeks later I'm in the hangar signing in for my flight and who appears? Miss Gams. I had to know if the story was true. I repeated it to her and she just gave me a little smile and said, "Yes. Wonder if they will get swivel seats in their next contract?"

Your Mind Is Where

I WAS BASED out of ORD (Chicago O'Hare) and had flown with the other two flight attendants on my crew many times before, so there was great comradery between the three of us. We were flying a Boeing 727 regular which held sixty-nine in the coach and twelve in first class. One might say it was cozy. We also were flying with the same cockpit for all three days of our trip. This was highly unusual because TWA had a chastity chairman who made sure that the cabin crews and cockpit never flew together that long. Now I'm kidding here, but actually it was unusual for us to fly on a domestic three-day trip with the same cockpit for all three days and for them too.

So, day one started with some kidding around, day two we were all starting to really tease one another and by day three nothing was too sacred not to poke fun at. It had gotten so bad that our captain, who sported a small thin mustache, had been nicknamed Herr Captain. I know bad pun on Herr Hitler, but he took it all in good fun.

Now picture day three. We had been flying many legs on days one and two, and at this point in time we were getting slightly punch drunk with fatigue. I'm working the first class door in Oklahoma City, greeting and meeting our passengers, and checking their boarding cards to make sure they were on the right flight. When what happens? A tall, thin, clean cut, young man in a suit with a white shirt and no tie squeezes between a boarding passenger and me. Yikes! Tight squeeze!

There was a bulkhead at this door blocking my view down the aisle, but we only had a load of approximately forty-five people with no one in first class, so finding this yahoo wouldn't be difficult.

A few minutes later there were no other passengers boarding and I walked around the bulkhead to go find my new friend, who thinks he doesn't need to show me his boarding card. Easy find, he was sitting in the last row of first class in a window seat.

Trying to maintain my cool and be professional, I walked over to him, slightly bend down and said, "Sir, may I see your boarding card please." He continues to look out the window and ignore me. I asked him the same question again. No response and he didn't even look at me. I'm getting pissed to put it bluntly! I step into the row, lean down further, tap him on his shoulder and say, "Sir, I want to see your boarding card and I want to see it NOW!" Total soldier's stripes in my voice! It was obvious that I wasn't fooling around anymore. I meant what I said.

He looks up at me and says, "Do you know who I am?" What flashes through my mind was, I don't give a damn who you are, but I controlled myself from saying it. Instead, I said, "No, I do not know who you are, but I want to see your boarding card now."

This guy looks at me and says, "My mind is up here," holding his arm and hand straight up over his head, "and everyone else's mind is down here," now lowering his arm and hand back down to his waist. "My mind can control the world and the Russians and Red Chinese are after me."

I looked at him and without skipping a beat said, "You're right, you don't need a boarding card." At which point I immediately went up to the cockpit, closed the door behind me and said, "LOON UP IN FIRST CLASS." Now remember we had been kidding around with the cockpit crew for three days. Of course, they all laughed thinking I was kidding. I said, "I'm serious!" When I explained to the captain what this man had said, he replied, "Get the agent and get him off of here right now! He's not coming with us even if he has a ticket. And after he's off make sure he didn't leave anything strange on the plane."

I go out to the agent at the podium and tell him the captain wants this loon of a passenger off the plane. The agent looks at me and says, "Oh, he has been trying to get on planes all morning around here." I'm thinking what the heck is wrong with you people? Why aren't you watching out for him? But I kept my mouth shut.

The agent followed me down the jetway and I stayed clear of the aisle when he was escorting Mr. Looney Tunes off. Then I went to check out under the seat areas, in the seat pockets, overhead bins, and even in what we called a dog house where the oxygen bottles were stored behind the last row of first class. Everything seemed to be normal, so I went into the cockpit and sat down in the seat behind the captain and said, "Everything is fine, the loon is off the plane now." I also mentioned that the agent had told me, that this man had been getting on airplanes all morning and being removed.

Well, we had about another ten minutes before departure, so I'm wasting time in the cockpit because I didn't have any passengers in first class, when one of my flying partners came into the cockpit. She says to me, "You've got the strangest passenger in first class." Before she could say anything else, I said, "Oh no. His mind is up here and yours is down here." She looks rather startled and says, "Yes."

I thought the captain had an electrical cattle prod under his seat. He jumps up and leaves the cockpit. I'm now standing out in the aisle seeing this same kook and the captain is marching out to the terminal to have a tête-à-tête with the gate agent. Would have liked to have been a fly on the wall for that one.

The agent returns with an airport policeman and they escort off our passenger, whose mind is up here and yours is down there. Who knows if they arrested him? Not my problem then.

Note: Years later I was working as an instructor for Lockheed Martin who had the contract to train all of the new federal TSA agents after 9/11. I used to tell some of my flying stories to the students to keep the classes from being too boring, and this one in particular was a good way to explain why profiling passengers by how they look doesn't work. Nice looking young man, in a suit, white shirt, clean cut haircut, shaved and crazier than a loon!

Natural Blonde, Don't Tell

I WAS THE FSM (flight service manager) on a Lockheed-1011 from Los Angeles to Dulles airport which is outside of Washington D.C. This flight was always full and always rushed. By the time we landed in Dulles I was desperate to use the facilities.

My jump seat was in first class, and the minute we touched the ground and turned off of the active runway, I jumped up and ran into the lav directly behind me. I finished, stood up, tucked my shirt hem under my chin while straightening my shirttail, with my pantyhose around my knees. Didn't believe in undies then. No judging!

Picture me now facing the lav door, when a man who had been seated in first class opens it. OMG! He quickly closed the door, went back to his seat and I stood there thinking that there was absolutely no way I could come out of that lav.

But … I still had to make the landing announcement and open the first class door for the agent who was meeting the flight. So, what is a girl to do? I decided that a sense of humor would be the way to go.

I left the lav and walked directly to his seat and whispered in his ear, "Just don't tell anyone that I'm not a natural blonde." He burst out laughing and my guess is that he still tells this story too.

Who are you Jerry … You Own What

IT WAS JUST another day in a flight attendant's life. We had a full load of passengers and knew we were going to be very busy. Of course, this was in the days when flying was a little more glamorous and lots of real food was served. But then I digress …

We finished our first class service and the passengers were relaxing now watching a movie. My flying partner and I were relaxing too, if you want to call it that. She was sitting on her jump seat which only held one flight attendant and I was sitting on a metal carrier. Yes, you read right, a metal carrier. This was a metal box that held supplies such as soft drinks, wine etc. that we would pull out from a work area, put a pillow on top of it and that became a seat. Surprisingly, we had pillows for our passengers then. Ah yes, my seat was so comfy, but then that is what we had to do if we wanted to sit together and kibitz.

Well, who appears in our luxury suite, yes I'm being sarcastic, but one of our passengers with a drink in hand. In those days, pre 9/11, passengers could get up and stroll around without the flight attendants telling them to sit down all of the time. And yes, in those days, the passengers loved talking with us and we even liked talking with them. Something that I noted has completely gone by the wayside in aviation now. However, let me continue …

We had a passenger manifest, but would also take names in first class when we were taking dinner orders. There was no one of note meaning of movie star power etc., it just seemed to be your usual group of businessmen in first class. So here we are, the three of us chatting away, when the flight engineer comes out of the cockpit, yes to use the lav. He looks over at the three of us and has a rather quizzical look on his face. Nothing was said and frankly it was a very quick glance.

My flying partner was a real "kidder" and loved bantering with the passengers and this man was now open prey, since he was in our "luxury suite." We were all laughing and teasing one another. In fact, I remember her telling him, "Hey don't bad mouth your first wife if you want to get another date. Women don't like it when you badmouth the first wife." And of course, we all laughed!

Approximately fifteen minutes passed, and I excused myself and went up to the cockpit to see if they needed anything. The flight engineer says, "Is that Jerry Buss who you are talking to?" To which I replied, "Who is Jerry Buss?" The flight engineer rolls his eyes and says, "Never mind."

Not being particularly interested in continuing the conversation I left the cockpit, got the passenger manifest and resumed sitting on my metal box. I looked at the passenger manifest and there was no Jerry Buss on it. Sneaky little devil was flying under an assumed name.

So quite casually I said to this man, "Are you Jerry Buss? The flight engineer asked me. And if you are, are you a famous director or producer that we should know?" Aside: we were flying from JFK to LAX, so Hollywood would have been a good guess.

He looks a little like a deer in headlights now and says nothing. However, I'm not ready to let him off the hook. "Oh, come on, who are you? And are you famous?" Of course, my flying partner now is chiming in and saying, "Who are you? And who is Jerry Buss?"

After a few minutes of continuing harassment on our parts about his identity he finally said, "Well, yes I'm Jerry Buss." You know where this is going. "So, you are Jerry Buss. But who is Jerry Buss?" He finally says and I might add sheepishly, "Well, I own the LA Lakers, The Forum and the LA Kings." At this point my flying partner says, "Jerry, I'll repeat this one more time. Remember now just because you have money and hang out with rich athletes you can't bad mouth the first wife."

I thought Jerry was going to fall over laughing now! Anyway, Jerry was a really nice man, took our kidding as it was meant, all in good fun, and also gave it back to us. Rest in peace Jerry and thanks for a great memory.

P.S. Bet you are wondering? He did offer us free tickets.

Crew Advice

MY FLYING PARTNER and I were newbies. I had been flying for about two months and she four. Everything was going along fine in coach until a male passenger came back to go to the lav and suddenly fainted!

She grabbed a bottle of oxygen and was turning it on, while I got the mask over his nose and mouth. Then she said, "Call the cockpit to let them know." This being my first, "first aid" emergency experience, I was shaken up.

I called the cockpit and the flight engineer answered, "Boiler room." I said, "This is Nancy, we're administering oxygen to a passenger in the rear!" There was a slight pause and the reply was, "Honey, try his mouth."

I Can't Understand

ONE OF MY first layovers, when I was a brand-new flight attendant, was in London. I received a phone call which I later found out was my crew call. Note: A crew call was always given to each flight attendant to let you know that your flight was operating on time.

Here's what happened: I answered the phone and a woman said something to me which I asked her to repeat. She repeated it again and I said, "Miss, I can't understand you. Can you please put someone else on the phone?" A gentleman came on and told me it was my crew call. I said,

"Thanks, I couldn't understand a word that woman was saying. Was she speaking English?" He replies, "Oh, indeed she was sir, the problem was you were hearing it in American."

And Who Is He Traveling With Today

I WAS THE lead flight attendant in first class. Greeting the passengers as they came on, getting them settled in first class and then taking their meal orders. After we were airborne and serving drinks, I started to talk with a passenger in 1C (first row, aisle seat). He looked to be approximately forty-five and was traveling with a young blonde woman, maybe twenty-five who obviously was not acting like she was his daughter. You know the hand holding and those baby blues batting their eyelashes at him.

I told him that he looked like Joe Montana, also known as "Joe Cool," quarter back for the San Francisco 49ers. Then we started to talk about sports, and went on to Indy car racing where we each had friends who were very involved in that sport. End of story. Not! Oh, this gets so good!

Back story: now we would bid for our flights each month and usually would fly different routes from month to month for a variety of reasons. What do you think are the odds that you would have the same flight attendant on your flight two months later going to an entirely different destination? Maybe a million in one shot?

OK, now we are getting to the good part ... I'm standing at the forward door doing my usual greet and meet, "Hello, how are you today, etc.," when who appears on the jetway at the door, but Mr. Joe Montana look alike. I immediately recognized him, since we had had a long conversation about Indy car racing and the fact that he did look like Joe Montana.

"Well, hi. Nice to see you again," I say. His eyes looked like they had gotten two sizes larger, you know that look when someone is caught, but he is still mister cool. How he remembered my name is beyond me, but under severe pressure people can do extraordinary things and he says, "Mary, I want you to meet my wife." And at this point he turns to the woman behind him and says, "This is Mary, I just flew with her."

Oh, what a delicious moment in time. The wife was not blond, was not twenty-five, but probably forty and brunette. I smiled at her and said, "Oh, it is lovely to meet you." I was chuckling inside and wondering what his blood pressure reading was about that time? Now I was having so much fun in the moment. Oh, what are the odds?

As soon as I had a break, I pulled my flying partner aside and told her what was going on. She loved it too. Caught red handed! Should I blow his cover? No let him stew in his own juices. I'm sure fear was pulsing through his veins. Is she going to let on to my wife? Will she ask about my "blonde" daughter?

Ah, it was so much fun … watching him squirm. Just like a rat in a trap! As his wife meanwhile sat there and enjoyed her cocktail and meal, while I fawned over her.

I know you are all asking the question now, did I finally blow his story wide open? No, I felt sure his wife probably would find out on her own. They always do. But as he deplaned, he said, "Thank you." And we know why …

So, my darlings, if you are planning on bringing your mistress with you on a business trip, or just taking a fling with her, we know following your heart, it would probably be a good idea to go on separate flights. Just a suggestion.

I should have bought a lottery ticket that day. Odds!

Hijacked

IT WAS THE first week in April 1970, when the few hijacked planes in the U.S. headed straight for Cuba. There was really no training for either the flight attendants or the cockpit, about how to handle these situations. The flight attendants were only told to try to keep them out of the cockpit for as long as possible by talking with them, don't give the hijacker alcohol, if you can call the cockpit to let them know you have a hijacker on board that is good, and finally not to jeopardize your life. Oh, easy breezy, wrong!

This particular flight was a nonstop from San Francisco to Pittsburgh, on a Boeing 707 aircraft. We had an uneventful boarding and the final passenger count was just over half full. Almost immediately after takeoff a young man, with disheveled blond hair, wearing zippered boots, was branded as a "problem passenger" by the coach flight attendants.

Let me paint the picture for you: he would not stay seated, continually in the aisle, pacing the cabin, causing the flight attendants to constantly maneuver the beverage cart back and forth around him. Later he refused his meal, saying that "they" were trying to poison him.

I was working the first class aisle position on that flight which meant I was in charge. I didn't know about "all" of this, until one of the other flight attendants working coach came up front to tell me about how he was behaving and what he had said. She asked if I could go speak with him. Oh great! I'm five foot four inches and 110 pounds, how big is he?

Off I go praying that I would not meet my maker! His seat was approximately halfway back into coach and he was actually sitting now. I asked him if I could be of help. I distinctly remember the first thing he said, "Where is this plane going?" Taken aback I asked where he was going, to which he replied, "Pittsburgh." My comment was something along these lines of, "Then you're in luck because that is exactly where we're headed." Thinking I was being helpful now, I pulled out the *TWA Ambassador Magazine* from the seat pocket and opened it to the route map, tracing a line from San Francisco to Pittsburgh. Unfortunately, the only clear non-intersecting line on that map was from San Francisco to Boston which is probably what he saw.

He was acting so oddly and fidgety that I decided to ask the captain to have one of the cockpit crew go speak with him. The flight engineer appeared minutes later with his jacket and hat on, and headed on back to have a chat with this young man. Now out of sight out of mind, I am back up in first class working.

BUT ... within a matter of minutes, I saw those zippered boots out of the corner of my eye, while I was kneeling down in front of a carrier, getting out another bottle of wine. I took my time looking up, having decided that this kid was being a total bother and could wait. When I did look up, ready to tell him to head back to coach, all I remember seeing was the perfectly round O of a gun barrel.

Your mind does strange things under pressure. My immediate first thought was of my dentist's postcard appointment reminders, a cartoon character smiling broadly with a perfect O centered in the grin. "It's time for your dental appointment! Don't delay and end up looking like this!"

I slowly stood up, shocked into silence. The young man nodded his head sideways toward the cockpit door and said, "I want to get in there." Remember, no "keep them out of the cockpit at any cost" or "how to training" had been offered by TWA to the flight attendants in 1970. I sidled around him, knocked on the door, heard the click of the doorknob, meaning it was being unlocked and I opened the door. With his left arm, he pushed me forcefully aside and disappeared into the cockpit, slamming the door behind him. When I say this happened, one, two, three, that is the understatement.

A mere few seconds later the flight engineer was standing in front of me, telling me he had seen the whole thing from the back of the plane, where he had gone to tell the other flight attendants to keep an eye on this guy. Unfortunately, when he saw him going into the cockpit it was too late to let them know by using the intercom from the back of the plane. I could see him pondering what to do? He waited a minute then knocked, used his key to unlock the cockpit door and then disappeared inside, leaving me totally open-mouthed.

My flying partner in first class came up to me and the two of us stared at one another, probably waiting for that slow, wide turn to the south; next stop, Havana. Now the other two flight attendants from coach appeared and the four of us ended up in the first class galley, whispering, waiting for something—anything, to happen!

The only thing out of the ordinary was the sound coming out of the cockpit of warning horns blaring, alert bells ringing, more horns and bells, then nothing! It seemed like an eternity, when perhaps twenty minutes later we heard the three consecutive bells ring in the cabin. That was the call from the cockpit for one of us to go up there immediately to see what they wanted.

Here we go! With my stomach in knots, I knocked twice on the cockpit door, waited for the clicking sound that meant the flight engineer had unlocked the door and then I entered a seemingly normal cockpit. YES! Everything seemed normal.

Captain John turned around, smiled and asked if he could have his lunch. Uh … sure came out of my mouth, while expletives were flying around in my mind! I looked at the first officer and asked if he needed anything to drink, got a negative response and then asked the flight engineer if he needed anything and he said, "No." I must be dreaming this?

I forced myself to turn around and look directly at Blondie (his name was Lyn) seated in the additional crew member's seat which is directly behind the captain's, and asked him if he wanted water or soda. He just shook his head no. I exited the cockpit and was met by three bouffant-ed flight attendant heads, who all resembled Farah Fawcett from the TV show *Charlie's Angels*, peering out from the galley. "What happened?"

"John wants his lunch."

"WHAT? That's it. Where are we going?"

"No idea!"

I honestly do not remember anything about the rest of the flight because the situation was surreal! We went back to work as if nothing was happening. No one came out of the cockpit to answer our questions and there was NO sweeping turn to take us south.

Only one passenger saw Lyn enter the cockpit, an older, silver-headed woman, seated in row two on the aisle in first class. At one point, she pulled me down to her level and asked what was happening. I whispered to her, "Truthfully, I have no idea, but we certainly would appreciate it if you kept this to yourself." I probably gave her some song and dance about the captain being very professional and responsible. Captain John eventually came over the PA system letting us know that we would be landing in Pittsburgh shortly. Pittsburgh, geez PITTSBURGH! What would happen there?

Our flight landed and all of our passengers deplaned, and I gave our silver haired female passenger a "thumbs up" and mouthed a thank you as she exited. A gentleman wearing civilian clothes was standing on the boarding steps by the door, so I assumed that he was a federal agent not local police.

He said nothing to me, but knocked on the cockpit door and stepped in, as I saw him putting his hand on Lyn's shoulder, while saying, "Are you ready son?" That kind gesture made me feel so very sad. The station manager then boarded the aircraft and asked if any of us wanted to make a phone call to let our families know we were fine. As I didn't think my roommates would give a toot, I declined.

Yes, the crew did have a debrief with cocktails at the airport hotel that night, where we learned what had transpired in the cockpit. Here is what happened there: the first officer turned around when the door slammed shut and saw this young man standing there pointing a gun at them. He turned back around and said to our captain, "John, there's a kid behind you with a gun." To which John laughed and told him he was full of it. "No really, he has a gun." Shortly thereafter, the flight engineer returned into the cockpit and John asked him to check the fuel gauge, thinking we would soon be Havana bound. He then let Lyn, our hijacker, know we only had X amount of fuel left and asked him where he wanted to go? Pittsburgh was the reply. That gave them pause! Our captain replied, "Pittsburgh it is."

This cockpit was perfect when it came to dealing with problems. They calmly spoke with Lyn, but thought that maybe some horns or bells sounds could possibly frighten him into forgetting about hijacking the plane, so that was why they proceeded to set them all off after he first entered the cockpit. Of course, this only managed to frighten the four clueless flight attendants in the galley.

As they calmly talked with Lyn, they learned that he had returned from a tour in Vietnam only days before and was going home to Pittsburgh, where he knew his entire family was waiting for him at the airport. He was certain that the flight was headed elsewhere, remember that route map, and he could not take that chance and disappoint his family.

After a long conversation, our captain asked him for his gun, which Lyn passed without a word, and John slipped it behind his back. They simply chatted about who knows what for the next few hours.

Most of these recollections are as clear to me now, almost fifty years later, as they were in the week following the incident. Some memories were recently jump-started with re-reading a newspaper clipping from my little hometown paper; MEDINA GIRL, STEWARDESS, COOL DURING SKY-JACKING. Complete with my TWA graduation photo. Will she give up flying? Definitely not, she tells her parents.

Over the years, I have often wondered what eventually happened to Lyn. I know there was a trial, but I was not asked to testify. This was before people really discussed Post Traumatic Stress Disorder. Lyn probably was the perfect definition for it. Very sad! I sincerely hope that Lyn got the help he needed.

As for me, just another story from my flying career.

My Biography

Photo of Elaine Buchholz Nicolson serving a passenger.
Image courtesy of Jane Nicolson Holcomb.

MY NAME IS Elaine Buchholz Nicolson, and I was a Transcontinental & Western Air, Inc. hostess from 1943 through 1946. That was in the infancy of what would later be renamed Trans World Airlines to be known as TWA.

I was born in 1919 and some would say I was a "depression era baby" from the time of the early 1920s. My parents lived in the suburbs of Chicago, IL and I grew up in Maywood, IL. I graduated from Proviso High School in 1937 and went on to attend the University of Illinois Urbana-Champaign, but did not graduate. I really wanted to be a career woman and was not interested in marrying then. In that era, supposedly working women did not marry. I can hear some of you snickering now, but that was the societal norm then.

I, like so many other women, had few choices when it came to employment, especially since I was not able to graduate from college, due primarily to the expense. So, what is a woman to do? There were clerical jobs or sales opportunities in stores. Then I saw an ad that Transcontinental & Western Air Inc. was hiring for the position of being a hostess. I would love to travel. Should I, could I, would I be able to. I interviewed and waited for either a letter of acceptance or the "we regret to inform you."

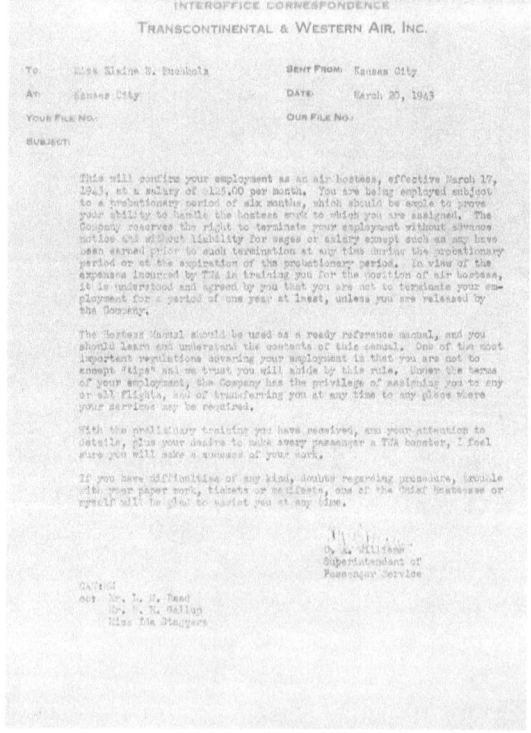

Image of employment letter courtesy of Jane Nicolson Holcomb.

What a thrill when my letter arrived and I was hired effectively on March 17, 1943 at the age of twenty-four. My salary was $125 per month and I was employed subject to a probationary period of six months, which as they said in my letter of employment should be ample time to prove my abilities to handle the hostess work. The company reserved the right to terminate me at any time during this probationary period, or at the expiration of this period. Now here is an eye opener and I quote here from the letter: In view of the expenses incurred by TWA in training you for the position of air hostess, it is understood and agreed by you that you are not to terminate your employment for a period of one year at least, unless you are released by the company.

Off I went to Kansas City with stars in my eyes ready to take on the world. What would the training be like? It would be an intensive six weeks, covering safety, dining and all of those many forms we had to be able to fill out. But the times are changing now too. Before I arrived, TWA devoted only two hours to personal grooming and now it would be sixteen.

Sixteen hours covering makeup, hairstyles, nails and personality (or how to smile), with even an additional personal one on one counseling. Speaking of hairstyles, no Lauren Bacall long and sultry looks for us. No exceptions! It was a three-inch what they called a feather cut and if you didn't want to cut your locks then it was time to go home. Our weight was never to be over 130 pounds and of course that was in relation to our height.

As was also explained to us, great care was to be used in taking care of our uniforms which the company expected to remain spotless, while we traveled across the country. I would find that to be no small feat later in my career.

One might say we all started to look alike, but the point of all of this was we were now to be known as those "glamorous girls in the sky." And to think I was on the cutting edge of all of this. I must add here that my picture was actually in the newspaper with our instructor adjusting my hat for its most becoming angle. This little memento, though very yellow, is still something the family keeps.

The course must have worked because while in Kansas City I met a young man who worked for the Naval Air Transport Service referred to as NATS. We dated while I was there, but after my graduation he made a concerted effort to show up often in a city where I had a layover. Talk about an interesting dating life. I guess you could say that was one of the advantages of being in the Navy Air Transport division during WWII.

Well, as they said in the day, "he finally popped the question." He asked me to marry him and I said yes. There was one big problem with this, you could not be married and continue to be a hostess for TWA. I confided to my supervisor that I had gotten married and to my astonishment she said, "Let's just keep this our secret." I don't know why, possibly because I was the Chief hostess on the east coast then, or maybe she thought I might need my job later if something happened to my husband during the war. But when the war was over my wings were "clipped." No more secrets. My supervisor and I had bent the rule long enough.

Oh, how much I would have loved to continue to fly, but the wonderful news was my husband got a job at TWA, as a dispatcher after the war. He retired in 1980 and we moved to Sun City, Arizona. Would you believe that thirty-two couples from TWA moved there too? Oh, we had so many wonderful memories of our friendships there. Yes, TWA was a family and we were all the best "ambassadors" for the company that we loved.

All these many years later, my daughter has my charm bracelet that is covered in charms from places that we visited because of TWA. She even has my nameplate that I had to slide into a slot in the cabin of the plane, so the passengers could see my name. And of course, most importantly she still has my wings that I proudly wore from 1943 through 1946.

No, I am not writing this because I passed from cancer when I was eighty years old. These memories are from my daughter, her keepsakes of mine and newspaper articles that have kept my TWA story alive.

My daughter Jane likes to refer to herself as a TWA kid. Thank you, Jane, for keeping my memories alive, for now your Dad and I are Traveling With Angels. Love your Mother.

Baignade dans la Seine à Paris

TO SET THE picture: it was a really warm night in Paris, sultry and hot. A perfect night for an adventure.

For those of you who are not familiar with the La Taverne du Sergent Recruteur restaurant located on the Île Saint-Louis in Paris, it had a wonderful prix fixe menu with "all" the wine you could drink. Well, after one such dinner, six of my crewmembers were walking back to the hotel and three of us thought it would be a "brilliant" idea to swim across the Seine River. Me being one of the three, and I admit the instigator. Plus, it didn't look that far across to us. Could it have been due to the unlimited amount of wine served at dinner that evening? Possibly, but all we could think about then was, oh what a story we can tell later.

So, we took off our outer clothes, removed our shoes and gave them to our support group that would carry them over the bridge and meet us at the other side. Me, all of a sudden, decided to be modest, and as I was taking off my skirt, I pulled my half-slip up and over my bra, as if that would make a difference. Really? Now in our skivvies and the plan finalized we slipped into the Seine.

There was only one small problem which turned into a major problem. The current was just a bit stronger than anticipated, and we ended up downstream of our destination without our support group AND our clothes! What is staring at us, but a rock wall that was too high and slippery to climb, so that option was out? Thank God a few minutes later our support group and clothes showed up, as we were dog paddling in the river, and trying to hang onto the rocks. But how were we to get out of the river?

Well, now for the weird part, I know you are saying "the weird part," how about swimming across the Seine at night in your underwear. But back to the wall, it was part of a small park and in that park were a couple of young men, who said that they were in Paris with some sort of Scout group and they had ropes. Hallelujah! The ropes were lowered and with the help of our new friends and the crew, we were pulled out and up to safety.

I have a feeling that these two Frenchmen have told the story many times of hauling three crazy Americans, half nude, at night, from the Seine.

Probably also saying one had her slip around her neck and we couldn't understand how she didn't drown. Me either!

Some additional notes ... The Seine is filthy. The next week I went back to the scene of the crime and saw many "things" floating by that I really did not want to know what they were. Seriously, don't swim in the Seine. Lastly, I know many of you were thinking why in God's name would she want to swim in the Seine River? Well, believe it or not when I started my flying career, I vowed that I would swim in every major river that was near a city where TWA crews laid over. Some people want to climb mountains. I thought I would be different and swim rivers. After my experience in the Seine that idea was quashed. As for the two others that joined me that night, we'll blame the wine. À votre santé

100 K ... Where

HAVE YOU EVER heard of the peninsula that is named Macau? I have, in fact I have been there.

Back story: TWA flew to the orient and among other places to Hong Kong. It was in the day and age when Hong Kong was referred to as a Crown Colony of the British Empire. Hong Kong was considered to have some of the best shopping in the world. From custom clothes, watches, china, crystal, cameras, jewels of all types, pearls, and everything was brand names and high end. You name it you could get it there. It also had some of the finest hotels in the world that catered to the wealthy. But one small extra attraction was close to Hong Kong. In fact, it was a short hydrofoil boat ride away. What was it? The peninsula of Macau that was attached to mainland China. You say who cares? Many, many people did! Because it had large gambling casinos and they were filled to capacity with not only locals from Hong Kong, but the tourists who were visiting there.

Note: In 1557 the Portuguese took over Macau, making it the first colony in East Asia. It was returned to China in 1999 after 442 years of Portuguese rule.

Well, it was in the early '70s and my husband and I decided that a trip to Hong Kong was in our future. He wanted to purchase some custom-made suits and shirts, plus a camera (obviously this was before cell phones). I on the other hand had researched Waterford crystal and had found out that it was cheaper there than in London. Remember Hong Kong was a British Crown Colony.

So where is Macau in this story? While we were waiting for the clothes to be custom made, we decided to take a hydrofoil over to Macau and check out some of the sites and a casino called Casino Lisboa. It had been built in the late '60s and then in 1970 a twelve story "round" hotel was added to it. It was stunning!

All in all, it was a great vacation, with a three-day stopover in Honolulu on our way home. To say my neighbors were jealous would be an understatement. However, for a TWA flight attendant this was our lifestyle.

A few years later, I was working a flight in first class going to Las Vegas. On the Boeing 707 aircraft, there was a lounge area across from the first class galley. It had four seats, two facing forward and two aft, with a large table between the seats, making it perfect for our passengers to have their drinks and meals together, play cards, conduct a business meeting etc.

On this particular flight there were four men sitting together there. They were Chinese, three gentlemen who appeared to be in their forties and one who was probably in his early thirties. The younger man gave me their dinner orders and made all of their requests in English to either my flying partner or me. I assumed that the other gentlemen did not speak English.

After the service was completed, I was picking up some dessert dishes from these four men when I asked the younger one, "Did you all enjoy your meal?" He replied, "We were just saying that our steaks were the best steaks that we've ever had on an airline." I told him, "I'm so glad to hear that. It makes all of my work worthwhile. You might not realize this, but we cook our steaks to order in a convection oven on the plane."

The conversation continued with some light banter, when I asked him if he and his friends were going to be staying in Las Vegas or going on. To which he replied, "We are staying at Caesar's Palace. They are very good to us there. We like to gamble at Caesar's because they give us a nice line of credit." I'm thinking, oh I guess you all are high rollers when he says, "Yes, we brought a hundred thousand dollars with us to start gambling with." My brain was starting to go on overdrive now. I hear myself saying, "You have one hundred thousand dollars on you right now?" He nonchalantly says, "Yes, in my briefcase under the seat."

Now I'm thinking, I can't believe this guy is telling me that he has one hundred thousand dollars in a briefcase on this plane! I look at him and say, "You really shouldn't be telling people that. We hit people over the head to steal a lot less money than that here." I might add that this comment didn't seem to faze him at all.

At that point, I asked him where they were from and he told me Macau. Another surprise after the 100K and I said, "My husband and I were just visiting Hong Kong and went to Macau." He asked me if I had gone to the Casino Lisboa and I said, "Yes, it was wonderful. And that round shape, well, I've never seen anything like it."

Now remember the other three men are not saying a word, when I hear one of them speak in perfect English, "I own the Lisboa. I would like you and your husband to be my guests the next time you are visiting Macau. Everything will be complimentary. But of course, if you lose any money playing in the casino, I cannot reimburse you," and he hands me his business card.

Then what do I hear, another one of the threesome saying, "I own the Canidrome dog track and would like you and your husband to be my guests on your next visit. And anything you win is yours and anything you lose I will make sure you are reimbursed." Then he hands me his business card. Now I hear the third man say, "Would you like to come gambling with us tonight at Caesar's palace?" I quickly was trying to compose myself and decline the offer. I said, something about it was very nice of them to take me gambling with them, but I was afraid that our layover was so short I just was not able to do that. Actually, all I could think was, "You've got to be kidding me. I'm not going out with four rich dudes from Macau to gamble in Las Vegas that I don't know." What about the business cards? I did hang onto them for a number of years, but we didn't make another trip to Macau. In hindsight that was a big fail on our part. Could we have had fun!

Now here is the crazy thing about this story. The gentleman who owned the Lisboa was Stanley Ho, one of the richest men in Hong Kong. Here I was carrying around his business card for years and had no idea.

Stanley Ho, Teddy Yip, Yip Hon and Henry Fok became some of the richest men in the world through their gambling empire in Macau. And I could have gone gambling with them ...

July 30, 1992
The Great Escape ... From the Crash of Flight 843

Photo of Flight 843 crash courtesy of Kaye Chandler.

I WAS THE last person to board Flight 843, San Francisco bound. Little did I realize my life was about to change forever. My name is Kaye Chandler and proudly I was a TWA Flight Attendant.

Introduction

February 11, 1970. began my first day of training as a Trans World Airline hostess. The term flight attendant came about a couple of years later when men joined the friendly skies. During the '70s, '80s and '90s TWA became sky king of the world, from London to Bombay to Hong Kong. Most of us were working as many international flights as we could, and glamorous does not even begin to describe the lifestyle of an international flight attendant. We traveled the world as most people take a trip to the grocery store.

Having just landed at Kennedy Airport from Madrid, I quickly changed from my uniform to street clothes and raced to the TWA domestic terminal, gate three, for flight 843 to San Francisco, only to find it was delayed. Passengers were in the middle of boarding and a few of the commuter crew members were gathered together, as always laughing, talking and waiting for their turn to board. Two longtime TWA flight attendant friends from San Francisco had the jump seats, so they would be sitting in the aft section of the plane. The bad news was the flight was oversold and the agents had actually paid a few people to take the later one. Therefore, my chances of getting on this plane were slim and none ... almost.

Boarding

As the last few passengers walked down the jetway, the boarding agent asked if I wanted to walk down with her and see if any empty seats might appear. She explained that boarding was a mess and their seating charts were way off. The agent and I were standing at the boarding door when one of the flight attendants from coach came running up from the back of the plane waving her arms and saying, "Don't close the door, we have an empty seat in the last row of coach." The agent looked at me and asked if I would prefer to sit in first class and use a surcharge (a small fee employees pay to upgrade). Absolutely! Then the agent briefly told me that she had moved a very rude and obnoxious woman up to first class and would rather return her to the back of the plane to the seat she had really paid for. Ironically during the evacuation this was the woman, who threw herself down in the first class galley kicking, screaming and refusing to evacuate, therefore requiring a couple of crew members to pick her up and toss her out the exit. So, I had my seat in row one, seat #2.

I raced for the lower galley to stow my luggage and quickly said, "Hi," to some of the crew that I knew. Note: the main galley on TWA's L-1011 were located one level down from the cabin in the belly. Many little secret stowage compartments existed there, for crew use only. The announcement to prepare for departure was made and we were all going to California now!

Settling in, I glanced quickly at my seat partner, an elegant looking woman, dressed in a designer Chanel suit complete with expensive Marsh-Jordan shoes. She was asleep. I took out my book feeling very pleased that I would be home in a couple of hours and riding comfortably in first class.

Lift-Off

The aircraft rotated for take-off and the #2 engine was fired up. (Later on, literally.) As the aircraft began to gather its V1 speed for take-off, I put my book down and listened. For whatever reason, something just did not sound right. Consider it years of experience or intuition, but something seemed very wrong. The plane began to lift-off the runway when suddenly it happened, we slammed back down and a loud bang was heard, followed by a second. The sleeping woman next to me woke, looked at me and asked, "What just happened?" My reply was that we were OK, this was just a new take-off technique (Ha—training, whatever you do, do not let the passengers know you are worried.) I looked out the window and saw the land moving past us fast, way too fast!

Now the plane was vibrating violently, and overhead bins were popping open, luggage was falling everywhere with more explosions of brakes, tires, whatever. Ceiling panels were jarring loose and falling down. Still the plane was not stopping. Throughout our venture down the runway, I kept explaining to my seat partner what I thought the loud explosions were and what I thought was going on. She asked me if I was a flight attendant and I replied, "Yes." She said, "Good." Like I had some magic wand to get us out of this disaster.

I looked at our flight service manager's face and could tell something was terribly wrong, as he was staring at the back of the plane. Then suddenly he was out of his seat, yelling to sit down, waving his arms about. The plane suddenly made an abrupt turn to the left, and he was thrown down onto the first class galley floor as the plane was now racing into the field!

He was trying to scramble back to his seat, barely getting his seatbelt back on when the nose gear collapsed. There was a loud groaning noise as the front of the plane rotated, lurching down with a thump. We had stopped and it was now deafeningly quiet. I tossed my book at the wall in front of me thinking this is one book I will never finish and then jumped up from my seat telling the lady next to me to move fast! She asked if she should put on her shoes. High heels, YIKES, they would tear the slide to pieces. I hear myself calmly saying, "No, leave them, you can retrieve them later."

Evacuate

Passengers were moving towards the #1 left exit door, behind me. I was the first to face the door and could hear our service manager yelling, "Keep everyone away from the door!" Another flight attendant was now at my left, eyes wide, with a look of "What the hell is going on?" I had my arms spread wide, to keep passengers back from the door, as this particular door popped inward and then up into the fuselage when I heard the captain's voice over the PA system telling everyone to evacuate immediately.

Our flight service manager pulled the emergency handle on the #1 left door as we all watched the slide slowly unfurl. I could see the other flight attendant grabbing the left door grip as I stood over the slide. During safety training when we practice evacuations, the joke is "follow me." My worst nightmare was happening now, I was dressed in street clothes, out of uniform and being the first was always a joke. However, I had no choice. I was to be first down the slide, move to the left at the bottom and help passengers evacuate. With the nose-gear collapsed, the distance from the left #1 door to the ground was only about two maybe three feet, so passengers were running down the slide and into the field.

I had stepped to the left of the slide, then looked at the fuselage of the airplane and froze. The entire aft section was a mass of smoke and fire and there was fire under the plane too! I thought my flight attendant friends were trapped, and being burned alive and I couldn't do anything to help them.

Then two explosions occurred on the left side, seconds apart. Smoke soared into the air. I had just witnessed the rear #3 and #4 left slide doors blowing up; surely, everyone was trapped now. I looked at the #2 left door just as it opened and saw a flight attendant, who looked like she was flying out of the emergency door exit, and all I could think of was, what was she doing? Miraculously she then pulled herself back in as the #2 slide was inflating.

My eyes turned toward an access road and I saw a bright chartreuse pick-up truck speeding towards us. My thoughts were, if this is the fire department, they are going to need more than one little pick-up truck to put this fire out. Reality, it took a fleet of fire trucks and forty-five minutes before the fire could be contained.

The Rabbit

I went into what is called "survivor shock" and I actually felt it happen. My friends were trapped and I was OK. Suddenly from underneath the fuselage a giant rabbit ran to me and stopped. He sat high on his haunches and our eyes connected. We looked at each other, both thinking the same thing, "What the hell is going on!" Later when I described my rabbit friend, I said he was about three feet tall. Oh sure, a three-foot rabbit, ha-ha!

Note: A few months later, I was on another TWA 767 aircraft and we aborted the takeoff, same runway, same airport, it was déjà vu. The crew knew my story and was concerned, as I was shaking. Later on, as I related my own story to this crew, I talked about the three-foot rabbit. Prior to this, any time I talked about the "rabbit," most crewmembers would look at me as if I was still on some funny stuff from the '60s. But then one of the flight attendants said, "Look at what I just read." She was reading about the history of Idlewild Airport, now called Kennedy, and years earlier a crate of Texas jackrabbits had broken open. Some of them had survived on the island for all of these years and they were described as being "three feet" tall! Whew, I wasn't crazy after all!

But back to my rabbit, he had centered me. As he hopped away, I realized that this plane was on fire, wings loaded with jet fuel and that this airplane was about to blow up with passengers standing next to the fuselage talking. I screamed with all of my might, "Run for your lives, get away from the plane, it could blow up!" I started running into the field and kept yelling; "RUN—RUN—RUN! DON'T STOP!"

Passengers, who were being evacuated through the left #2 door, were also gathering under the left wing! I immediately turned and ran to them all the while yelling, "Run, get away from the plane!" I remember stopping by the #1 engine, looking at the blades slowly turning with that click-click sound engines make when they are shutting down. God, how long will it be before this plane blows up? I hear myself still yelling, "Run away now," as I was standing there looking at the burning aircraft. It then became totally clear that people were everywhere, and they were all running away from the plane! This must have been the reason I was on flight 843.

A couple of years later, one of my flight attendant friends said she had a woman on her flight and this lady had been on flight 843. The woman told my friend that she would never forget the woman in the peach-colored dress yelling for everyone to run, run for your lives and realized foolishly thinking that just because she was out, she was safe. My friend told her that the woman in the peach-colored dress was really a flight attendant and she said, "Oh now it all makes sense."

The Field
In the field, I began to look for other crew members, or anyone who would need assistance who was injured. I found the lady, who had been seated next to me, and asked if she was OK. Yes. Then I ran into a flight attendant from Petaluma, CA, someone who I had worked with years before. She was returning to San Francisco after a visit with her family in Portugal and told me she was in the back of the plane, where the fire was, and that she was standing in the aisle when the plane left the ground after it crashed. Crazy what you think about in these situations, she asked if I had my asthma medicine with me, if not she would share hers (we were fellow asthmatics). Asthma medicine was the last thing I was thinking about and immediately thought if she managed to escape, could my fellow crew members and friends in the back have made it out as well?

Comforted by the knowledge that she and my seat partner were OK, I moved on to see if I could help, someone injured, a child lost, and also if I could find my friends. Suddenly I saw one of them, we ran to each other, hugged, and cried and she told me how horrible the back of the plane had been. People were screaming, flames were shooting under the cabin doors and the windows were melting. She said the entire back of the plane was cast in a strange orange glow from the fire. Moreover, she did not think she was going to make it because she was one of the very last to evacuate.

As we watched the plane burn, my friend looked at me and asked if I thought this crash would make the evening news. I stared at her with disbelief! "Evening news, this is international news. This is big!" She replied, "No, no I don't think so ..." as fire trucks were everywhere now to fight the fire with foam covering the burning jet and field.

We returned to looking for our friends when I heard her scream, "Oh my God, look BLOOD!" Right in front of us was a huge glob of a bright red substance. A man was on the ground trying to scoop up some of the glob. What? About the very same moment we both recognized what the glob was, spaghetti sauce! This passenger had foolishly risked his life for a jar of spaghetti sauce.

TWA Hangar 12

Mobile lounges were sent to the field to retrieve both passengers and crew; as we drove away watching the plane continue to burn there was one final mighty groan and the tail section dropped to the ground. It was over.

Eventually we returned to the main terminal where TWA support teams were there to assist everyone. The crewmembers were whisked away in TWA vans, back to Hangar 12. When I positioned myself in the last row of the van, I was seated next to two women, who I recognized but really had never met. They were TWA flight attendant supervisors and introduced themselves to me and I, in return, said, "Hi, I'm Kaye Chandler." They looked at each other with surprise, turned back and said, "So, you're Kaye Chandler." I never did quite understand what they meant. However, I had just nearly lost my life, met a three-foot tall rabbit and seen a man scraping spaghetti sauce off the ground, so it was just another strange moment in time.

Once back at TWA's Hangar 12, we all shared in the joy that everyone survived. TWA people were running up to us with hugs, kisses and tears. Even the lady, who cleaned the third floor of the hangar grabbed each of us, crying and hugging with such compassion.

We stayed at the hangar for a couple of hours. First, to write down our own experiences, then to call family and friends telling them we were all OK. There are not enough words to say how smoothly the flight attendant supervisors and our union representatives worked together. They kept shaking their heads in amazement that we all had survived and all of the passengers too. I don't think we, the flight attendants, really realized at that time that this truly was a miracle. Even today, it is still rather surreal.

Holiday Inn
Next, we were taken to the Airport Holiday Inn. The entire crew cannibalized the tiny gift shop, stripping it of mascara, toothbrushes, hairdryers and t-shirts to sleep in. I still have my Minnie Mouse t-shirt, which I slept in for a full year as my comfort zone.

Once settled in our rooms, we met downstairs in a conference room that TWA had quickly set up. Dinner was being served, along with a glass or two of vino or ale. And to think that just a few hours earlier, we were all standing in a field watching our plane burn and now we were sitting in a room, dining on pizza together. In retrospect, this was really rather difficult to comprehend. Anyone looking at the dinner pictures would question if the plane crash really existed, or we were just having dinner together.

Friday July 31, 1992
Friday morning, we met once again in the same room. Breakfast was served, but we were more interested in the collection of newspapers on the table. We were being called "Heroes." Front-page news! The TV's were all touting the miracle of "Flight 843" and footage of the burning aircraft dominated the screen. We decided to autograph all of the papers as a souvenir of our ordeal. I still have my autographed page today.

Note: The front-page headline of one the newspapers was "Evacuate," and the article under it was titled, "The Great Escape" where there was a picture of one of our flight attendants caressing the head of one of the unaccompanied children. The child was in the arms of a passenger and was safe.

After breakfast, we all returned to TWA's Hangar 12, The Rose Room, and shared our experiences, starting with our captain and then everyone told their own story. Listening as each crewmember related their feelings, thoughts and reactions was mesmerizing. Everyone seemed to have put their own safety aside; getting 273 passengers (90% non-English speaking) to safety was the priority. We laughed at how many of us had actually fought with the passenger with the antler hat. In addition, how we fought to keep passengers from evacuating with their "precious" carry-on luggage. However, we all teared up about the two unaccompanied children, who thankfully made it off safely.

Having listened, in awe, we all realized each of us had found some way to make a difference. TWA could hold its head up high! It had given each of us the tools to work with and we knew TWA always had the highest standards in safety training of any airline.

The crash was on a Thursday and all I really wanted to do was go home, but that would not happen until Saturday. Why? Because we had to meet with TWA, FAA, NTSB and IFFA (our union). Each of us repeated the details of our experience to all of them which was very time consuming, but most important.

A Little Trivia
May 1992, layover in Cairo—a toothless old Egyptian man had read my palm and he told me that a big event was about to happen. It did.

My mother was watching the Phil Donahue Show when they announced the crash, but she was convinced that I was still in Europe and decided to take the dog for a walk, so she missed my phone call. Poor dog, mother refused to walk the dog for an entire week.

After missing my mother, I was finally able to contact my mother-in-law. I explained what had happened and asked her to let the family know I was OK. She said she would share the news and then asked if TWA had made sure everyone had a decent meal! This is a woman who raised nine children and food was always a priority.

I got hold of my husband and he began the telephone conversation by telling me about his day. I politely listened for a few minutes, periodically trying to interject to tell him I had been in a plane crash. Not really hearing me, his response, "No problem. Your brother called and left a message about something mechanical and could you pick up some Swiss Army knives on your next trip to Switzerland." Finally, he glanced at the TV and saw the local news footage of a TWA L-1011 burning in the field, a light bulb moment! Now it was my turn to talk. He was on the next flight to New York.

Four years later my husband also flew to New York July 19, 1996, two days after TWA flight 800 fell into the Atlantic Ocean. He was there to meet me as my Rome flight landed at Kennedy Airport. Doomed flight 800 was supposed to land in Paris and continue to Rome, it was my crew that was to bring the fallen 747 back to New York, it never happened. Moreover, I never returned to Rome again.

Conclusion

Not an overly religious person, I somehow must believe there was a higher power involved in TWA's Flight 843 miracle. For whatever reason I was supposed to be on Flight 843, July 30, 1992. Maybe to share our story and keep the grand name of TWA alive.

TWA's Emergency Response Team

IN 1992, TWA flight # 843 crashed on the runway at JFK on takeoff. All 293 passengers and crew managed to survive even though the L1011 was engulfed in flames and only three emergency exit doors were usable.

A supervisor for flight attendants at JFK was charged with the responsibility of dealing with the unexpected issues that evolved. What became apparent was the fact there really was not much of a system set up to deal with the passengers or the crew in a unique situation. TWA with the leadership of this supervisor, created a specially trained team of TWA employees. They were taught how to handle passengers, families and crews who had been in a plane crash.

TWA at this time was the only airline to have a specially trained trauma team. When the disaster of TWA flight 800 happened a few years later, these TWA employees were called upon to meet the needs of the passengers' families and the employees' families who now had lost one or more members.

The TRT helped to escort family members, attend the memorials, transport remains and council where needed. They made sure that family members had hotel rooms, access to meals, vital information and whatever else might be needed. These people also offered comfort and were a contact, so the families knew that TWA cared.

During the tragedy of flight 800 you were TWA's true unsung heroes!

Cats On the Catwalk

WE KNOW YOU all want to know about the naughty, so here we go. Many of you have never had a flight on a 747, but to say it is big, well, a small town could travel on it. The passenger load can be anywhere from a minimum of 416 to as many as 660 on some other airlines. In addition, to take care of these people you usually have a "minimum" of twelve flight attendants. People could vanish and then reappear! Let's put it this way, they could be discreetly absent for a while and we are speaking of the crew too.

But getting back to TWA's 747, the flying public has no idea about what is above them in the ceiling. You can actually gain access to this area, above the passengers' seats, by a hidden staircase in the rear of the aircraft. And no, we will not give you any more information on how to find this staircase. Why? Because after you read this, we do not want you getting any ideas!

So, picture yourself having gone up these stairs and now what do you see? A catwalk that runs all the way to the business section of the aircraft. Very private! No one can see you or hear you.

Let us call one of the flight attendants working this flight, "C" as in cat now. "C" and another one of the flight attendants were dating and "C" now decides to introduce her to the "catwalk." Meow, what will these two little pussy cats be doing up there? Wait! What do two frisky cats usually do? You guessed it!

While they were in the "act" the plane hit some clear-air turbulence and guess what? There are no seat belts and this catwalk is narrow with minimal railings. They are in the prone position with nothing to hang onto, but each other.

You know where we are going? They are tossed off the catwalk in the turbulence and go crashing through the ceiling. They land in an older woman's lap, "C" with his pants down around his knees and the young lady with her panties in her hand. Fortunately, no one was hurt.

Thank God there were no cell phones!

The Yellow Rubber Ducky Pants

I WAS FLYING JFK to LAX on a Boeing 747 for the month. Everything had been going smoothly until this one flight.

Most of you don't know that the crew had to meet for what they called a crew briefing before flights on a wide body aircraft. We had a flight service manager (FSM), who conducted the briefing. He/she would give us the passenger count, celebs or important people on board, then we would bid in order of seniority for where we were going to work on the plane, and usually reviewed some safety questions. Today, the FSM had informed us that the aircraft which was coming in from Rome was going to be late. Then she went on to say, "Don't worry about being at the gate to get on the aircraft an hour before departure. The aircraft is late, it has to be cleaned and meals boarded. Just show up at the gate in ninety minutes."

The crew split up since we had time to kill. Some of us were reading, others were making phone calls and some of us were just talking about this, that and whatever together.

Fast forward, I got up to the gate area at the appointed time and some of my crew was already there. As I weaved my way through a sea of humanity, pulling my crew kit behind me, I passed by a group of people, who had a small baby in a car seat on the floor. I was thinking to myself you better watch that baby with all of these people moving about, someone is going to trip and get hurt. BUT THEN as I got closer to the infant, I smelled it! What was it? Let's put it this way, why doesn't someone change that baby's diaper. It was awful!

At this point I see my flying partner that I had been working with all month and we locked eyes and I rolled mine. She had a slight smirk on her face when I got up to her and I whispered, "My God why doesn't someone change that baby's diaper?" She looks at me and says, "Well, guess what? It's not the baby." I'm thinking, what? It's not the baby then what is that terrible odor? She then continues, "You aren't going to believe this, but it is a man standing right over there, who smells so bad and he is coming on our flight."

"Oh gee, don't tell me he is in first class?" I was working the first class cabin position and all I could see was major trouble here! Oh Lord, give me strength. She immediately replies, "No he is in coach, but the service manager just got on the plane to talk with the captain. We can't take him with us. He is covered in feces." I almost yelled, FECES!

The captain gets off the aircraft and goes out into the gate area, takes one whiff and immediately goes back to the podium where the gate agent is and says, "We aren't taking him, period." The gate agent tells the captain that TWA had sent out a letter to all of the gate agents telling them they couldn't refuse boarding to anyone, because the company had too many lawsuits going on right now for denied boarding. The captain is irate and demands to speak with the agent's supervisor. The supervisor told him that he had to take this man. It then got so heated that the captain demanded to talk with someone in management at our corporate office in NYC. That went nowhere too, as he was told by all that we had to take this passenger. Insanity yes! We had to take a passenger, who was covered in feces, from JFK to LAX. Think about that one.

So, what do we do? You aren't going to believe this. A mechanic comes up the jetway stairs and gives a pair of rubber yellow pants to the gate agent; picture now those yellow rubber ducky pants that street guards used to wear at school crossings years ago when it was raining. They were elasticized around the waist and ankles. Well, these also were the pants that our mechanics and ramp personnel wore over their work clothes during rainstorms. Replete with a matching jacket and hat, très chic. Excuse the sarcasm. Note: The passenger was not asked to wear the jacket and hat. I can see you now LOL. Anyway, this guy puts on the yellow rubber pants over his slacks and then boards the aircraft. Unbelievable but true.

Finally, we take off with a full load of passengers. I'm working first class and was very busy, and as far as I was concerned "nothing" behind that blue curtain that separates first class from coach really existed. UNTIL, we landed at LAX and I was walking with the rest of the crew through the terminal. I casually said to one of the coach flight attendants, "So, how was the guy in the rubber pants?" Now I have to say this crew looked like they had just finished working two coast to coast flights, not one. Total exhaustion!

This flight attendant looks at me and says, "Oh, he was the very least of our problems. We had two passengers, who almost ended up in a fist fight, and we had to threaten them with having the police meet the flight. Then we gave oxygen to two people. And some of the serving carts were broken, so it took us three hours to do the service and people were really getting pissed off."

And then she says, "While I'm on my hands and knees and have half of my body stuck inside one of those damn serving carts, trying to pull out the last tray and meal, there is banging on top of it. I pull myself out, look up, and this man is standing there and he says, You've got to do something. There is a man in the back lav and he is nude."

I'm looking at her like thank God I wasn't working in coach today! "So, what did you say to this guy?" She said, "I really wanted to say I've got two words for you and they aren't let's dance. But I said, sir, you know what lav he is in, just don't open that door. Leave him alone."

My head was exploding now with all of this and I looked at her and said, "It must have been the 'yellow rubber ducky' man who was trying to clean himself up." Then I had a come to Jesus meeting with myself and thought, "I think the glamour is really gone now. Maybe it is time to give this up after twenty-five years."

Believe me there were a number of debrief cocktails that night and thankfully, we were able to laugh about the whole sordid mess. Feces and all.

Don't Let Them Stop You

I WAS FLYING with one of my friends to London out of Chicago. We arrived in London after being up half the night and took our three-hour nap. Later, when we were meeting for coffee to wake up, we decided that Harrods was on our radar. No, we didn't need anything at Harrods, but who doesn't like to explore all of the goodies in Harrods. Really, that should have gone unsaid.

So, we arrive at Harrods and go inside. What greets us? Virtually no people shopping! What the heck is going on here? I looked at her and she looked at me and I said, "We don't have to fight the masses. Look at the purse counters, we can actually see the purses and not wait behind a herd of people. Is there some type of holiday that we don't know about?" She laughs and says, "Who cares. This is great!"

We meander around the purse area, stroll through cosmetics, and then decide to get on the elevator to go up and look at Waterford crystal. Now picture an elevator car that is practically the size of a cattle car. They are huge! Next, picture the doors opening and a tiny grey haired woman standing in the back of the elevator car.

We get in, push the button for our floor and of course then the silence starts. I'm thinking to myself this whole situation is really strange. Why is Harrods so empty? It is never empty.

I turn to this well dressed, older lady and say, "Excuse me. We are Americans and have been in Harrods many times, but we've never seen it this quiet. Is there a holiday that we wouldn't know about, so people are not in London shopping?"

She looks at me with rather steely blue eyes and says, "No, my dear. There is no holiday. They just announced on the telly that the IRA has said they were going to bomb Harrods. As soon as I heard that I put on my coat, grabbed my purse and came straight here in a hackney." Then she said, "I'll never let them stop me."

I'm thinking the IRA said they were going to bomb Harrods. Now! Geez wouldn't you know it that's why the place is so empty. I look at my BFF and say, "Are we shopping?" She looks at me without batting an eyelash and says, "We're shopping."

I turn to our elevator companion and say, "We're shopping too." To which she replies, "Never let them stop you girls."

Next stop crystal!

Moral of story: About a week after 9/11, I was in California and was to fly back as a passenger to New York. I called my husband and said, "You know I'm not feeling comfortable flying right now. I'm not sure if I will come back to New York." Then I thought about that little lady many years before. She obviously had gone through WWII and wasn't going to be intimidated by the IRA. I immediately straightened up. She's right! Never let them stop you! I was on a really empty plane the next day to JFK.

It Is a What

I WAS WORKING first class on a flight to DCA, Ronald Reagan International airport in Washington D.C. Now you have to know that this flight was an extremely short airborne time, so as they say, "time was of the essence."

I was finally at the last row taking drink orders when the joker in 5A could not decide what he wanted to drink. While I ran through the drink options, I held back my impatience. As he is mumbling about this, that and whatever I just wanted to scream, "This is a short flight and I've got dinner and drinks to serve. What do you want to drink!" But I bite my tongue. Finally, he just said, "Surprise me." I'm thinking, "Oh really."

Picture me in the galley, mixing up my magic potion. I serve him the mysterious drink, watch him take a sip and then ask, "How do you like it?" His reply, "It's really good, what is it called?" I just look him dead in the eye and respond for everyone to hear, "It's a Screaming Orgasm, I thought you could use one."

Needless to say, the entire first class cabin cracked up. I had to mix lots of them, so everyone could try it. I still to this day cannot believe that I did such a thing, but then again …

Here is the recipe or Google for more information:

1 oz. Vodka
1 ½ oz. Irish Cream liqueur
½ oz. Coffee liqueur
Pour over crushed ice.
Happy screaming!

Good Morning Mr. Hughes

Photo of Howard Hughes in the left seat. Courtesy of the TWA Museum.

THE TWA ADMINISTRATION Office at 11500 Ambassador Drive, Kansas City, MO is now a registered historic building. It was designed and built by Howard Hughes. Let me tell you how Howard Hughes was ever the futuristic thinker. Here is my story ...

I had worked in this building for Worldspan, formerly called PARS, which was the TWA reservation system and was spun off from TWA in 1991. The day we moved into this building as Worldspan employees, I walked in with a friend of mine by the first name of Judy, who worked for TWA and now worked for Worldspan, as I had. We entered the big metal doors, walked ahead to where the open-air atrium jetted up four floors to a massive glass paneled ceiling, with streams of sunlight highlighting the big tree coming from a huge planter box in the marble floor. In front of us was a "reflecting pool" that expanded to take up the center of this space forcing you to walk around the edges. It was said by former TWA employees that back when TWA owned the building, people would be walking in reading the newspaper and walk right into this reflecting pool. Today, they'd be heads down into their cell phone and do the same thing.

But back to Judy and me walking in that day. As we got to the edge of the reflecting pool, Judy looked up around each floor and said, "I see dead people," we both laughed aloud, but she got me thinking, she was right. Every day I walked those halls, I imagined the TWA employees all working there, talking in the hallways, sharing their stories and I felt "they were there."

Now to the part of the story that will blow you away, it was what I found out from the head of the facilities. Worldspan was having a huge open house for our families and friends, to come see the newly renovated offices and this historic building. I was part of the planning committee for this event, so I started doing research on it and knowing it was historic, I reached out to our facilities department to see if they had any interesting facts. WOW, did they!

The ever-thinking brain of Howard Hughes was in overdrive in the design of this building and the TWA reservations systems building next door that stored all of the TWA airline reservations. That building had fourteen-inch thick, lead-lined walls to protect it from a disaster or data breach. But it gets even better. Kansas City was expanding and growing in the area of this building and the brand-new Kansas City International Airport (MCI) was being built right across the new I-29 freeway. With the power of persuasion ($$$) Howard Hughes had on Kansas City, he had a special enhancement he had to have for his new TWA building and the reservations systems building. In that building, he had his mechanics install jet engines and a "bank of car batteries." Mr. Hughes was the forward thinker! In the event of a natural disaster such as a severe storm or electrical grid outage, this first of its kind unique backup system would start the jet engines, to keep a charge on the batteries, while keeping the valuable TWA reservations system "alive" and "business as usual." Today the system is gone and has been moved to an Atlanta location and that lead-lined building has a new owner. Told you it would be mind blowing what he designed.

Now back to the TWA "ghosts" in the building. Just something I did, something that nobody saw or heard me do, as I walked the stairs up to our second floor office, I would stop, reach down and touch the retro linoleum stairs original to the building and say, "Morning, Mr. Hughes." Why? Because the "Number One Ghost" people saw there was that of Howard Hughes. They told us they'd be working and "feel" him or "see an image" of him in the halls of the basement area. I guess I was just hoping in my daily routine to have him appear and tip that famous fedora brim of his hat to me, as I walked up past him on "his stairs."

Princess Diana

THIS WAS REALLY the most amazing experience while on a London layover. It was April 1990; I was flying with a very good friend on this particular trip and we were discussing what we wanted to do in London. Would it be Harrods for shopping, a play that night or some sightseeing?

Our layover hotel was the St. James Court located down the street from the Queen's St. James Palace. When we arrived at the hotel, we were greeted with incredible security and found out at the desk that the state dinner for the President of India was being held at the hotel that night. Why this hotel? Well, it was chosen because at the time it was owned by the Taj chain, a group out of India.

The staff at the hotel informed us that it was "very rare" for all of these dignitaries and royalty to attend the same event due to security reasons. The street was to be blocked off several hours before the dinner, and all hotel guests had to enter and exit out of a side door of the hotel and be screened.

But our plans for our layover were made when they told us the time to stand on the other side of the street, if we wanted to watch everyone arrive and get out of their cars. Who wouldn't want to see Queen Elizabeth, Prince Phillip, Prince Charles and Princess Diana!

Well, I'm here to tell you that Diana was more beautiful in person than pictures. She was in a full white formal gown with long white gloves and a beautiful tiara. In other words, "drop dead gorgeous" and the paparazzi were frantically taking pictures of her.

I scarcely remember Maggie Thatcher, who was Prime Minister of England then, and a host of others after seeing the Queen and Princess Diana.

On August 8, 1997, I was flying to England again and it was the night Diana died. The entire crew went to Kensington Palace to see the memorials and the mountain of flowers, candles and notes to her. All I could think of was that beautiful woman in that fabulous white gown and tiara radiating warmth and poise. So sad …

What Is the Passenger Count

BEFORE COMPUTERS FOR the masses and cell phones, yes people we had to function without these things, we never knew what the passenger load was going to be. So, our first question to the gate agent when he or she was letting us on the plane before the passengers was, "What is the load?"

The usual response was the count in first class and then in coach but not on this day. It is still indelibly imprinted in my mind what this agent said, "Well, let's put it this way. There's an ass in every seat and a face in every window." I have to say I laughed out loud.

So, the next time you're a passenger on a flight that is full just remember that description. It does paint the picture.

Good times …

The Truth Hurts

A FRIEND OF mine had gained a little weight over the summer of 1990 and was called into the office to discuss the situation. She walked in for the meeting and was met by a very arrogant, and also overweight, herself, supervisor.

This supervisor spoke to her in a condescending tone of voice, while telling her how important it was to maintain her weight. How we had an image to uphold and you had to be sure to maintain a positive self-image.

She then walked her over to a full-length mirror and gazed into it, while standing alongside my friend and said, "OK, I want you to look into this mirror and tell me what you see. And you MUST be brutally honest in your answer." My friend thought for a minute and then said, "OK, I see two fat women." The supervisor asked her to please leave and she was never contacted again.

This supervisor must not have heard the old adage of, "Don't ask a question if you can't handle the answer."

Baby's Daddy

I WAS WORKING a flight and our flight engineer was quite the kidder. We had been harassing each other all day on the plane with silly comments and also told one another a few jokes. It was breaking the tedium of a rather boring day. When all of a sudden, I thought I've got a way to get him!

This was in the days when we had pillows and blankets for our passengers. I got into the overhead bin and took out two pillows. Then I unwrapped my serving smock and placed the two pillows over my stomach, tied the smock over them and asked my flying partner, "Do I look 'really' pregnant now?"

She was laughing and said, "Yes, you definitely look pregnant. What are you doing?" I said, "Just watch, I'm going to get him now." Picture a woman, who looks like she is ready to deliver, slowly waddling like a duck down the aisle toward the cockpit, with her hand held up to her back like her back hurts. Got the picture?

I walked the entire length of the aisle from the back of coach through first class. When I reached the cockpit door, I looked backwards to see if I was getting the needed heads out in the aisle to watch me. Ah yes success, there were many.

The secret knock to get in the cockpit was done. Really complicated, it consisted of two rapid hard knocks and then none. The cockpit door was opened by the flight engineer. Instead of walking into the cockpit and closing the door I left it wide open, stepped inside the cockpit with my hand still to my back, turned and looked down the aisle, smiled at all of the leering passengers and then pointed to the flight engineer. At this point I stepped back, grabbed the door knob and closed the cockpit door.

Inside the cockpit now, the captain and first officer, who had also seen what I had done were in hysterics. The flight engineer was beet red but he also started to laugh.

My Turn! Got-cha!

Still Gives Me Nightmares

IT WAS THE 1970s and I was working a flight that stopped in St. Louis before continuing on to LAX. In STL, the gate agent had gotten on board and said we were having VIPs on today in first class, a celebrity and their friend who was traveling with them. You will understand why I do not want to divulge their name as you read this.

The celebrity and their friend were pre-boarded by one of our PR people. Both were very polite and low key, and frankly, it was great fun to see this person since I had grown up with their music and loved it! Now celebs normally never sat in an aisle seat, I am sure the reasoning was so the public could not get to them easily. However, this one actually sat in the aisle seat and their friend took the window seat.

The plane was full and I noted when some of our passengers passed the celeb you could tell they were taking note. Menus were passed to our passengers in first class and I am now in the aisle taking orders. I take the celeb's order and the friend's, who are seated in row two, and then turn to the other two passengers, a couple, in the same row to take theirs. This is where my nightmare started!

This man, who is seated across from the celeb now says in a very loud voice, "I want to tell you something young lady, just make sure you serve us first before you serve those and now he used an extremely offensive racial slur! Yes, it was that word! Have you ever felt your stomach churning and then flipping upside down, your face flushing and your brain spinning while you are trying to remain calm? Well, it was all happening to me now!

Background: This was in the day and age when you tried to do everything to cover up ugly scenes on the plane. I found myself leaning over and saying in a very calm, quiet voice, "Sir, that will not be a problem, may I have your orders." All I am thinking is please Lord I hope they did not hear that but how could they not? Today that old goat's ass would have been taken off the plane, but back then we really did everything to try to appease people.

In the galley, I am telling my flying partner about this awful passenger. I told her instead of serving the traditional way we will just change it and no one will even notice. Example: Instead of serving Row 1, seats A and B and then seats D and F, we would serve D and F and then A and B. Easy right?

Everything is going along smoothly. We had served cocktails and appetizers, then we brought out the salad cart and of course, the important issue of serving passengers in the reverse order was working. UNTIL, my flying partner was making up the entrée plates. She had made up the celebrity's and friend's plates but the "nightmare" passengers had not gotten theirs yet. I made the fatal mistake of saying, "Oh, I don't want their meals to get cold while you are making up that jerk's. Everything seems to be fine out there. I'll just take these meals out while you make up that jerk's and his wife."

Now, I serve my celeb and their friend, then go back to the galley to get the "nightmare" passengers meals. As I am placing their plates with their entrees onto their tray tables, he picks up his glass salt and pepper cellars and "throws" them in the aisle on the floor. While yelling, "I told you not to serve those God-Damn, again the extremely offensive slur word, before you served us."

Taking a very deep breath to compose myself, and acting as if nothing has happened, I pick up their entrée plates before he had an opportunity to throw them, returned to the galley and put them down on the galley serving area. My flying partner looks at me and says, "Oh, my God! What is happening?" I said, "I'm picking up the rest of their glasses, silverware and plates. He is throwing things. Under "no" circumstances do you talk to them or give them anything else. They are no longer visible! I'm going into the cockpit to tell the captain what is happening out here and get one of them to come out and tell him to shut up! You continue serving the rest of the first-class passengers."

Well, you aren't going to believe this one! I surely did not. After explaining how I needed help with this jerk because he is throwing things in the aisle now, and using racial slurs about our passengers and swearing, you know what I hear? This ... the captain looks at me and says, "I'm sure you can handle it, we won't be coming out into the cabin." I thought I was going to stroke out now! I looked at him and said, "If I could handle it, I wouldn't be in here asking for your help!" To say that I slammed the cockpit door would be an understatement. It was lucky to have remained on its hinges.

At this point, I went back out into the cabin, directly to our celeb and their friend, and started apologizing profusely. They were so kind and just told me not to worry, everything is all right. Everything is ALL RIGHT! I don't think so! Soldiering on we now come out with our dessert cart and what happens? This jerk stands up and starts spitting on it. YES, he was spitting on the cheese, fruit, ice cream and anything else on that cart. At this point I had put myself into some type of Zen state, as if this is all very normal. I look at my flying partner who is assisting me with the cart and calmly say, "Would you please take this cart back to the galley and refresh the items on it. I'll be back in a moment."

I walk up to the cockpit door like nothing has happened. Knock, knock, twice in a row on the door (our secret knock to get in). The door opens, I calmly walk into the cockpit, close the door and then it is like Mount Vesuvius erupting. I am screaming at the top of my lungs, "The bastard is spitting all over my dessert cart now. I'm here to tell you I can't handle it! One of you better get out here now and stop this situation!" Upon which I leave the cockpit and turn into a supposedly sane person, acting again as if everything is very normal.

Now here is another detail of this story that I haven't told you. Our flight engineer is black. Who comes walking out of the cockpit now in his uniform with his hat on but our flight engineer? He walks straight back to the jerk, just stands there and stares at him. It seemed like an hour frozen in time when it probably was only a minute. However, the look on this old geezer's face was one that I cherished! He was stunned and now speechless!

Our flight engineer then turns to our celeb and their friend and says very causally, "Hi, my name is ____ and we've met before. It was at a party at so and so's house and I was actually there on a date with one of your backup singers. You probably wouldn't remember me but you also sang that evening. It was great." The celeb extends a hand and says, "Oh, thank you so much. Yes, I do remember that party. It was such a great time." They talk for a few more minutes and he returned to the cockpit.

At this point, I went out to the celeb and said, "I just want to apologize for everything that has happened on this plane today. On behalf of TWA, and all of its employees and my crew, we are deeply sorry and so embarrassed. I hope that you will accept my apology from the company." I have to admit here I had some tears in my eyes because of all of this stress.

You know what the celeb said to me? "You have been wonderful and handled this situation gracefully. Please don't worry about it." Then I thought I was really going to cry and had to quickly exit up to the galley.

Now the nice thing, if you could say nice thing, that happened on that flight was after the service was completed many passengers in first class got up, went over to this celeb, and their friend and apologized for this man's despicable actions and words.

A TWA PR person met the flight to escort my VIPs off the plane and again they thanked us for being so nice. Before we had packed up our suitcases to get off, the PR returned and said to me, "I just want to make sure that it was the passengers in 2D and F that created that problem." I said, "Yes," and then he said, "They will be put on our 'do not fly' list. They will never fly on TWA again. They'll be rebooked on American." Thank you, no passenger or crew should have to put up with that!

Years later, I was at a concert that this celeb was putting on. Always such a class act, both professionally and in person. Many thanks for your kindness to me in such a dreadful situation.

Dining With The Rich and Famous

IT WAS IN the early '70s and my husband was a young and upcoming executive with a large company. One of things he did was take customers out to dinner, and when it was possible he would invite their wives to come too, and of course I was there to spread the love also.

This one particular evening we were taking two couples out and we were going to Chasen's restaurant in Beverly Hills. Now to say Chasen's was an institution for the Hollywood crowd would be the understatement of the year because it was open for business for fifty-nine years before closing in 1995. This venerable institution had opened in 1936 and was located at the corner of Doheny Drive and Beverly Boulevard at the edge of Beverly Hills, so you can see why all of the rich and famous dined there. If only those tables and booths could have talked ... what did they hear when some of the greatest stars to appear on screen had dinner there? We will never know ...

But back to me. I had never been to Chasen's and was looking forward to this. Upon arriving, our guests were not there yet, so we took a seat at the bar. What is suspended from the ceiling over the bar, but a large plastic Boeing 707 airplane painted in TWA colors with a TWA logo on its tail. My husband points at this and I have a quizzical look on my face. Why? What? I don't know.

Our guests arrived and we were seated in a large booth that was quite comfortable for six people. Everything was lovely and our waiter was very attentive. We ordered our dinners and when our appetizers appeared, what were they served on? None other than our TWA Rosenthal china, replete with the TWA logo on it. This was the same china we used in first class. What? Then the salads, entrees, desserts are all served on TWA china too. Even the coffee was served to us in a TWA Rosenthal cup and saucer. Our guests were teasing me and asked if I had some type of pull in the kitchen. I have to admit I was mystified by this whole thing. And to be frank I was thinking I can't believe we are in this high-end restaurant in Beverly Hills and I have to eat off of china that I was just serving my passengers on. Can't I get away from TWA for just a few hours? The good news was the food was delicious.

Now the bill comes. No problem, my husband whips out his Diners Club card, puts it inside the folder that the bill was in and leaves it for the waiter to pick up.

The waiter picks it up and returns in just a few minutes, leans down, and discreetly says, "I'm sorry sir, but we do not take credit cards only cash." Gulp! We had spent probably $400 minimum on dinner and wine and remember this was in the early '70s. Well, neither of us had that type of money on us in cash and our guests were now combing through their wallets to chip in for dinner. We couldn't come up with the cash between the six of us and actually started to laugh when one of us said, "Who's going to stay tonight and do the dishes and clean up this place to cover our dinner bill?"

My husband meanwhile hails our waiter and asks to see the maître d'. He explains our problem about not having the cash between the six of us when the maître d' says, "Sir, we can accommodate you if you have a TWA Getaway card for credit. We will open a private account for you like we have for our other guests and you can charge this bill to it. We'll then send you a bill and you can send us a check."

Thank the Lord and pass the plate! No problem there, we got out our TWA Getaway charge card and a private account was set up for us at Chasen's. This was mind boggling ...

It wasn't until years later that I found out the connection between Chasen's and TWA. Chasen's actually had a contract with TWA to do their catering out of LAX. Leave it to our owner and Hollywood director/producer Howard Hughes to have Chasen's providing our catering.

Thank you TWA for saving us from doing dishes with our guests that evening ...

Note: One of Chasen's signature dishes was their chili. Allegedly, Elizabeth Taylor loved chili so much that in 1962, while in Rome on location filming for *Cleopatra*, she paid $100 to have Chasen's chili shipped to her on dry ice. She said, "I love chili and knew I had to try Chasen's chili if it really is that good."

Note: You can google Chasen's Chili recipe. Have a '60s party and serve it. You and Elizabeth Taylor, why not?

Pigs In a Blanket and We're Not Talking Appetizers

IT WAS AN all-nighter flight from west to east coast and the load was about half full. Now some of you might think that you are very anonymous on a plane, but guess what? You are not. Within ten minutes your flight attendants know where you are seated, who you are flying with and how you are dressed. Think I'm making this up, non mes amies, I'm not. When we are walking up and down those aisles during boarding, checking where you are stowing your carryon baggage we are observing all.

So, during this process my flying partner noticed a man boarding by himself, sitting in a coach aisle seat and then a woman boarding five minutes later, who sits in the window seat in the same row. There was not much interaction between them until after they were airborne. Picture them chatting away now and having some drinks. And then some more drinks, and then some more ...

We had finished the service and pillows and blankets had been handed out for the passengers' beddy-bye time. All seemed well, until ... my flying partner decided to do a cabin check. These were required to make sure that someone did not need something, everyone was well and frankly, they weren't burning the place down with one of those cigarettes that they were allowed to smoke at the time on a plane.

Now she is making her way down the darkened aisle, looking left and right when she slightly trips on something. Thinking it was a blanket that had fallen into the aisle she reached down to pick it up. She starts to pull on it when what to her wondering eyes does appear, but a pair of men's slacks. A pair of men's slacks? What?

At this point, she looks into that row and sees these two passengers are under a blanket together. Oh gee, you have to be kidding. Have some pride people, at least you could have gone to the lav for a quickie!

As they were in the middle of a lustful moment, she quietly takes the slacks, rolls them up and proceeds to go up to first class. In an empty row, she opens the overhead bin, moves the pillows and blankets over and puts the slacks behind them. They would never be seen again, until the cleaners would be on the plane hours later. Bet they would be surprised to find a pair of men's slacks in the overhead bin, but then maybe not? I hate to even think what they found left on planes.

Anyway, as she strolled back through the cabin she saw that the couple was still under their blankets enjoying one another shall we say? She is thinking, "Oh, this is going to be fun in a few hours or who knows maybe in minutes." When she gets back to our jump seat, she proceeds to tell me what had just happened and then she says, "I told the other flight attendants in first class about this. I'll handle it when he rings his call button for his pants." Oh, cray-cray times now!

Well, our two little love bugs did not "uncouple" until the morning light started to appear. Now we hear the ring, ring, ring of the call button. She gets up with a smirk on her face, knowing who was probably ringing.

"Good morning sir, may I help you?" He looks disheveled and confused and says, "Yes, when I was sleeping, I decided to take off my slacks, so they wouldn't get wrinkled. I put them on the floor and I can't find them now."

"Oh NO, let me help you look for them," she says with that note of concern.

Now she is crouched on the floor, feigning to look for those missing slacks. "Sir, I don't see anything," then she pops up at the row in front of him and says to those passengers, "Have you seen a pair of men's slacks?" Then to the other side, then behind him, repeating the same question, all with the same response, NO. "Sir I don't know what to tell you, no one seems to have seen any slacks. Would you like me to make an announcement on the PA asking if anyone has found a pair of men's slacks?" He is stammering now, "Uh, no that won't be necessary."

"All I can suggest is that you keep that TWA blanket and wrap it around yourself to deplane in. I would be happy to write up a flight report and let the company know about your missing slacks just in case they are found. All you have to do is give me your name and address. Would you like me to do that?" Guess what? His answer was NO.

I'm in the galley now preparing trays of coffee to help our passengers awake before landing when she returns. I said, "What were you doing out there?" When she told me everything, I just told you, I had to control myself not to laugh out loud. Picture me holding my sides now and laughing silently, which made me "snort" through my nose. What an appropriate sound. He was a pig, I hope his wife was there at the gate to pick him up at the airport and he had to explain about his slacks. To have been a fly on the wall for that one.

Bet you'll think twice now when eating "Pigs in a Blanket" at a cocktail party.

P.S. Wouldn't it have been fun if he had actually given his name and address to her. Why? Because we could have sent him his pants back addressed to his wife, saying, "Thanks for such a good time on the plane last night. Maybe next time we should use the lav. Here's to the Mile High Club!"

Escapades In the Desert

I WAS BASED in New York in the early '70s and my first flight, as a TWA flight attendant, was to Las Vegas. Ah, yes Vegas in those days was filled with celebrities, people dressed to go to the shows, and the food was spectacular and cheap too!

It is like yesterday when I remember this flight since I was a total rookie going to Las Vegas. The senior flight attendants informed me that I was working coach and of course, they were working first class. Frankly, I thought that was a good idea and was relieved since I didn't know anything about how to put on a really great first class service then.

After we were airborne and our service was completed in coach, I went up to first class just to check it out and I noticed there were several good-looking men seated there. Who were they? Well, I was about to find out. An hour before we landed one of the flight attendants from first class came back to our galley in coach and said these men would like to take us out for dinner in Vegas that night. I could feel my eyes starting to get wider then. My first flight and someone wants to take us out for dinner in Vegas!

Well, I came to find out that the flight attendants in first class knew these men because they had been passengers on many of their previous Vegas flights. They assured me there was no funny business going on, they just wanted to take us out to thank us for the great service. Wow! Was this what my new job was going to be like?

We arrived at our layover hotel, which was the Tropicana, rushed up to our rooms and changed into something more appropriate for dinner in Las Vegas. Now back down in the lobby one of those gorgeous men was there to meet us and ushered us out to a waiting limo! You have to be kidding me, I'm in Las Vegas in a limo going out for dinner. We arrived at an Italian restaurant and inside the maître d' greeted us and it was obvious that he knew our escorts. The restaurant had "red velvet walls", those big booths and the next thing I knew Steak Diane was in front me. This was heady stuff for a first trip as a newbie!

BUT the evening wasn't over yet. We are back in the limo now and off to see Don Rickles. Only one of the most well-known comics on the planet at the time! No seats for us in the peanut gallery in the back of the theater, yes, we were seated in a booth near the stage.

Don could easily see our booth and I'm sure he spotted our table since I was the only African American seated there. Well, if you ever saw him in person or on any of the TV shows, his act consisted of heckling anyone and everyone. You guessed it! Don Rickles heckled me, yes, he heckled me. Best night I ever had, being heckled by Don Rickels, a memory I still look back on and laugh about because he was one of my favorite comedians.

But the night didn't end there, these guys gave us some chips to gamble with and off to the craps table we went. I'd never played craps! Oh well, another learning experience. At this point, I have to admit I was getting really tired. Finally, we all decided to turn in. SEPARATELY, I might add.

The next morning, we met these men for breakfast and I, being a naïve nineteen year old, blurted out, "Are you guys in the mob?" I know I was an idiot! Well, there was a pall in the air, you could have heard a pin drop at the table, and it seemed like an eternity passed, when everyone finally started to laugh.

In retrospect, they could have buried me in the desert, and no one would have ever known.

It Was a Long Hot Summer

BACK IN THE summer of 1967, to be precise July 12th through the 17th, the Newark race riots were going on. They were one of 159 riots that swept through cities in the United States during that "Long Hot Summer of 1967," as it was later dubbed. Over the four days of rioting, looting, and property destruction in Newark, twenty-six people died and hundreds were injured.

During this time, I was based in Newark, NJ and lived in the Weequaic Towers which were across the street from Weequaic Park. I was a new flight attendant and on reserve (can be called out for any flight) and got the call from scheduling to work a flight from EWR to LAX.

From where I lived, which was directly across the street from the corner of the Weequaic Park, there was a bus stop where I would catch a bus to the airport. There I was standing, out in the open, waiting for the bus when someone fired a shot at me. Guess it must have been my lucky day because they missed and the bus arrived immediately thereafter. Well, being the good flight attendant that I was, I just showed up for work after being shot at and took out my flight. After all, did scheduling want to hear about the fact that someone had just tried to kill me. Probably not! The flight still had to get out on time.

As you might have surmised, I did not own a car then. So, I called my mother, who lived in southern New Jersey, and asked her if she could pick me up at the airport the following day when I came home, and take me to her house, until things cooled off in EWR. Needless to say, my mother immediately said yes.

I told her to come early, and she could go up to the deck of the airport, and watch planes take off and land until I came in. When I finally met my Mom, the first thing she said to me was, "Oh, Cyn, you missed it! What did I miss Mom?'" She replied, "Oh gosh, this plane came in on fire! There were ambulances and fire trucks and foam all over the place. It was scary!" I replied, "No, Mom, I didn't miss it. It was my plane."

It was a very long hot summer in 1967 ...

P.S. I'm sure you are asking now if we were all alright. Yes, the crew and passengers were all fine. Gunfire and planes on fire didn't stop TWA or me.

#MeToo

IN THE VERY early years of my flying career, which was from 1971 until 2009, I was working on what we called a Boeing 727 stretch aircraft. There was a work area behind the coach galley where supplies were stored, and it was right before the lavs and our jump seat. There were also two passenger rows right across from this work area.

Prior to landing, a male passenger came back to this spot where I was standing and approached me. Before I knew what was happening, he leaned over and said, "How often do you have to f— these guys?" I was incredulous! The word "WHAT!?" loudly flew out of my mouth. Then he jerked my forearm, pulled me close to him and repeated the same question in my ear.

Without another thought, I reacted by yanking my arm free and then slapped him as hard as I could. His glasses flew out into the aisle. Another male passenger who witnessed the scene, but did not hear the insult jumped up and grabbed him as I burst into tears.

I turned to the intercom system that was next to our jump seat to call the cockpit, to tell them what had just happened, but I was unable to speak coherently on the interphone when the flight engineer answered. As I turned to run up to the cockpit, I saw this man's glasses in the aisle and was about to purposely smash them, as they were in my path, but quickly changed my mind, figuring I was already going to be called on the carpet for my actions.

In the cockpit, I told them what had happened between sobs. Thank heavens, the captain was one who did not hesitate to back up his crew. He immediately stormed out and had words with this man. Upon exiting the plane this passenger made the declaration, "TWA will be hearing from my attorney." I know, amazing!

Well, this was not today it was 1973, so I felt I needed to high tail it to the hangar, to my supervisor's office there and tell her what had just happened on my flight. She was at a loss for words, but really had no idea how my issue would be handled. Consequently, enough time passed and a determination was made by my supervisor that hearing from his attorney was not going to happen.

However, my supervisor had notified the manager of TWA flight attendants in Chicago about this incident. The manager made the decision that since I represented TWA while in uniform, I should recognize that this kind of "bad conduct" was occasionally part of what we had to endure in our roles as flight attendants. She said she had no recourse but to place a letter in my company file, even though a complaint letter never came in from this passenger. In the letter she said that I had not conducted myself properly and had embarrassed TWA.

Well, when I learned about this it was just one more indignity that I felt I didn't deserve, nor should I have to put up with. What next? I went to my union rep immediately to file a grievance. Surprise, an arbitrator later found in my favor and her letter was removed from my file. Can you imagine today if a passenger spoke to a flight attendant like that, let alone laid a hand on them, what the repercussions on the passenger would be? How times have changed!

Just hashtag tag me, #MeToo.

The Gipper

THE MORNING STARTED out like any other. Get up early, drive to the airport, park in the employees' lot, take the crew bus over to the terminal for check in on a wide-bodied aircraft, the Lockheed 1011. There were the usual ladies that I flew with. It was a closed club to most flight attendants for TWA, who were based out of Chicago. You had to be in the top one hundred in seniority to hold this flight. Why? Because it was a turn around. In other words, fly to Las Vegas, sit on the ground for two hours, and then fly back to Chicago. Wham bam you are home by 9 PM. You did this eleven days out of the month. We hear you saying to yourself, "Not bad." But believe you me, we earned every penny.

The passengers going down we're in the "partaay" mood, drinking, playing cards and in good spirits. Then there was the return trip or what we called the second leg, coming home with another full load, but this time they had lost their money, drank to much, slept too little and generally were in a foul humor. Plus, we did this trip back-to-back. In other words, you flew it two days in a row. The second day coming home believe me, you had to bite your tongue.

Then there were some Las Vegas trips like this one that made it all worthwhile. We were in the briefing room the first day of one of these trips, when our flight service manager told us we are going to have Ronald Reagan on the flight down to Vegas. Whoa, now this would be more interesting! Especially since I had heard him speak to a Republican crowd at the Cincinnati convention center. Ten thousand people, balloons dropping, marching bands in the aisles and they were screaming for more Ronnie!

Well, I happened to be the most senior that day. This meant I could work anywhere on the aircraft. Therefore, Ronnie was going to be in first class and I would be too. Here is the back story: Reagan was going to a Republican convention in Las Vegas to speak since he was getting ready to throw his hat into the ring for a second time for President.

Now back to the flight, he was boarded by one of our PR people before any of the passengers got on. Not only was he being pleasant and well-mannered to all, but his aide that was accompanying him was too. He had that Irish look about him, red apple cheeks, a twinkle in his eyes and a smile on his lips. You just automatically like him!

When I gave him his menu, yes, we did have those in first class then, I told him that I had heard him speak in Cincinnati and that he had 10,000 people standing on their chairs clamoring for more and how exciting it was. Reagan was looking at me as if to say, "Wow, I did that?" No bravado or aren't I great attitude.

So, we take off and do the first class service. Nothing too exciting there. I went into the cockpit to check to see if the pilots wanted anything else to eat or drink. Totally ho-hum at this point. But here is where the story gets better.

As I left the cockpit, Reagan was coming around the bulkhead. Yes, probably to use the lav and stretch his legs. I said something to him and he replied back and the next thing you know we were having this nice intimate conversation. We talked about history repeating itself, the VietNam war and other things. However, in the conversation he said, "Do you know who Jimmy Stewart is?" Do I know who Jimmy Stewart is? Of course, who doesn't know who Jimmy Stewart, the actor is. But I didn't say that, I said, "Of course." Now, some of you who are reading this might not know who Jimmy Stewart is but trust me, everyone at that time knew who he was. Reagan continues with, "Well, you might not know this, but he is one of my very best friends."

He then does a perfect imitation of Jimmy Stewart's voice as he says, "You know Jimmy Stewart was a pilot in the Army—Air Core. He loves flying and it makes him angry when all anyone talks about is the food they ate on the plane and doesn't appreciate the marvel of being at 33,000 feet in the air in a capsule, flying above the earth." It was great.

Needless to say, I was having a marvelous time talking with Reagan, but then who wouldn't. Probably at least fifteen minutes had passed when another flight attendant came walking around the bulkhead and knocked on the cockpit door to get in. The door opens and the flight attendant starts to enter the cockpit, when the captain turns around in his seat and sees Reagan and me standing there. Oh, this is where it gets even better!

The captain says, "Governor Reagan, would you like to come into the cockpit and sit for a while." Reagan without missing a beat says, "Oh, no thank you I'm talking with Stephanie."

SCORE! Reagan chose me over the captain! I could feel a slight smile at the corner of my mouth and tried not to give someone a high five.

Of course, later when I went into the cockpit the captain was, shall we say, irritated. "What were you talking to Reagan about?" I smiled and said, "Oh politics, Vietnam, and Jimmy Stewart." He squirmed in his seat and looked ticked off!

Years later when President Reagan passed, I watched the many eulogies that people were offering during the day of his burial at the Reagan Library in Simi Valley. The one really overriding thing that resonated with me, in all of them, was what a gentleman he was; kind, considerate and caring. Then it dawned on me why he didn't accept the captain's offer to go into the cockpit, because it would appear that he was dismissing this female and would rather be with the men in the cockpit. All of those many years I had thought he had used me as a way to keep from getting stuck up in the cockpit with the guys. No, it was that he was a true gentleman.

I've told that story to others in the past and people asked me if I got his autograph. I never asked for an autograph from any of my passengers. I felt that it was an intrusion. Plus, an autograph would never have been the same as having talked with a future president of the United States. That is something I will never forget. Something very special …

Fashion 101

I WAS WORKING a 747 from Athens to JFK and the entire back of the aircraft was filled with Laotians refugees, who spoke little to no English. They were all dressed in very stiff new western wear. Now remember these people were just out of the rice fields and used to wearing very soft, pliable clothing.

Now speaking of clothing, these were the days when the female flight attendants would take off our uniform pants and put on our serving smock to work in. Much cooler as in temperature.

We were on our final approach into Kennedy and it was time to put my uniform pants back on. Well, I was all the way in the back of the plane, where duty-free was sold. This was also a quiet spot and protected from public view. I'm getting ready to put my pants back on with my smock off, thinking I was "by myself." Au contraire ma cherie!

Here is the picture: I am standing in the back with only a blouse, lacey undies and my panty hose. Suddenly I hear a lav door open, this very ancient Laotian man comes out of the lav trying to figure out how to zip up and button his brand new, very stiff Levis.

He sees me trying to get my pants pulled up "fast." Therefore, he has now assumed that this is the official dressing room. He watches me button and zip up my pants. Then he looks at his pants and a light bulb goes off, button, then zip. But he was still struggling with this new concept of attire.

I could see he needed some assistance, so what is the ever-helpful flight attendant going to do? You got it, I helped him with the zipper detail. Buttoned and zipped, he then gives me this very wide, toothless smile and bows, so I bow back, then he bows again and we both repeat this several times.

All I could think of was, what if someone from the crew just happened to be bounding back in time to see me and this man buttoning, zipping and bowing. By the way, how many times should one bow in a situation like that? Too late now!

Bet he had a story to tell his family later. Welcome to America ...

Simply Works

I WAS WORKING on a 747 and our flight service manager was extremely "suave" and spoke four different languages fluently. I noticed when the passengers were boarding, and there would be a woman complaining about something that obviously he couldn't help her with, he would listen intently, and when she had finished he would say, "Darling I would love to help you, but I simply can't." What could they say to that, nothing.

After hearing him say this a number of times I went over to him and said, "Where have you been for the last fifteen years of my flying career? That is the greatest one liner I've ever heard and it sure works." In a matter of minutes, a woman from coach appears in the first class cabin. She babbles on and on to me about some problem she is having in coach, which by the way there are only 10 other flight attendants back there that could probably have helped her, but I digress. I listen to her intently and then give her the line, "Darling I would love to help you, but I simply can't." She looked at me for a split second, while my comment sunk in, then said thank you and left. I looked over at him now and winked. That simple statement worked for the rest of my flying career!

Try using it sometime, it will get you out of a lot of things you don't want to do.

You Can't Make This Stuff Up ... Tales From a TWA First Officer

I REMEMBER THOSE fuzzy layovers at the Continental Hotel on Guam and lots of other stuff, including flight attendants flying the aircraft. Yes, crazy times! One particular incident when I was a first officer on the Boeing 727 at La Guardia stands out though.

The captain calls the first class flight attendant to the cockpit and tells her his brother, who is also a TWA captain, is meeting the aircraft when we land at LGA. He says we look exactly alike and to treat him well. "Can you please give him a hug when you open the door after we pull up to the jetway in LGA." You could easily tell she thought he was full of it and just kind of nodded her head.

We land at LGA, taxi into the gate and the jetway is pulled over, but then the captain moves the aircraft forward a bit, opens his window in the cockpit and tells the agent, who is standing on the jetway, "not" to open the door yet, just wait for him. The agent is a bit perplexed, but sees the captain getting ready to exit through his cockpit window onto the jetway! That is exactly what he did, and then he went over and opened the forward door from the jetway.

Well of course the flight attendant sees the "brother" on the jetway and can hardly believe it is true. However, she gives him a hug anyway, having no idea that the captain has pulled a fast one on her.

These two are really like twins! Now the captain's brother and she stand there and say goodbye to the deplaning passengers. Then he says, "Let's go into the cockpit and say hello to my brother." No captain, an empty seat and the window is open in the cockpit. I could see the look on her face, one of what the heck is going on? Then the cockpit crew erupts into laughter and she realizes that she has been tricked. She did have a good sense of humor though and started laughing too.

This same captain would put a rubber chicken under the cockpit windshield wiper and tell the tower and maintenance he had a bird strike.

As I said, you can't make this stuff up.

All It Took Was a Dime

I WAS A union rep for the TWA flight attendants based at JFK. In the '60s and '70s there was a weight requirement that you could only be two lbs. over your hiring weight. This obviously created many problems for a lot of flight attendants. Unfortunately, it might be described as that era in the airline's history of the Gestapo always checking your weight and appearance!

One of our flight attendants was a beautiful British woman, who was put on the dreaded "weight check." She was also taken off payroll and put on probation, meaning there was the possibility that she could lose her job, if she didn't lose a certain amount of weight at a specified time. Needless to say, this cost her a lot of money.

Photo of Stan Herman TWA uniforms
courtesy of Linda Chabrja.

As that fateful weigh-in date arrived, I took her to the grooming supervisor's office during lunch, while no one was there, to see her get on the scales to weigh in and to find out if she had met the requirement. No, she didn't, what to do?

Now this was before digital scales. Remember those old scales with the weights where you moved a weight on the bottom for the hundreds and the top one was for the individual pounds. I said, "Don't worry, I'm going to get you through this." I took a piece of Scotch tape and made it double sided, then put a dime on the tape and pasted it to the back of the top weight. It could not be seen and since you do not touch the back of the weight when you move it, I felt confident that we would get away with this.

It was now the time of reckoning! She put on quite the show of removing all items from her body, i.e. shoes, watch, scarf, earrings and rings before getting on that scale.

She stepped on the scale and the supervisor moved the weights! Tick, tock, tick, tock, I was holding my breath now, what would the weight be? Would the dime keep that metal weight from moving? Yes, she was nine pounds below the requirement. We did it! The grooming supervisor congratulated her, but as the Gestapo always did they called her in again a few weeks later for another weigh in. I once again accompanied her and again the same weight. Still nine pounds lighter. The dime was still working its magic. Everyone was all smiles, the supervisor congratulated her and we went on our merry way. If I had kept liquor in my office, I would have had a celebratory drink then!

Several months later, I was in the grooming supervisor's office and what did I see? A mirror had been placed behind the scale. Hmmm, somehow they must have discovered the dime and wanted to make sure that our trick could not be used again. Oh well, it worked for a while.

"A dime in time" or "A dime for every nine pounds!" You pick …

I'm Going to Die in Entebbe

MY HUSBAND AND I were going on a picture-taking safari in Kenya and Tanzania. We had flown over to London and had spent a few days and then were taking a foreign carrier (which I will not identify) to Nairobi which made stops in Rome and Entebbe. Our travel agent had told us not to get off of the plane in Entebbe since they didn't like Americans. Did give us pause, but we were young and you always think things can't happen to you.

From London to Rome was basically uneventful. I had told one of the flight attendants that I had a broken seat back that wouldn't stay in a locked position for takeoff and landing and it needed to be fixed in Rome. Not a problem on that leg of the trip because I could move to the center seat next to my husband.

Well, we land in Rome and no mechanic ever comes on board to fix the seat. The plane was going to be full from Rome to Entebbe and sure enough a man appeared, who had the center seat assignment. Not being a fool, I suggested that he take my aisle seat and I would sit next to my husband. He seemed delighted with that and plopped himself down. Seat back not staying in a locked position didn't seem to faze him at all.

But it gets better. Muhammad Ali was fighting George Foreman in the famous fight in Kimshasa, Zaire which had been dubbed "The Rumble in the Jungle." In Rome the plane filled up with lots of partying Italians, who were going to the fight. They had obviously been imbibing before they got on and proceeded to place their "many" Chianti bottles in the overhead storage rack which at that time was not enclosed. Only coats, hats, and light objects were to be placed up there. Did anyone care, as in the crew? Obviously not and I prayed we didn't hit any turbulence where they would start flying through the cabin like little missiles!

Now we take off for Entebbe. The wild Italians were up and out of their seats partying in the aisle with drinks in hand; when finally, late into the evening they along with most of the other passengers dozed off after the meal service. What next? I had made a trip to the lav and what did I see? Both of the flight attendants were asleep in their jump seats! Oh, perfect as in not! Ironically, I had just read in their in-flight magazine how well trained their cabin crews were. Really? Methinks not, as I noted that they also had cartons of soft drinks piled up in front of the exit doors! This is where ignorance is bliss. I unfortunately was not ignorant and had come to the conclusion that if we made it to Nairobi, I might be staying there permanently for fear of getting on another one of this carrier's planes!

OK, but it gets better. As we approach Entebbe, we are flying into a terrible rainstorm. It was literally like someone was outside throwing buckets of water at the windows. The rain was pounding the plane. Of course, everyone was asleep, including my husband and I was reading the same paragraph over and over again in my book. The plane was black inside except for my reading light. No dim lighting had been turned on for landing in the cabin, as it should have been by the "well trained" flight attendants. To say I was slightly anxious would be putting it mildly. In fact, I was convinced that we were probably going to meet our maker soon!

The plane was shaking and rolling; my husband stirs at one point and says, "What's going on?" I wanted to tell him that we were probably going to die in Entebbe, but why do that. Let him die in peace was what was screaming through my mind at that point. So, I just said, "Oh nothing honey, go back to sleep." Which I might add that he did! I'm back to rereading that same paragraph.

Now, I'm the only one on the entire plane who seems to be awake at this point. The "well trained" flight attendants had not even bothered to come through the cabin to check on seat belts, seatbacks, us, nor as I said, turned on any interior lights for landing. And then it happened, we aborted our landing!

What does that mean? We were close to the runway for landing, and then all of a sudden the captain pulled up the nose and we started going back up rapidly. Now what went through my mind is not repeatable. I was sure we were going to die now. Does my husband wake up—NO!

Well, the captain goes back for a second try and this time we land. OMG, terra firma. I wanted to go out and kiss the ground, but we are in Uganda. The travel agent said, "Do not get off of the plane there. Edi Amin does not like Americans." Plus remember there was still a torrential rain storm going on.

Most of the passengers deplaned at this time, including all of the crazy Italians with their chianti bottles in hand to continue on to Zaire and I got up to stretch my legs before our next leg to Nairobi. Would you believe my husband was still sleeping? I walked to the open back door for some fresh air. Now you have to picture an airport that is the size of a postage stamp. So obviously, there are no jetways. The rain was pouring down and I peered out to see a 6'5" man in army fatigues with a machine gun. Yikes, you better believe I'm not getting off of this plane. Oh, Lord just let me make it to Nairobi!

Well, end of story we finally get to Nairobi and have the best vacation of our lives with another couple, who was meeting us there.

I might add that she was also a TWA flight attendant and the first thing she said to me when we met in Nairobi was, "How was your flight? My God I was scared to death on mine, I thought it was the end! And now we all have to fly back together on that carrier."

Picture us nine days later: My girlfriend is sitting across the aisle from me on the plane. The captain revives up the engines. She looks at me and I look at her. Both of us are rolling our eyes now. She extends her hand out to me and we hold hands across the aisle, as the plane takes off down the runway. The good news was we didn't have to stop in Entebbe on our way to Rome. There was a God! And we still laugh about this today.

Moral of the story: Fly on American carriers.

POSTSCRIPT
The G O A T

MANY YEARS LATER who do I have on flight, but "The Greatest of All Times," Muhammad Ali. He was so handsome and had the most wonderful smile. I thought to myself, if only my girlfriend was here now, she would get his autograph for her husband. You see he was a major fight fan and when we were in Kenya, "The Rumble in the Jungle" took place. The newspaper in Nairobi the next day had a huge front-page picture of Ali on it with the headline ALI STILL KING!

Her husband had purchased five copies of the newspaper, just in case if something happened he would hopefully still end up with one. When he got home, he had the entire front page framed and it was hanging in his office.

Never liking to ask for anyone's autograph I decided this was a once in a lifetime chance and I had to go for it. I explained to Muhammad Ali how we had been in Kenya during the fight, and how my friend's husband had the newspaper's front page framed in his office and he would be thrilled to have his autograph.

Well, to my surprise and delight he asked me if I had anything he could write on and he would be happy to give me an autograph for my friend. TWA at that time had writing paper and postcards that we gave to the public to use inflight and I prayed there was still some left. Viola! A postcard, perfect!

He signed it:

> To: Sandy
> Peace in the world!
> Muhammad Ali

Sandy took his framed newspaper to the framer, had them open it up and placed the postcard inside with the newspaper. It is still proudly hanging in their home today.

This Is the Last Straw

MALE FLIGHT ATTENDANT: One day while working the bar cart, I'm going through coach serving drinks. A lady in an aisle seat orders a soft drink. I hand it to her along with a napkin and she says, "I'd like a straw." I said, "I'm sorry ma'am we don't have any." She said, "I see those little straws on your cart, just hand me one." I said, "Ma'am really we don't have any." She said, "Look, this is real simple, just hand me one of those little red straws there that you have with the napkins," as she was pointing to the plastic stir rods.

To which I replied, "OK Ma'am, but if you can suck anything through this, I'd like to have your phone number."

TWA Wants to Know My Hair Products

THE BEGINNING OF January I saw that TWA was advertising in our local paper that they would be having interviews in Philadelphia, PA for "hostesses," as they then called the flight attendants. It sure sounded good to me, so I decided to try it. This required taking the train from Harrisburg to Philadelphia for the interview there, as well as their testing. To say I was excited would be an understatement. Even if I wasn't accepted it would be a fun day.

After the interview and testing was finished, I went back to Harrisburg and waited. It seemed like an eternity, but it was a mere two days later when I got a phone call saying I had the job. They would be sending a ticket to come to Kansas City, the second week in February, to start training. I was walking on clouds. Little me from Harrisburg was going to join those glamour girls in the sky!

Flash forward: In Harrisburg, I boarded the good old Connie (Constellation) airplane at the airport. I had never been on a plane in my life, let alone been to the Midwest where I was sure there were real cowboys with bibbed overalls, cowboy hats and boots. This was a new adventure, was it really happening to moi? I already had dreams of going to Paris then. Well, remember I said I had never flown before, so I proceeded to throw up all the way to Kansas City. What a mess! And on top of this the flight attendants told me I was never going to make it. This was not starting well.

When I arrived in Kansas City, I took a cab to the Georgian Court, as instructed by TWA, where I would be staying during training. Oh, this new adventure was really happening and I had already forgotten about all of that airsickness! The next day I met everyone in my training class and realized they were just as excited as I was.

All was going well, as everyone made it through our classes the first week with flying colors. However … just when class was about over, on Friday, I was called into the office to talk with the head of the training center. This would be as if you had been summoned to see the principal at school and I was terrified! What had I done? Picture me with sweaty palms sitting across from this woman, at her desk, when I hear her say, "Do you highlight your hair?" Why was she asking that? Hmmm, the only nice thing they said to me during my initial interview was that I had beautiful hair, so I guessed they wanted to know what products I used on it. Wrong! Was I naïve, really the head of TWA's training center wanted to know what I used on my hair? NO! Nevertheless at this point, as I started to relax, I told her what products I used.

Well, my dream bubble was about to burst when I was told that I wasn't allowed to stay in training because my hair had color in it. Yes, you read right! What? I had no idea. I was never told that and I never saw that written anywhere. I started to cry. Then she handed me a ticket and said that there was a cab outside that would take me back to the Georgian Court. I was to pack my clothes and the cab would wait to take me to the airport for a 5:00 PM flight home. They would hold all the classes at the training center because they did not want me to see anyone before I left. I hear myself saying, "You mean I can't say goodbye to my friends?" To which she replies, "No, we're sorry. It would be way too upsetting." I was devastated, even though they said that I was more than welcome to return once the only color in my hair was my own!

The day after I arrived home I had my hair cut as short as I could and all I could do was wait for it to grow back. At that time, we got a small paycheck, in training, so once I received my check for my one week of training I could go and apply for unemployment. I collected that every week until I went back to Kansas City the third week in June. Short hair and all I passed their inspection.

I look back on this and have to smile. My how things have changed and maybe, many years ago, I was part of that.

TWA Crew Hijacks Airplane

IT WAS NOVEMBER of 1973 and I was flying what we referred to as a "double crossing." This particular trip was a series of charters that the company had put together to make up a double crossing. We left JFK in the evening, flew to Frankfurt, Germany, laid over for twenty-four hours, and then flew back to Detroit to layover for twenty-four hours. However, we weren't through yet. Then we flew to Pisa, Italy where we would drop off our passengers, to ferry the aircraft (that is a term meaning no passengers on board only crew) to Vienna, Austria and layover for twenty-four hours. Our final day we would fly to Boston, where again we would drop off our passengers, go through Immigration and Customs, then ferry the aircraft down to JFK. If you add up the days away, we came home on the fifth day. Believe it or not this was a plum trip. Lots of flight time in just five days. So, you were half dead by the time it was over, but that was of little concern. It was all about accumulating as much flight time, in as few days as possible, meaning more time off between trips. Little did we know what an adventure we would be on.

On the first part of the trip the captain asked the entire crew to meet in Frankfurt to go out for dinner. He was a very senior captain and I might add really looked out for his crews. Why did he want our entire crew to go out for dinner together? To discuss November 5, 1973, 12:01 AM. You are now saying what?

Well, the TWA flight attendants were set to go out on strike when we were airborne going to Pisa, Italy. Therefore, the important topic of conversation at dinner was, if we actually went out on strike, we would be airborne at the time and would not find out until we landed in Pisa. We needed to have our plan finalized, would we stay in Pisa, Italy, or ferry the plane to Vienna, Austria as we were scheduled to do. There was lots of good-hearted banter comparing Pisa's Leaning Tower to Vienna's Lipizzaner horses. Where to go? The consensus from the entire crew was forget the Leaning Tower of Pisa, we would rather see Vienna.

Now for those of you who are not familiar with airlines and strikes, when a particular union strikes and the company shuts down there are obviously employees, i.e. cockpit and cabin crews, spread around the TWA system which means all over the world. Flights known as "sweeper" flights would pick up crews around the entire system to bring them back to the states. It was also a way to get a number of planes back into the country and to our domiciles for when the strike would end. Why do you need this much information? You'll understand in a minute.

A few days later, off our little merry band goes taking a full load of charter passengers to Pisa, Italy. Now Pisa at this time was a tiny little airport and TWA did not have service there, so they had brought in an agent from Milan to help with this flight. Our purser spoke fluent Italian, and when we landed he opened the door to be greeted by an agent that he knew well from flying into Italy, many times. The agent said, "You went out on strike last night." Our purser immediately opened the cockpit door and told the cockpit crew we were out on strike.

Remember our plan was now to just continue to Vienna, as our schedule required, instead of saying we are on strike and aren't going. The passengers deplane, the cockpit goes into the ramp office to file their flight plans to Vienna, the flight engineer does his outside walk around the aircraft, and the flight attendants proceed to kick off their shoes, plop down in first class seats and get ready for the ferry flight to Vienna.

The captain and first officer return to the cockpit along with the flight engineer, they start up the engines and tell the purser they are ready to leave. Meanwhile the agent is standing on the steps that had been brought up to the forward door for the passengers to deplane. He is gesturing with his hands and obviously upset that the crew was going on to Vienna. Our purser is literally closing the door in his face and saying in Italian, "I hope this strike is a short one. See you soon." And off we go to Vienna …

We arrive in Vienna and are like kids in a candy store. Believe it or not, none of us had been to Vienna before. The entire crew decides to go on a tour. Now remember we have never gone to bed. Off on the tour bus we go, Lipizzaners here we come. Four hours later, we returned to the hotel. The captain and first officer say, "We had it, we have to go to bed." Two of the other flight attendants and the purser say they have to go get some sleep too. That leaves the flight engineer, another flight attendant and me. We are not down for the count yet! Heck, who knows when this strike is going to be over and we might as well get some Christmas shopping done.

The three of us grab a quick bite and now proceed to jump in and out of shops. We were like the Three Musketeers, or the remains of the crew "on a mission." Laden with gifts, we return to the hotel and drop them off in our rooms. What next? Sleep? You have to be kidding! NO sleep for us. We ask the concierge at the hotel for a recommendation for a restaurant and out we go for dinner. We wined and dined on Wiener Schnitzel, Krautrouladen, and Schweinsbraten. The rule we made-up was, you were only allowed to eat a third of your entrée and then had to pass it to your right, so that we all got to try everything. Finished with dinner, now what? Back to the hotel. We enter the lobby and can hear a band in the bar. It is like "Lorelei" calling us from the sea. Who needs sleep? The bar awaits us with a few nightcaps! We have been up for thirty hours at least and it is now 11 PM local time, FINALLY we decided it was time for bed.

Up we go on the elevator and strangely enough we were all on the same floor. Note: that usually never happens. I get to my door, whisper good night to my comrades and open it to see a white sheet of paper on the floor with a handwritten note on it. It was from our purser. I whispered to them to come back, and told them the purser had left a note for me and it involved all three of us.

It seems that TWA did not like the fact that the crew had hijacked their plane and had gone to Vienna. No sense of humor back in New York! The purser said in his note; no matter what time you get back to your room please call me. The captain wants to have a meeting. So, I did as asked. The conversation kind of went like this: "Are you just getting back to your room?" Me, "Yes." "Have you ever gone to sleep?" Me, "No." "Are the flight engineer and the other flight attendant with you?" Me, "Yes." "Well, get over to my room now! The company is really pissed that we took their plane to Vienna and the captain wants to have a meeting. I'm going to call him now." Me, "OK." I'm now hearing mumbling before he hangs up, "Damn I can't believe they never went to sleep!"

Now here we were at the big meeting in the purser's room with the entire crew and I might add they were all looking at us like, "These idiots have never gone to sleep!" The purser reads this long and I mean "really" long message from the company, which I will condense, saying we did not have their permission to take the plane to Vienna. Furthermore, since we were now in Vienna, we were to work our scheduled flight home with the charter passengers on it. And if we did not and planned on staying in Vienna, all of the sweeper flights were now back in the states, and they were going to leave us there and had instructed the hotel (Intercontinental) that they would no longer pay our hotel bills.

Of course, the captain already knew about this, as well as the rest of the crew, who had not "partied hearty" with us. The captain said, "I've been through these strikes before. We will just go to the airport and I'll pay to have the plane gassed up. The company will pay me later. These bastards aren't going to leave us in Vienna. And furthermore, before we leave I will call the American Embassy, and tell them TWA was going to leave us here and we thought about declaring ourselves destitute."

Well, cooler heads were prevailing, and our purser said he would call our union's New York strike headquarters to see what the union wanted us to do. Surprise, the union already knew all about us. Yes, we were the only crew, who was not home yet. The company was mad to put it mildly and the union just thought it would be easier for us to work our flight home. They couldn't guarantee us though if we would get paid for it. The captain finally acquiesced and we all went to our rooms for that much-needed rest. I will add here that I had the best sleep on a layover I ever had. It was eight hours of sleeping like the dead! When that wakeup call came, I actually felt like I was ready to go.

Now the second part of the adventure kicks in …

In the morning, off we go to the Vienna airport. There were supposed to be two TWA charter planes to take passengers to Boston. Well, the other charter crew never showed up with a plane, as we did. So, those passengers were put on a Pan Am flight and we had our passengers.

I will never forget it. The passengers were boarding and saying, "We thought you were on strike? We are so thankful you are here. We thought we were going to be stranded." Our purser got out the crucifixion nails and crosses then for our martyrdom. His reply, "Oh, we did not want to involve the public with our dispute with the company. So, we decided to work our flight home." These people were kissing our feet!

We got up in the air and the purser made a PA announcement that we would be serving them lunch, and then the bars on either end of the plane would be opened up and if they would like something to just come to the bar area. As he said to us, "We probably won't get paid for this. Forget the liquor carts, they can come to us." Well, come they did and since it was a charter all of the liquor was complimentary. And did we make sure everyone got plenty!

Then a woman said to me, "You know the silverware on those trays is just a little smaller than normal. My grandchildren would love them." Me, "Oh darling, here are the carriers. Just open the doors; here is the hot water to rinse them off with because I don't have any clean ones. Put them in one of the barf bags and take them home." Well, she and her girlfriends are like fine oiled machines, going through that galley, grabbing up the dirty silverware, rinsing it off in hot water and filling their barf bags. Trust me they all had service for eight settings at least! I guess lots of grandchildren? Later I see them taking pillows and blankets from the overheads. Someone on the crew had said, "It was alright."

Next what do I hear? A woman's intoxicated voice coming from the PA system in the rear of the plane. She says, "Ladies and gentlemen. These people were soooo wonderful to work this flight, so we could get home and they don't even have a job when they get home. And, (slur, slur,) they don't even know if they are getting paid for this. More slur, slur, so I'm coming through the plane to collect money for them." Well, our passengers were quite benevolent, or sloshed, or maybe both, but we all walked off the plane with $100 apiece. Now that was 1973 and that was some nice money then!

At this point I went up to the cockpit to see how they were doing and the captain asked me how the passengers were. I explained to him what I just told you and he laughed. He said, "Let them strip the plane, if they want it, let them take it." And take they did. I still wonder how they explained all of their ill-gotten gains to customs.

Now we are about thirty minutes outside of Boston, when the captain got on the PA system and made the following announcement, "Ladies and gentlemen, I just thought you would like to know that you are now on the last TWA aircraft that is airborne anywhere in the world." Wow, there was a hush on the plane while that sunk in. It was really like the twilight zone, surreal!

But our adventure wasn't over yet. Remember we still had to ferry the plane from Boston to JFK. We cleared Boston Immigration and Customs and went back on the plane. Off to Kennedy we go. We arrive and our cockpit pulls the plane up to the TWA terminal. There is a plane at every gate! Gee, now what? The captain is talking with our ramp office and to be frank they were giving him the runaround. According to them it would be at least thirty minutes, maybe an hour, to get one of the planes out of a gate, so that we could park and get off the plane.

Remember the captain was going to gas that puppy up in Vienna and leave regardless of the company's edict. This answer went over like a lead balloon. I paraphrase his remarks back to the ramp office. "You've got five minutes to get some mechanics out here to push a plane out of a gate, so that we can park.

My crew is dog-tired. We are finishing up a five-day trip and just came from Vienna via Boston. If I don't see some mechanics out here on the ramp moving a plane in five minutes, so that we can park, I will instruct my crew to pull all of the emergency handles on all four slides, and we will evacuate this plane and be out of here! Do you understand me?!" You could see mad scurrying now from mechanics and a plane being pushed out of a gate for us.

End of adventure, No not quite! We were parked at a gate in five minutes and getting off that plane, but there was one more detail, there was no crew bus running from the terminal to the hangar where our cars were parked! This required another call from the captain and believe you me I wouldn't have wanted to be on the end of that conversation.

Forty-two days later, we ended the strike in mid-December, but I already had my Christmas shopping done. Bet you are wondering if we were paid. Yes, we were and it was a nice surprise since there was no paycheck coming in during the strike.

P.S. I bought some Christmas ornaments in Vienna on our shopping spree. Now every year when I put them on my tree, I remember a really special time when we hijacked a TWA plane. Cheers to a wonderful crew!

Voulez-vous un café

WHILE STANDING ON an armrest, reaching up to the storage area on a Boeing 747, a male passenger walked by me and stuck his hand up my skirt. And I might add, it was not a few inches if you get the picture. I can see the look on your face now. Imagine the look on mine!

I heard a few gasps from the other passengers, who saw this, while I almost fell off of the armrest from shock. Then he turned back and winked at me. You've got to be kidding me. I wanted to kill him. Now you can imagine the thoughts that went through my head. Revenge! You've heard the old adage, "Never tick off a food handler."

Right before I reached his row to serve coffee, I returned to the galley to get a fresh, full, piping hot pot of coffee. Delicious! With a big smile and my "chirpiest" flight attendant voice, I offered him a cup of coffee. I'll never forget that big grin he had on his face. He must have thought I was delighted with what he had done. NOT!

He lifted his cup for me to fill and completely by accident, I must add, the whole pot fell right into his lap. Horrors! How could that have happened? "Oh, NO!" I exclaimed, followed by profuse apologies for it seemed to have hurt a tad. As I picked up the coffee pot from his lap, I offered to get him some paper towels, followed with a wink ...

As I said, "Never, never tick off the people who have control over your food."

Time Change ... Can Lead to Troubles

I WAS BASED in LAX and was flying a flight to Philadelphia. Of course, you all know there is a time change of three hours between the cities. Therefore, if you arrive at your layover hotel in the city and it is 9 PM there it is only 6 PM in LAX. Early for a Los Angeles based crew.

We had a very long layover and didn't leave until late the following day, so what is a crew to do? Well, the captain asked if any of the flight attendants wanted to go out for a drink on the layover with the cockpit crew. I, along with my flying partner, said, "Yes, we'll go." Seemed rather harmless, have a few drinks and then go back to the hotel. Now here is a small fact that many of you probably don't know. Most of the time we never drank in a hotel we were laying over in, because God forbid one of your passengers sees the crew whooping it up in a hotel bar and the next day they recognize you in the airport. Not good!

But getting back to my story. The three pilots and the two of us meet in the hotel lobby, and the captain tells us he had spoken with the concierge, and he had given him the names and addresses of three different bars. Off we go ...

The first bar had a live band, and before you knew it a number of men came over, and were asking my flying partner and myself to dance. We kept declining, but it didn't seem to make any difference that we were there with three men. After a while, it was getting annoying and the captain said, "Let's get out of here and go to another bar. I think these two (meaning us) could get us into trouble here." He dropped some money on the table for our drinks and we were out of there.

Now where? It is only midnight in PHL, 9 PM our time. The captain said, "The concierge said there is a small quiet bar right around the corner from here." What a great place it was, picture red leather booths, paneled wood walls that were filled with pictures of Frank Sinatra, and the Rat Pack crowd of Dean Martin and Sammy Davis Jr. There was an old-fashioned jukebox that you didn't have to put money in to play a song and it only played Frank's, Dean's and Sammy's music. Only problem was that it closed early, 1 AM Philly time, which was still only 10 PM, our time.

So, at 1 AM we left. Now where? The captain says, "There is another bar around here. It's a private club, but the concierge said to tell them he sent us and they would probably let us in."

We walked another block or so, turning down an alley that I might add was poorly lit to arrive at a large wooden door. There was no address, no signage, nada. The captain knocks on the door. Really more like a light bang. Nothing! Then he bangs on it a few more times. All of a sudden, a small wooden peep hole opens in the door. All you can see are two brown eyes and then we hear a man say, "Who are you?" The captain says, "The concierge at the Warwick Hotel told us we could get a drink here." The brown eyes are moving from left to right and back again, constantly moving and checking us all out. Then we hear him say, "Where are you from?" The captain says, "We are from LA. I'm a TWA captain," he points now, "this is my first officer, he is my flight engineer and these girls are our flight attendants."

After what seemed like an eternity of silence, more eye movement and checking us out the peephole slams shut. Then we hear the sounds of bolts on the inside of the door being moved. The door swings open and a large man in a suit says, "Just walk down the hallway, turn to your left, go down the stairs and you'll find the bar." We all mumble thank you and start to walk down this narrow hallway. The walls were cement, the floor too and it was not very wide. I'm thinking, what is this place? When all of a sudden, we walked down the steps he was talking about, and we entered a massive room filled with people, a huge bar, and a live band! We were in an after hours SPEAK EASY!

Well, the guys are throwing down the martinis, and my flying partner and I are sipping on vodka and tonics. Get the picture. We are still sober and the guys are not! Finally, we convince them at 3 AM, Philly time that we need to go back to the hotel.

We're outside now and the pilots are walking together, who knows what they were talking about, and my flying partner and I are walking behind them. We are talking about how hungry we are, remember it's 3 AM in Philly, but only midnight our time. Do we order room service? They probably are closed. What to do?

We made our plan, ditch the pilots, go find some type of a diner that was open, and get a hamburger. How to ditch those three?

She says, "When we get to the elevator let them go in first, hang back. Then we'll let the door close and we'll wave bye-bye to them." It worked! We could hear them saying, "Where are you guys going?" as the doors closed. Thank God, now let's get some food.

We left the hotel and decided that we had seen a hamburger joint down the street. Perfect! We find it; order our burgers, fries and soft drinks to go. A short walk back to the hotel and "heaven" was just minutes away.

As we left the restaurant, we started pulling fries out of the go bags and were munching away, when a cab came screeching up to the curb right next to us. The cabbie lowers the window and says, "What are the two of you doing out on the streets at this time of night?" Remember it was after 3 AM now in Philly. It was like your father swooping into a party that you weren't supposed to be attending and telling you to get in the car you're going home. And that is exactly what he did.

We hear him saying, "Where are you staying?" I babbled something about we are at the Warwick Hotel right around the corner, but I really wanted to say, "I'm sorry father."

Then he yells at us to get into the cab and he will take us over to the Warwick. Well, you do as your father requests. We climb into the back of the cab and he proceeds to lecture us for five minutes about how you don't walk around Philly at 3 AM in the morning etc.

The two of us are mute in the back seat, like chasten children, as he pulls up to the hotel. I hear myself saying to him, "Thank you, how much do we owe you for the ride?" He turns around, looks at the two of us like you are lucky I'm not your father because you would be grounded for a month and says, "Nothing! But I don't want to see you out on these streets again at night. Do you understand me?" Both of us just nodded yes, exited the cab, walked in the front door of the hotel and looked at one another like, "What the hell just happened?"

In retrospect, he probably was our guardian angel ... you don't walk around Philly at 3 AM!

P.S. The pilots never asked us the next day where we went. Wonder why? Could it be because they had been over-served?

Howard Hughes and the Mechanics

AS YOU ALL should know the "famous or infamous" Howard Hughes owned a controlling interest for a number of years in TWA. Mr. Hughes was not your usual owner of an airline.

Since I was based in LAX for a number of years, as a flight attendant, we occasionally talked with the mechanics when they got on board to do their work. During one of these casual conversations my flying partner asked this senior mechanic if he had ever met Howard Hughes. He said, "Oh sure, I've met him a number of times. He would show up in the middle of the night in a big black limousine at the hangar. He'd get on the planes where we were working and would look at the log books for that plane. Then he would watch us work on a repair and even make suggestions. He was quiet, but fairly sociable. He'd hang around for anywhere from an hour to two hours, and then get back in his limousine and leave. We always knew it was Mr. Hughes in the middle of the night when we saw that limousine pull into the hangar."

Photo of Howard Hughes exiting an aircraft courtesy of the TWA Museum.

How many CEO's or major owners of a company show up in the middle of the night. Only Howard Hughes who was a genius with planes.

Captain Who

WE WERE "NEW HIRES" and it was the good ol' days of paper pay cards that the flight engineer had to fill out for us, a detail you will understand a little later. The first class flight attendant, who was going to make the announcements, would have to go up to the cockpit and get the captain's name, flight time and cruising altitude. Here is where the story begins:

My flying partner, who was going to make the announcements, went up to get the info and when she asked the captain his name, he told her, "Well, I'm Captain Garue, G-A-R-U-E, but believe it or not, there are actually two Captain Garue's working for TWA. So, when you make your announcements, be SURE to use my first name as well as my last." She assured him that she always uses "both" the captain's first and last name in her announcements and asked him what his first name was. He said, "It's Ken," and the plot thickens.

The plane is being pushed back from the gate now, and she dutifully got on the PA and said (if you haven't figured this out yet, read the next line out loud), "Good morning ladies and gentlemen. Captain Ken Garue and his entire crew would like to welcome you …" then she stopped, wondering why the entire cabin was laughing now. She did a quick recap and realized what everyone thought she had said.

The cockpit could listen to our announcements if they wanted and I'm sure they were listening in and laughing. When she went back into the cockpit, they pointed out to her that the captain's REAL name was on the pay card the whole time. I'm sure there were a lot of wisecracks about the first officer being Mr. Greenjeans on that flight.

Hazing of new hires, a rite of passage.

Que Sera, Sera

AH, TO BE a TWA flight attendant in the glamour years. The years when Howard Hughes, motion picture producer and director, owned TWA and all of those Hollywood celebrities flew his airline. The '60s and '70s when people thought being a flight attendant was the epitome of sophistication. Yes, you might have graduated college but guess what? The newspapers put your picture in the paper, with your announcement of becoming a stewardess, not when you graduated from college. There was a professional picture of you in your uniform which you submitted, your biography and where you were going to be based. The entire city knew you were one of the few who had made it into that rarified air. And it was a big deal! In 1968 over 100,000 people interviewed for a flight attendant position with TWA. How many did they hire? Approximately 1,000 from all over the US, plus some from Europe. You had a better chance of being admitted to an Ivy League college then, than being hired by TWA.

Picture of Stephanie Johnson, age 5, author of the story,
practicing to become a flight attendant

Let's face facts, it was the profession that fascinated the general public. Those glamourous girls seeing the world, meeting and greeting the rich and famous. Now those were star-studded adventures that most people would never have and only dream about.

Here is where my TWA tale starts for me: sometimes it is just a suggestion that makes one think and act. It was spring of 1968 and I was studying in my room at the sorority house with my roommate. When out of the blue she says, "Let's go interview with the airlines." Airlines? My reply was, with a slightly stunned tone of voice, "Doing what?"

"Well, we can be stewardesses and fly for TWA. We can fly around the world." Hmm, something I had never thought about before. Now this might be fun.

She continues, "I saw in the newspaper that TWA is going to be interviewing at this hotel in the city. Let's go." My attitude was, sure what do we have to lose. So, a few days later we were in a hotel suite with a lot of other young women. We filled out an application and then patiently waited for the interviewer to call us, one at a time, into another room for an interview.

The interviewer was a young, handsome man in a suit and tie and he obviously had done a lot of interviewing by his suave manners. After about ten minutes he said, "Well, I would love to send you to Kansas City for a second interview, but if you are hired you would have to start training in two weeks. I seriously don't think you are going to leave college in your last quarter, when you only have eight weeks left before you graduate. If you really are interested in this job we'll be back. Just keep checking the newspaper and then come for another interview." So *"Que Sera, Sera,"* whatever will be, will be.

Now as it was getting closer to graduation the idea had become intriguing. Why not do this for a lark? Fly around the world for two years and then get a real job.

You guessed it. About six weeks later there was an ad in the paper. Of course, in the meantime my roommate had gotten engaged and was not interested in pursuing this lark. But the seed had been planted in me. Off I go! This time the interviewer was a woman. When I told her about interviewing previously, and the interviewer telling me to come back if I was truly interested, the interview kicked into high gear. Before you knew it, I was taking some written tests which tested my mathematical and verbal skills. She told me how much TWA paid, where their bases were, and some other facts which really meant nothing to me at the time. An aside: that pay issue, little did I know that would be much more complicated than just a monthly salary. She then continued that I would be receiving a letter with a ticket to fly to Kansas City, for a second interview, in approximately two weeks.

The letter arrives with the ticket and now I'm a semi rock star in the sorority house. Previously one of my sisters had been hired by Pan Am and one by American. Pan Am sounded interesting but American, basically a domestic carrier then, plus TWA flew around the world. TWA was definitely my first choice!

Off to Kansas City I went. They put us up in a downtown hotel room that we had to share with another interviewee. I had felt a little strange about sharing a room with a total stranger, but it was really a "test" by TWA. At the interview the next day we were asked about our roomie. How did you get along, did you like her etc. Why this interest? Because TWA flew both domestically and internationally, and on domestic trips you had to share a hotel room with another flight attendant. They didn't mention that in the interview. Note: This stopped in the early '70s when TWA along with the rest of the airlines couldn't discriminate by sex in hiring anymore. They started hiring men to be flight attendants and obviously couldn't demand that women had to share rooms with male flight attendants. So, single rooms for all started.

Now back to the interview: I noted that every interviewer that day was a man. We know today that would be considered odd. When your name was called in the waiting room, they were careful to walk behind you to an interview room. Why? It hit me later, they were checking out your legs. In that day and age, you were hired because you had good looking legs, an attractive face and were the right height and weight! No one under 5'2" or over 5'9". There were strict guidelines on weight for those heights too. TWA wanted you to have at least two years of work experience or two years of college. They loved it if you could speak a foreign language. No foreign language or some but not fluent, no problem. They'd pay for language lessons.

Little did we know what awaited us in Kansas City after that "congratulations" letter arrived saying you had been hired, here is your ticket and what you were to do when you arrived in Kansas City. I'll tell you about the nightmare of training next. But before I do, check out the application for employment questions that follow. You won't believe them ...

TWA Application in the '60s

Personal Information:

Name, Present address, Social Security #, Citizen of the U.S.A? Yes/No, Birth date

Age, Height, Weight, Color of Hair, Color of Eyes

Measurements: Bust, Waist, Hips.

Have You Ever Been Arrested? (Other than minor traffic violations)

Do You Wear Glasses or Corrective Lenses? Visual Acuity (without glasses) If Known (Example: 20/40) Right Eye, Left Eye, Both Eyes

Do You Have Any Missing Teeth? Give Location, Have They Been Replaced? Permanent Bridge, Removable Bridge

Do You Have Any Visible Scars? Give Location

List Any Serious Illness and/or Physical Limitations

Number of Days Lost Because of Illness During Last three Years

Have You Discussed This Application With Your Parents? Do They Approve?

State Father's Occupation, Mother's Occupation

Number of Brothers, Number of Sisters, Number of Children Younger than You

Have You Ever Been Married? Date of Marriage, Number of Children

Present Marital Status: Single, Married, Widowed, Separated, Divorced

If Divorced When Was Divorce Final? Type of Decree?

Are You Willing to Be Based in Any Part of the U.S.A.? How Soon Can You Accept Employment?

Have You Ever Previously Been Employed By TWA? When? Where? What Position?

Have You Ever Previously Made an Application to TWA? When? Where? What Position?

Do You Have Any Relatives in TWA's Employ? Name, Relationship

In What Countries Have You Worked or Traveled?

Educational Record, Name, Location Years Completed, Graduated, Year

Grammar School

High School

College

College (Part Time or Evenings)

Special Courses

Degrees Held or College Credits

What Languages Do you Speak? 1. Fluently 2. Slightly

Employment Record (List Most Recent First—Explain Periods of Unemployment)

Date: Month & Year, From & To: Employer Name of Company and Immediate Supervisor, Address, Monthly Earnings, Job Title, Type of Work Performed, Give Exact Reason For Leaving (This Information will be Checked)

Postscript: APPLICATION—For every TWA hostess the beginning is always the same—the application, the interview, and the anticipation.

And no one told you that they would actually measure you at your second interview in MKC. Nor about that paper they would ask you to sign, saying you would leave at 32. Details …

The Nightmares of Training

I TOLD YOU I would go into the nightmares of training or was it prison time? Upon arriving in Kansas City to start my six weeks of training, I was told to go to a downtown hotel where I would be staying for one week, and then moving out to the Dos Mundos apartments for the last five weeks. Note here: this apartment complex was totally rented out by TWA for only their hostess trainees.

The hotel was fine, not the Ritz mind you, and I was rooming with another trainee. Of course, we had maid service and could eat in a restaurant in the city. No meal preparations needed and we were within walking distance of the training facilities.

But then that week was up. It was out to the Dos Mundos apartment complex where our prison time started. Remember I had graduated from college and in college I didn't have any hours. Mais ma chéri that was coming to a screeching halt at the Dos Mundos. We not only had hours as to when we could leave in the morning, but when we had to return by a certain time at night. And there was a gate to the apartment complex replete with a guard in uniform, who checked your ID before you could enter or leave. You were not allowed any guests unless they had been preapproved by the TWA supervisors, "our wardens", who lived there. Male guests were limited to your father and he better have the right identification to prove it. No dates, no boyfriends, no brothers, no males period! As for those hours on weekdays, you had to be back in that apartment complex by 9 PM, and on Friday and Saturday you could stay out until midnight. Sunday was back to a 9 PM curfew. But to make sure that you could not cheat, wait for this … there were actually bars on the outside of the windows of each apartment. Metal bars! Just like prison!

Every morning after we would leave our apartment for our limo ride to training, more about that in a minute, a supervisor (aka warden) would come in to check it out. Your beds had to be made like those in the military. All the clothes hung up in the closets. The bathrooms had to have the towels neatly folded, hanging on the towel rods. No makeup on the sink, and God forbid that there were any dirty dishes left out in the kitchen because now we had to prepare our own meals and clean up after ourselves. Food, well you walked to a grocery store to get it, TWA didn't provide you with that either. Lest we not forget the living room, it had to be neat as a pin too, no papers left out, better be in the trash can under the kitchen sink or off with your heads. And just in case House Beautiful wanted to come in and take pictures, the pillows should be arranged neatly on the couch. Any of these not performed would be noted by said warden and put into your file. You were threatened with not being able to graduate if you were messy!

But it only got better. How could that be? I'm being factious. Every day we arrived at the training center, "not" in a limo, but on an unairconditioned bus that they provided for us. It was a lovely thirty-minute ride in June because as we all know it was so delightfully hot and humid in Kansas City then. The windows on the bus were always half closed because we had spent so much time in the morning doing our hair and we didn't want it to get windblown. Why all of this fixation with hair? Well, it would be checked out on a daily basis at the training center. Remember every hair in place at all times!

Then it was more fun. Hours of courses in safety, ditching, dining and yes grooming. It wasn't that the material was that hard, gawd knows because I could compare it to an eighteen-hour course load in college, but it was that everything always had to be perfect! And when I say perfect, I mean it. And back to that grooming detail, you even had a grooming supervisor, who would make surprise visits to other classes you were taking. She would walk up and down the rows of seats, as you held out your hands, so she could check your nails and see if they were polished correctly. And what does your makeup look like? It better look just fine, even though it is eight hours old by now on your face. No greasy spots on your nose or forehead. Horrors! And remember it is always about that hair. Is it straight and straggly now or out of control curls? Better not be!

And then your attitude. What attitude? Yes, you should always be smiling and happy that you are there. Never ever question anything they are teaching you. You are a sponge and only allowed to soak up what they want you to. There are no discussions in class about how something is done. It is only done one way and that is TWA's way. This was further dramatized to all of us, as they explained to one of my classmates that she asked too many challenging questions and they thought she would be happier at Pan Am. Bam, you're fired sweetie from training. Now I personally had figured out at the beginning of training, just go along to get along. Obviously, this woman hadn't figured that out. Her downfall!

Finally, we were graduating. It was like a hundred-pound weight had been taken off my shoulders. As my basic training instructor was pinning on my wings, I got tears in my eyes. She looks at me and says, "Oh, we will miss you too. We all loved you." All I could think of was, just let me get out of here and on a plane to LA to my domicile. This has been hell! I'm not crying because I'm sad, I'm crying from relief! But I just smiled and said, "Thank you."

There was one salvaging grace at the end of this not so lovely time in my life. TWA had given us company passes to use to get out to our new domiciles. A number of my classmates had already checked in for our flight to LAX, including my roommate from the Dos Mundos. All had been given coach seats. When I checked in, the agent said, "Would you like to sit in first class?" Sounds good to me! Now I have a first class seat and I ask my roomie where she is seated. She says in coach. Hmmm, I go back to the gate agent and ask him if my roomie can sit up there with me. He hands me another first class boarding card for her like it is no big deal. Why me? Heaven only knows, but there were fourteen other newbies who were jealous and sitting in coach.

Flash forward: approximately, eighteen months later one of my sorority sisters had been hired to fly for TWA. We had always kept in contact and when I found out she was in Kansas City for training I met her, when I had a layover there. She had been doing the hotel living for a few weeks then and wasn't out at the Dos Mundos apartments because they were full. When she opened her hotel door, she looked awful. Picture exhaustion and dark circles under her eyes. I gave her a big hug and she said, "I thought you had been exaggerating about how awful training was. How could it be any worse than some of our college courses? I just didn't understand. You didn't exaggerate one bit. This is like hell!"

I hugged her again and said, "Don't worry, it will be over soon. There is a God." And then we both laughed.

Guess what? We both flew for over twenty years. Did we have great hair?

Perks of the Job

Tom Stout (left), TWA's sales manager in Hollywood, Richard Zanuck, president of 20th Century Fox Films, Corp., and hostess Stephanie Johnson, during their joint sales call.

YOU ALL SAW a few pages before a little five-year-old girl dressed in her white dress, carrying white gloves, wearing a hat replete with daisies on it. She was standing on the steps of an airplane seeing her father good bye on a flight. A photographer had been hired by the airport to take pictures on that particular day, to later be displayed on the wall of the airport. That little girl would have been me. Flash forward to 1970 and she was now doing publicity work again, except this time for TWA. Here from the TWA *Skyliner* company newspaper, March 7, 1970 is an article about that little girl who was now grown up and visiting with the President of 20th Century Fox Film Corp.

LAX HOSTESSES, BOOST SALES WITH VIM, VIGOR & VITALITY

Los Angeles—A sales and service program here is providing a unique opportunity for flight hostesses to lend their charm and personalities to the job of boosting TWA's sales. The program teams up a hostess with a sales representative for joint calls on commercial accounts in the Los Angeles area. The girls not only enhance their knowledge of the airline, but in the process, they also teach the sales rep partner a thing or two about the in-flight services side of sales and services.

"The girls don't just come along," says Stan Burton, manager of commercial passenger sales. "They intuitively become active members of the sales force." He added that the accounts, many of whom are top executives, "enjoy the chance to talk with a flight hostess and can appreciate her job."

Hostess supervisor Tish Anderson, who coordinates the visitation program here, commented that the girls "enjoy the change—and there's no shortage of volunteers."

One reason for this enthusiastic response is that many of the calls are on television and motion picture accounts. The hostess-sales-woman often finds herself invited on a personally-conducted tour of the studio or TV production facility.

Equally exciting are sales calls at the major aerospace industries in southern California. Many of the girls have been

privileged to have seen the Lockheed 1011 production line and interior mockups.
—Mike Leone

Note: On this particular sales trip I met the president of 20th Century Fox Film Corp., Richard Zanuck. After that I toured the set of ABC-TV's *Land of the Giants*, where I had my picture taken with all of the actors in that series. Followed by lunch with some more of the executives at 20th Century Fox. And I got paid to do this!

Oink

I WAS WORKING coach on a domestic flight and there was a Frenchman seated at the bulkhead. He was loudly complaining about the price of an alcoholic drink on the plane and how we Americans were essentially all rip off artists. He went on and on, ringing his call button every five minutes, and constantly making demands about this, that and whatever. Nearby passengers were rolling their eyes.

After an hour of demeaning my country and making a total nuisance (and I'm being kind here) out of himself, I'd had enough! So, I told him to consider the $1.50 for the cocktail a small installment on their World War II French debt to us.

The passengers around him when they heard my quip, clapped, which made him even madder. But it subdued him a bit, as he still just sat there grumbling about how "impertinent we Americans were."

A few weeks later, I was called into my supervisor's office to read the complaint letter he wrote about me. After I finished reading it, she asked me if I actually said that. I cannot tell a lie and fessed up. Then she started to smile and we both ended up laughing.

Her advice, NEVER, NEVER say that again. Apparently, some of the passengers seated around him, unbeknownst to me until that meeting with my supervisor, had written letters to the company detailing the exchanges and his aggressive, anti-American attitude. Thanks, you saved my bacon or maybe my foie gras, wink!

Dallas Cowboys

I WAS WORKING a flight where the passengers were boarding through the second left hand side door on the L-1011, not the first class door. This required our first class passengers to walk through business class to their seats in first class.

As I was standing up by the galley near the cockpit, talking with my flying partner, who walks into first class from business but a total hunk! I'm thinking, "Wow, that guy looks familiar." All of a sudden it hits me. It's Dandy Don Meredith. Wow, it's Dandy Don! I turned to my flying partner and said, "I think we have Dandy Don on today." She says, "Who is Dandy Don?" What a twit! I tried not to roll my eyes and said, "Never mind."

Now for those of you youngsters, or those of you who don't follow football, Dandy Don Meredith played at SMU during his college days when the students started referring to it as Southern Meredith University because he was so popular. He was the very first player signed for the Dallas Cowboys when the team was being put together. Dandy Don went on to play for them for nine years, from 1960–1968, as their quarterback and was even more wildly popular in Dallas.

Dandy Don's next stop was color analyst work for the NFL from 1970 to 1984, as he and Howard Cosell really put Monday Night Football into everyone's home. He was the comic relief and foil to Howard's imperial broadcasting approach which made the show such a hit. Dandy Don also dabbled in acting, but he was really becoming well known for doing commercials for Lipton Iced Tea in the '80s. In fact, it seemed like every time I turned on the TV there was Dandy Don sipping on a glass of iced tea.

Anyway, back to Dandy Don on my flight. He had on a pair of jeans with a belt that had a large metal belt buckle, a checked shirt, gorgeous rough suede jacket with fringe on the arms, cowboy boots and was wearing a pair of blue tinted Porsche sunglasses. Start your engine ladies! He also was sporting a short beard. Whoa cowboy!

So, I took a menu back to him, as he was getting seated and welcomed him on board. I said, "I'll give you a chance to look at the menu and I'll be back in a few minutes to take your order." I'm thinking, oh yes this is definitely Dandy Don.

I return a few minutes later and ask him if he would like something to drink before his lunch. He says, "Yes, I would love a margarita. But you only have those ones in a little bottle. They really aren't that good." I pipe up and laughingly say, "Yes, and I'm sorry our blender is broken too." He laughs and then orders another drink and then his lunch entrée.

I'm positive now this is Dandy Don from his voice and I say, "Perchance are you Dandy Don?" He looks at me and smiles, and puts his fingers to his beard and says, "Would Dandy Don have one of these." To which I reply, "I'm not sure if Dandy Don would be sporting a beard, but Dandy Don should have ordered ... now think long and drawn out, I C E D ... TEEEEEEA."

He starts to laugh and nudges me with his cowboy boot on my shin. I smiled and laughed back at him and said, "I thought so." Dandy Don was on my playing field now and I was having fun harassing him. Our conversation continues to the point where I asked him if he was married and he turned bright red. I said, "Not for me. I can find you a nice girl," as I flash my wedding rings. At which point, one of my flying partners started to walk by and I said, "Well, take her for instance." I thought he was going to die from laughing now.

Oh, Dandy Don you were so funny, good looking and really a gentleman. Monday Night Football has never been the same without you and Howard Cosell. Rest in Peace and thanks for the great memory ...

From Tragedy

IT WAS IN the '80s and I was working a flight out of Tel Aviv when I started talking with one of the passengers. I could not help but notice that this gentleman had a number tattooed on his arm. In the course of the conversation, he told me that his entire family had been killed in a concentration camp during WWII. It was a sobering conversation, but then he smiled about halfway into it and said, "I met my wife in that camp then too. We live in Los Angeles now and have three beautiful and happy children. I spoil them rotten and I don't care that they are spoiled."

I hope that he had many grandchildren and great grandchildren that he could spoil too.

The "Royals" or the Royals

IT WAS IN the '80s in the fall when the Kansas City Royals baseball team was in the playoffs for the World Series pennant. I knew nothing about baseball and hadn't been keeping up on the series. Plus, I was only flying our Chicago to London trip and it was not a big point of conversation in England. Another important fact: I had become a big fan of Princess Diana and thus the royal family, and had even started subscribing to Majesty and Royalty Monthly magazines, both all about the British royal family.

So, here we are working back from London to Chicago: after takeoff, we leveled off and began our initial beverage service. I reached a row where we had a passenger who was from the Midwest (U.S.) and eager for some news from back in the states. I was pouring him a drink when he asked me, "Do you know where the Royals are?" I replied, "Why of course. They're at Balmoral," and here is the rest of the conversation:

Passenger: "Where is THAT?"
Me: "In Scotland, Balmoral Castle."
Passenger: "What are they doing THERE?"
Me: "They go there every summer."
Passenger: "The whole TEAM?"
Me: (Thinking to myself, if you want to refer to them that way), "Yes, all of them."
Passenger: "What do they DO there?"
Me: "Oh, they like to picnic and fish in the River Dee."
Passenger: "REALLY?"
Me: "Yes. They love it there."
Passenger: "Do they take their families?"
Me: (I'm picturing Diana, her two cute boys and their cousins) "Why of course."
Passenger: "Who PAYS for that?"
Me: "Well, I imagine the taxpayers."
Passenger: "TAX payers? Why would THEY pay for it?"
Me: "Well, the Royals ARE a bit of a tourist attraction."
Passenger: "They are?"
Me: "Absolutely."
Passenger: "The baseball team?"
Me: "Baseball team! What?"
Passenger: "Yes, the Kansas City Royals."
Me: "I'm talking about the Royal FAMILY!"

By this time, there are howls of laughter from the passengers within earshot. It was like a "Who's on first, who's on second?" skit. He and I then erupted into laughter as well. I made his drink a double and told him it was on the house since it only seemed fitting after all the consternation I'd put him through. Later I called the captain and asked for information about the K.C. Royals. The man deserved to have his earnest question answered. Unfortunately, the Royals were losing to the Phillies.

Tienen Inodor Viajara or a Well-Traveled Toilet

WE WERE RETURNING from San Juan, Puerto Rico to JFK, on a Boeing 747, with a full load of passengers. I was standing at the forward first class door with the flight service manager welcoming passengers on board, when an older gentleman appeared in front of us pulling a trolley.

Now you all know how slow boarding can be with many people and their baggage, plus on top of this it was very hot. Therefore, in our defense it took a minute or two for us to realize that this man was struggling with his trolley because he was pulling a very "weighty object" on it.

Boy, were we in for a surprise when the passenger finally pulled his trolley onboard. We did not know whether to laugh or cry when we saw what was strapped to it. It was a toilet! Yes, a toilet. It was not wrapped in any protective packaging, just strapped to this trolley. I am thinking now, I have seen it all. Really a toilet?

We tried to tactfully explain to the gentleman that he could not bring that on board. However, here was our second problem, his first language was Spanish and he spoke limited English. "Why? Porqué? I want my toilet on the plane. It can go in the overhead bin."

Could you imagine, another passenger opens the overhead bin and a toilet drops out, or worse still the overhead opens during takeoff or landing and a toilet flies through the air like a torpedo! Not to mention the fact, how would we ever get it up there? I saw a workman's compensation case coming from a job-related injury on this one.

Unfortunately, this gentleman still did not see any problems here, in fact he suggested that we could store it in the lav. Of course, we always take the lavs out of commission to store extra toilets in, or large objects that will not fit under the seat, or in the overhead bins. NOT! And there was also the detail of it being against company policy, plus one more minor point we had a full load of passengers and we would need all of those lavs to accommodate them.

Needless to say, he was not happy with any of our answers and kept insisting that we take the toilet and stow it in the aircraft's cabin. "Mi hermosa inodro, my beautiful toilet, is going to get chipped or cracked if you put it with the cargo below."

The flight service manager now had had it and went out to the gate agent, probably giving him a new orifice for letting this man try to bring on a toilet and not stopping him. Fortunately, the agent spoke fluent Spanish and told our passenger that the toilet was really a NO GO in the cabin and it would be checked in the belly, when upon arrival at JFK he could pick it up in baggage claim. Or, his other alternative was if he did not like that idea then he could always not take this flight. He finally saw the errors in his decision about trying to bring a toilet as carry-on luggage and decided he really wanted to go to JFK.

Can you imagine today some agent saying to him, "Sir, will your grande inodoro fit in that box next to the agent's podium that we use to measure carry on luggage? If it doesn't fit then it cannot be brought on board." Wonder if the "hermosa inodor" made it without a chip? I hope it did.

P.S. When I am boarding an aircraft now and see all of the passengers weighed down with bags, it often makes me think about the grande hermosa inodor and puts a smile on my face.

Still Makes Me Sad Today

I HAD A child on my flight that had Down's Syndrome. He was so sweet, about six years old, dressed in a darling sports jacket and slacks, white shirt with a little bow tie, dress shoes and a coat. His father handed him off to the agent at the gate, who brought him onboard. I could not believe my eyes when I saw this unaccompanied little child. I asked the agent, who was meeting him at our next stop and he replied, he was going to a private school there and someone from the school would be meeting him. In reality his family was basically shipping him off.

My heart just ached for him, so young and so innocent. He was in a coach row by himself and barely could see out the window. What to do? I told the other flight attendants that I was moving him to the last row in coach, so we could keep an eye on him. I picked him up and said, "Honey I'm going to put you in the back with us, then we can talk and play together." When I picked him up, he grabbed me firmly around the neck with his two little arms and placed his head on my shoulder. I just could not believe that his family was sending him away! This adorable child who was so loving.

As I said previously, we had a very light load that day and my flying partners told me, we don't need you, you take care of him and we'll do the liquor service. After we were airborne, I just sat with him while he used the TWA coloring books we had for children then, and talked and stroked his hair. That haunted me for a very long time and even today I can still see him in his adorable little outfit and bow tie. Was a killer when I had to hand that child over to the next agent. I always hoped that he was able to return to his family. Very, very sad … even now.

Rookie Mistakes … Learning the Ropes

WE WERE ROOKIES in the fall of 1960. Everything about us was brand new from our crisp green uniforms to our contagious enthusiasm. Puddle jumping on many flights across the Midwest in search of New York was not work, we thought it was a lark then. On the occasion in question its song was about to become even sweeter and then … a sour note!

This particular trip was a "turn-a-round" starting in Kansas City. We deposited businessmen in towns across the Midwest before arriving in Newark, NJ. There we would rest a few hours before retracing our same route home.

Newark however that day was under siege by Mother Nature. After several hours of uncertainty, our flight was canceled; we were released from duty and sent to the St. George Hotel in midtown Manhattan for a layover of indeterminate length. This is known in the airline world as "going non-routine" and is generally dreaded by all crews since you were now at the mercy of crew scheduling. Meaning they could send you anywhere. Forget your plans that you made for your days off. Nevertheless, as I said we were rookies and it was NYC! I had been there once before and had been unabashed with my amazement and excitement. My flying partner was a Brit and had never seen the city and I couldn't wait to be her guide.

Unprepared for a layover since we were supposed to be returning back to our base that same day and not prepared for inclement weather, we stopped first at a sidewalk kiosk where we each purchased a warm sweater. I might add here that this taught us a good lesson about always being prepared for the unexpected when you pack your crew kit for a trip. Now sweaters in hand we set off to see the sights. Much of our attention was focused skyward as we wandered in the sea of skyscrapers. We visited St. Patrick's cathedral, gazed into all of the many shop windows and finally ended up at Rockefeller Plaza. What now? Radio City Music Hall and off to see the Rockettes. What a perfect ending to a day of unsurpassed excitement for these two rookies! We returned to our hotel happy but very exhausted. After rinsing our stockings, showering, washing our hair and yes, the proverbial rolling your hair in curlers (remember it is the '60s), we fell into our beds and slept like we were dead.

You know when you are really tired, sleeping soundly and a phone rings, it seems like mere moments from when you first fell asleep and you aren't thinking clearly. My Brit flying partner was closest to the phone and picked it up. I heard her mention some numbers, say thank you and hang up. She then mumbled some info from crew scheduling to me and we both turned over to go back to sleep. One hour later the phone was ringing again and I heard her say, "Oh no captain, we aren't going until tomorrow morning," and then she says to me, "The cockpit crew is leaving tonight."

I couldn't get back to sleep and I wasn't so new, not to sense that something was wrong. I got out of bed, tapped her on the arm and said, "Where is that information from scheduling?" As we reviewed it, we both realized we were in deep serious trouble! I called scheduling and was told the unwelcome news that we should indeed have been on our way with the captain and the crew. OOPS!

We threw on our uniforms, including wet stockings, ICK! Yanked the curlers from our still wet hair, grabbed our metal flight kits, and raced for the elevator and the lobby. Of course, the cockpit crew was long gone. It was 3 AM and there was not a cab in sight. This bedraggled, unprofessional and by this time weeping duo raced for an intersection where we found a cab, jumped in and ordered the cabbie to take us to the Newark airport and FAST!

Between sobs, we alternated chastising and consoling each other through that endless ride towards a hoped for redemption. It was not to be! The airport was as dismal as when we had left it many hours before and there wasn't a human being in sight. Refusing to believe the obvious, we raced into the TWA ramp office. "Where is our plane?" At LAGUARDIA??? We were in the wrong state!

Back through the airport we ran and jumped into the lone cab that was miraculously waiting there. The cabbie said, "You lucked out. I wouldn't have been here, except I had to use the restroom." "How much to take us to La Guardia, quick?" we both yelled. It was $17.00! More than we had between us now. Not about to give up, we asked for alternatives; our jobs were at stake. The cabbie explained that he could take us to the Port Authority in Manhattan, where we could get a bus to La Guardia. In unison we yelled, "Do it!"

Red eyed from crying and terrified, we arrived at the west-side terminal where more bad news awaited us. Buses to LaGuardia leave from the east-side terminal! Didn't the cabbie know that?

TAXI!!!!!! Another race across town and we are now penniless.

A call to crew scheduling from our newest location confirmed the worst. Our crew and our plane were long gone. It hadn't been decided what to do with the wayward hostesses who would be us. Exhausted physically and emotionally we sat and awaited a verdict.

Eventually, we were assigned to our first and we knew, probably our last "dead head" which means flying like passengers, back to Kansas City and judgment. In disgrace and in disgraceful condition, we flew toward doom and soon learned we were famous. "Oh, you are the two who ...!" Fearing that we were going to be fired it was like being resurrected when mercy was shown by the hostess supervisor in Kansas City.

Our wonderful captain wrote to the company on our behalf, and even asked that our cab and bus expenses be reimbursed. And we got it! I flew for six more years and my lovely Brit flying partner, who now became my new best friend, flew for twenty-two. We trust TWA wasn't sorry that they gave us a second chance.

The Vietnam Years 1965 to 1968

I HAD BEEN flying out of SFO since 1961. In 1965 the Military Airlift Command, known simply as MAC, opened up a pacific base outside of San Francisco for flights, from the Travis Air Force Base to Vietnam. TWA had a contract with the United States military to haul troops on our aircraft, staffed with our pilots and hostesses to Vietnam.

These flights were considered plum assignments because of all of the flight time you earned in an eleven-day period. The eleven days on duty started from the Travis Air Force Base outside of SFO to Honolulu where we laid over. From there we continued on to Okinawa and laid over. Out of Okinawa we flew a round trip flight into Bien Hoa Airbase in Vietnam, returning to Okinawa eight hours later where we laid over again. From Okinawa we flew to Honolulu with another layover and finally home to the Travis Airbase.

I remember these flights and layovers so well for many reasons. Let me take you on some of them now.

Our first day we would leave the SFO airport in a limo arriving at Travis Airbase near Sacramento, CA for a late-night departure. Our special passengers were all Army soldiers. It was about a seven-hour flight to Honolulu, where we stayed at the Reef Hotel for our layovers and more often than not found ourselves at Duke Kahanamoku's nightclub, being entertained by Don Ho accompanied with a number of Mai Tai's. Are any of you old enough to remember the song, *Tiny Bubbles*? Everyone would sing along with him for this one.

Next stop was Kadena Airbase outside of Okinawa, Japan. Yes, the military let us shop at the base and we would also go into town. In Okinawa I would take one of my husband's suits to be copied by their excellent tailors, and by the time we returned from Vietnam for another layover the suit was finished. And of course, we all had to purchase the Popa-san chairs. I'm sure everyone was staring, when our limos were returning from Travis to SFO on route 101 with Popa-san chairs tied to the roof. But my best buy by far was at the Kadena officers club. I bought a full set of my Gorham silverware and a candelabra as fancy as Liberace's, for $125.

Out of Kadena we flew to Bien Hoa Airbase in Vietnam. It was approximately twenty miles east of Saigon which is now named Ho Chi Minh City. I was in and out of Bien Hoa Airbase, from 1965 through 1968, and lost track of how many times I landed and took off from there. TWA paid us an extra $25 in our paycheck for every time the wheels touched the runway there. It was called "hazard duty pay." What did our soldiers get for fighting in Vietnam? Combat pay which added $50 to $65 per month to their check. I would say that was precious little.

Believe it or not, one of us was allowed to sit in the cockpit for landing or take off. I remember the tower in Bien Hoa always saying, "Good-bye and climb expeditiously." Why? Because the end of the runway was not secure. Oh, how young and naïve I was. I never thought anything could happen to us. That would change.

One time looking out the window on a beautiful sunny day as we were approaching the airport in Vietnam, I saw a little village with a pretty church in the middle of it. Where were the people? Instantly I saw the entire village explode in flames! It was a reality check for me at that point; yes, you are in a war zone. Fly expeditiously rang in my ears.

Each flight as we were approaching the Bien Hoa Airbase, we would ask all the soldiers to lower their window shades after we landed. I'm sure they thought that it was so horrible on the ground that we didn't want them to see it too soon. The real reason that the shades were lowered was that it was so terribly hot and humid outside; we were trying to keep the airplane from getting any hotter while we sat on the ground for only forty-five minutes unloading the soldiers and loading the boys going home.

Most of the soldiers hadn't seen an American female for a long time. As they boarded, we gave them our best smiles as some of them stopped in their tracks and stared. Probably another reason was that we weren't twenty years old either. I remember thinking it was hard to imagine that many had literally just come out of a fighting jungle a few hours earlier.

After takeoff, the bathrooms soon smelled like pot, but we said nothing. These war weary young men fell asleep immediately and I always thought these soldiers deserved some good dreams on their way home.

Many of you don't remember Vietnam, but little did I know at the time that on Jan. 31, 1968 the Tet offensive would start and one of the military installations attacked would be Bien Hoa Airbase. The attack lasted twelve hours with the American forces being outnumbered 5 to 1. During this battle 139 North Vietnamese and Viet Cong soldiers were killed and twenty-five taken prisoners of war. Four U.S. soldiers died that day. When I heard this, those words "fly expeditiously" rang in my ears again.

I had met my future husband in Honolulu on a layover while I was flying these MAC flights. We married and I continued to fly them until I became pregnant. TWA's policy in 1968 was to fire pregnant flight attendants. I decided to fly one last MAC trip before telling them I was pregnant. It was the flight to remember: about three hours out of Okinawa on our way to Honolulu the captain called me up to the cockpit and asked me for my lipstick. Every good hostess always carried lipstick in their pocket. Then I saw that the windshield was developing cracks. He was trying to see if it was the inside or outside pane of glass that was shattering, by rubbing my lipstick on the inside glass. Shortly after that, I was told that the dials were showing we were losing hydraulic fluid. At this point, the captain said all of the hostesses were to sit down in their jump seats and be prepared to put on their oxygen masks if they fell. He was concerned that we might have a decompression in the cabin. All I could think of was, those poor soldiers had survived Vietnam and now this.

The crew descended the plane and we were now flying at a very low altitude in case God forbid the windshield blew in. When we got closer to Hawaii, the captain radioed the tower requesting the use of the long runway (there were only two). The answer was NO, President Johnson was landing that afternoon and the runway had to be secured. Knowing President Johnson's propensity for straight speaking, I'm sure if he had heard this he probably would have said, "You've got a disabled plane full of returning VietNam soldiers. Let them land the damn plane wherever they want to."

THE END OF THE STORY: we landed with the captain trying to look out the side window as the front windshield had a thousand cracks in it. The hydraulic fluid left was just enough to stop the plane on the short runway. There was a higher power looking out for all of us that day! It was saying, "Fly expeditiously."

Postscript: Remember I told you I was married and now pregnant on my last trip. It was the end of 1968 and TWA fired me with no chance to return as a flight attendant after the baby was born. Thirteen years later the U.S. Supreme Court ruled that male flight attendants were not fired for becoming fathers, but female flight attendants were fired for becoming mothers, this was discrimination. Four hundred TWA flight attendants who were fired for becoming mothers prior to this ruling were entitled to get their jobs back. Two hundred came back and one of them was me. I flew until retiring in 1996.

In 1993 my daughter Susan was taking a class at the University of California Berkeley and the assignment was "Interview a Woman in the Work Force." She interviewed her mother, a flight attendant now, not a hostess, about discrimination against female flight attendants. Her classmates had never heard of this kind of discrimination. From no marriage for years, to we'll let you be married but no pregnancy, maintain a certain weight or we'll fire you, and guess what when you turn age 32 regardless of your work record you are out of here, yes they were all reasons to be fired. Her professor spent three classes discussing Susan's paper and the professor wanted her to publish it. Today my daughter is a history professor at NYU. She has published a book about the essential role of women in forming the new colony of New York in the sixteen hundreds.

How times have changed ...

My Encounter with John F. Kennedy, Jr.

SETTING THE STAGE: TWA flew an all-nighter flight in 1989 from LAX to JFK. It was flight #702. These all-nighter, coast to coast flights, were known for their "quirky" passengers, especially when it was a full moon. But may I say this flight turned out to be one of the best of my career.

You all must know who John F. Kennedy Jr. was? For those of you who know no history, he was the son of President John F. Kennedy and I'll add here, one of the most gorgeous men on the planet then. He was also dating Darryl Hannah, the movie star, so their pictures were constantly on the covers of the tabloids. To say he was a celebrity would be an understatement and as such was pre-boarded in first class before the rest of the passengers.

Here is where the story begins: The other flight attendant who was working with me in first class was brand-new and was star struck! Literally could not function when she saw him. So, even though I was working the galley position not the cabin I took it upon myself to go ask, "Mr. Kennedy may I offer you a beverage?" He replied, while looking me in the eyes, "Please just call me John." To which I replied, "Please just call me." And we both laughed.

He asked for a glass of red wine which I served him, and I returned to the galley to inventory what had been boarded for the inflight service. Two minutes later he approached me in the galley with a red wine stain on his white t-shirt that had the word NAKED in black across the chest.

John, notice how I used his first name now, asked me if he could get into his garment bag to get a different shirt and I showed him where it was hung. He then proceeded to remove his t-shirt (OH MY GOD) in my galley and then leaned into the closet to get his garment bag.

Be still my heart! WHAT A SIGHT! I jokingly said to him that if he gave me his t-shirt, I would send it out to the cleaners for him and have it available on arrival. He did just that. He gave me the shirt right off his back and told me to keep it.

I have that t-shirt to this day, red wine stain and all, sealed in a bag. My biggest regret is that I didn't have him autograph it. Lucky me, I had him on several more trans-con flights and he was always the perfect gentleman. And yes, John always remembered me and the red wine.

Maybe I Missed My Calling, Just Call Me Renee Fleming

I WAS WORKING a flight and everything was uneventful. Happy passengers, happy crew and on time. But then ... we are on descent and you could feel the wings tipping back and forth. Yes, we had major crosswinds. The plane hit the runway with a thud, and then we landed again, and one more time for a cheap thrill!

Back story: I always would sit in the impact position during the last minute of approach and do a mental review if God forbid something should happen; check for fire and smoke, none then open the door, pull the inflate backup handle if the slide didn't inflate, slide inflated then start evacuation. My hands would be firmly clutched to the edge of the jump seat and I would stop any conversation I was having with the flight attendant who I was sharing a jump seat with.

So, I'm in the impact position and we are landing not once, not twice but three times. My flying partner grabs my thigh and squeezes it so hard that later I actually had five bruises on my leg from this. Probably could have taken a picture of them and used them for fingerprint identification at a crime scene. That was how hard she squeezed me. Plus, picture my feet flying off the floor with each bounce on the runway.

Now, I had landings like this before, you fly long enough and you are all going to have one, but what I did this time even surprised me. As the other flight attendant was squeezing the blood out of my leg, I let out a high extended "C" that any soprano opera star would have been envious of. No, I really did. Where did that come from? Who knows?

We pull off the runway to taxi to the gate and I look down the aisle to see all of the passengers, in the aisle seats, have their heads poked out looking forward at me, with that look on their faces that says, "What the hell just happened?" At this point one of my first class passengers said in a loud voice, "You missed your calling, you should have been an opera star." I laughed and yelled back at him, "Just wanted to give you a little extra for your money today." And everyone laughed.

As the passengers were deplaning a few of them mentioned the poor landing, in their "expert opinions." (Note: Sarcasm) First of all that is bad form on a passenger's part, remember that people, only the flight attendants are allowed to make remarks about landings, and we don't say them to the public. Now for all of you as passengers remember this too, any landing you walk away from is a good landing! And that was my reply, as always with a smile, to the ones who thought it necessary to remark on the expertise of the cockpit crew. What I really wanted to say was, "Hey nitwit you try one with some bad cross winds." As always, thanks to our captain for getting us there safely.

Now I'm looking for my audition tape for the Met. Just kidding ...

Five Foot Nine, Three Inch Heels and a Bottle of Jack Daniels

First Class bar in TWA's 747.
Flight Attendant pictured is <u>not</u> the author of this story.
Photo taken from TWA *Timetable* courtesy of the Jon Proctor Collection.

A FRIEND OF mine was the flight service manager (FSM) on a 747. In other words, she was in charge of all. In the good old days, there was not only a small bar lounge upstairs behind the cockpit for the first class passengers, but they even had another large bar area with an actual stand up bar behind the first class section. Wouldn't want our first class passengers to not have three places to drink; their seat and two bars.

FYI, the FSM was in charge of inventorying all of the liquor, first class and coach plus all of the money in coach. This was no small task on a 747!

Anyway, she goes to the large first class bar where there was a really junior flight attendant working to tell her that she would be back to inventory the liquor and to start to take down the bar. Note: We actually had 5th bottles then at that bar, not little miniatures. As I said, it was really like a bar.

Well, one of the passengers had been "over" served by this junior flight attendant. Which I might add we were not supposed to do. But being junior she didn't know how to tactfully tell this man that he was cut off. On the other hand, the least offensive way was to just start watering down his drinks. No fuss no muss, worked all of the time!

But I digress ...when the over-served passenger hears this, he demands another drink. What to do? The man is drunk! This was totally obvious and my friend (the FSM) tells him that the bar is closed now. And what does he do? He starts cussing at her and then tries to climb over the bar to grab her. This was not well thought out on his part, let's put it this way, it was a very bad idea. She picks up a Jack Daniels 5th and turns it upside down to make a club out of it and then says, "You take one more step toward me and I'll use this." Amazing when one is looking at a large liquor bottle that can be used as a club how fast they can sober up. He backs up and she suggests that he return to his seat now or the police would be meeting the flight. Probably more like she ordered him to go back to his seat. Surprising what a woman who is 5' 9" in three-inch heels with a bottle of Jack can do! As for the newbie flight attendant, she got an eye full, lecture and now knows to water down drinks. Ah yes, good times ...

To Be or Not To Be

EVERYONE ALWAYS IS wondering, were the cockpit crews and cabin crews really cozy on layovers? What happens on layovers stays on layovers, well mostly. This is a case of "not" cozy.

Prelude: I was a new hire. Otherwise known as a "newbie." Fresh out of upstate New York, in my early twenties, and being rather sheltered this new world of travel was most exciting. TWA had built us up in training that thousands and thousands of people had interviewed for our jobs and we were the elite. In actuality, it was true. Not the elite part so much, but in the fact that thousands (as in as many as 100,000) had interviewed for approximately 800 positions the year I was hired.

We had been groomed to the TWA standards, trained in safety and dining for five plus weeks and were now thrown out into the real world. We were still young, impressionable and to be truthful gullible. Ready prey for some more sophisticated people to try to take advantage of us. And yes, some tried.

I was the most junior flight attendant on this flight and who asked me to dinner but the captain. Me? Wow, I was flattered. There were other flight attendants prettier than me in the crew, much more worldly and had been flying for a number of years, but he had asked me to dinner. Of course, I said yes.

At dinner, he seemed to hang on my every word which probably at the time consisted of stories from high school and college. Very interesting to someone in their 50s. You think?

After dinner he walked me to my room and as I was thanking him for dinner, he said, "Aren't you going to invite me in? I could make you very happy tonight."

WHAT? What did he just say? I looked at this fifty plus year old face and saw my older relatives, i.e. my dad, uncles and grandparents now! As I said, I was hardly a woman of the world and what did I say, nothing, but in my nervous confusion I looked at him and burst out into laughter.

He turned, said nothing and left red faced. I in turn grew up that evening.

You Brought a What on Board

HAVE YOU EVER opened the overhead storage compartment door and heard a hissing sound? Me neither. You are not going to believe this: we were airborne and one of our passengers opened the overhead compartment over his seat to retrieve something. He heard a hissing sound and saw a large iguana staring at him. I'm not kidding!

In shock he jumped backwards, lost this balance, hit his head on the armrest and was knocked unconscious. The captain made the decision to land the plane at a close airport that was not our original destination, so that this passenger could receive medical attention. Fortunately, the man woke up, but the paramedics said he had a concussion and they took him off in the ambulance.

Getting back to the idiot, oh sorry, the passenger who brought this iguana on board, he claimed the agent told him it was all right and just to put the iguana and the bag it was in, in the overhead compartment. Sure! Now that was the biggest load of BS I had heard in a while.

Can't you just hear this passenger today claiming it is his therapy animal and he needs it close by to help him relieve his stress? That is as bad as someone who recently wanted to bring a peacock on board as a therapy animal. Give me a break ...

But getting back to the iguana, remember it had gotten out of its container and now was freely strolling around in the aircraft. It took the mechanics four hours to find that iguana ensconced behind the paneling over the forward boarding door. Can you imagine boarding an aircraft and then all of a sudden seeing an iguana flicking its tongue at you from the ceiling over the door? Now that would wake you up.

What happened to the passengers on that flight? Fortunately, there was another flight leaving that had room for them, so they were able to get out of town without an iguana. As for the iguana's owner, he should have been sent a bill for the delay, but knowing TWA they put him on the next flight too and then flew the iguana free to this man after they found it. The crew knows what we would have liked to have done to this passenger, and his pet iguana and it wasn't exactly that.

Patsy and The Pope

EVERYONE LOVED POPE John Paul. He was charismatic and kind in every situation. He loved to reach out to his flock and made several major trips to America. It was just one of these trips that brings me to my memories of Patsy, me, and the Pope.

Patsy and I were working in first class on a transcontinental flight to JFK. Who might be among our passengers but the two biggest honchos with the airline our CEO and CFO. And yes, they were very nice gentlemen.

The talk among all of the TWA employees was about having snagged the biggest celebrity of the time, none other than the Pope, to take our airline for his tour in the U.S.A. To say this was a major coup would be putting it mildly. All of the carriers had wanted this charter.

Anyway, Patsy and I had been discussing the Pope's upcoming American trip and we had wondered how to get our names in, as crew for the Pope's charter. Clearly this was a long shot, but I quickly decided that now was the time to take advantage of having the big shots on board. I pulled Patsy into the galley and whispered, "Now is our chance to pitch ourselves as crew members for the special Pope charter. Are you in?" Patsy was not shy and immediately replied, "Let's do it."

As you all know, there was a period in flying history when flight attendants were not only young, but perfectly groomed and always ready to strike up a conversation when it was appropriate. And boy did we feel like it was appropriate now!

So, Pasty and I got ready for the kill. We casually engaged the TWA execs in conversation. Quickly, I zeroed in on the upcoming charter in question with a nonchalant remark. "We heard that the Pope will be using TWA to travel to and around America. We are so thrilled for the company to have this publicity." To which the CFO who looked very proud at that moment said, "Yes, that's correct. We are going to provide the Vatican with three jets for his trip. Each jet will be refigured to take care of the Pope, the traveling clergy and press. And we will be serving food that has been expressly ordered for the Pope."

My BFF, Patsy, smiling ever so sweetly, now says, "How are you selecting crew members for these charters? Are you only going to use TWA flight attendants that are Catholic?" I immediately chimed in with, "That's a great idea, Patsy, as Catholics, they would understand the ins and outs of protocol in dealing with the Pope, cardinals and priests. And it would mean so much to a Catholic. Really a dream of a lifetime." At which point the CFO says, "I'm a Catholic and I can tell you I was thrilled to meet him in the Vatican when we were planning this trip."

Patsy and I are smiling now. Cha-ching! Maybe this was going to work? So, Patsy chimes in with, "We are both Catholic and would love to be on the Pope's charter." Now the CEO who had been sitting there quietly says, "Well, I am not Catholic, but my wife and I were also thrilled to meet with the Pope." Ouch! Awkward moment now, as we feel our Catholic faith "hook" slipping away. But it was still worth another try, "Well, we would be honored to be chosen. We would be thrilled to work on the Pope's charter. Please keep us in mind and here are our names and domiciles. It was a pleasure to meet you." Back in the galley by ourselves, we both agreed that we gave it our best effort. But it was going to be a very, very long shot at best.

Now fast forward to the Pope's charter one month later. Patsy and I are working together again, "So, did you see who they announced would be working the Pope's charter? Our supervisors." Yes, our management took the opportunity to don brand new uniforms and work the chartered planes for the Pope's visit. How could we be so naïve to think that they would choose "real" flight attendants to work the Pope's flight? And guess what; to our knowledge not one of them was Catholic.

The good news, the press did not miss this little faux pas. They noted that the flight attendants were not "regular" working crewmembers but their managers. The pilots, however, were selected out of a Catholic pool of pilots and brought their family bibles for the Pope's blessing. Can you see this scenario happening today? We think not.

In a follow-up on another trip to America by Pope John Paul he was also flying on TWA. A good friend of mine was chosen to work the charter. She has now passed away but it was the memory of a lifetime for her. This time the press published beautiful photos of the Pope, the TWA crewmembers and my friend on the specially configured 767. It was only fitting that the Pope, Traveled With Angels.

The Golden Globes

I WAS BASED in LAX and couldn't believe what luck my roommate and I had. We were asked to be hostesses at The Golden Globe Awards. No, not kidding here!

TWA was the sponsor that year and they wanted two flight attendants to appear in uniform and greet the nominees as they entered. We were only twenty years old; can you even fathom how exciting this was for us? Here comes Andy Williams who was the host and then it started! Everyone was there, Steve McQueen, Dean Martin, John Wayne, Rock Hudson, Jack Lemon, Julie Andrews, Natalie Wood, Elizabeth Taylor and so many more. Who was our favorite? Natalie Wood, she was gorgeous.

But it didn't stop there. We were also invited to attend an after party, so we had brought a change of clothes. Us at the after party. Truly heady stuff!

So, what do I remember most about that party, well ... a really big time movie star who made western movies was over-served. The two of us were sitting in some fancy booth when he stumbled over and sat down right next to me. Let's put it this way because of his size it was quite intimidating! Magically someone appeared and whisked us off to the other side of the party room. Thank you to whomever you were.

What a celebrity scene, one I will never forget ...

Sparks On My First Flight

IT WAS BACK in the 707 days in 1970. I was a brand-new purser on a TWA flight to Zurich. Have to admit, I was intimidated as the only male crewmember, except for the pilots on this flight, with a group of "savvy" senior female flight attendants. To make matters more complicated, on top of this, there were some sparks flying between me and one of the ladies.

After we arrived in Zurich, a few of the hostesses (that is what they were called in the '70s) offered to take me out to see some of the sites which included a beautiful train ride through the mountains. We followed this up with dinner and a few bottles of wine. Now those sparks were really igniting with that one hostess.

As fate would have it, the "spark ignitor" and I were alone on the elevator going up to our respective floors in the hotel, when what did I hear, "Would you like to come to my room for a nightcap?" Well, you know where the nightcap leads and it was not "G" rated.

Before you knew it, it was morning and the phone was ringing in her room. It was TWA crew operations in Zurich, calling to tell her, this was her crew call and the flight was operating on time. S—, I forgot all about a crew call being placed to your room!

Then they asked her if she had seen me since I was not answering the phone in my room. Her reply, "Yes, he's right here," and handed the phone over to me. I could hear the operation people laughing on the other end of the phone and they said, "This is your crew call, pick up in an hour." Thank you was all I could say as I handed the phone back to her.

I threw on my underwear and pants, then grabbed the rest of my clothes and shoes. I only had to go up one floor and made a "fatal" error in judgement. Instead of taking the stairs, I decided to take the elevator. I frantically jumped into one, pressed the up button for my floor and the elevator went straight down to the lobby. We've all been there when that happens but this time it was awkward!

The door to the elevator opens for the lobby and some of my crew was already downstairs meeting to go for breakfast. One of them happens to turn around and look at the elevator with me standing there, barefoot, clothes in hand, looking like the fool that I felt like. Curse words are flying through my mind at this point.

The door seemed to be open for hours as I started repeatedly hitting the button for my floor and then the close door button. That is one of those moments when you say time was standing still!

Later that morning, as I sheepishly got on the crew bus to go back to the Zurich airport, the entire crew greeted me with really big smiles. My "spark ignitor" just winked.

Now all of those many years later I can laugh about this and yes, the spark ignitor and I did date after that. We loved our Zurich layovers together. Stop smiling …

Red Carpet Treatment

PICTURE A MALE flight attendant at the boarding door …

Just another day of dealing with the public. As we were boarding, I was standing at the front first class door to meet and greet our passengers, when a drunk man who could barely walk came down the jetway and approached me. Oh boy, not this. I found myself standing in front of the boarding door now with my arms blocking his way. Once they get on it is always bad news. Fortunately, there was no one behind him then and I immediately said, "Sir, we are going to have to go talk with the gate agent about getting you onto another flight." To which he replied in his drunken slur, "I am the CEO of a company and you should be rolling out the red carpet for me."

Oh really flew through my mind, and I said, "There's a red carpet in the terminal for you." I know smarty comment, but he was ticking me off now. I continued with, "I think it would be best if you went back out to the gate area and you took the next flight." At which point he took a swing at me, missed and fell down because he was so drunk.

Trust me I didn't bother to see if he was OK, I just marched out to the agent and said, "You let a drunk get on board, he just tried to hit me and now he is lying on the jetway floor. Call the airport police now." I got the last laugh as the airport police took him off in handcuffs. Buh bye Mr. CEO. Federal law doesn't like passengers attacking crew members. That is a NO-NO! Wonder if his jail cell had red carpeting?

Plunk Your Magic Twanger, Froggy

IT WAS THE Vietnam era and some of you might remember those orange clad "monks" who were Hare Krishna wannabes. Now I mean no disrespect for the Hare Krishnas or their religion, only that there were some unscrupulous men out there who were taking advantage of people and purporting to be something they really were not. Let's put it another way, I'm a Chinese astronaut if they were really "monks."

So, where better to solicit for money than an airport. These men were aggressive in their soliciting and knew who to go after. Sometimes it was the young returning soldiers from Vietnam but usually it was the elderly, someone in a wheelchair, young families, teenagers, etc.

These so-called monks were at most of the major airports, but our St. Louis station seemed to be especially inundated with them. There was an area right before the secured TWA concourse where they hung out, so they would literally corner and pressure their prey. Needless to say, they left the crews alone but still to be honest it really ticked us off watching them. It was predatory!

Anyway, some of our pilots came up with a great idea. Remember those little clickers that looked like tiny, tin, toy frogs. They sold tons of them to TWA employees; it became a movement of sorts. Every time we would see the fake monks we would start with our clickers. Trust me they knew that sound well after a few weeks. I hope that they had nightmares about crews approaching and millions of little clickers going off.

But I digress, if we saw one of them really hassling a reluctant, nervous passenger, we'd go up and start clicking at them and "escort" the passenger into the concourse, usually with some excuse like they were being paged. It infuriated the predators when their prey escaped. I guess the clickers and our non-relenting harassment finally got on their nerves because they started to follow us to the TWA concourse line, yelling all manner of expletives while we just walked straight ahead, clicking away. I know, amazing.

Finally, their cover was blown, for it showed the pseudo monks true natures. Shortly thereafter, some type of law was passed that you couldn't solicit in airports. I would hope our clicker brigade had something to do with that.

If you are old enough to remember Froggy the Gremlin that was probably where those pilots got their idea for those clickers. Plunk your magic twanger, Froggy … puff the monks were gone!

Terror on Takeoff

I WAS WORKING TWA Flight 159 on November 6, 1967. We were flying from New York to LA with a stop at the Greater Cincinnati airport. Our passenger load was very light with only twenty-nine passengers out of Cincinnati to LA and there were seven crew members on board, consisting of three pilots and four flight attendants.

We were ready to leave Cincinnati but were held on the taxiway waiting for a Delta DC-9 flight to land. Our plane was a Boeing 707, called a water wagon. FYI these were older 707 aircraft with engines that water was injected into the compressed airflow, to increase the flow mass, thereby providing more thrust for takeoff. We got very used to the pilots revving the engines for a while before starting the takeoff roll.

As flight attendants we did not know what was going on outside of the plane because our jump seats for takeoff and landing did not have windows at our jump seat level. We had no idea that a Delta DC-9 which had landed was now mired in mud, just off the runway. All we knew was that we had been cleared for takeoff and had started rolling down the runway.

The next thing I and the other flight attendant sitting next me on the jump seat felt was the nose lifting, and then there was a "big bang" on the right side of the plane. Everything seemed to shut down and then the braking and reversing of engines began.

Now we could see a fire on the right wing and could tell we were not going to stop in time. The plane was careening right off the end of the runway where it went over a hill. It then struck the ground, shearing off the main landing gear and displacing the nosewheel rearward. We later found out that the plane after striking the ground then became airborne again for sixty-seven feet before coming to a rest 421 feet from the end of the runway.

When the aircraft finally stopped, I jumped up, opened the aft door and pulled the slide out of the ceiling. When I went to lock it on the floor, I realized we were only about two to three feet off the ground because the landing gear had been ripped off. No need for a slide, just jump out. I directed my passengers to jump and run away from the plane. Little did I know what awaited us.

Outside of the aircraft we were in mud that was so thick we were all sinking to our knees. It was very slow going and terrifying, as we tried to struggle through the muck and mire to find safety. Finally, after what seemed like an eternity, we made it to the top of the runway to turn around to see our aircraft burning.

As it turned out we only had three exits out of six that we could use for evacuating. The forward cabin door was blocked because the nose gear had been pushed up into it, making it impossible to push the door out to be able to open it. The right wing was on fire so the emergency wing exit could not be used there, and the aft galley door had flames shooting by it so that door was unavailable too. We were left with the forward right galley door, the left-wing exit, and the aft left cabin door. Amazingly we only had ten injuries and thankfully, only one fatality.

After several hearings in Washington DC, it was determined that Delta had not totally cleared the runway. Their plane was stuck in the mud and its jet exhaust continued to pose a hazard to any aircraft using that runway because it would cause a "compressor stall" to the other plane. Delta was held at fault. They settled with the deceased passenger's family for supposedly $105,000 in civil court and settled with TWA for $2,216,000 for the loss of the Boeing 707 aircraft.

Note: Our co-pilot was in charge of the flight that day and decided to abort. He and our captain were questioned over and over about his decision at the hearings. I thank him every day for his quick thinking! Who knows what might have happened if we had taken off?

Make My Day

THIS WAS BACK in the days when we would routinely "hold the flight" for late passengers.

The aircraft doors were all closed for departure and we were starting our emergency demonstration when the agent moved the jetway back to the plane and two more passengers were boarded … with attitude, I might add.

At any rate they stormed back to their seats that were located by the aft galley on the MD-80. One of them opened up the overhead bin right above him and it was full. He slammed it shut, threw his garment bag onto the galley floor nearly hitting me and demanded that I find a place for it.

Needless to say, I was not happy with this, in fact I'll be honest here I was pissed, but I walked up two rows where there were no passengers seated and opened a bin, which "big" surprise, had space in it. I "pointedly" turned to him and said, "Here you go!" He looks at me and then his bag as if I'm to retrieve it and put it in the overhead bin.

Well, you obviously have no idea who you are dealing with, do you Mr. Nasty? At this point I smiled and said sarcastically with an edge to my voice, "You have two choices, one either put your bag in this overhead bin or the second one is I will open the door, kick it out onto the ramp, where the baggage handlers can collect it. Your choice."

I was kind of sorry he opted for the first choice because swear to God, I wanted to open the galley door and kick his bag to the tarmac so badly! Don't mess with 5'4" in heels …

Just Another Flight Until...

WE HAD BEEN bouncing around the good 'ol USA for four days on a Convair 880. It was our last leg from Las Vegas to LAX and we were expecting a full load, but we got an unexpected surprise. One of our passengers in first class was none other than Dean Martin. Now for those of you who don't remember the "rat pack" days of Frank Sinatra, Dean Martin, Sammy Davis Jr., and Peter Lawford they were infamous in Las Vegas, movies, and TV specials. Plus they were pals with President Kennedy before his death since Peter Lawford was Kennedy's brother-in-law.

But back to our trip. The boarding agent told us we were having Mr. Martin and his manager in first class, now things were looking up. We went from dog tired, to woo-who this might be fun!

Well, Mr. Martin lived up to all of the hype; good looking, knew how to dress, spectacular tan and very personable. He was sitting in row one, in the aisle seat, and his manager was in the window seat, so they were very close to our galley.

Everyone was on board when the captain announced we were going to have a mechanical. Large groan from the cabin followed. Now Dean Martin on his TV show was always carrying around a lit cigarette and smoking it, as well as when he was performing in Las Vegas. Guess what? He was a chain smoker. Mr. Martin says to me, "Honey I need to have a cigarette. I'm going back into the concourse, but I will be standing right at the window watching the plane. As soon as the captain is ready to leave, just come out onto the steps, wave at me and I will get back on immediately." Point here: there were no jetways at the Las Vegas airport then, passengers boarded on steps the agents brought up to the doors of the aircraft.

Well, who am I to say no to Mr. Martin, "No problem sir, I'll let the captain know that you are in the waiting area in the concourse." Off goes Dino (his real first name) and now I find myself talking to his manager. He is telling me that Dean Martin had just finished filming a movie called *Airport*. It was adapted from a book named *Airport* written by Arthur Haley.

So, I'm sitting in Mr. Martin's seat next to his manager now totally engrossed in our conversation, as he was explaining to me that one of the characters in the book was based on Roy Davis who was the director of maintenance at O'Hare for TWA. Haley had gone to Chicago and evidently spent a few weeks with Roy just watching, observing and asking him questions.

A little background about Roy Davis. He was an institution unto himself. If our cars in the TWA employees' lot wouldn't start because they had been sitting outside in minus ten degree weather while we were flying a trip, just go inside to his office and tell his secretary that we needed a jump start for our cars. There would be a mechanic there in a few minutes with a large truck and cables. Crew bus was on the other side of the airport at the terminal and you were running late. Roy would make an exception for you and get one of the mechanics to run you over from the hangar to the terminal in a truck, so you wouldn't get into trouble. That was just the type of man he was. Plus, it was amazing, if he learned your name, he learned it for life. He had a heart of gold!

An aside: there was a classic story about him and this is important because you must know he always had a cigar in his mouth or hand. Anyway, a new mechanic sees him walking across the tarmac with a cigar in his mouth. What this newbie didn't notice was that it was not lit. He commented to another TWA mechanic about the dangers of smoking on the ramp, you know what he heard back? "That's Roy Davis. The ramp wouldn't DARE blow up!"

Roy Davis, yes, he became a character in Arthur Haley's book *Airport*, he was the mechanic who was chewing on a cigar and getting a plane off of the runway in a snowstorm. And of course, the mechanic had a TWA hat on. Who could play Roy? The famous actor George Kennedy.

But I digress: as I'm sitting there unbeknownst to me Mr. Martin had walked across the ramp and up the stairs. Everyone on the entire plane had seen him when they were boarding and were now aware of him walking back onto the plane. All of the aisle passengers' heads were looking out from their seats to see Mr. Martin.

I hear my flying partner now say to me, "Hey look down the aisle." I turned in the seat and I saw around fifty faces looking back at me. Then I feel a heavy weight in my lap. My head swings around and who is sitting in my lap putting his arms around my neck but Dean Martin. He starts to laugh and then says, "There is something wrong with this picture," and gets up. Then he says, "Give me your hands," pulls me out of the seat and he sits down when I hear him say, "OK, now you sit in my lap." I can feel myself blushing as I sit down in his lap and my flying partner is snapping away with her little camera that she always carried with her. I might add the flight engineer had come out of the cockpit too and was taking pictures.

I used to love to tell people that Dean Martin had sat in my lap and then I sat in his. You should have seen the looks on their faces. And I still have that photo today ... good times.

P.S. If you haven't read the book then watch the movie *Airport*. Both are great.

We Had It All

IT WAS THE beginning of my lifelong love affair with aviation, and I knew I was embarking on something special and the years since did not disappoint.

A few years after graduating from Ozark Flight Attendant Training, Trans World Airlines bought us and soon thereafter, I went from working DC-9 jets here in the USA, to working jumbo jets to all corners of the world. TWA afforded me the opportunity to live a life I never could have imagined.

Let me share with you just a few things that make me who I am today: the city of Tel Aviv, Israel where I have sat in the manger where Christ was born in Jerusalem, prayed at the Western Wailing Wall surrounding Temple Mount in Old City Jerusalem. Visited the Church of the Holy Sepulcher that is built over the remains of Golgotha, also called Calvary, the hill just outside of Jerusalem where the Romans crucified Jesus and the location of the tomb where the body of Jesus was laid.

Athens, Greece that city of wonder where I walked the ruins of the Acropolis citadel and the Parthenon temple. Dined on Moussaka and watched some people throw plates on the floor in tune with the music being played in restaurants.

Marveled at majestic Rome, Italy with the Colosseum built during the Roman Empire and today having thousands of cats roaming in it and begging for tidbits of food. And of course, I visited Vatican City where I stood in St. Peter's Basilica and viewed Michelangelo's Sistine Chapel frescoes.

And I will never forget Zurich, Switzerland with Chagall's stained-glass windows in the Fraumünster Church in Zürich which was built on the remains of a former abbey for aristocratic women. It was founded in 853 by Louis the German for his daughter Hildegard. "853" think of that! In addition, I'll always remember sailing on Lake Zurich and yes, I even did some cow tipping with sleeping cows on a hillside.

Visiting Amsterdam, Netherlands to see the Van Gogh Museum and tour the Anne Frank House. Oh yes and sat in a bar where patrons openly smoked marijuana (full disclosure, I did not) and walked the famous Red-Light District to see those ladies of the night advertising their wares in the windows. (Full disclosure again I did not participate).

The lovely rich in history city of Madrid, Spain where I admired art at El Prado, Reina Sofia and the Thyssen Bornemisza museums, or simply called the Thyssen which is an art museum in Madrid, Spain, located near the Prado Museum on one of city's main boulevards. And I even attended a bull fight in Las Ventas.

TWA afforded me these and so "many more, wonderful adventures." I am not bragging; I just want you to know how blessed I have been in my life and share with you some of it. Life can take many things from you, but all of the great memories remain yours. Thank you, TWA, for my great love affair with the world.

I Lived the High Life

Turbulence, tight quarters and talkative soldiers made every flight an adventure for a 1940s stewardess

I WORKED AS a hostess in 1943 back when that job was considered one of the most glamorous jobs a young woman could have. After growing up in Gary, Indiana and attending Purdue University for a year, I'd decided I wanted to do something for the war effort, so I applied for a job with TWA as a hostess or ground agent.

When I got the telegram inviting me to interview for hostess training, I was very excited. But when I saw the other applicants in the waiting room looking so poised and sophisticated, I didn't think I stood a chance. To my surprise, I was the only one chosen from the bunch. Later I found out it was because I looked "wholesome." Probably being from the Midwest had something to do with that.

Our uniforms consisted of a sky-blue skirt and jacket, with a navy camisole and an overseas style hat. Nylons were so scarce because of the war that if I got a run in them, I would cry. I remember my roommate coming home from a flight and taking off her nylons just in time for me to put them on! Our shoes were plain brown oxfords ... "ugly" but practical during turbulence, when we were being buffeted back and forth while passing out "burp cups" to airsick passengers.

TWA hostesses showing off their military pride with a salute
in their 1940's summer uniforms.
Photo courtesy of the TWA Museum.

The trusty DC-3 was what we flew and our crew of three consisted of a pilot, copilot and me, the hostess. Our passengers were mostly military personnel, who had priority with the airlines and we often had to "bump" civilian passengers. I empathized with the soldiers and airmen who were either going to war or coming home but I will admit sometimes I was emotionally drained by their stories.

Yes, flights then were longer, more turbulent and less predictable but I thought they were exciting! The less exciting part of the job was the burp cups and passing out chewing gum to help ease the pressure of stopped-up ears. And then, there was our galley which was drafty and cramped and had a strong "metallic" smell in it. I have to admit that sometimes the food, especially the scrambled eggs, tasted metallic too and nothing looked appetizing on those cardboard trays. Would you believe we were responsible for the flatware kit too? Every night I'd have to take it to my hotel room to wash the flatware in the basin! So much for sanitary and then there were our suitcases. Room for my clothes? Well, it had a divider inside and only half was for my personal things. The other half-contained flight reports and forms to be turned in when we landed.

In those days of smaller planes and fewer passengers, hostesses could give more personalized service than they are able to do today. I would visit with so many interesting passengers and they would sometimes show their appreciation with letters of accommodation. I still recall a Christmas flight when I took little wreaths and pinned them above each seat. That small gesture for the holiday certainly made everyone's lives a little more special, including mine.

Yes, those years were truly the time of my life from flying the first delegates to the United Nations and occasionally having celebrities like Howard Hughes on board! Though bad weather often stranded us in dull places, having a long layover in an exciting big city was adequate compensation. Especially for a girl from Gary, Indiana.

But my last memory is truly one of the best. It was a stormy night and a tall handsome naval officer boarded my flight. From then on, my flying days were numbered ... a few months later I married that good-looking Navy pilot.

In the years since, I've seen airliners increase greatly in size and sophistication. Still, the jumbo jets with their luxurious accommodations and super power just don't thrill me like that modest DC-3 once did, as it quivered at the end of the runway ready for takeoff. Yes, those were days ...

The author of this story is now traveling with all of the TWA angels in the sky in a modest DC-3.

Why

I WAS FLYING from Frankfurt, Germany back to JFK and the flight was going to land almost an hour early due to favorable winds. Everyone was very happy about this, but as I was walking down the aisle, a younger gentleman asked me where he would go for his refund? When I asked why he wanted one, he said, "Because I am not getting my full time in the air."

Can't make everyone happy …

Damien, Yes that Damien

LATE ONE NIGHT on the last leg of a four-leg day, an agent in St. Louis came down the jetway at the last minute dragging a miniature passenger—what appeared to be a little boy of around ten. His name was Damien. She shoved him in the door, grimly said, "Lots of luck," and quickly shut the door behind him.

Proceeding with caution, I put him in an open first class seat. Actually, it took two of us to put him there because he started kicking and screaming the moment we looked at him. One of us wrestled him down and the other one tried to buckle him up as the plane taxied into position.

He successfully drowned out most of my PA announcements, and I gritted my teeth as we took off with him standing up in his seat, and throwing his gum at the businessman behind him and constantly dinging the call bell.

The flight was a living hell, but the crowning touch came during landing. On our final descent, he made a quick dash and locked himself in the first class lav of this 727. I quickly grabbed a metal dinner knife from the galley to unlock the lav door. Note: There is a tiny slit that you put a sharp object in, so that you can slide the lock back to open the lav door from the outside, when the door is locked from the inside. Now you know an airline trick.

I opened the door; he saw me standing there with the knife and proceeded to scream at the top of his lungs, "Somebody HELP me please, she's got a knife and is trying to kill me!"

An entire plane of shocked passengers leaned into the aisle to see me standing there holding a knife in my hand. I was mortified; there I was obviously looking intent on mayhem. I should have just killed him anyway since he'd announced it to the world.

The captain heard the entire commotion through the door and had police meeting the flight. As soon as the cabin door was opened, the kid tried to bolt off, saw the police and careened back into the lav. CLICK!

I was drained and no longer cared. I said, "He's all yours—lots of luck."

A Sad Holiday

ONCE BACK WHEN I had just started flying, probably in the early 1970s, I had a turnaround from ORD to PHL. In other words, we were just flying from Chicago to Philadelphia, sat on the ground for a short period, loaded new passengers and went back to Chicago. The bad news for the crew, it was during a holiday when you wanted to be home with your family.

Now this was in the days when passengers could be brought on the plane by a family member to say their good-byes. In Chicago, a woman was pre-boarded and her sister had gotten on the plane with her to do just this. Our passenger who would be flying with us was an older woman, and she was also deaf and mute. In addition, unfortunately none of us knew how to do sign language.

This woman explained to us that her sister was going to Philadelphia to stay with her brother for "a while," and that she had been taking care of her for a long time. As this woman was deplaning, she gave my flying partner an envelope, saying there is information about her in here.

We did not think much about it at the time and started boarding other passengers. Finally, during the flight, my flying partner opened the envelope to find a five-dollar bill, a letter giving her brother's phone number in the Philadelphia area, plus an explanation that she had been taking care of her sister for a long time and it was "his turn now!" From the sound of this letter, she was sending her sister off to the brother permanently, not what she had told us during boarding that her sister was just going to stay with her brother for "a while." Did her sister know this?

We went up to the cockpit and showed the letter to the captain, and he called ahead to notify the TWA ramp office about this situation. When we landed, the agent said they could not get hold of the brother at the telephone number that was in the letter. Oh no, we just had to hand this woman off to the agent. It was devastating! We feared that this sweet woman probably had no idea what was happening to her either.

We never did learn if they found her brother, but it was a terrible holiday for the crew. When you are placed in this kind of situation some guilt always remains with you, even when you cannot help. I hope that all was resolved, that she spent a wonderful holiday with her brother and most of all she was able to continue living with a family member.

Ex-Boyfriend
All Male Crews Were My Saviors

IN 2020, DREW Carey, the comedian and television game show host most of you would recognize, ex fiancée was murdered by a stalker. This gave me a flashback into my previous dating life.

It was just a normal flight. I was flying with two male flight attendants that I really did not know. On the ground, before the passengers had boarded, we introduced ourselves to one another and decided what positions we were going to work on the plane. I was senior to them and I chose to work the galley position. Now to paint a picture this plane was a Boeing 727—regular. It had one galley in the center of the aircraft to serve both first class and coach. On the ground, it was my responsibility to check out the galley to make sure that not only first class but also coach had the proper amount of meals boarded for the passenger count and we had all of our supplies. I was doing this with the galley curtain closed during boarding, so I saw none of the passengers getting on.

When everyone was seated and boarding was completed it was my responsibility to perform the emergency demonstration for first class. Then I sat in my seat which was actually an aisle seat in a coach row right across from my galley emergency exit door, for takeoff. All was normal so far.

After we were airborne and I was in the galley starting to prepare for the coach service, a man appeared and was standing in the aisle looking at me. Who was he? A former boyfriend. To say I was surprised would be an understatement. Our relationship had been rocky. To put it bluntly I had gotten a call one afternoon at my apartment from a woman who claimed that she was his wife. You can imagine my shock! Needless to say, I confronted him about this call. Of course, he professed his innocence, claimed he was not married and it was just a jealous ex. Well, I might have been twenty-three and he was thirty, but my better judgement told me there was something "very wrong" here. I broke off the relationship. Who sends me flowers? Yes, you guessed whom. Who was always calling? You know whom, but I was having none of it.

Then he called and had the nerve to ask out my roommate who was also a TWA flight attendant. I guess he thought this would make me jealous and I would start taking his calls. Remember this is before caller ID and cell phones.

My roomie and I both finally decided it was time to get an unlisted phone number and we actually moved because he would show up unannounced, and be knocking on the apartment door saying he needed to talk with me. We would peer out the peephole of the door and not answer.

He was so intimidating and even said one day in a total snarl, when he was standing outside the door, "I wish I could have gotten you pregnant, so you would have had to have married me." Sick!

The good thing about working for TWA was that they would never give out our phone numbers or addresses to anyone, so the move stopped all of this unwanted aggression! Until this flight.

Remember I said, I did not see any of the passengers during boarding, and it wasn't until we were airborne when I was in the galley setting up everything for the service when this former boyfriend appeared. I was stunned! The definition of stunned is so shocked that one is temporarily unable to react. That would be me at that moment.

I hear him saying, "Hello, how are you?" It was one of those surreal situations, as I'm trying to compose myself, and my reaction was to lie and say, "I'm sorry I don't know you." Moreover, here are some of the passengers who are only a few feet away from us listening to this conversation. He replied, "Oh come on, you know who I am." Then he notices my wedding rings and says, "Oh, you're married now. You must have been on the rebound from me then." What conceit and ego, let alone to be saying these things in front of all of these total strangers on the plane. I was mortified!

Well, how to get rid of him? I replied. "I don't have time to talk now. We have to start our service. I'll talk with you later." Later as in over my dead body! To say that my stomach was churning would be putting it mildly. Thank God, he left and returned to his seat which was at the end of coach. I immediately told the two male flight attendants that there was an ex-boyfriend of mine in the back and if he asked anything about me to tell him that you don't know my last name, where I'm based or anything about me. Nada, nothing!

I should have been working the liquor cart in coach, but asked the flight attendant who was working first class if I could trade positions with him, so I could work first class and not spend time in coach. You guessed it. When they were serving drinks from the liquor cart, the ex-asked them where I was based and what my last name was. They said, "Sorry, never flew with her before, don't know where she is based or her last name."

Needless to say, I told them I wouldn't be going near him and since it was a very short flight before you knew it, we were sitting down for landing. As soon as the aircraft was parked at the gate, I made a beeline for the cockpit, opened the door quickly, closed it and sat down in the additional crew member's seat behind the captain. He turns around, looks rather surprised, and says, "Are you trying to get away from an old boyfriend?" I could only assume that one of the male flight attendants had told him what was going on in the cabin. I looked at him and said, "YES." I told them none of us are leaving this cockpit until the passengers are all off the plane. And the cockpit door remained shut!

I told my all-male crew, "I know he will be waiting for me out in the gate area. Please don't let him get near me." I was not wrong. He was out there in a half-empty terminal, just standing there, all six feet four inches. Now picture this, me surrounded by five men. The captain, the first officer, the flight engineer and my two male flight attendant partners. The EX did not try to approach me.

He followed us out to the front of the airport and watched as the courtesy van from the hotel was picking us up. Even though he did not know my married name, I was still afraid he might follow me to the hotel. When I checked in, I gave the hotel explicit instructions that I would only take a phone call from TWA's scheduling department. How did I think he would be able to track me down in the hotel and call my room? I didn't know, but I wasn't taking any chances. Fear can make you non-rational. My wonderful crew realized that I was afraid of him and said, if I needed them just to call one of their rooms. Thankfully, that never occurred.

It is a terrible feeling to think that you are being stalked. Fortunately, time, marriage, change of last name, moving across the country with my husband and having a company that would not give out any information about its employees really helps. Today with so much on the internet, people can track down anyone easily. They can make your life a living hell if they want to.

I can only imagine what some woman or man must feel in this type of situation that continues on and on and on. I was one of the fortunate to get out …

Marine Style ... OOH-RAH

IT WAS A sunny, warm afternoon in St. Louis and I was working the first class cabin on a Boeing 767. The gate agent had informed us that we had a full load and he was ready to start boarding. Then as usual, our flight service manager made an announcement to the cabin crew telling them the passengers were on their way.

It was the typical boarding process that moves along at a snail's pace. Everyone waits for what seems like an eternity as someone is always taking their sweet time trying to find their seat, or putting away their personal belongings. However, everyone seemed to be in a good mood when they boarded and this boded well for a good flight.

Our passengers were now all on board and our flight service manager had disappeared to somewhere else on the plane to follow up on something. I was busy taking dinner orders in the first class cabin, when I saw our first officer come out of the cockpit, and at a fairly fast clip walk down the opposite aisle from me toward business class and disappear from my view. What was he doing went through my mind, but I still had a number of things to do and was busy, so I just continued my work.

Well, what did I hear next? The flight service manager saying on the PA system, "Ladies and gentlemen, will you please leave your personal belongings on board and deplane the aircraft immediately through the first class door that you entered through. Please do this in a calm and orderly way now."

I immediately turned to my flying partner, who I was working with, and whispered to her, "I think we are having an evacuation at the gate." She said, "Damn straight, get them moving!" I said, "Go to the first class door and tell them to keep going all the way out to the concourse. I'll keep them moving in the cabin." At this point, the captain joined her at the door, and I could hear him giving the passengers instructions to move out to the concourse and the agents would tell them what to do.

In first class, I saw a group of my perplexed passengers still sitting there and I said in a loud voice, "Ladies and gentlemen please leave the aircraft now. Do not take any personal effects with you. Please leave now."

Passengers were starting to file by and the aisles were filling up as I could hear the flight attendants from business class saying in loud voices, "Please get off of the aircraft now. Do not take anything with you!"

The coach flight attendants at the rear of the aircraft were also starting to move people out of their seats at this time. To everyone's credit no passengers were complaining, trying to take anything with them and were deplaning in an orderly manner.

Within a matter of minutes, everyone was off the plane, including the cabin crew and only my flying partner and I were left. I looked at her and said, "Hey before we get off, look down that aisle and I'll look down the other one too just to make sure all of the passengers are off."

But NOOO, there is "always" one that can't follow instructions. Plus, the million-dollar question that I still wonder about today, where had she been hiding while the rest of the passengers were deplaning? I guess I'll never know.

Anyway, getting back to this woman. I see her standing on an armrest while trying to remove something from the overhead bin. I turned into a combo of Jack Nicholson, John Wayne and a Marine. In a really "loud, low voice" as I was pointing my finger directly at her, I yelled, "YOU." She turned and looked at me and I yelled again, "YES, I SAID YOU. GET OFF OF THE AIRPLANE NOW AND NOW MEANS NOW! HAUL ASS!" Picture a platoon of Marines being led by Jack Nicholson or John Wayne yelling, "OOH-RAH!" That is how loud I was.

This woman had a rather blank stare on her face and again, I yelled in Ooh-rah fashion, "I SAID NOW! HAUL ASS!" She literally jumped off the armrest, ran past me and off the plane. My flying partner actually started to giggle and said, "Where did that come from? That was great."

As we walked off the plane, I looked at her and said, "Well, remember they told us in training they don't care what we say or how we say it during an evacuation; just get them off the plane. But to be honest I don't know where it came from." And then I started to laugh too.

OOH-RAH!

P.S. Why were we having a gate evacuation? One of our baggage handlers had been in the belly of another aircraft that was parked next to us loading bags, when he spotted something that looked suspicious. Well, it was of enough concern that they evacuated "all" of the other parked aircraft at that end of the terminal too. As the passengers left the airplanes, they were moved out of that part of the concourse. Have to give the gate agents credit here, they moved hundreds of people out of that end of the concourse without any problems either. We left three hours late and it was free drinks for all. Good news was nothing was found in the belly that was an explosive. Just another day in our flying office …

They'll Get the Trucker First

IT WAS A beautiful weekday and I was scheduled to fly out that evening on an international trip. My day would start out by leaving five hours before I needed to check in for my flight. Why so much time? Well, I lived in the Wilmington, DE area and the drive up to JFK took two hours and thirty-five minutes. Yes, I knew the exact time it took, every twist and turn on the I-95 and the NJ Turnpike, and then there was the Goethals and Verrazano bridges and finally that gawd awful Belt Parkway filed with potholes, the longest seventeen miles of my life to finally get to the hangar. I could have driven it all in my sleep.

Why did I need five hours though? Well, the drive was two hours and thirty-five minutes with no problems as I said, and then I would check in with scheduling, check my company mailbox, go to the TWA employees' cafeteria for an early dinner and finally take the crew bus over to the terminal to meet my crew for our briefing. Five hours gave me the time I needed. Moreover, since I was not going to see food until around 11:30 PM at night on an international flight I really wanted that early dinner experience.

So, everything with my drive on the NJ Turnpike was fine. I was blowing down the road now, a woman on a mission so to speak. Entertaining myself by listening to plenty of tunes to break the boredom. I was about an hour thirty minutes into the drive when the four lanes of the turnpike started to all slow down at once. If you do any long distance driving you will find that you should immediately get over into the slow lane of traffic. Watch the next time you are in a traffic jam—what lane moves better? The slow one.

I'm in the far-right lane now, the traffic is moving at a snail's pace and then eventually we are just sitting there. All four lanes dead! No movement period! I get out my bid sheet for the next month to look it over, so I can begin thinking about what I would like to fly for the following month when I hear a truck's horn blasting away. One long sharp blast, then a second and then a third. What the—? I look in my side door mirror and what do I see? A huge semi-truck driving down the breakdown lane approaching me. The driver had obviously lost his mind.

Decisions, decisions! Should I jump out after he passes me and just follow him down the breakdown lane? If there is a NJ Highway patrol officer down there, they will go after him first. I will cry hysterically, tell them I'm a flight attendant and have to get to JFK or I'll be fired. Please, please, please don't give me a ticket!

My decision is made in a split second. Jump on his tail end and suck up his exhaust now. I no sooner did that than four other cars jump out and are following the two of us down the breakdown lane too.

We drove about a half a mile when all of a sudden, he veered into the four lanes of nonmoving traffic. It is like Moses parting the sea. And trust me I'm one of the Israelites following him. Cars are scattering like dominoes and I'm still on his tail end sucking up exhaust. The other four cars behind me chickened out and disappeared from sight. Now we are in the breakdown lane on the left-hand side. He is blowing his horn again like a demented person. Of course, I can see nothing ahead of us—I mean nothing.

All of a sudden, he drives past an overturned semi on the turnpike that is blocking all of the lanes. There were probably at least three NJ Highway patrol cars blocking off the traffic. The trucker pulls out onto the turnpike now and starts to accelerate.

It was now or never! I put the pedal to the metal and took off. I'm doing about ninety and there are absolutely no cars in front me. Have to admit it was rather exhilarating, the NJ Turnpike with no cars on it. I look in my rearview mirror to check my escape. My plan is working; they went after the trucker! I continued to drive at ninety for about ten minutes when I decided that I had probably made up my lost time while sitting on the turnpike. Ah, back on schedule and I can relax, I will be having dinner at the employee's cafeteria in about another ninety minutes.

Sometimes you just get lucky ... I know it was a crazy thing to do but TWA took a dim view of being late. I still wonder what ever happened to the trucker? Probably not good ...

George Hamilton

BY FAR, MY favorite working trip was a polar flight, from Montreal to Rome, on May 2, 1961. Reason I remember that date is from my photo album.

George Hamilton was the only passenger in first class where I was working. He was going on location to film *Light in the Piazza*. We laughed at nothing and everything for hours at 30,000 feet.

TWA supplied a Polaroid camera at that time for us to take pictures of the passengers and give them these as souvenirs. Another hostess snapped ten or more photos of Mr. Hamilton and me, which I still have. Unfortunately, they are now deteriorating! However, I don't need photos to remember us doing the life vest and oxygen-mask demonstration together and making a fake toast to who knows what?

Mr. Hamilton was friendly, unassuming, and kind. He was also a sentimental sort of person for he wore a gold chain with an amulet and said he would never take it off.

I still remember that he invited me to the set in Rome, but at the time, TWA had a rule about dating passengers that was a No-No. However, it was also easy not to accept because I was in love with someone then, someone who strongly and ironically resembled George Hamilton.

Still love seeing you on television and in the movies. And when I eat Kentucky Fried Chicken, I always think of you now. Toasting a true gentleman ...

Boys Will Be Boys

HOW ABOUT A passenger getting embarrassed? I was working a flight and had four men in coach who were traveling together. They were having a good time and taking turns buying drinks. It was now time for this one man to buy the next round.

You aren't going to believe this one. He pulls out his wallet to get money to pay me, opens it up and tries to take out some bills, when what also pops out? WAIT! A very "well-traveled never used condom." It falls on the floor! Oh my, now I am going to have a good time with this.

I leaned over to pick it up and as I handed it back to him, I said, "See you haven't had much luck in a few years." His friends were dying with laughter now and we razzed him the entire flight. On descent when I was checking seat belts for landing, I could not resist and wished him luck.

His little faux pas turned a dull flight into a fun one. At the end of the flight, I bought his drinks for the entertainment value he had brought that day. OK and a little mea culpa too for harassing him.

I Am Only Worth How Much

IT WAS BACK in the '70s and I was working a Peace Corps charter to Monrovia, Liberia. (Republic of Liberia). We had a seventy-six-hour layover there and decided that it would be a great adventure to take a dugout canoe trip down a small river called the Du. Our destination was a remote village referred to as Bassa village of Go Wein.

Here were some of the guidelines they gave us before sending us on our way with our guide: You will be visiting an isolated rural community that has remained virtually untouched by modern life, so we ask you to please make this interaction a positive experience for everyone involved. Cultural sensitivity is really important. Your tour guide will help you in this, but a few basic expectations apply:

1. Please speak to everyone with respect, especially the village chief and elders.
2. Please be aware that you are guests in the community and act considerately at all times.
3. Ask permission before taking photographs of people (they will be happy to oblige!).
4. Make sure you leave no rubbish in the area and ensure that any human waste is buried well away from the village.

Ultimately, the goal is for you to have an enjoyable, and rewarding experience and for the host community to benefit from your interaction. This should be the benchmark for your behavior.

Well, that certainly sounded easy except for possibly burying the human waste?!

So, I along with another flight attendant and our captain got into one of the dugout canoes and started paddling along. Now picture the riverbanks which are home to the tribes and their families. Everyone would gather on the banks of the river waving at us as we cruised by and us to them.

We finally arrived at the Bassa village where the tribal chief met us. After a few minutes of conversation with him, conducted through our guide, he informed us that the chief wanted to buy me from the captain. Yes, the one with the hair like snow. (I was a blonde.) He thought I was worth two pigs and a goat. Willing to pay more because of my hair!

The captain "respectfully" declined, and fortunately for me no deal was struck. I was reminded of that many times for the remaining part of our trip. Two pigs and a goat, puhleeze I'm worth more than that!

How much do you think you are worth?

I Always Wanted Wings

IN THE MID '60s there were quite a number of so-called Airline Academies who advertised training to be a stewardess and claimed that with one of their diplomas any airline would gladly hire you. This was misleading because everyone with a bit of insight knew that all carriers preferred to train their own staff and these schools were really money wasted. Fortunately, my parents said if you really want to be an airline stewardess you have to apply to each carrier and forget these bogus airline academies and their ads.

Now I started scanning the newspapers classified sections on a routine basis to see when each airline would be in town for interviews. Having German, as my mother tongue (my parents had emigrated from Germany when I was a young girl), I really wanted to work for either TWA, Pan Am or a foreign carrier.

My wish was granted when I saw an ad for TWA hiring stewardesses. My dreams came true because after my interviews I was hired. To say I was excited would be putting it mildly. But my dreams were shattered when I found out that after training in Kansas City, TWA would base me anywhere they had an opening. This would be for a minimum of six months, or possibly as long as a year, before I could transfer back to New York where my parents lived. In my nineteen-year-old ignorance and naiveté I didn't expect this because I had planned on being based in New York and continuing to live in comfort with my parents.

What to do? After thinking about it and talking with my parents, a higher power or just good luck must have been on my side. When I called TWA to tell them I decided not to take the job, the next thing I knew they offered me a job in reservations. My training would be at the TWA Hangar at JFK and I would be able to continue to reside with my parents.

This was an amazing time for me and there I made my first acquaintance with TWA's generosity. The entire training class was offered first class, round trip tickets to either Los Angeles or San Francisco for the purpose of getting to know TWA's service and the organization.

In addition, we were given passes for New York Airways that at the time was operating helicopter service between the New York airports, Wall Street and the top of the Pan Am building, which was thrilling and also a bit scary to land on. To be in Manhattan within twelve minutes, no less on a helicopter! Very exciting for a nineteen-year-old.

After six weeks of basic training, where we were drilled in how to sell seats in the domestic reservation department, I started working at the WestSide Airlines Terminal and later moved to 2 Penn Plaza.

Now most of you wouldn't know this, but we were given a made-up name and a call sign. "Good evening, TWA, the all-jet airline, Miss Manchester speaking," was my greeting with every call. I chose the name Manchester because I thought that everybody knew how to spell and remember this name. Remember service was everything in those days and it better be personal too!

Sometimes, a supervisor would listen in to make sure you were going through all of the sales points and NEVER EVER call a flight by only its flight number. It was "Star Stream flight 800" to Paris, etc. etc., and always mention the choice of five entrees and the headphones for entertainment. Gawd forbid if we missed something. You'd hear your real first name with the request of please go unavailable directly after that phone call. Your call had been reviewed, you missed something and now you would be reviewed.

I also learned that the stewardesses weren't the only ones who had to deal with cranks. We had one particular weirdo who phoned every evening asking, whoever was "lucky" to get him, "What color panties are you wearing?" My standard answer was always, "I'm not wearing any," and hung up.

After six months, I was promoted to Sky Chief, which dealt only with corporate accounts and travel agencies. We still had to go through the "All Jet Airline" and "Star Stream" procedures and I remember well travel agents responding with "Don't give me that crap. I know it …" Yes, we just gritted our teeth and tried to have a smile in our voice.

Finally, my promotion came to work at the TWA ticket counter in the Airlines Building on 42nd St. This legendary building had airlines like Eastern, American, United etc. in it. At last, I had the uniform and winged name badge! I might not have been a stewardess but I loved my job just the same.

Thank you, TWA, for all of the wonderful memories and the dear colleagues I worked with. For putting up TVs in the ticketing hall, so no one would miss seeing the first man walk on the moon. When Martin Luther King was killed, we all cried and hugged one another. And the same terrible tragedy with Bobby Kennedy. When snowstorms shut down airports and we were deluged with calls from the public, or working those ticket counters when our colleagues couldn't get to work, so we worked overtime hours to take care of our customers. I remember them well.

You're probably wondering if I regretted never being a stewardess? No life takes us in different directions and I still worked for one of the finest airlines in the business. I left TWA and moved back to Vienna and when I went to Swiss Air to interview for a job, as soon as they found out I had worked for TWA, I was hired! No better recommendation needed ...

No You Don't ... Get Out of My Way

ONE OF THE last exercises prior to graduation from flight attendant training was to practice an evacuation. There was a mockup of an aircraft interior with seats, galley and doors. Very realistic.

My training roommate was chosen as one of the crew to perform the evacuation and I was one of the passengers along with the rest of my class. When we got to the mockup trainer, we were told that several guests would also be part of the passenger group. Guests? Who? Believe it or not our guests were none other than the pilots from Air Force One who were in training with our pilots in MKC and wanted to observe. TWA did the training for Air Force One at that time (1966). Not too shabby, the U.S. government must have thought highly of us.

Anyway, back to the mock evacuation: my roommate was positioned at the Convair 880 door, and I might add here that this door was really heavy and you had to throw some weight into it as you opened it. The command to evacuate was given when all of a sudden one of the Air Force One pilots got up and was going to attempt to assist her. Not a good plan on his part! She literally threw him across into the galley, opened her door and we all started to evacuate.

After the mock evacuation was completed, the Air Force One pilots attended a critique of it by our instructor. Well boys you got a wakeup call. Our instructor informed them that the hostess had done her job as she was trained to do, that she knew how to open the door and performed all of the evacuation procedures perfectly.

I always wondered if those pilots had a different view of "hostesses" (as we were called then) after that experience. Something tells me they did.

Georgia On My Mind, or Maybe It Is Just the Bumps

RAY CHARLES WAS traveling in first class on my flight and unfortunately, I was working in coach that day so I wouldn't have an opportunity to chat with him. I was in love with his music, and decided that I had to go meet him and let him know I was a fan. As I approached his seat, what did I see him doing? He was reading a *Playboy* magazine and it was in braille. Yes, braille!

Being slightly the smart aleck, I said, "Aha! A man who really reads *Playboy* for its articles." He laughed and said, "Oh, no honey, I just like to feel the bumps."

I instantly broke out in laughter and finally pulled myself together to tell him that I loved his music. I still laugh about it today.

Love you Ray!

Christmas Eve ... Bah Humbug

IT WAS MY first year with the company and first Christmas being away from my family. My roommate who was also a new flight attendant was really bah-humbug about the holidays, and was not taking it well about being away from her family either.

Well, what to do? I relentlessly pestered her about getting a live Christmas tree. We can't be in this apartment without something that says

Christmas. I was a broken record until finally, she gave in. But we couldn't afford a container for the tree, let alone ornaments, so the tree sat in our apartment on wooden slats that it had been nailed to. In addition, I might add drying out rapidly from the heat of southern California and no water! Details ...

Decorations consisted of a few red bows I made up and scattered around on it. No lights, no ornaments, nothing else. I know it sounds rather pathetic, but the tree sat in our living room by the front window as a small tip of the hat for Christmas. And we did enjoy the scent of the drying pine. LOL!

We were both on standby and knew it probably would happen. Ah yes, the magic ringing of the phone from the scheduling grinches calling us to fly on Christmas Eve, returning two days later on the 26th. Good times, not! Full loads on the 24th, bad weather and dealing with some people that had lost the holiday spirit.

Soldiering on, as passengers boarded with their bags full of gifts and luggage, it was our job to wish them a Merry Christmas and serve them with a smile on our faces. That is what we were being paid the big bucks to do and no, we did not get holiday pay for all of this. And then there was the fact that we would be in a hotel for Christmas Eve and the next two days fly a few more lonely souls around. A big downer to put it gently!

So, we bounced around the countryside and finally it was our last leg of the day. The gate agent told us we only had twenty-five people boarding. Well, that was a relief! It was 8 PM now and most of the world was at home, enjoying their evening except for these twenty-five poor souls, who God only knew why they were flying on Christmas Eve.

Our passengers boarded and looked as excited to be there as we were, which was a big NOT! When all of a sudden who comes walking down the jetway, but a person dressed as Santa Claus replete with a full white fake beard. They even had a large red sack thrown over their shoulder.

I said, "Well, hi Santa, welcome aboard. Merry Christmas." To which I hear a woman's voice reply, "And a Merry Christmas to you too! Ho, ho, ho ..." Now picture our Santa who was only about five foot three inches, slight in build, red hat and white beard, with a pillow over her stomach under her red suit, which was held in position with a big black belt.

Our Santa proceeded to walk to coach and find her seat while I informed the cockpit that we had a special passenger that night, Santa. The pilots laughed and said, "Well, we better make sure Santa gets there." Then the captain got on the PA and told everyone on board that cocktails were free this evening. Now this perked up our small crowd from their rather dour expressions. Free cocktails can always help! But what now do I hear coming from the coach cabin? The sound of laughter. No, it wasn't our passengers laughing then, but someone had a laughing box and had set it off for just a few seconds. Then a few minutes later, there was the laughing box going off again. One of my flying partners comes up to me and says, "That woman dressed like Santa has a laughing box and is setting it off."

At this point, I can hear our other passengers starting to laugh. Then the two of us started to laugh. You can't help yourself when you hear a laughing box. Fifteen minutes later we take off to the sounds of a laughing box.

Yes, the absurdity of having to fly on Christmas Eve, with a woman dressed like Santa and her laughing box was just what we needed to perk us up. We laughed our way to Philadelphia.

Before we landed, as the captain was going to sign my liquor papers authorizing the complimentary drinks he said, "We need something for ourselves to enjoy in the hotel," and he gave me the cockpits orders for miniatures otherwise called booze. He said, "Be sure that the cabin crew gets something too." A captain who cared! Possibly things were looking up now. No such luck! We arrive at the hotel to find out that there are no restaurants open for Christmas Eve or Christmas day either. Room service was available, with only hamburgers and cold sandwiches. Gee, Merry Christmas …

But as we gathered in the captain's hotel room, to enjoy our Christmas toddies and room service burgers, we laughed about that woman who made our Christmas Eve trip a little more tolerable. My dear if you are reading this, thanks! You did light up the plane that night.

I almost forgot, she handed out candy canes to all of our passengers too. She was a great Santa!

For All Flight Attendants Who Were Ever on Weight Check
"A Christmas Lament"

T'was the week before Christmas and all through the house
Were delectable goodies that would tempt any mouse
The cookies were baked in the oven with care
In hopes that we'd eat them and our uniforms still wear!

Most flight attendants were nestled all snug in their beds
While visions of sugar plums danced in their heads
And I in my stretch denims (I looked like a beast!)
Had just settled in for a dynamite feast!

When out on the lawn there arose such a clatter
I sprang from the table to see what was the matter
When what to my hungering eyes should appear
But ORD's supervisors with all of their weighing gear!
And before I could throw all my food in the trash
They entered my home-down the chimney in a flash!
They carried in scales, tape measures and such
They told me my stockings were already filled too much
And just when they were about to "pinch more than an inch"
John Nelson arrived and became sort of a Grinch.
Then laying a finger aside of his nose
Up the chimney John and all the rest of them rose.

On Bradford, on Kreimer, on Chandler and Nelson
(and Warren and Smitty and Gene were all helping)
To the top of the roof and the top of the walls
Now dash away, dash away, dash away all!

And I heard John exclaim as they rode out of sight ...
"Merry Christmas to all ... we won't weigh you tonight!"

Yes, Virginia there can be a Santa Claus. He comes as a TWA supervisor with his supervisor buddies but then in the spirit of Christmas decides to leave. No weighing that night.

From Subway to Burgers

IT WAS A morning flight to Las Vegas from ORD on a L-1011. Those of us who were working coach and business class were waiting for the liquor carts and food carts to come up from the lower galley to start the breakfast service. As we were standing there just aimlessly talking about this, that, and whatever, I started to smell something coming from the cabin. I said to one of the other flight attendants, "Wow that is strong. It smells like it should be a hoagie sandwich. Who has a hoagie for breakfast?"

Curiosity got the better of me and I went out into the business class cabin and started to make my way forward. When I finally got to the very first row, there was a man seated with an unwrapped hoagie, getting his napkins ready for a fine dining experience. I couldn't help myself, I leaned down and whispered in his ear, "How dare you bring that wonderful smelling sandwich on this plane. People are going to be disappointed when we don't offer them a hoagie."

He laughed and I said, "It's going to be a few more minutes before we bring out the carts. Would you like something to wash that down with?" To which he replied, "Yes, I'd love a Pepsi." "Well, sir we only have Coke, would you like that?" He just smiled and said, "No problem." I gave him a can, a glass with some ice and said, "Buon appetito." You will understand later why he ordered Pepsi.

The service is now finished and I'm standing by the lifts that we used to go to the lower galley when this same passenger comes back and says, "Can I have another Coke?" "Sure, and by the way, you were fortunate we didn't have a riot on the plane because people did comment about the smell of the hoagie, and peppers, and wanted to know why they weren't getting that." We both laughed about it and then started chit chatting.

I find out he is a big executive with none-other than Wendy's. (An aside: Guess what Wendy's serves? Pepsi.) Of course, I really had to harass him about bringing on a hoagie from another fast-food company! Then I told him my husband loves Wendy's burgers for lunch, but that they were just too big for me to finish. I said, "Why don't you have a Wendy's Jr., like Burger King does? Little kids can't eat a big Wendy's burger even if it is a single." He says, "Well, their mothers can cut it in half." I told him, "You are missing the boat here. You really need to get a Wendy's Jr. on your menu for kids and for people like myself, who just want a small burger."

After about ten minutes of conversation he says, "Give me your mailing address and I'll send you some coupons for Wendy's for you and your husband." Great, who is going to refuse free coupons for a good burger? About two weeks later the coupon books arrived with a thank you note for my great service and also my suggestion. Guess what? Within about a year's time Wendy's had a Wendy's Jr. on their menu. You all can thank me now …

The Rules Are the Rules

IT WAS THE late '50s and TWA was owned by the dashing Howard Hughes. Needless to say, the majority of us had never met him personally, but we all knew he was the main figure behind the scenes for the company. What Mr. Hughes wanted, Mr. Hughes got.

Pittsburgh was a large hub for TWA at the time and I was working a flight out of that station. This is where my story begins: I was in the first class lounge getting things ready when I noticed a man boarding the aircraft. What? The agent had not told me he was starting boarding.

I turned to this tall, handsome man and explained that he had to wait until the flight was called, and then I asked him to please return to the boarding gate area. He asked if I knew who he was. I will admit when passengers gave me that line, "Do you know who I am?" it just didn't go over well. It was bite your tongue time because I was thinking, "I know you are another guy who thinks he is more important than the rest of the passengers."

At this point, you probably already know my reply. I tried my best to not be too snippy and told him it made no difference. The rules are the rules. Well, the tall, handsome man left without a further word.

The next thing I knew the gate agent appeared and said, "Do you know who that is?" Oh please, that question again! I have to admit I was getting really aggravated with, "do you know who that is" and I told him I didn't give a dxxx. He says, "Well, you better that was Howard Hughes." You could hear a "gulp" coming from me now! Well, when Mr. Hughes re-boarded, he thanked me for doing my job.

Thank you, Mr. Hughes …

A Handful

I HAD BEEN flying for about a year and on this particular trip was flying with my roommate Kathleen, a stunning brunette. The gentleman in seat 4C had called me over to thank me for the great service and he said "You really do a wonderful job, but why do you waste your time working here? You could do something that makes a lot more money." About this same time, Kathleen walked by me with a coffee pot and said, "Excuse me sweetie," and grabbed a handful of my derriere as she passed. The passenger said, "OK, never mind."

Runner and We Aren't Talking Nike Here

FOR YEARS I flew out of Chicago and flew mostly what we called a turnaround. We had three of them that were flown by the top one hundred in seniority at the base. These were the three with no layover: 1. ORD to LAX to ORD, 2. ORD to PHX to ORD and 3. ORD to LAS to ORD.

Photo of 1st class L-1011 swivel chairs with dining table.
Taken from TWA *Timetable*.
Flight Attendant pictured is *not* the author of this story.
Photo courtesy of the Jon Proctor Collection.

One of these "turns" was our notorious flight number 711 to LAS on a L-1011. We left at 9 AM, flew to Las Vegas, sat on the ground for two hours, and then flew back to Chicago and I was home in the driveway by 9 PM. Sounds easy breezy but trust me those passengers going down were party, party, party and coming back they were grumpy, grumpy, grump. They had lost their money, drank too much, stayed up too late and were not in a good mood. Plus, the loads were always full.

Now this is very important. The L-1011 aircraft had eight seats in the center of first class. These seats actually could swivel. We had the ability to pull up a post in the center of the four seats and put a large table top on it. Picture two round tables in the middle of the aircraft with four seats around them. Got the picture now of seats being able to turn around and swivel.

On this flight many times we had passengers in first class who looked like they should have been in the movie *Saturday Night Fever* with John Travolta. They had the shirts unbuttoned half way down their chests, piles of gold chains on and always the pinkie ring. We had learned over the years that they were "runners." And they were very well "connected" in Chicago and Las Vegas. Capisce? They usually came on with a Red Coat, who was a TWA agent who wore a red jacket and handled all of the "important" people. We were told by the Red Coat to make sure the "runner" always got a bottle of champagne to take off the flight. After a while if you flew this flight enough you started to recognize them.

This particular flight coming back from Las Vegas to Chicago as usual was full. There were no requests for the table set ups, so all of the center first class seats were positioned looking toward the front of the cabin. One particular passenger in a center seat kept giving the flight attendant, who was working the cabin position in first class, a hard time.

There was a "runner" sitting in front of him who could hear the conversations. After a while he stopped this flight attendant and said, "Is that guy behind me giving you a hard time?" She said, "It's OK." Well, about five minutes later the guy is still being a jerk and what does the runner do? He hits the swivel button on his chair. The chair turns totally around so that he is now looking at this horse's petute behind him. And what does he say? "I'm sick and tired of you giving the flight attendant a hard time. If I hear another word out of you, you will find your feet in cement and be in the bottom of the Chicago River. Got it!" Then he hits the swivel button and turns around. Guess who shut up? We loved our "runners!"

The Flight Gods

MOST OF YOU wouldn't know but flight attendants bid for their flights. These flights were awarded by seniority and you would fly them with the same crew for a month. Sometimes the flights you would bid were only for one flight attendant. What? Confusing, but this was called an "extra" position. As the extra you never stayed with one crew for the entire two to four day trip, but would bounce around from flight to flight as the extra. Why did they need an extra? Because these flights were usually always full and required more than the normal amount of crew to be able to get those inflight meal services done.

Why all of this information? Well, it is part of my story: It was the late '80s and I had bid flights that called for the "extra." To be honest I hated it because of the fact that you flew with so many different crews and they would just make you work wherever they wanted you to.

I was St. Louis based and when I boarded the plane to meet the JFK crew, who was already on board, I was greeted with, "You're late." I wasn't because I had to get there from my previous flight that had just landed, but that was a moot point.

To be honest, the other flight attendants were shall we say not hospitable, and I was informed that I would be working first class. I really didn't care, as it was my last day of an awful four-day trip that had been full of delays. I just wanted to get the day over with.

Well, this crew must have misread the passenger manifest list because I ended up with only one passenger and guess who it was? Rob Lowe! Moreover, to make it even more delightful, coach was fairly full. No idea how that happened, but who am I to question the "flight gods" when dishing their doses of sweet karma?

Rob Lowe was incredibly lovely and I must add handsome too. We chatted at length most of the flight about this, that and whatever. And I must add, this was probably the only flight I never went back to assist in coach. As I said, those "flight gods" dished out a touch of "karma" to the other flight attendants and who I was to mess with karma!

Now I always blow a kiss to my television screen when Rob appears. Love those flight gods …

New Yorkers Are Awesome

I WAS HIRED in 1985. My second flight ever was from JFK to Vegas, with a Lockheed 1011 plane full of New York passengers ready to drink, gamble and party. Being the junior flight attendant to bid for my working position on the plane, I was quickly left with the galley assignment. The flight service manager refused to let me take that assignment, as I was so green, and the ensuing arguing among the flight attendants broke out. Most were shouting, "I don't want to work galley!" It eventually got settled by the flight service manager cajoling one of the more senior flight attendants to take pity on me.

On the return flight home, I was not so lucky. I was assigned the galley for the breakfast service. It was a trial by fire and what a nightmare! I ended up "burning" all the omelets, every darn one of them. When I finally made it out of the lower galley (it was in the belly on a L-1011) and up to the cabin to help serve, I got nothing but "dirty" looks from the crew, as they were all fielding passenger complaints right and left about their burnt breakfast. NOW this rather unfriendly and hostile crew generously told everyone it was the galley girl's fault.

After the service, I asked the flight service manager if I could get on the PA system and apologize. He gladly agreed, as he was sick and tired of fielding all the complaints as well. I walked to the front of the plane, got on that PA, stated my name and that it was my second flight as a brand-new flight attendant, and I was deeply sorry for burning their breakfasts. As I made my way to the back of the plane, passenger after passenger seeing my nametag on that navy-blue apron that we wore, stopped me and thanked me for apologizing. "Doll, it could happen to anyone." And, "Oh, it was the best omelet I've ever had." And so on. Their generosity of spirit was amazing. New Yorkers are awesome!

Best Forgotten

MALE FLIGHT ATTENDANT: This one is a L-1011 lav story. I had just finished my crew break on a flight to Madrid. The passengers were all tucked in, some watching the movie and others doing whatever.

I headed back to the rear lav to freshen up a bit before resuming my duties. Still in a daze from my nap, I casually looked at the lock on the door and it said unoccupied. So, I placed my hand on the doorknob to enter, when a passenger approached me and asked for water. This request diverted my attention as I directed her to a service center where she could get her beverage.

Now still slightly groggy, I turned the doorknob to open the door and started to step into the lav, when I saw that there was a heavy-set woman sitting on the toilet. This was definitely one of those moments where you just wanted to quickly close the door and disappear. But no, that was not going to happen.

What I had not realized was that in stepping into the lav I actually stepped into her slacks that were down around her ankles. Yes, I did! She was startled and screamed, for a man now had his foot and half of his leg inside her clothes. Needless to say, these peals of screams woke me right up.

Now the problem was that in her fright she closed her legs with my right leg tangled all up in her slacks and panties too. I tried pulling my leg out, but her big thighs held me firmly in place! As I pulled, I noticed that I was literally pulling her off the seat. Which I might add was no easy task. I finally said, "We must work together here ma'am, release my leg and I'll step out." That was not that easy either since she had to get my leg out of her slacks and panties.

Later, on the flight, when our eyes met there was that uncomfortable familiar look. What a YouTube video this would have made. Probably could have gotten a million hits!

She Won't Remember You

I WAS WORKING in first class on a flight to JFK when who was boarded but Patty Duke. Some of you might not remember who she was but she was a pretty big deal, movies, TV etc. At that time, she was also president of the Screen Actors Guild. She was very petite, short, rather quiet but also polite. We exchanged pleasantries during the flight and she frankly was very undemanding. When she deplaned, I told her how much I enjoyed having her on board and wished her a nice day.

A few days later, I was working my scheduled trip and on my return to JFK I literally ran over to another gate, with a company pass, to fly out to LAX to meet my husband. I hadn't even changed out of my uniform since there was no time. I thought when I was on the plane, I would change into layover clothes because a cocktail sounded like a good idea, but the thought of undressing and redressing in that lav just wasn't appealing. So, I stayed in my uniform for the flight knowing full well when I landed in California it would be cocktail time!

Arriving in Los Angeles I had to get myself over to the United terminal. Why? Well, my husband was coming in on a United flight. I know you are all wondering why he wasn't on TWA but it wasn't convenient for his business trip. And frankly, he traveled so much on TWA he really did pay them for my salary.

But getting back to me. I go into the United terminal and head back to the gate area; this was in the day and age when you didn't need a ticket to go back there. I was waiting at my husband's arrival gate when his plane arrived. A number of passengers started to deplane and I knew he would be off soon since he was in first class. BUT who do I see, getting off now, Patty Duke!

Patty had gone out on TWA and was now returning by United. My husband gets off the plane and I greet him with a little kiss, and then he says, "Guess who was in first class with me?" "I know I saw her deplane, Patty Duke. I just had her on flight a few days ago too."

We are now down in baggage claim to pick up his checked bags and Patty is standing near the baggage carousel. I said to my husband, "I'm going over there and tease her about flying on United." To which he replies, "She isn't going to remember you." I snort in contempt and say, "Puhleeze, who do you think you are dealing with? Of course, she will remember me."

I walked up behind Patty, now remember I told you she was not tall and I on the other hand was five foot 10 inches in my heels. I quietly stand behind her, lean down and whisper in her ear, "You little traitor. Flying on TWA and then on United." She turns around quickly to see me standing there with a big grin on my face now. Obviously, she remembered me because she started to laugh and said, "How are you?" I said, "I'm fine. But you know you can't get away with anything. What are you doing on United?" She laughs again and says, "What are you doing here?" I said, "Well, besides checking on you I came over to United to meet my husband. He was in first class with you." Then I point him out.

She waves at him and says, "Speaking of traitors, what was he doing on United?" So, I had to explain why? Then I told her, "He said you wouldn't remember me and I just had to prove him wrong." She laughs and says, "Prove him wrong, of course I remember you" and gives me a big hug. I wished her a nice evening and then said, "I don't want to see you again when I'm in the United terminal." We both laughed and she threw me a kiss and I walked back very smugly to my husband, mouthing, "So, she wouldn't remember me? Nader, nader, nader."

Encanto

CHRISTMAS EVE, 1996 in New York City. There was a relentless, blinding snowstorm and I could barely see across Lefferts Blvd. when the call came in with my assignment to fill in for a commuting flight attendant, who was unable to make it to JFK to work flight 12. This was a coveted 747 San Juan trip with a layover at the renowned Caribe Hilton. It would be both my first trip ever to the Caribbean and my ticket out of the apocalyptic storm, I was thrilled!

I hung up the phone and then wondered how I would ever make it a few miles down the ice slick, Van Wyck expressway to the JFK airport. After repeated calls and abrupt hang ups to the Kew Gardens car service, the transportation company of choice for most airline crewmembers in Queens, I decided to go out and hail the ever-elusive cab. That proved to be fruitless. Now with wheeled luggage and a garment bag in tow, I slipped and slid on the sidewalk until I finally found a public bus stop.

An hour later, after an agonizing crawl that never exceeded five miles per hour on the Q-10 bus, which went through all of the side streets of Queens, my luggage and I were unceremoniously dumped into a three-foot, slushy, brown snowbank directly in front of the TWA Flight Center. It was the Aero Saarinen's 1962 architectural masterpiece with its elegant, soaring lines designed to reflect the graceful contours of a bird in flight.

I could hear loud voices that rose from the bedraggled and wet crowd, shouting in rapid fire Spanish at the TWA ticket agents and one another. This would be a very, very long night, for I soon realized the visions of sun and fun in paradise were beginning to vanish from my mind.

Flash forward: to my great relief, once we took off (three hours late) I discovered our Puerto Rican passengers to be some of the sweetest people I had ever met. Although half of them poked me in the small of the back or in the ribs and hissed things like "Mira Mira! Psst Psst!," or snapped their fingers and bellowed "Papi!", at me, I forgave them.

Their enthusiasm and childlike wonder of people, who traveled once a year for some and once in a lifetime for others, contrasted so joyfully with the jaded passengers, who I dealt with on other domestic flights that I couldn't help but like them. Yes, we were now late but not one person complained, as they were just so grateful to be going home to spend the holiday reunited with family and loved ones.

One passenger on this particular trip as I was standing at the back of the plane after the service, all of a sudden was standing in front of me. He was a tall, dark-skinned Spanish man in his late forties. I had been so busy on the rushed, chaotic flight that I hadn't noticed him even though he was on my side of the aircraft. He smiled a dazzling, warm smile which was paired with such a self-assured confidence.

Before I could make sense of the moment, he was actually standing over me, for he was very tall, and taking my hand in his own and was saying, "Feliz Navidad, Mijo."

I nearly fell backwards, but composed myself and replied, "Gracias, Senor, Feliz Navidad, to you as well." I then apologized for the late arrival. "No importa, Mijo. It's Christmas," he joyfully replied, squeezing my hand and stepping still closer. I smiled despite myself and a quick glance around showed that no one paid us any attention. I don't know which was redder at the moment, my face or the TWA logo lit up brightly high upon the 747's tail.

"You live in New York, Mijo?" "Yes," I replied. "You are not from New York though; this I can tell. You are far too sweet." "I'm from California," I replied, blushing because I could never remember having been called sweet. As we talked for a while, I began to relax into the conversation and forget my self-consciousness.

We shared our stories, speaking intimately in that way that only strangers can. I found that he was the son of a poor farmer, growing up near El Yunque, the jungle at the interior of the island. He had run away young to New York City when he realized his own emerging sexual identity was on a collision course with that of his devout Catholic faith, plus his deeply ingrained sense of loyalty to his familial obligations, as the oldest son in a Latin family.

He arrived in New York broke, alone, and with no direction or guidance, and fell prey to many who took advantage of his beauty and naivete. He found his way into the club scene where drugs and alcohol ravaged his life and soul. He contracted HIV/AIDS. He was dying, physically and spiritually, alone in a cold harsh city, and he had accepted this as his fate and penance.

It was the unconditional love of the very family from whom he had fled that transcended the darkness. When one day a knock at the door of a friend's squalid tenement apartment, where he was staying, turned out to be his beautiful sister who had spent weeks on the streets looking for him. She took him home to Puerto Rico where the women of the family nursed him back to health.

Now, in the back of this 747, stood a true testament to empowerment and healing; a vital healthy man, reconciled in his faith, with his family and at peace with his identity. He was a professor in a prestigious university where his journey through adversity allowed him to reach others.

What started out as a flirtation had quickly turned to admiration and respect. I saw this man as a strong role model, and mentor and such an example of accomplishment. I had hung on his every word as he told me he lived in New York and San Juan because I had never known anyone who lived in two cities. He said he flew TWA between the two cities regularly and that while he was headed to his family tonight, he would look for me on a future flight and that perhaps we could have dinner in Condado sometime after a flight.

Now it was time for the flight to land and as quickly as he came into my life then just as quickly, he was gone. In retrospect, I'm sure a higher power had put him on my flight that evening to give guidance and perspective to a young gay man.

As for Puerto Rico, the island and the people captured my heart with their infectious and heartwarming ways. They call Puerto Rico "Isla del Encanto," the island of enchantment and it certainly is.

Que dulces estan estas memorias de la vida. Me encantan todos. Gracias.

It's Vegas Baby

WE HAD A long Las Vegas layover and a few of us decided to take advantage of being TWA flight attendants there. Most of the name casinos, if we told them we were TWA flight attendants, would let us into the main show rooms with big name entertainers for free. What a perk! Who to see? We decided that it would be Robert Goulet at the Sands. Talk about a hunk with a big baritone voice, who was a Broadway star, Grammy and Tony winner, and not hard on the eyes either.

My flying partner, who was a very attractive woman and was always wearing the latest fashions, had brought a new dress for the layover. She told me that she had hemmed it at home because it was too long and it needed to be shorter. Short was in then. Turns out it was way too short now. Minor detail, she had not tried it on after she had hemmed it. Major problem!

Photo of TWA advertisement for coast-to-coast flights in 1969.
Flight attendants shown wearing paper dresses.
None of the flight attendants pictured are authors of this story.
Photo courtesy of TWA Museum.

As we were being escorted into the theater to some of the best seats by the maître d' hôtel, she was keenly aware of her skirt length. Picture her walking on spiked heels, totally erect to make certain that her derriere was not exposed. Yes, we are talking only inches to spare! Heidi Klum would have been proud of that runway walk. The good news here was she did have on pantyhose but still …

The maître d' sat us at a table right near the edge of the stage, our seats couldn't have been better. Cocktails were ordered, and we started talking about how great we thought Mr. Goulet was and how lucky we were to be seated where we were. I'll just call her Ms. Gorgeous who was now enjoying a gin and tonic and a cigarette. Remember it is Vegas baby and smoking was allowed everywhere then.

Picture a grand piano on the stage and a band in the background playing. Mr. Goulet walks onto the stage from the wings, starts with his opening song and wows the audience. A few songs later he started walking around the primo tables, when he stopped and started singing to Ms. Gorgeous! You could see that she was nervous because her hand was trembling as she tried to remain nonplussed by this attention. She brought her cigarette to her lips, took a strong puff on it and inhaled deeply. Then trying to look sophisticated, she blew the smoke out her nose only to end up burning the inside of it!

What does Ms. Gorgeous do? She immediately grabbed an ice cube out of her drink and put it on her nose, as Mr. Goulet had to stop singing because he was laughing so hard. He asked for her name and then started to pull her hand asking her to come with him. She tries to say no because it was all about that insanely short dress now. He is not taking no for an answer.

While Mr. Goulet starts singing to her again; he leads her onto the stage with a spotlight following the two of them. Yes, a spotlight that was really showing off her short dress and the possibility of some other things. I must tell you that she was doing an excellent job of keeping her derrière covered though, until he turned to lift her onto the piano … OOPS … but the audience loved it by the sounds of the whistling and clapping! I'm sure they were thinking of Folies Bergère, but I think Mr. Goulet thought some of it was for his athletic prowess in lifting her onto the piano. Probably a big not! There she stayed … legs crossed like a lady, until he finished his song. Unfortunately, she still had to get down off the piano. Instantly the room erupted with more whistling and clapping! "What happens in Vegas stays in Vegas," well maybe.

The Eyes of Warriors

Note: I was the service manager and the only male in the cabin crew.

TEL AVIV WAS an extremely senior trip. Why? Because you flew to Paris's Charles de Gaulle Airport spent the night, then picked up the flight the next day and continued to Tel Aviv where you would stay at the Hilton Hotel. The next day you would fly back to Paris, spend the night and then return to JFK. So, you were gone a total of five days and had five days off at home.

We would stay at the Tel Aviv Hilton and in those days of the early '70s we would sign for our food either at the hotel, or we could sign and eat at a very nice restaurant called the Kasbah. This was a "perk" of flying international flights then.

At the Kasbah they would have a table just for the crew and usually our captain would sit at the head of the table. This particular evening, I was sitting to his right and the rest of the crew was scattered in different seats at the table. A little side note: we signed for the food but the liquor was not covered, but interestingly enough sometimes on the bill it would show "thirty oranges." Surprisingly that would cover the price of the wine.

While we were dining, I observed a fellow at the bar, who really did look suspicious. He was sitting by himself and kept looking over at us. Obviously, I knew right away that he was waiting for the right time to come and approach the table, in most likelihood to probably try to pick up one of the flight attendants. We got to the dessert course, and as I imagined the fellow stood up and started walking towards our table.

I attempted to get up to inform him that this was a private party. When suddenly, the captain gently grabs my left arm and taps on it, as if to say it's okay and then whispers in my ear, "That's General Moshe Dayan, he comes every night hoping to get lucky."

Well, General Dayan came to the table and asked to sit with us. Immediately the waiter had a chair available for him. I could see a scar running across his face and then realized that this scar ran from his hairline, across his eye, and all the way down to his chin and that was why he wore a patch over his one eye. He had a very gentle kind face, but his one eye that you could see could only be described as "steely." It was as if it was saying, if

I have to, I will kill you. It was a determined look of strength, as only a true warrior has.

Well after dessert and coffee, we all left except two flight attendants who were still talking with him. I have no idea how their evening ended. However, I know, I will never forget my encounter with this famous individual, who was one of history's greatest warriors.

Later on, after I retired from TWA, I was visiting my brother. He belonged to a poker group and in the poker group was another famous warrior, General Norman Schwarzkopf, who I got to meet. He was married to a former TWA flight attendant and as the story goes Brenda was with a group of TWA flight attendants when she met Schwarzkopf at West Point.

Back story: there was a TWA flight attendant who was dating a cadet at West Point and a number of cadets needed dates for an event, so she invited five TWA flight attendant friends to be dates for these cadets. One of which was Brenda and her blind date was a young dashing cadet, Norman Schwarzkopf, who she later married.

But the key to this story is the look I will never forget of General Moshe Dayan. That look of a "steely stare" but a gentle kind face, just like General Norman Schwarzkopf who was a giant of a man, but yet had that sweet smile and kind face with those same eyes like the "finest steel!" The eyes of the warrior!

I'm a lucky guy, TWA showed me the world and introduced me to people I could never imagine I would meet.

Thank You to My GI Joe Hero

IT WAS 1944–45. I was working a DC three flight from Kansas City to Pittsburgh. There were only about fourteen passengers on board and some of them were returning soldiers from the Pacific war. These men were all eager to talk with me, not about the war, but about their families, life in the states now and how glad they were to be coming home.

One soldier had gotten up to stretch his legs and had come back to my workstation on the plane. He was casually leaning against an inside door on the left-hand side of the plane and was holding on to the door's knob. I was standing in front of him with my back to the other passengers as we were talking. All of a sudden, I heard a loud noise when he grabbed the front of my clothes and pulled me so tightly against him that our noses were touching. Then he threw me down the aisle so hard that I landed four rows forward with my legs up in the air. All I could think of at the time was people could see my underwear!

As I got up, I sat down immediately in a seat as the soldier was pulling himself up the aisle and sat in a seat behind me. I was trying my best to collect myself when the soldier said, "The outside door is open and you have to tell the pilot."

I have to admit I was afraid to get up now, but I steeled myself and went forward to the cockpit where I knocked on the door. Much to my relief the copilot answered my knock and I told him that the passenger agent hadn't properly locked the outside door and it was open now!

Well, needless to say we did not continue to Pittsburgh but diverted to Chicago. The door had to be repaired and I stayed with the passengers as the captain and the soldier went into our ramp office to explain to the company what had happened.

I was probably a little bit in shock, but was trying to act as if everything was normal as we finally continued our flight to Pittsburgh. Thank heavens that this soldier was holding onto that inside doorknob and had laid back against the door as he pulled me to him and threw me down the aisle. He saved my life and was not only a hero in WWII, during the Pacific war efforts but was my hero too!

The company offered me a few days off after I returned to Kansas City, but I declined because I thought it was a good idea to fly again right away, "courage over worry." And frankly what is an open door on an airplane in comparison to what my GI Joe hero survived in the Pacific.

The author of this story is now flying with the TWA angels and it was donated by a good friend.

The Decision Was Made For Me

I'M ONE OF those people who likes change to a point, and loves and needs some variety, or so I thought. After I had flown domestic trips for six years, I was going "mad" flying to the same old US cities and serving the "same" old food and snacks. I needed a change.

My first thought was to go and visit other domiciles and then transfer to one. Maybe that would be enough. But Boston was really the only one that interested me and after spending time with a high school classmate who lived there, for some reason I decided against the east coast. Not even all of that "cheap lobster," which I used to bring home when I had a Boston layover, could entice me. Something just didn't click.

Coming back to Chicago I was very disappointed and somewhat aggravated by the entire situation. I truly thought about ditching this career, but I had nothing else I wanted to do, so I took a breath and carried on.

Then one afternoon in flight operations, I saw the crew desk was scrambling and one of the charming schedulers, we knew them all by name and loved them, well, at least I did ... leaned over the counter and said, "Do you have a passport on you? Want a five-day Cairo trip leaving from Kennedy tonight?" Note: Years ago, on TWA we were required to carry our passports with us at all times.

Well, I said, "Sure," thinking that sounded much more exciting than the Cincinnati airport popcorn being the only highlight of my scheduled evening.

Anyway, from that moment on, I got to experience real change and excitement! The trip was JFK to Rome, Athens, Tel Aviv, Cairo and back. I was flying with some very seasoned ladies, who not only welcomed me but basically took care of me for the next five days. I could not believe how gracious they were and soon you'll know why.

On our international flights, you had pre and post briefings and seeing as this was in 1977 there was a lot of security talk. I had only flown domestic trips for six years and frankly started to get a little nervous then, but the crew reassured me it was just protocol to be careful.

Let's cut to the chase, Rome and Athens were "OK." Yes, I'm finding out that I'm not the adventurous person I thought I was, but rather chose to follow the crew everywhere so as not to sit in a hotel room in a magnificent city by myself. However, I was also just starting to feel the effects of some significant jet lag, so I wanted to keep busy.

The next day put me over the top. We arrived in Tel Aviv and disembarked between lines of soldiers with machine guns. A bit unnerving to say the least. Then the crew told me that in the airport we would walk arm and arm together like a long chain. Don't get separated! Easy to say but try doing that while carrying a Samsonite suitcase that doesn't have wheelies on it and also your purse.

Then I remember the long, dusty ride on the crew bus to our hotel. Now I've always been the kind of person to notice when I'm uncomfortable, making me also note every mile between myself and "the plane to take me back home." But along the way, the girls all talked about the "stuff" they had to do at the "market" and that I should go with them.

Well, again I was not about to stay behind alone. After we checked into the hotel, the crew was "out of the gates," picking up cartouches, brass, spices, food and whatever, while I tagged along unexcitedly, tired and yes, I'll admit a tiny bit scared.

Here, I am in the hubbub of the market with the flight attendant that I pretty much hung out with when she says, "Wait here, I'll be back in a flash. Just have to pick up something." I did NOT MOVE. The next thing I know a man in broken English is saying to me, "Come be my bride," while others were gawking at me. Even gawking men and offers of marriage couldn't make me leave that spot because I was too terrified, I would get lost. Finally, after what seemed like an eternity she returned and I almost screamed, "Praise the Lord!"

Then because I didn't really look like I was having a good time, wonder why, she made me buy something. Sure, souvenirs always help soothe your rattled nerves. I ended up bringing back a brass plate bigger than a satellite dish that years later I could not stand the memory of, never used or displayed, and so I sold it at a garage sale. Obviously, I'm not really the kind of person who collects "stuff" on her travels around the world.

Finally, we got back to the hotel after our shopping expedition. I was so over tired that I slept very little that night and in the blink of an eye we're back on the plane to go to Cairo. We arrive in Cairo and are having our debriefing from the captain when he says, "Remember you sleep in your panty hose and keep your suitcase packed." WHAT! Here I was with a beautiful view from my window of the pyramids all lit up, and really didn't care because I had to wear panty hose to bed and all I could think of was I wanted to be home. Now it was another semi sleepless night!

Next day on the way back to JFK I was on the jump seat, nauseated, vomiting and so sick. Again, wonder why? Possibly no sleep really for days! The crew acted like they were my parents and no matter how much I apologized for not working, they just took over. Of course as we all know, everyone got fed and left happy because we were TWA.

Needless to say, when I got home, I didn't want to look at any of the schedulers in case they asked me how I LIKED THE TRIP. I learned my lesson and continued flying domestic trips until I finally had enough seniority to fly our Chicago to London trip. I did so for the next eight years and never went further east! So much for change, variety and new adventures. But it was still better than Cincinnati popcorn in the airport …

I Can See Clearly Now

WE USED TO have a captain that would sit in his seat for boarding and wear a blind person's glasses. YEP, a real kidder!

The looks of the passengers as they boarded were priceless. They would be all smiles and then take one look at the captain through the cockpit window when they were on the jetway, before stepping onto the aircraft and their faces changed! Smiles to, "What the hell did I just see?"

I'm surprised that we never got written up (slang for a passenger writing a complaint letter to the company) for that stunt. The entire crew was in on it too. Those were days, pre 9/11 when the crews could still have fun on a plane.

Flying Miss Daisy

I WAS WORKING on a Douglas MD80 that was an early morning departure from St. Louis to San Jose. It was a light load and most of the passengers were still sleepy and very quiet. But not one!

There was a little lady who resembled Miss Daisy in the movie *Driving Miss Daisy*. She announced to us on boarding that this was her first flight and proudly told me she was 87. You would have thought she was like a kid in a candy store! Have to admit she was terribly cute as she walked up and down the aisle stopping to look out of every window. Then she asked if we had any "souvenirs" and I gave her some wings, the same ones we gave to the kids on flight. The silverware and coffee cup on her tray seemed to appeal to her too and she asked if she could have them. What are you going to do but offer her some napkins to wrap them up in?

We actually gave her a bottle of champagne to take off the plane to celebrate her first flight with. I can hear her now, "Did I ever tell you about the first time I flew on an airplane?" She was cute!

My Hiring Adventure

I WROTE THIS letter to my parents in 1960 when I was twenty-two years "young." It was written in a different era: when excitement and thrills didn't come too early in one's life; when travelers were dressed to the nines; pre-sophisticated million milers; pre-jaded world travelers; pre-hijackings and terrorists; pre-women's lib when "girl" was an acceptable word and when examining a woman's figure wasn't politically incorrect. This is a tome written about my experience of being sent to Kansas City to be interviewed by TWA. Well, maybe not a tome.

Dear Dad, Mom and Family,

You have been selected as the lucky first group to review my latest novel: a tragedy entitled, "Kansas City—There I Went!"

Chapter One

The events leading up to my trip to the Midwest could have been ruination; that is, if I were the type of person to let minor matters affect me. What did I care that my hair looked a fright? Would they really notice? Who cares about sleeping soundly before a big interview? Who needs it? Black circles under your eyes can be covered up with makeup. Why was my stomach in knots? Why couldn't I eat? What should I wear? Does it really make a difference? And on my way to the airport, why should I worry about a silly old plane that was taking off in an hour, when I was having a hilarious time helping my cab driver discover why his car wouldn't start. Fun times!

Now to get back to the story: I was not going to be discouraged. Excluding a few minor would be obstacles, I arrived at the airport in fine form. In my fitted grey suit and my white accessories, I caught the eye of every old man in the airport.

As I stood on the sidelines, anxiously awaiting an answer to my question, "Is there room for me on this plane," I noticed another girl whose expression told me she was waiting for the same answer. I approached her and discovered we had more than one thing in common. You see, both of us had the same destination in mind, Kansas City, Missouri. As luck would have it, both of us were going to be interviewed by TWA for consideration as hostesses.

What a relief to have found her and to be traveling together! I have to admit that it was comforting to see that she was also nervous and it wasn't just me. Loretta was by now my new best friend and we got the last two seats on the plane. Upon boarding, I said "Goodbye" to all of my nerves, my worries and tensions. At least for then.

The flight, which was uneventful, took three hours. However, due to time differences, we got there two hours after leaving D.C. We were served a delicious meal: turkey, dressing, peas, sweet potatoes, jelly cake and coffee.

To my relief the stewardesses, who TWA calls hostesses, seemed just like the girls I went to school with. One major spark of encouragement.

Chapter Two

The airport at Kansas City was a luxuriously modern building that looked as if it belonged to Mars more than Earth. We wasted no time there however, but headed straight for our hotel.

Loretta and I didn't write TWA on our foreheads, but it must have shown in our eyes. No questions were asked about who we were or why we were there. Everyone just took it for granted, but then why wouldn't they? Twenty somethings all checking in around the same time? But I must tell you the hotel treated us like royalty even though we had to share a room with another interviewee. Fortunately, I had Loretta to share with.

No sooner than we stepped inside our room the phone began to ring and we were welcomed by several other prospective hostesses. Everyone was gathering in their room to get acquainted. One by one, more and more girls arrived. They represented every section of the country: Florida, New York, Massachusetts, Wisconsin, Arkansas, etc. Everyone felt pretty much the same way, wanting to succeed but afraid to hope too much.

Anyway, after several hours of continuous talk, some brilliant person made the suggestion that we take advantage of this trip and see some of Kansas City. So, we all went out to explore and proved one thing: we might make hostesses but there wasn't a trail blazer among us. No Lewis and Clarke enthusiasm! Afraid of getting lost? Too tired to walk? I don't know? At this point, we divided into two groups. One group hungry, one group not. I joined the not group and went to a Marlon Brandon movie but afterwards was starving. So, it was off to a restaurant with a few of the other girls.

Then realizing that my faculties were becoming dull from lack of sleep I hobbled back to the hotel, with my bed, the foremost thought on my mind. This time I did get to stay in my room long enough to see it. But you've heard of the best laid plans of "mice and men." In Kansas City it happens to women, specifically me! There were more late-comers to be met and inspected. Several more hours passed with lots of talking when finally,

Loretta and I managed to make it back to our room and drift off to dreamland.

Chapter Three

At 6 AM, I was rudely awakened by the sound of fire engines—or was it an ambulance? It could not be just an alarm clock. Yes, it could. It was!

I staggered out of bed and was fully dressed before I opened my eyes. When I looked into the mirror, I found myself in a charcoal and white sheath dress, with a white jacket and white accessories and I did it all in my sleep. Hopefully, beauty personified. Again, the taxis were waiting and we were taken directly to the airport without instructing the driver. At our destination, I was hit square in the face with the horrible realization that the big moment was now at hand! I began to feel my nerves, and those tensions had caught the 4:15 out of D.C. and were nearing Kansas City. However, I gathered myself together and walked courageously through the door.

After roll call, we (about thirty of us) were escorted to a classroom where we got off to a rip-roaring start with an intelligence test. Then we were lectured for forty-five minutes about what was expected of us and what we could expect from them. We were told the good and bad about the life of a hostess. There were questions and more questions; answers and more answers. Some I liked, some I did not. If rejected, we will not be told why. A thought flashed through my mind, "How can you tell a girl she has a face that would stop a clock? Please don't let that be me."

After class, I was subjected to a "medical examination", which consisted entirely of: have you been a patient in a hospital, why were you admitted and for how long, have you had any more trouble? All of this took until ten o'clock. The rest of the day was spent waiting and waiting and waiting and waiting ...

Each girl had to have two interviews. They wanted both a male and a female opinion. The man was a cinch. I felt completely at ease and I thought I did well. The woman was a different story! I had to walk and pivot. She felt my backbone and examined my teeth. She inspected my hands and even my knees. I felt like a witness in a murder trial. I left her feeling more discouraged than I had been through the entire trip. The cheerful, consoling, "You'll hear in two weeks," did not cheer me a bit. Oh well!

Chapter Four

At 3 PM, Loretta and I said "goodbye" to the fateful city and headed homeward. We had one stopover, in St. Louis. The pilot showed us around the cockpit. The three stewardesses were darling and very friendly. We were served one more scrumptious meal: shrimp cocktail, veal chop, baked potato, apple pie and more.

It is all behind me now; over but wondering and waiting. It would be interesting to know who the lucky girls will be. As for myself, I would like very much to get a "We are pleased to inform you" type of letter. However, if the regrets come, I will not be too disappointed and I am certainly not sorry that I tried.

It was fun being miserable.

The End

P.S. When I said, "book," I meant it. I won't be able to use my hand for a month. P.S.S. I MADE IT! I just got the letter of acceptance.

Footnote: Loretta and I received our wings on July 14, 1960.

Tidy Whities Not So Tidy

TWA HAD A notorious night flight from New York to San Francisco, flight number 15. In the early '70s this was a Boeing 707 which departed JFK around 10 PM, stopping in Chicago, then continuing to Los Angeles and finally landing in San Francisco sometime around 5 AM. It was a marathon of a trip! And totally exhausting.

I was working in the coach cabin and on descent, having checked seatbacks, seatbelts and carry-on luggage placement, I noticed the aft lavatory door was locked. The seat belt and no smoking sign was on and we were close to landing. I pounded on the door to see if anyone was in there. No response, then I yelled, "Is anyone in there? Are you alright? You need to go back to your seat immediately!" Then I heard a man grumble and make some rather "rude" comments as he refused to come out of the lavatory.

Gears down, we were close to landing. Nothing that either I or my flying partner could do, but secure ourselves in our jump seats across from this lav despite the fact this man was still in it. Touchdown! Suddenly the lav door swings open and this rather hefty man jumps out, pulling up his pants and mumbling some more rude comments at us.

What now? We smelled a smokey odor coming out of the lav. Our first reaction was that it has to be a fire. We immediately called the cockpit and said we could smell smoke and maybe something was burning. As the passengers were deplaning, the captain was making his way back to the tail of the aircraft. We had already started looking around and decided to pull out the trash can. Bingo! There they were, Mr. Important's tidy whities, which were less than tidy, in the trash can with a big hole burned in the middle. We doused them immediately with some water to make sure there was no danger of a fire. What a way to end our flight! At this point we were all totally exhausted, and left the tidy whities and proceeded to get some well-deserved sleep.

About two weeks later, when I was checking in for my next trip, there was a note in my mailbox to please see my supervisor ASAP. Notes like this were not good to find in your company mailbox. Not knowing what this was all about, I went down to my supervisor's office. As I walked into it, I noticed quite a few eyes were turned my way. Hmmmm ... Now what could this be all about.

My supervisor asked me to sit down, and told me that the office had received a telegram and apparently TWA was being sued. I will never forget the wording of this telegram, "While in the bathroom a stewardess loudly and rudely pounded on the door telling me to return to my seat. Her pounding startled me so much that it caused me to drop my lit cigarette into my shorts causing a fire which burnt my designer suit, and I was unable to complete my bowel movement. I am suing TWA for damages done to my designer suit and the embarrassment along with pain and suffering."

I just sat there and started laughing. And I might add that my supervisor wasn't able to keep a straight face either. I couldn't help myself at this point and said, "You've got to be kidding me." Then I shared what actually happened and told them that the captain and the other flight attendant would back me up. But here is the really fun part of this story and what really made this entire scenario even more laughable; this charming man's designer suit was a lovely beige colored "polyester" leisure suit. Such a real fashion statement.

Coins

ON A FRANKFURT to JFK 747, I passed by a young man trying to get into the lavatory, but he wasn't having any luck. He asked me why the open/close slot was not accepting his ten pfenning coin to open the door. I said nothing, opened the door for him, and left. Sometimes things are just left better unsaid.

The Most Beautiful Blue Eyes

I WAS WORKING a flight where we had a heavy load. The passengers were boarding and who got on but Polly Bergen and her husband.

For those of you who don't recognize that name, Polly Bergen was an American actress, singer, television host, writer and entrepreneur. She won an Emmy, was nominated for a Tony and a Golden Globe. Ms. Bergen also started her Polly Bergen Company cosmetics line, created jewelry, shoe brands and authored three books on beauty. Most people would recognize her from the '50s through the early 2000s. So, trust me I recognized her immediately and she was stunning.

Back to the flight; years ago, we hung people's coats and jackets in the closet, who were first class passengers, as they were boarding. We would "never" let them wad up their good jackets and coats in the overhead bins. I asked Ms. Bergen if she would like her coat hung up. Now let's talk about this coat. I take the coat from her and immediately think this is the softest fur I ever had touched. I know anti-fur people you are going nuts now, but this was way before it was socially unacceptable to wear fur. But getting back to the coat, it had a beautiful red lining and it could be zipped off at the knees. What do I mean? You had the formal look for evening down to your ankles and the less formal look in the day time by simply zipping off the lower part below your knees. Insane, I know!

But as I said it was the softest coat I had ever felt and trust me years ago having mink coats in first class was standard wear. Upon closer inspection I realized this was SABLE! I'm hanging the coat in the closet and leaning into the closet at the same time, so that I can stroke this coat, when I hear one of my flying partners saying, "What are doing inside the closet?" I pull my head out, grab her arm and hand, and whisper, "You've got to feel this coat. It is sable!" Now half her body is in the closet and she is saying under her breath, "Oh my God this is so soft."

Now getting back to Ms. Bergen and her husband, they were class acts. They were not demanding, and were immersed in conversation and paper work most of the time, probably about her cosmetic line. We arrive at our next destination and they de-plane saying, "Thank you very much for a nice flight."

Oh, but not the end of the story. A few months later I'm working another flight and there is a very well-heeled couple in first class. They looked like they just walked out of Neiman Marcus, replete with Tiffany jewelry and exquisite Ann Landers manners. As I'm taking drink orders in first class I noted that she had the most beautiful blue eyes, just "like" Polly Bergen's.

I couldn't help myself and I said to this woman, "I just had Polly Bergen on flight and she has the most beautiful blue eyes. Your eyes are just like hers." This woman looks at me and has a slight smile on her face and says,

"Thank you so much for that compliment. I'll have to tell her what you said. She is one of my best friends." Well, that was a surprise! What were the odds?

Silhouettes

IT WAS CHRISTMAS Eve and we were on our overnight layover in Cairo after flying from Paris. A few of us decided we wanted to go out to the pyramids for a camel ride. Now the taxi ride out there is just as much of an experience as the camel ride, and if you have ever been on a taxi ride in Cairo you know what I'm talking about.

We survived the taxi ride to the pyramids and found a guide that would take us out for a couple of hours. Picture a dark night with a little bit of moonlight and the stars were out in amazing fashion.

Here we were on three camels and a donkey, in the desert surrounding Cairo, going by the pyramids on Christmas Eve. Three camels and one donkey, starting to sound familiar? Remember it was Christmas Eve and we were having fun with the idea of the "three wise men and a donkey."

Our guide was leading us and we asked if we could go out by the pyramids. He said it wasn't allowed after dark, but if we wanted to add a little more incentive he would do it. Needless to say, we went to the pyramids.

Talk about a very surreal experience. Here we were on three camels and a donkey, in the desert of Cairo, going by the pyramids on Christmas Eve.

Now it gets interesting. We got out to the pyramids before the "Pyramid Sound and Light Show" had started. I noticed that we were riding between the big bank of flood lights that lit up the pyramid for the Sound and Light Show and the pyramid. All of a sudden, the lights go on and we are spotlighted, as if we were on a movie set, but we were far enough away from the audience that we didn't think they could see us. As we slowly were passing by though I looked up at the pyramid and low and behold, there we were. Our silhouettes were plastered across the face of the pyramid! We all just started laughing with the irony of our giant shadows of three camels, one donkey, all with riders, going past the face of the pyramid on Christmas Eve.

I've always wondered what the audience was thinking at the show when they saw this. As I said it was a very surreal experience and because it was Christmas Eve, I have to admit a religious one too.

Just another story from a great airline, TWA, and as we all remember what Pope John Paul called us when he was traveling with TWA, it was Travel With Angels.

You Want to Live Where ... You Want to be a Mother

WHEN I STARTED flying in 1962 as a flight attendant, you had to live within fifty miles of where you were based. In saying this, I know that there were a few people that didn't follow that rule. They got around it by keeping a post office box where they were based, so all mail from TWA came to that box, and to further cover their tracks their bank was where they were based too.

Why is this important? The man that I was planning to marry lived and worked in the Philadelphia area, which was ninety miles from JFK where I was based. What was I ever going to do? I knew if I faked it, like other people did, I would be the one that got caught and I would lose my job. I had to be up front. I needed my wonderful job and I needed the money.

As an aside: We were to be married on December 29, 1964, and I was lucky enough to have that day off even though I did fly on Christmas. Can you believe that I was flying on the 25th of December and getting married on the 29th? I could have been caught in a blizzard somewhere and missed my own wedding. Now that would have been another tale!

But getting back to my conundrum, as I said, I couldn't fake where I was going to live, I'm too honest and knew it would eventually catch up with me. Therefore, at the beginning of December I summoned up the courage to tell my supervisor that I was getting married and would be living outside of Philadelphia, which is approximately ninety miles from JFK.

I pleaded my case and explained to her that we needed my paycheck and I didn't want to lose my job, "Isn't there anything we can do about this?" She thought about it and said that she would talk to the other members of In-Flight Services (those were the supervisors for the flight attendants) but she was sure that I would have to quit. The company would never go for that. I said a prayer when I left her office because I just could not lose hope.

The fateful phone call came and my supervisor explained to me that they had set up an appointment for the afternoon of December 27th, for me to meet with everyone in the in-flight office. They were going to give me a chance to plead my case. This was two days before my wedding when I had to drive from Harrisburg, where I was to be married, to JFK, but then I had nothing else to do. Note, sarcasm in my voice now.

The truth was even if they had chosen my wedding day to talk to me, I would have gone. It was too important to say that I could not make it, but I think in retrospect that is what they might have been hoping for, i.e., she's getting married on the 29th, probably won't show on the 27th. Ironically, being a flight attendant for two years had given me quite a strong backbone, so I was not going to give up and I would be there on the 27th!

At that point, I was thinking I had too much to win for myself, never thinking that this would also be a monumental change for everyone that was a flight attendant with TWA, which also morphed into other airlines changing their policies too about commuting to work.

The morning of the 27th arrived and I drove to JFK not wanting to be a minute late for this meeting, even though I was there hours early. Finally, I was sitting in a room with all of the supervisors from In-Flight at JFK, which at that time was probably only about five and told my story. They all listened and asked many questions. When it was all over, I won! BUT "not" until I signed a paper saying if I was ever a second late for a check-in I was fired on the spot. No excuses just turn around and go home.

Needless to say, it was the best wedding gift I could have been given. I knew it wasn't going to be easy because we only had one car, so it was a cab to the train to go from Philadelphia to NYC, then the bus from the city out to JFK. There was no place to sleep at the hangar except on reclining chairs in the crew restroom and I had no money to pay for a hotel, but I made it work!

The rule of not living any further than fifty miles from your base for flight attendants changed within the next year. I don't know if TWA saw that it could work or recognized that they let their pilots commute from anywhere they wanted to live and were not confined to fifty miles from their base, but once TWA adopted it so did all the other airlines.

Was I really the reason for this huge change? I can't be 100% sure, but I do know that I was the first flight attendant at JFK working for TWA that they "knew" was commuting more than fifty miles. Look at what that turned into, people commuting from all over Europe, Hawaii, the islands, etc. You name it and people could live where they wanted. I'm very proud that I was part of that change and maybe just maybe the reason for it.

Postscript: In July of 1967, I became pregnant. As a flight attendant, being a "mother" was grounds for termination. You could not have children either biologically or adopted. In other words, you could not be a mother, period. Therefore, I flew for another six months until my pregnancy was visible. When I went into the JFK flight attendant office to tell them I was pregnant, I was terminated.

Now the unfairness in this was that our pursers who were all males, no female was hired as a purser and our pilots who were all male then too, no women were hired in that position either, could be fathers. So, why couldn't a female flight attendant be a mother? Of course, why couldn't a woman be a purser or pilot? And then, why couldn't a male be a flight attendant? As you know that has all changed. But the driving force was because of the Civil Rights Act of 1964 Title VII. For those of you who are unfamiliar with this, it is a federal law that prohibits employers from discriminating against employees on the basis of sex, race, color, national origin and religion. But still, surprise, TWA had to be taken to court for me to get my job back.

The momentous day wasn't until November of 1978 that I got it back through lawsuits claiming discrimination for TWA female flight attendants, who were mothers and were fired for that vs. male employees who were fathers and not fired. I'll never forget that day when the court ruled in our favor, it was like getting the "pot of gold" at the end of the rainbow. I always loved flying and I was going back!

Some of you might think we got a large monetary settlement. No, that was not the case; some women got $1,000 to $3,000 depending on how long they had been terminated for and how many children they had. Our flying seniority that we would have accrued if working was also prorated, therefore, we did not get back all of the time we had been off either. But for the 250 plus/minus of us who came back we were thrilled just to be back with the airline we loved.

Again I was instrumental in helping to change workplace rules. And how long did I stay with TWA? I retired in 2003. It was a great ride and I still have special friends from my flying days. Would you believe that a thousand of us just met for a reunion in New York at the TWA Hotel? I don't know whether secretly TWA put something in our veins to make us so loyal to the company, or possibly we just ingested too much jet exhaust, but we are all still sisters and brothers. A closed fraternity that only an ex-TWA flight attendant would understand.

Note: If I had become pregnant after October 1970, TWA had abandoned its "no-mothers" policy. In addition, they finally were letting women be pursers but it wasn't until years down the road that we started to see female pilots in the cockpit. Title Vll of the Civil Rights Act of 1964 was at last finally taking hold everywhere on the plane.

Sonny

THE PASSENGERS HAD not boarded, now picture a very senior flight attendant stooping over and picking up something off the floor at the first class door when a new hire, or as we would say very "junior" new flight engineer gets on the plane. She looks up at him and says, "Good morning." He is startled to see, shall we tactfully say, a rather senior woman who had been flying for a long time. BUT he makes the fatal mistake of opening his mouth and saying, "How old are you?"

Without skipping a beat she replies, "Let's put it this way sonny. If I was in the cockpit I would be in the left hand seat." He never said another word.

Angels Do Indeed Fly

I WAS A flight service manager on an L-1011 and one of our passengers had gotten on with shall we say an attitude problem. Very impressed with himself, Gucci briefcase and all.

After we had been airborne for a time, he approached me in the galley and said he did not feel well. Within less than a minute, he collapsed with a grand mal seizure. We immediately made an announcement for a doctor on board but there were none. By the grace of God though, two of our senior flight attendants were former MASH nurses who had served in Viet Nam.

I'll never forget how they leapt into action, took over, dead serious, cushioned him on the floor, secured his head, spoke so gently, soothed his fears and had this other worldly focus. The professionalism was outstanding. I was totally awestruck by the two of them.

We were close to landing now and had to decide what to do with our passenger, who was still lying on the floor with cushions surrounding him. As a crew, we completely changed our safety protocol for landing. We rearranged the flight attendant exit door coverage because the two flight attendants, who were the former MASH nurses, felt the passenger should not be moved yet from the cushioned floor area to a seat. In order to keep him more secure for landing they wanted to stay with him on the floor. The captain approved.

This passenger was not only "greatly humbled and thankful" to these two flight attendants, as he was taken off the plane by the paramedics, but I am sure eternally grateful for the quick actions of two very amazing women. I can only imagine what they endured when in Viet Nam, but they did validate that TWAngels do indeed fly and miracles can happen at any altitude.

Pope John Paul II

You will note in our stories that most authors have remained nameless. This particular story requires that we print it as received. We would like to thank Virginia J. Kelly for sharing a once in a lifetime experience that she and her husband, Bill, were so fortunate to have during their career with TWA as flight service managers. Enjoy the read ...

Flight 8699, October 8, 1995, Aircraft # N601TW, Baltimore to Rome, Italy
By Virginia J. Kelly, Flight Service Manager

Photo of Pope John Paul II with flight attendants Virginia and Bill Kelly.
Photo courtesy of Virginia Kelly.

BEING ASSIGNED TO a Papal Charter had been my dream for a long time, even more so because of my respect and love for Pope John Paul II.

Bill, my husband, who was also a flight service manager, and I had put in a request several months prior to the charter that TWA was to fly for Pope John Paul ll, to work the flight as flight attendants. We hoped that a combination of our languages (Greek, French, Lithuanian), our having been married in St. Peter's Basilica in Rome and our records with TWA would help us be selected.

At one point, without my knowledge, Bill went to Pat Rice who was the manager of In Flight and Judy Zimmer the general manager. He asked them that if only one of us could be chosen, which he assumed was the case, to please choose me and not him. They told him that there were many qualified people and that nothing was for certain.

It was Pat Rice, weeks later, who called to inform me of our assignment. A precedent was broken by giving me the flight service manager position, since a male flight service manager had always been used in the past internationally. In my opinion, it was time for an older woman who was also a flight service manager to be in charge. I might add the crew consisted of many flight service managers who had worked previously as flight attendants. Later, it was told to me that the company and our union did the selection process together.

A week before the charter, I injured my foot by putting a chair leg on it and sitting down. What pain! What a mess! But nothing was going to keep me from flying that charter, so I did not mention this to anyone at the time.

In Florida where we lived, Bill and I kept in touch with JFK and STL supervisors as to plans, services and procedures, studying all as it became available. This would be the most unique and special flight we ever worked.

On October 6, 1995, we flew to New York and went to TWA's Hangar 12. The preparations on the aircraft were unbelievable ... the enthusiasm, the work, the happiness of everyone involved was unprecedented.

The following day, October 7, 1995, our crew from New York left on TWE to Baltimore. (Trans World Express, a commuter airline.) We stayed at the Marriott Inner Harbor Hotel, across from Camden Yards, where the Holy Father would be appearing the following day.

The STL based flight attendants, who were working the flight the next day, joined us for dinner and afterwards some of us went to a moving Mass at the National Shrine of the Assumption of the Blessed Virgin Mary. Our crew belonged to many different religious faiths and this was not part of the criteria for being chosen.

The next morning, October 8th, was spent in briefings. We received extensive packages about the flow of services, procedures, protocol, etc. The crew members chose working positions on the plane; Harold Newton would be working the galley in first class, Bill Kelly would be the first class aisle flight attendant, and Ratan Bhappu the extra, or as we called them the floater, who would help in the entire aircraft. Karen Sikora would be in the next galley, with Carolyn Hamilton and Anna Delmolino working in the next area with her. Mary Ellen Norton-Hayes would work the aft galley, with Susan Exum and Oksana Faller working the aisle positions in the aft section. I would be in the aisle in the aft section and wherever needed.

At 4 PM, three Super Shuttle vans transported the crew and TWA officials to the BWI (Baltimore) cargo facility. Prior to boarding "Shepherd I", the Secret Service checked each crewmember and TWA passenger against a master list, which had been screened in advance.

The chefs then came on board to provide us with even more detailed information about the food and its presentation. Then the press boarded early and we served them hours before the plane actually departed.

The air really started to feel different as a helicopter with the Holy Father landed. This was actually happening now! There were ceremonies and speeches with Vice President Gore there to see the Holy Father off. Interestingly enough the Cardinals and other high officials boarded first.

Prior to the Pope's boarding, our Captain, Fred Arenas, told us that he wanted the crew to stand in a row like a reception, starting by the door. As the Holy Father started slowly coming up the stairs, I was overcome by the honor of being able to be in his presence. I spoke to him in Lithuanian, "Sventas Tevas, Sventas Tevas, Aciu, Aciu." Then I kissed his ring and genuflected.

Bill genuflected, kissed his ring and greeted him in English. Our Captain, Fred Arenas did so in Spanish and so on.

We only had four first class passengers besides the Holy Father. They were Monsignor (now Cardinal) Dziwisz, Cardinal Angelo Sodano (then Secretary of State), Cardinal Edmund Szoka and Cardinal William Baum.

Once seated, the Holy Father asked Bill for a wet cloth to wash his hands. As I said, we had an extensive menu and presentation decorum to follow and all seemed to enjoy their dinner. The Holy Father then changed into his nightclothes to rest in bed for about three hours. Yes, he had his own bed complete with a seat belt in it. As an aside that bed is now in a museum in Kansas City. In the morning, before arrival he had a light breakfast and read a Bible.

***

We had brought a box full of rosaries to be blessed. Bill was worried that there would be no time for this. Unbeknownst to me and I only became aware of it much later, during the night Bill placed the box under the Holy Father's bed under his head, later moving it under his feet. After I found this out, I was worried that it would look suspicious to have Bill on the floor putting a box under the bed. Thankfully, no one saw him do this. I know you are wondering why, his reasoning was he felt that if the Holy Father couldn't bless these rosaries at least they would have been in his presence.

During Bill's conversations earlier with Monsignor Dziwisz, it came out that I had been born in Vilnius, Lithuania. Monsignor Dziwisz asked Bill to have me come up to talk to him. Most people from Vilnius speak Polish, unfortunately, I did not. But all turned out well anyway, I could understand him and he could understand my English, so we were fine.

As it turned out The Holy Father signed books, photos, and blessed religious artifacts so those rosaries were blessed for us. Bill had also brought our wedding photo taken in St. Peter's which The Holy Father autographed with "Cum Benedictum. Joannus Paulus II 9.10.95."

To our surprise we were told to get ready for short audiences. When it was my turn, I sat down next to the Holy Father and he took my hand! I never expected that! I spoke in Lithuanian, "Sventas Tevas, Aciu, Aciu" to which he replied, with a most dazzling smile and outstretched hands, "Lietuva, Lietuva."

He then proceeded with the following, "Tegu buna pagarbintas Jezus Kristus." I answered, "Per amzius, Amen." It was an old Lithuanian prayer that my aunt and godmother, Dagmar Svoinickas had taught me. The Holy Father now took his thumb and blessed me by making the deepest cross on my forehead; it was as if an indelible mark would be left. During this audience, those watching thought the Holy Father and I were singing songs.

Everyone had an audience in a myriad of languages and we were all so touched. It seemed that the Holy Father related to each person on the level they needed.

Cardinal Sodano, then Secretary of State, praised TWA, and the service and offered a tour of the Vatican to the crew. What an honor! All of our "guests" were extremely complimentary.

The trip was coming to an end when The Holy Father indicated he wanted to speak on the PA. He came forward, and put one hand on Bill, and one on me, and said, "Good couple. God Bless You." As he touched us to steady his arm, I gave the PA to him upside down. Bill turned it around and The Holy Father smiled. He then spoke in Italian, thanking everyone and said, "GOD BLESS TWA."

This trip, with the most wonderful crew, was the highlight of my TWA career.

Virginia J. Kelly

From the First Flight to the Last

MOST OF YOU wouldn't know but many pilots and flight attendants did not live where we were based. I was based out of JFK and flying our international trips but lived in Kansas City. We were referred to as commuters.

By chance, I was commuting from JFK after an international trip and went through ORD where I was connecting to my flight home to KC. I arrived at my gate in ORD and was surprised to find that it was the last leg of the very "last" flight of TWA's 707 aircraft. It was returning to the overhaul base for retirement.

Cake was served at the gate to all of our passengers and we were given a marker to sign our name on the airplane as we boarded. Since I was still in uniform the crew adopted me and I helped serve champagne in-flight to our passengers. They all knew they were making a little history that day.

What really made that flight special? One of the flight attendants, who was working this flight, was Ms. Ida Staggers, she had worked the "maiden" flight of the first TWA Boeing 707 in January of 1959. Ida was an "icon" for TWA flight attendants and was one of the most senior in seniority in our ranks. I feel sure that the company had asked her to work this flight because of her history with the aircraft. Always the consummate professional and here she was working the very last leg for a TWA 707 aircraft.

If you have not visited the TWA Museum at 10 Richards Road in Kansas City, MO you really should. You will see a signed postcard from our entire crew on that historic flight, in a display case there. However, trust me that is only a minor display at the museum of our storied airline.

World's Best Flight Attendant

ANOTHER STORY ABOUT, flight attendant, Ms. Ida Staggers who was one of our truly special flight attendants. Enjoy ...

I was in sales and marketing for my twenty-one years with TWA but one of the most moving stories for me was about Ida Staggers. She was one of the very early flight attendants with TWA.

I'll try to reconstruct the story: It was at a meeting in the early '70s of the San Fran management team where we held a mock trial accusing Ida of being the world's best flight attendant, she denied the charges.

As one of the witnesses for the prosecution, we called to the stand a flight attendant who worked the MAC flights (Military Aircraft Command), as did Ida at the time. The witness recalled a Christmas Eve when she was picking up a MAC flight in Guam. She and her fellow crew members were all feeling sorry for themselves for having to work that night. When they got to the top of the stairs to enter the TWA 707 who popped out but Ida. She had a big grin on her face and a Christmas ornament in her hair.

The witness recognized her immediately, and in her shock said, "You are number one on the seniority list. What are you doing here tonight, on Christmas Eve?"

Ida looked at her with an equally puzzled look and replied, "It's my number one seniority that ensures that I can be with our boys on Christmas. I wouldn't miss this for anything!"

The embarrassed crew looked at each other and entered the plane, which had been decorated throughout with wreaths and other Christmas decorations. They were surprised again and asked if TWA had done all that. Ida explained that no she did it. The witness concluded that this event had taken place a number of years ago and that she now herself had not missed a Christmas Eve flying MAC flights since then.

We had generals and other military people testify, and in the end Ida was found guilty on all counts of being the "World's Best Flight Attendant."

It was a very emotional and fun evening.

Mission Instructions Received

AS I WAS meandering through Costco today, I noticed a wild bird casually jumping around on the floor looking for some tasty morsels when I had a flashback.

I was working the Boeing 747 first class galley on a flight from LAX to JFK. The aircraft had been late coming into LAX for this new departure, so everything was behind schedule. Our cleaners had stormed through the aircraft getting it ready for the passengers before they boarded. Additionally, our commissary personnel were loading the galleys, when the gate agents started boarding VIPs. Those agents were hell bent and determined that the flight would go out on time. Because of all of this last-minute preparation both the first class boarding door and the door opposite it for the commissary truck were both open.

As I said, the agents had started boarding our VIPs and one of them was the actor Peter Graves. Some of you might remember that he was in the original *Mission Impossible* series on TV, way before Tom Cruise was making *Mission Impossible* movies. Now think you are watching TV, or for our younger readers you are at the movies and that *Mission Impossible* theme song starts. A fast-paced montage starts unfolding and Peter Graves, known as Phelps in the series, receives his instructions from a voice delivered recording which then self-destructs at the end.

Now back to our plane. A bird flies into the first class cabin through the open galley door. It flies around the cabin for a minute or two with our first class passengers letting out shrill squeaks and covering their heads as the panicked bird flies from row to row, diving back and forth.

Peter Graves and I might add here, with his beautiful head of thick grey hair, immediately accepts the mission as the tape is getting ready to self-destruct. He not only catches the bird, but gently tosses it back outside. And there was applause from all who witnessed this.

The galley was loaded, all passengers were on board and we departed on time. Just another *Mission Impossible* accepted by Peter Graves. Great TV series and now great movies.

Do You Know What She is Driving

FLASH BACK ... I had a little red Fiat sports car when I first started flying. Unfortunately, I demolished it in an accident. Yes, no fun times there. I knocked out a tooth, had to have seven stitches on my lower lip, four on my chin, a sprained jaw, two black eyes and bruises all over my body. The good news was I had on my seat belt, or I probably would have been killed. Yes, being a flight attendant, this was just the first thing you always remembered to do, put on your seat belt!

But my second red car seems to be the one that got me into trouble too. And no, I did not get in an accident in this second car. The issue was it seemed to be a magnet for men.

What was it? A burgundy Corvette with an upgraded very powerful engine. Oh, did it sound great when you turned over the engine to start it. You wanted to just listen to it for a minute before taking off down the road. It was the real deal, Zoom, Zoom, Zoom! And of course, a stick shift. How was I able to afford this on a flight attendant's salary? I couldn't, it was my husband's.

Now most women do not know how to drive a stick, but I had a boyfriend in high school that had a sports car with a stick transmission and he taught me. So of course, driving my power buggy was no challenge. I only had to learn not to stomp on the gas too hard, or the car would fish tail.

Oh, that Corvette would draw comments from the TWA pilots all of the time at the hangar when I was parking it before a flight. "Pretty big engine in that car for a little girl. Is that your car or your husband's or boyfriend's?" Etc. Etc. Etc. My reply to them was usually, "Yes, it will get down the road and yes, it is my car." I couldn't resist because I knew it irritated them.

Now here is where it gets fun … I'm driving to the airport for a flight. Close to the TWA hangar at LAX, where the employees parked, was a long stretch of road; four lanes wide, two on either side, probably about a mile and half long between two traffic lights, totally straight and there were no other cars around. I pull up to the first traffic light, which was red, and a few seconds later a truck pulls up next to me. Then I hear the person in the truck racing their motor as if they want to drag race with me. Really?

The light changes and the truck takes off. I put the Vet into first gear, and then a little Devil jumps onto my shoulder and says, "Take him!" But on the other shoulder the good Angel appears and says, "Don't do that, remember there might be a cop around." But the Devil was screaming, "Go, Go, Go for it!"

The little Devil wins! I smashed down on the accelerator; the car needed a tune up and I could see some black smoke come out of the tailpipe. I put the car into second and now I've got the accelerator floored. I skip third gear and go straight into fourth. I glance down at the speedometer and I'm doing

90 as I fly past the truck! Couldn't help myself and I was laughing as I'm doing all of this, and obviously the Devil was enjoying himself too!

The second traffic light is approaching me rather quickly (do you think so?). I take the car out of fourth, shift down to third while braking, and then go into second to really slow down. I make the turn to go back down another small road to our hangar. The truck is long gone! Really, whom did they think they were playing with? The Devil is nodding his head in approval.

An hour later, I'm on the plane and we are getting ready for the passengers to board. As a courtesy, we would go up to the cockpit to introduce ourselves to the captain prior to boarding. I told my flying partner I was going to run up to the cockpit for a second to say, "Hello" and I would be back.

Ah yes, I said this was the fun part! I walk into the cockpit and the first officer turns around, sees me, and says to the captain, "Do you know what she is driving?" I just got a big grin on my face and said, "Oh, you must have been in the truck. I'll talk to you boys later." Cha-ching! One for the Devil ...

Happy Motoring! Zoom, zoom, zooooooooom.

Bang Bang

ON AN L-1011 there was a lot of racket going on in the one of the first class lavs and even the door was bulging. I knocked on the door and asked, "Are you OK?" The occupant said she was fine. Shortly thereafter the cockpit rang three bells which meant they needed something. As I entered the cockpit the flight engineer said, "What the hell is going on in the lav, someone is banging against the lav wall and my whole panel is vibrating." He was super Po'd!

So, back to check on the activity in the first class lav, again I asked, "Are you OK?" A breathless woman said she was fine and soon returned to her first class seat. Within a minute, another woman exits. They offered no explanations, we asked for none. Vibrations in the cockpit stopped. Hmm ...

Third Hand

IT WAS THE early '80s and I was working first class on an L-1011. My flying partner was quite the kidder. In fact, harassing the passengers and making them laugh out loud seemed to be her forte. And I might add she did it very well.

On this particular flight, who did we have in first class but Jimmy Connors. You know that guy who won all of those tennis tournaments, like Wimbledon, the U.S. and French Opens. Just those minor types of tennis tournaments. Yes, we are being sarcastic here. He was really a big deal in the tennis world.

But I think the thing that really impressed us was he was in first class, with his wife Patti (former Playboy model and gorgeous), their two small children (son who was about three years old and daughter who was still an infant), their Schnauzer puppy and the nanny. Now, many celebs or people of means would put the nanny, children and dog in coach while they dined and wined in first class. Not the Connors! They had all six seats across the first row in first class. Plus, both parents were totally involved with the children and the puppy. To the point that they would change seats with one another and the nanny to interact with the children.

Jimmy at this point was sitting with his son. Which I might add he was a very well behaved child and a little cutie. We had the dessert cart out in the aisle serving ice cream sundaes with all of the goodies. Now remember, I said my flying partner was quite the kidder with everyone and was very good at it.

We get the dessert cart to Jimmy Connors, and his son and my flying partner asks them if they would like dessert. Jimmy's little boy's eyes got huge and he nodded his head yes. She made up a delicious looking sundae for him, and he sat up really straight to reach the table and his dessert. Jimmy was helping him when my flying partner asked him if he would like dessert.

Jimmy says, "No thanks, I'll wait until he is done. I've got to help him with this." To which she replies in a totally back handed way, (I know bad pun), "Yes, it looks like you need a third hand here. Hmm, maybe if you had had a third hand you could have been a great tennis player." I thought he was about ready to drop the spoon now and he just roared with laughter.

As I said, the Connors were delightful. Totally relaxed, non-pretentious and fun. But here is another part of my story. A few years earlier, I had another world ranked tennis player on board. She was traveling with her manager and felt it was beneath her to talk to the help, which would have been us. So rude!

I'm now sitting with Jimmy chatting away about this, and that, and I brought up this woman and told him about how she had treated us on the plane. He said, "I'm not surprised, she acts like that all of the time." I'll let you figure out who this mystery woman was.

Thanks for a great memory Connors family. You were all delightful!

Blind As a Bat ... Then Maybe Not

WE WERE FLYING an all-nighter from LAX to JFK and had a passenger in first class that was blind. My flying partner and good friend told me that she actually had this passenger on previous flights and really did not care for him.

He would put headphones on and sing aloud to whatever he was listening to while people were trying to sleep, drink heavily, and then stand around the galley listening to us and being obnoxious.

Well, it was the middle of the night and he was in the galley. There were a few of us standing by him and I decided to try to make everyone laugh. I started to slowly lick my lips and do a bad imitation of Marilyn Monroe movements. I was having so much fun now I started licking my finger and rubbing my breasts very provocatively. The only thing I refrained from was singing Happy Birthday Mr. President, but that did not stop me from mouthing the words.

Boy, did I think I was funny and the other flight attendants seemed to be getting a kick out of my performance too, when the man said, "This is damn good first class service."

"What?" I mouthed in shock to my friend, which I might add here she was deadpan the whole time. Then I mouthed, "I thought he was blind." She starts to walk away with a little smirk on her face, and then turns around and mouths back to me, "Oh, he can see a little."

I never came back to first class again that evening even though I was working there. This falls under the category of "never assume."

Everyone Needs a Big Brother and the Kindness of Strangers

I HAD JUST started flying and the world was my oyster. So many things to see and so many places to go. But before I begin let me give you some background.

My roommate during training was a redhead from New Orleans. She was a sophisticated woman and a little older than the rest of us. As she said during training, "I could have worked for Delta Airlines, but who wants to see Atlanta or Cincinnati, when you can see Paris or Rome."

So, fresh out of training we decided to share an apartment. We chose one close to the airport and relatively cheap since there were only two of us. Most of the new hires would have six women in a two-bedroom apartment. Frankly that didn't sound very appealing!

Now this apartment building was primarily filled with "stews" (flight attendants), pilots and a few mechanics. Everyone seemed to know one another, and we had become friends with one of the single pilots there. He for whatever reason had nicknamed me Sam and her Red.

He was the big brother that I never had. Watched out for us, told us his opinions about who we dated, helped us buy our cars and taught me to like Bombay gin on the rocks with a twist of lemon. He was a good "big brother."

Well, Red and I had been flying close to six months and decided that we would go to Acapulco. Red made all of the hotel reservations and figured out how to fly down there on another carrier who was offering airline employees cheap rates. One of the perks of working for an airline.

Off we go for five days of fun in Acapulco. It was five days for me; Red had seven days off and told me she was going to stay for those extra two days. Oh, it was great! The bars don't really start getting people in them until 10 PM and then the partying starts. You can literally dance all night if you want. Great beaches and water skiing during the day. People selling cheap jewelry on the beaches that you just can't say no to. Only thing you had to remember was don't drink the water!

Well, it comes to my fifth day and I'm off from Acapulco heading over to México City to go back home to the states. All is well until I arrive in Mexico City where the airport is jammed with people. I went to the ticket counter to check in for my next flight to LAX, with my reduced rate ticket, which was also a "standby ticket" and this is where the drama began.

I'm informed by the ticket agent that the flight I thought I could get out on was oversold and he would put me on the stand-by list. This is not looking good! Well, I stand by for two more flights and now I have to admit that I'm beginning to get a little panicky. You see I had to fly the next day and frankly TWA didn't care about any of your vacation problems. When I say they didn't care, I mean they didn't care. You are supposed to show up for your flight and the only excuse for missing one is that you are calling in DEAD! Or at least sick!

Major point here: understand that I'm still on what they called probation and anything such as not showing up for a flight is definitely not going to look good on my record period. My airline career is in jeopardy now … I could hear the words, "You're fired!"

Now when the same check in agent tells me I probably won't be getting out that day I was ready to commit suicide. Well, maybe not suicide but trust me I was thinking I've got big time issues here. I asked him what a full fare ticket cost and he told me that there were seats available if I wanted to pay for a full fare ticket. YES! I will!

I pull out my checkbook and my driver's license and he says, "I can't take a check on an American account." I feel like I'm having an out of body experience now, "What! But I only have my checkbook with me." He says, "No credit card?" I shake my head no. In fact, at this point I only had a few pesos left.

Here was my problem, I had forgotten to bring my credit card, but thought no big deal I have plenty of cash on me, and Red had said, "Not to worry, I'll pay for the room, and we can put things like meals on my credit card and you can pay me back when we get home."

But back to the drama, the agent is looking at me now as if what am I going to do with this girl. The next thing I remember him saying is, "OK, my very good friend is the bank manager at a bank right outside the airport. I'll take you over there, and hopefully he will cash your check and you can pay for your ticket in cash." So, off we go in his car. Thankfully, it was not another error in judgement of getting into a car with a total stranger in Mexico City, but in my defense at this point in time I was desperate. These are things we never tell our parents about.

We arrive at the bank and the next thing I know I'm sitting across from a stern looking man who says, "I understand that you only have a check and cannot pay cash for your ticket." I'm nodding my head yes now, and trying not to cry because at this point, I'm thinking I'm going to lose my job and also be spending the night in that damn airport sleeping in a chair. And I don't even have enough money to pay for a meal!

The bank manager looks at me and says, "Do you swear to me that you have $200 in your account?" I told him, "I swear to that and look at my check book. See the checks I have written and what I have left. There is more than $200 in this checking account."

He says, "Let me see your passport." Then he tells me to write out the check for cash, he writes down my passport number, and tells me that I better be telling him the truth and then hands me $200 in Mexican currency.

I wanted to kiss him but knew that would be inappropriate! OMG! Just let me get home and I will never leave my credit card behind ever, ever again.

Remember the agent who really took me under his wing? When we returned to the airport, he gave me a voucher to go to the best restaurant in the airport to get something to eat, and also gave me my boarding pass, so I didn't need to stand in another line. Sometimes we have to rely on the kindness of strangers.

Now where does my big brother (pilot) come into this? When I finally got home, I ran into him in the courtyard of the apartment building. I told him what I had been through and how I had to fly the next day. He took out a $100 bill from his wallet and handed it to me. "Sam, this is your back up money. I want you to put it in your wallet and it stays there all of the time for emergencies. Do you understand me? When you get back from your next trip and get paid then give me the $100 bill back. But make sure that you put a $100 bill in your wallet to replace it."

He then says, "What about Red? Where is she?" I replied, "She is still in Acapulco and doesn't know about any of this."

"Well, give me the name of the hotel where she is staying. I'll call her to make sure she has money or enough credit on her card to buy a ticket to get out of Mexico." He's shaking his head now and saying, "Why do I see me wiring her money?" And he had to the next day.

Everyone needs a good big brother and sometimes the kindness of strangers ...

It Was the Fifties ... with Silver Tip Roast, Sleeping Berths and Movie Stars

THIS WAS THE era of the Connies and sleeping berths in first class in the fifties. Yes, you think all of that just started recently with private sleeping areas for first class passengers. Oh, no it didn't! There were four berths, two on either side with curtains that covered them for our first class passengers who paid for the upgrade. Oh if only those berths could talk!

Then there was our famous owner at the time, Howard Hughes, who was referred to as Uncle Howard by the TWA employees, and stories were told that he would take a TWA plane to the islands for days and weeks at a time. Movie stars flocked to fly on TWA! We were the airline of the stars. Probably Howard Hughes connections in Hollywood had a lot to do with that too.

Photos of large 1st class lavatory and sleeping berth.
Photos courtesy of the TWA Museum.

Was first class elegant? We had menus and offered among other entrees "Silver Tip Roast" which we carved at the first class passengers' seats. You do not care for beef, then try the Lobster Thermidor, which was a really big hit! Mums champagne flowed and we had most of the makings for a full bar. Yes, it was elegant.

As for memories, I'll start with one of my first flights on a Martin 404. Our flight was late on arriving and I announced to the passengers that we would be on the ground for thirty minutes. That was the original scheduled time for the ground stop, but the agent wanted to get the flight out on time, something I had failed to take into consideration being a new hostess. So, the ground stop ended up being fifteen minutes. Have you ever seen a passenger running down a runway to catch a flight? Well, I did, and he didn't make it!

You think bomb scares started in the '60s and '70s, no I had one in the '50s but fortunately nothing was found. Then there was a flight where I was so airsick, I could not get up to serve the passengers. Who did? The co-pilot. The passengers got a kick out of that.

Speaking about the cockpit, the flight engineer on a Super G that I was working had to use an ax on the front lav door to remove a passenger who had passed out in it. Yes, it is true! Then I remember when lightning hit the plane during one of my flights. Fortunately, nothing happened except the awful smell of phosphorus.

But the really great experiences were with those movie stars from the '50s! Are you old enough to remember Ester Williams? I can hear some of you now saying, WHO? Well, she was a big deal in the fifties. As a young woman, she had won many swimming competitions, among them three United States National championships. The story is told that she was spotted by a MGM talent scout, while working in a Los Angeles department store. Yes, those stories of movie stars being found at lunch counters and working every day jobs possibly may be true. Stardom didn't take that long to achieve as MGM created a special subgenre just for her known as "Aqua Musicals." Her big splash, I know bad pun, such as *Million Dollar Mermaid* turned her into "America's Mermaid," because it appeared in these movies that she could stay underwater forever. The synchronized swimming and diving extravaganzas in those movies dazzled audiences. Plus, her being gorgeous didn't hurt either.

But back to my flight with Ester. She was traveling in first class on the Connie and had been using one of our sleeping berths. After we landed in Los Angeles, she waited until everyone deplaned and then went to the first class lav to change into her clothes. All of a sudden, the lav door opened and she said, "Can you zip up my dress please?" Zipping away, I thought, OMG, wait until I get back to NY to tell my roomies this, SHE DOESN'T WEAR A BRA! But then it only got better!

Who gets on the plane but Jane Russell. Now for those of you who don't know who Jane Russell was, she was really the most gorgeous, curvaceous movie star on the planet then. Howard Hughes (remember Uncle Howard) made her famous in a movie called *The Outlaw* which he produced and directed. Then she went on to do more movies with another one being a box office smash called *Gentlemen Prefer Blondes* with Marilyn Monroe. Talk about two curvy, sexy women together.

OK, back to Ester and Jane. Jane was Ester's ride home. As Jane got on the plane, I hear this voice yelling, "Where the hell are you bitch?" It was good-natured because there were hugs and kisses between the two. I'm standing there in awe trying to pick up my jaw from the floor of the plane! Ester Williams and Jane Russell standing right in front me.

Then I had Marilyn Monroe on flight. This was another OMG moment. Remember she was married to Joe DiMaggio, The Yankee Clipper. The photographers were swarming the plane, taking pictures of them saying their goodbyes. She was quiet and subdued, quite the lady and very beautiful.

Lastly, there was June Allyson and her husband Richard Powell. They were both extremely well known for all of their work on stage, in films and TV. Powell was also a director and producer. They had reserved two of the berths in first class and were seemingly sleeping for the evening flight when June Allyson appeared in the galley and said, "Can you give me a cup of coffee. I'm wide awake and might as well stay awake." The next thing I knew she was in the cockpit in her housecoat,(today we call it a lightweight robe), telling jokes the whole night to the crew as Dick Powell was snoring gently away in his berth.

But one of the best times I ever had celebrity wise was on a layover in Los Angeles. I was working coach on this particular flight and after we landed I was informed that the entire crew had been invited to Chasen's restaurant for dinner. Chasen's was only the best restaurant and waterhole in West Hollywood to see all of the celebrities in LA. Plus, guess what? Chasen's was TWA's caterer out of Los Angeles then. Just another celeb connection for our airline.

How was our dinner at Chasen's? It was wonderful and totally gratis but at the end of it, Mrs. Chasen invited us back to her personal office. This was rarified air! Her office walls were covered with pictures of all of the celebrities who were her friends and dined there regularly. And who was in her office but Louis Jordan's wife, "Quigue" watching TV! All I remember was standing behind her watching Louis Jordan accepting an award. It was all overwhelming, me in Mrs. Chasen's office watching TV.

Those were the '50s! What wonderful memories TWA gave me. It was quite a ride for two years, thanks TWA for everything …

Baby in an Umbrella Stroller … Remember Those

WE WERE FLYING a Boeing 707 from Paris to Rome to Tel Aviv. A very heavy-set Muslim woman, dressed in a traditional hijab, with several children in tow boarded to go to Tel Aviv. She was also carrying a baby and pushing an umbrella stroller that was filled with blankets. Getting her and her children settled was an adventure to say the least.

After about ten minutes, we finally had them all in their seats with their luggage, toys, etc. stowed. My flying partner took the stroller and proceeded to put it in the already bulging aft coat closet that we had for carry on garment bags. At that time, this was the luggage of choice for all business travelers before wheelies had been invented.

But getting back to Momma, she was chirping away and we couldn't understand what she was saying. A man who understood Arabic told us, "She said, we put her baby in the closet," we replied back to him, "No, she has it." He just shrugged. Hmm, maybe we better go look just in case. Sure enough, there was a baby hanging in the stroller with the garment bags. Whoops …

How Not to Celebrate Your Wedding Anniversary

IT WAS DECEMBER 1st, 1974, my first wedding anniversary. Where was I? On a plane going from San Francisco to New York. Yes, I was too junior (meaning not enough seniority) to be able to get that day off to celebrate with my husband at home, but I was meeting my maid of honor in NYC that evening for dinner, so all was not lost.

We were flying on a 747 and I was working the first class galley position, but during boarding I ended up standing in the rear cabin for a while. As I was trying to make it back up to first class, I saw a very tall, thin man who was looking for his seat. After I directed him to it I noticed that he seemed to be short of breath and looked tired.

I couldn't leave him without talking to him for a few minutes to make sure that he was OK. He told me that he had been living in the United States, and was moving back to India and he was just very tired. I offered him a glass of water but he refused, and said he needed to rest for a while, at which point I reminded him that if he wanted anything just to ring his call button.

Boarding was completed; we did the emergency demonstration and proceeded to our assigned jump seats for takeoff. Initially after we were airborne, there was some turbulence and the cockpit made an announcement for the cabin crew to remain seated until we were told it was safe to get up. It was a good half hour before the captain gave us the all clear to begin our service and I was busily setting up my first class galley, when a flight attendant who was working that back cabin came up to me and said, "Weren't you a nurse?" I nodded yes and said, "Why do you ask? Well, there is a man in my zone who I can't wake up. Can you come back and take a look at him for me."

Oh no, it was the man who was moving back to India. He looked the same but his skin was cold and there was no pulse. We had a deadheading pilot (which means traveling like a passenger but on company business) who was sitting in that row at the window seat. He said he had fallen asleep after takeoff and hadn't noticed anything wrong with this passenger before he went to sleep. He said, the passenger just looked like he was nodding off for a nap too.

From my nursing career I knew that the man was deceased, but immediately called for a doctor on board and fortunately, there was one. He concurred that the man was dead, but from what, we didn't know. The cockpit was notified and much to my relief they returned to San Francisco. Why do I say that, well I had heard horror stories about dead passengers just being covered up and the flight continuing to its destination. Thankfully, we hadn't been airborne all that long, and the captain made an announcement to our passengers saying we had a sick passenger on board and we would be returning to San Fran.

After we parked at the gate the police came on board, inspected the passenger, the surroundings and then carried him from the aircraft. We were on the ground for around an hour giving the police our statements, refueling, and getting new flight plans to start all over again. But then as fate would have it, we arrived in the New York area to a sleet storm, which added another hour of holding time to this flight before we could land. Would you be surprised if I told you upon landing 360 passengers burst into applause!

Remember my maid of honor was meeting me and we were going out for dinner. I wasn't very hungry. I made sure from that day forward I would never fly again on my anniversary!

My Mother Always Said It Is a Small World

I HAD BEEN flying for approximately a year and was based out of LAX. The grooming supervisor, yes you read right we had a grooming supervisor, who would periodically call you into her office to be checked out, i.e. uniform was it clean and neat, did you have on the correct jewelry, weight, hair, nails, makeup and a girdle!

This "once over" had never happened to me, so I must have been passing with flying colors. In fact, she came up to me one day when I was checking in for a flight and asked if I would like to do some "special assignments" for the company. Would I! Yes, was the answer because you got 2.5 hours of flight time for each one you did. EXTRA MONEY! And considering that usually by the end of the month before that pay check came in, I had to decide if I could afford a hamburger, or had to eat a grilled cheese on a layover, so that extra pay was a big deal.

What were some of the things I did? I would go out to the movie studios with one of TWA's sales reps and pose for pictures with stars such as Rachel Welch and the President of MGM studios. Then we would have lunch with their executives. I said really nothing and just smiled pretty. I think the Rep liked that about me. I kept a low profile. So, I got asked back to do these a lot. I also appeared on the TV show, Truth or Consequences hosted by Bob Barker. Again, just eye candy in my uniform for that particular part of the show. It was fun and again, 2.5 hours of extra flight time. No grilled cheese for me that month!

Another one of my assignments was with a second TWA flight attendant in LA. We went to the hangar where a Boeing 707 was parked, totally shiny and looked like it had just come out of the Boeing plant. Some of you might remember "The Three Stooges", Larry, Curly and Moe. Well, they had a pilot idea for a TV show where they would be flying around the world on TWA, and the show would have their usual antics and silliness in it.

I along with the other flight attendant were there to lend authenticity to this pilot because we were in our uniforms. We just stood on the steps up to the plane, waved at them and again smiled pretty. Neither of us expected an acting career to come out of this, but we loved getting that overtime pay.

You might be wondering what happened to that pilot? The Stooges had begun the production of it which would be for a syndicated, half hour, 39-episode TV series called Kook's Tour. It was basically a travelogue-sitcom that had them traveling around the world with episodes filmed on location. Of course, they would always be on a TWA plane. Unfortunately, Larry had a stroke which ended his acting career along with the plans for the TV series. The producer Norman Maurer took some of the available footage and made a 52-minute special out of it. It was released on a video cassette in 1973. I never knew about this, and when I heard about it years and years later I wondered if the two of us made it into the special since we were taped waving at them from the plane. Who knows?

But my most stressful special assignment was when I went to a career day at a high school to represent the company and tell everyone about having a career as a TWA flight attendant. My Mother always said, "Remember it is a small world you have to watch everything you say and do." That statement never rang truer than in this episode of my special assignments.

I had gone out on a date, my first date actually, with my future husband. It was for a St. Patty's Day party. The night was filled with "many" Irish coffees and plenty of great food offered by our host and hostess. We had hit it off so well at the party that we were the last to leave and I got home at 2 AM. Now I was supposed to be at this high school at 8 AM for the career day symposium. I had estimated that it would take me 45 minutes to drive there. This was "way before" GPS, therefore, I was relying on their directions to find this school and wanted to give myself plenty of extra time to get there.

Terrified that if I tried to sleep for only two hours I might sleep through the alarm and if I missed this assignment, I would never get another one again. I put into place my plan. I didn't go to sleep, just stayed up the rest of the night. Yes, no sleep for me!

Off I went to the school exhausted; made it there on time, met the principal, then found myself sitting on a stage with some other people, who were there too for career day presentations. I was introduced, gave a short speech, then went to a classroom where students could come in and speak to me on a one on one basis if they liked. Remember, I'm in my uniform, trying to look as professional as possible, after never having gone to sleep and I might have enjoyed a few Irish coffees too. Finally, the torture ended and I drove home to collapse in my bed and sleep for the rest of the day.

Two days later I'm checking in for a flight at the hangar. One of our schedulers says, "Hi, I wanted to tell you that my daughter just loved you at career day." Gulp! I'm thinking, "Oh gee, I hope I didn't smell like an Irish Coffee. How red were my eyes?" Then he continues on, "She thought you were so poised and pretty. She wants to be a flight attendant now."

Thank God races through my mind. And then my Mother's words of advice came to me, "Always watch what you say and do for it is a small world." And TWA made it a very "small world" for all of us.

Sláinte (Cheers in Irish for your next Irish coffee)

What Is That Little Spot of Yellow

Photo of advertisement courtesy of TWA Museum.
The flight attendants pictured are not the authors of this story.

IN 1977, TWA opened a new domicile in St. Louis. I had been based in ORD for a year, but as I was born and raised in St Louis, I thought it would be nice to go back home as it was a new domicile and TWA was taking care of the expenses for the move. The only downside was that my boyfriend was still in Chicago, so I bid trips with as many long layovers in ORD as I could.

One month I bid an extra flight attendant position, which meant that I was never with the same crew for the entire month and I was flying on all kinds of different aircraft too. But who cared because it had one beautiful eighteen-hour layover in ORD. My boyfriend was so excited and had made big plans for us that evening.

Unfortunately, there was no room for any slight margin of error on the day of this layover and the margin got increasingly narrower, until it disappeared into the red zone! You'll understand what I mean in a minute.

The flight I was working on, the so-called direct, but not non-stop 727 aircraft, went from St Louis to Tulsa, then to Oklahoma City and on to Las Vegas. My last leg was a quick connection with me changing planes to a Lockheed 1011 from Vegas to ORD. Much to my mounting worry, we were late into TUL, left late and were later into OKC, left even later, and as we landed in LAS my flying partner looked out the window of the first class door and said, "I think that your L-1011 just blocked out from that gate."

"Whaaaattt! No way, I'm going to make it." She couldn't imagine how! The agent opened the first class door and I shot out into the jetway with my luggage, before the passengers, and ran down the jetway steps outside onto the ramp. The L-1011 was just sitting out there on the tarmac, engines running. I ran to the front of the L-1011, looked way up to the pilots who were both leaning up to their windows now looking down at me. I kept pointing to myself and then up to the airplane. I was mouthing to them, "I should be up there."

I must have been just a spot of yellow to them (I was wearing the yellow Stan Herman uniform we had at that time) but it seemed that they had gotten the message because, lo and behold, a hydraulic truck pulled up next to me and the driver said, "Get in. I'm supposed to deliver you up to that plane."

The pilots decompressed the cabin, told the service manager to disarm the first class door and the hydraulic truck hoisted me up to it. The service manager opened the door and I said, "Hi, I'm your extra." He looked up to the clouds and exclaimed, "Thank you God!" Now this was an oversold flight and the flight attendants were none too happy that their extra hadn't made the flight. More work for everyone with all of those meals that had to be served in coach. Needless to say, they were thrilled to see me.

A while into the flight the flight engineer came back into the cabin and said he didn't know what to do in filling out my pay card. This was way before everything was computerized, and we actually carried around a large paper pay card that the flight engineers would fill out for each leg of our trip and the captain would sign. Then we turned them in when we got back to our domicile. So, here was the conundrum, he said, "We blocked out before you blocked into LAS. How could you possibly have been on two different flights for the same five minutes?" A baffling situation indeed. Hmmm … this would require some creativity.

I don't remember how he chose to fill out that pay card, but I feel fairly confident that an eraser might have been used. But I clearly remember what a grand evening it was in downtown Chicago that night!

It is amazing, isn't it, how we seem to achieve the impossible in covering our assigned flights when we REALLY wanted to?

Fire … My Match Collection

I WAS COMMUTING from Orlando to NY and there were flights almost hourly to JFK and LGA which was a great thing for commuters.

Back story: I was a newbie and collected matches from all of the hotels we stayed in, and kept them in a plastic zipper pocket in my crew kit. I must have had fifty or more there. Don't ask why I kept them there, I still don't know.

Anyway, back to going to work in NY. I boarded the flight to JFK and sat down in the last row of first class. The agent came on and said she did not get my ticket from me and asked me to get it quickly, so she could close the door and the flight could depart on time.

I frantically opened my crew kit (we called our suitcase that) where I had the ticket and started rifling through it. Viola found! I grabbed the ticket, gave it to her, and quickly closed my crew kit back up. I thought all was well until a few minutes later, I could smell burning. I'm looking all over. What is that smell?

Luckily, there were only a few people in first class, two rows ahead of me. I look down and I see smoke coming from my crew kit. You have to be kidding me, OMG! When I shuffled through the bag for the tickets, I must have ignited the matches.

I quickly opened my crew kit and threw my on-ground beverage, which was a soft drink, inside it and then slammed it closed. What now? I see the working flight attendants walking through the cabin sniffing. Sniffing, sniffing, sniffing! About ten minutes later, the captain comes on the PA and says, "Ladies and gentlemen we were ready to leave but we have a sulfur smell that we can't isolate on the aircraft. Mechanics will be on shortly."

I'm still on probation and you could get fired for anything! I'm saying to myself, "Holy shit. What now?" I was so stupid and a chicken little that I didn't want to admit to this, let alone go up an hour later to the cockpit and say, "You won't believe this but ..." So, I gathered my belongings and told the flight attendants, "I think I'm going to go take the LaGuardia flight next door. Have a good day," as I slithered off the plane not wanting to be noticed.

When I arrived at LGA I found that they had cancelled the flight I single handedly helped to cancel. I think the statute of limitations is over now and it is safe to tell the story.

Thank you. I feel so much better now. Sorry if any of you were on that flight all of those many years ago! My bad ...

In Sickness and In Health

ONE EPISODE ON the plane that sticks out in my mind was being a flight service manager on a L-1011 from SFO-JFK. A very tall man from the Ambassador (business) class came up to use the forward lav. He was standing by the phones. Yes, we had phones for a while on that plane.

When they were first installed on board the reps for Lockheed flew with us to make sure we could explain to the passengers how to use them. (And believe me they weren't cheap!) However, the best part was we all got to place one call for free. You can imagine when we called someone on the ground and told him or her we were calling from the plane at 33,000 ft., now that was a total shock in the '70s.

But getting back to this passenger, he was about 6'4." I had a liquor cart by the first class boarding door and was collecting coach liquor sale money, from a real cute blonde flight attendant that fit every blonde joke you have ever heard.

My back was to the gentle giant. Well, the giant fainted ... passed out ... whatever. His back hit my back. I was thrust against the liquor cart but bounced right off of that sucker while the big man kept falling.

The landing position for me was my skirt was about waist high and my legs were straddling his neck! His glasses were askew and his eyes were rolling. I started shaking his face asking if he was OK. As he was starting to come to, the blonde leaned over the cart and sounded like a Valley Girl from California, "I think his condition would improve if you would get off his face." Did you ever want to just, pardon me here, "bitch slap" someone? I controlled myself and said, "Help me up!"

As I was struggling to get up and he was gaining consciousness I'm sure we made quite the picture. Fortunately, he was fine and had a sense of humor as he later requested that I not tell his wife about our rather compromising position.

Michelangelo in Cairo

HERE IS ONE I'll tell you about our captain. He won't mind as he told the story himself for weeks afterwards.

We were laying over in Cairo and he had been given one of the suites with a kitchen, living room, bedroom, luggage room and bathroom. Quite the suite! But when you wake up in the middle of the night, you can do a lot of wandering around to find the "john." In the process he missed the "john," opened the hall door and found himself standing in the hallway "naked as a jaybird" with the door shut and locked behind him.

There was no night hall guard in sight and he wandered around in his nakedness looking for some way of getting out of this predicament. Finally, he found a closet with some old sheets and wrapped himself up in one, until thankfully, a hall security guard appeared, to let him back into his room.

He made the mistake of telling this story himself, the next day, on the way to Riyadh. Oh, we couldn't let this go by. What to do? When we got back to Cairo very late that night, my flying partner and I got some fig leaves off the trees that were in front of the Nile Hilton. After having a sandwich, we went up to the captain's room and slipped several of them under his door along with a poem. Which we will definitely not repeat here. The next day he asked everyone who it was. We played dumb and someone said to him, "Maybe it was the hall security guard?" And everyone laughed.

We continued slipping fig leaves under his door at night for the rest of our Cairo layovers that month. Suspecting toward the end of this month that he had started staying up and watching, so he could open the door on us when we were sliding the leaves under it, we would quickly scurry off like bad kids to slip into an indented space to hide in, a few doors down from his.

We got away with it several times until one night he must have staked himself out right by the viewing lens and caught us. As the door flew open, he yelled, "Gotcha!" Thankfully, he did have his pants on.

Oh, how we laughed and giggled like teenage girls. We had him going most of those layovers over these fig leaves!

And you wonder what we did on layovers?

Hermés ... No Not Necessary

IT WAS THE end of a three-day domestic trip, Columbus, Ohio into JFK. I was working the first class galley position and would be taking care of the first class passengers by myself while my flying partner went to coach to help them.

After we were airborne, I was getting some supplies out from a side compartment that was in front of a passenger seated in row two in the aisle seat, 2D. I just happened to look at him, and he was looking at me, and I smiled and said, "Hello, how are you this afternoon?" He said, "I'm fine, thanks for asking."

I'm busy serving drinks and finally when I got everyone served, I started going through first class again offering my passengers more ice and mix for their drinks. I just happened to say to 2D, "Are you going home to New York or going on to Europe?" He says he is going on TWA to London. Now I love London, one of my favorite cities and I said something to that effect to him. He replies, "Are you familiar with Hermés?" I laughed and said, "I'm familiar with Hermés but Hermés is not familiar with me."

He then went on to say, "You've been so pleasant to everyone on board today. One of my best friends owns the Hermés store in London. I'd like to send you a scarf just to say thank you for the great service. What is your favorite color?"

I was slightly taken back but immediately said, "Sir, that is so thoughtful of you but I get paid to be pleasant to my passengers. I couldn't accept a scarf even though it is very kind of you to offer."

He looks me in the eye and says, "No, you don't understand. When you were getting those things out of that storage area you said to me, 'Hello, how are you today?' You could just as easily looked away, got your things and never said anything. I noticed that you were also talking with the other passengers too. That is really good customer service."

Again, I went back and said, "You know I just can't accept a gift. My flying partner is back in coach helping them while I'm up here being offered a silk scarf from Hermés. I would feel very guilty." He looks at me and smiles and says, "OK, then when she comes up here ask her for her address, and her favorite color, and write it down on a piece of paper along with yours and I'll send her one too."

My flying partner comes up from coach after helping them and I tell her about the scarf offer. She is looking at me with a quizzical stare and says, "You've got to be kidding?" I shrugged my shoulders and said, "I'm not. Better go back there and thank him."

Two weeks later what arrives in the mail? You guessed it a manila envelope and inside it is an Hermés envelope with my beautiful red scarf. No note, nothing. But I did see the return address was from Columbus, Ohio and he was the President of a "big time" company.

To say I was surprised when the scarf arrived, would be an understatement! My Mother had taught me well, the art of writing a thank you note, so my skills were put to use.

And you're wondering did my flying partner get her blue scarf too? YES …

O Dark Hundred
Airline Jargon For Very Early In the Morning LaGuardia Airport

A PASSENGER STROLLS down the jetway pushing a carpet sweeper. Yes, a Hoover upright! Couldn't help ourselves, we all started laughing. Guess the gate agent thought we wouldn't mind? Sometimes it just isn't worth the argument. The flight to O'Hare was half-empty, so we just strapped it in an empty seat in an empty row. Best passenger on the flight.

She Was Past Cheeky

I STARTED FLYING as a purser at the beginning of July in 1965 at the tender age of twenty-one. Hardly a man of the world then. The first six months of employment with the company you were on probation and felt like most of the time you were walking on eggshells. God forbid that a passenger should write a complaint letter about you, that would surely be the end of your flying career.

In the purser position, you were in charge of the service, safety, selling duty free items and the flight attendants. Otherwise called everything.

Approximately two months into my probationary period, I was working a flight from JFK to London which was full in first class and the coach section was about half full. Approximately four rows from first class, entering into coach, was a woman seated in an aisle seat who was a relative of Winston Churchill's. Note here, I did not know this, the last name on the passenger manifest did not say Churchill. Evidently, she was a fairly frequent flyer with TWA which I also didn't know and her reputation preceded her "as in being difficult," another thing I didn't know about. Remember I'm a total rookie here.

Have any of you ever heard of Roy Orbison? He was one of the biggest Rock n' Roll stars at that time. Well, he was sitting across the aisle from her and his entire band was with him filling up a number of rows of seats in this part of the plane too.

Now back to Miss Difficult. She started acting up in various ways, and disturbing people around her with her complaining, and demands for this and that. I had to keep going to her to see what the problem was and what I could do for her. Meanwhile Roy Orbison and his group were getting a kick out of this and started egging her on. Thanks Roy! But in Roy's defense he finally said, "Not to worry if needed they would back me up."

Remember I said that I was in charge of selling duty free items on the plane. Well, Miss Difficult at one point bought a carton of cigarettes from me, but would not pay for them. I attempted a few times to ask her politely for the money, but she always just dismissed me. The final time I asked her she threw the entire carton in the air backwards and hit another passenger in the head with them. I could see my flying career ending now! Fortunately, that passenger just tossed them back to me and never said a word. That was when I knew there was a God on that plane.

Finally, I told the captain what was going on and he said he would call ahead and advise the ground personnel in London to have security meet the flight. When we arrived, who met the flight? TWA ground personnel with a large arrangement of flowers for her, treating her like a celebrity. That was when one of them whispered to me who she was. I'm thinking, "Oh, wonderful," as in NOT!

I had no other option than to write up what we called a flight report about the incident of her throwing the carton of cigarettes and never paying for them etc. If I didn't and the passenger who had been whacked in the head with a carton of flying cigarettes decided to write a complaint letter I would be out of here. As per company instructions all reports had to be delivered to the flight attendant office in JFK upon our return, in this case from London. I planned to do it personally because as I said, I was worried about losing my job and wanted to make sure they understood exactly what had happened.

As I sat across the desk, watching a supervisor read my flight report, he started to laugh. And then what do I hear him saying? "Oh, we get reports on her all of the time when she flies with us. We're used to it. Don't worry about it." And, I thought I would be in trouble!

Definition of cheeky: slightly rude or showing no respect but often in a funny way. As I said she was past cheeky. And definitely not funny!

Poor Little Rich Girl

IT IS JUNE 17, 2019, and I just turned on the television to learn of Gloria Vanderbilt's death at the age of ninety-five. Immediately I had this flashback of having her on one of my flights. Isn't it odd how some people make such a distinct impression upon us that so many years later we can actually still see them.

I couldn't tell you where we were flying to but only that it was on a Lockheed 1011 in the early '80s. The gate agent had told me that we would be having Gloria Vanderbilt on flight that day in first class. My first reaction was, oh I wonder what she is like? Will she be full of herself? Being a socialite, having tons of money, her designer jeans being worn by most every woman in the United States, etc., etc. etc. Hmm this should be interesting.

Well, we had a light load of approximately fifteen people in first class and Ms. Vanderbilt got on the plane with no fanfare, no entourage, no secretary and no attitude. She was beautifully but casually dressed; her skin had not one flaw on it and looked milky white and smooth. She was "very slim", lady-like in manners, rather soft spoken but not in a shy way, and she carried herself with a quiet style that only old money had. One would say that your first impression would be this is a woman who has class, taste and refinement down to a T.

Ms. Vanderbilt was carrying a few small bags and was seated in the last row of first class at the window. I went back to ask her if I could hang her jacket for her and if she would like something to drink. She politely declined both. I returned a few minutes later to offer her a dinner menu and to my surprise, she told me she had brought her own food. Gloria Vanderbilt brought her own food ... then she said, "If you could bring me a glass, some silverware and a dinner plate after we are in the air I would appreciate it." Of course, I would be happy to and if you need anything else just ask. As I walked away, I was thinking well this is one for the books, Gloria Vanderbilt brought her own food.

After we were airborne, I went back to Ms. Vanderbilt and asked her if she would like her table set up now, or would she like to wait for when we started the service. In her beautiful, soft voice, she said she would like to have it now. No problem, off I went to get her tablecloth for her drop down table, water glass, plate, cloth napkin and silverware. As I was setting up everything for her lunch I said, "If you need anything else please ring. And are you sure you don't need some water?" At this point, she had her bag open and had started pulling out food that was obviously "not" airline or fast food, complete with a bottle of water and she said, "Oh, I brought my own thank you."

I have to admit I did giggle a little now at her and said, "You are prepared. Our food is really good but this looks like it is much healthier." She smiled at me and said, "Yes, I do try to eat well."

I checked on her a number of times during the flight and she never wanted anything. Always a polite decline and when she deplaned, she said, "Thank you for your lovely service." Wow, she was the perfect passenger.

As I said earlier, she was quiet, elegant, old money with style. Rest in peace Ms. Vanderbilt, what a life you lived!

P.S. Just a little touch of TWA gossip:

In a story first reported on Nov. 7, 2004 on CBS News *Sunday Morning*, Gloria Vanderbilt told Erin Moriarty of *48 Hours* more about her book, *It Seemed Important at the Time: A Romance Memoir*. The then 80-year-old heiress, who had been married four times, admitted in her memoir to also having thirteen affairs.

Backstory: Vanderbilt grew up in the '40s, a time when the moneyed set of New York mingled with the glittering stars of Hollywood. And Gloria did admit in her book and also in the Moriarty interview to mingling.

She told Moriarty that she had an affair with the dashing Howard Hughes when she was still a teenager. "I would have married him in a minute," she says.

Now that would have been interesting, Gloria Vanderbilt and Howard Hughes married. Hmmm.

She Needed Some Tender Extra Care

BACK IN THE day many passengers who probably should have had someone accompany them traveled alone.

I had a teenage girl, who was maybe seventeen, and had a learning disability board a flight from Albuquerque to Los Angeles. She had an escort for boarding and I was told that she had been at a facility and they had discovered she was pregnant. She was being sent home and her grandparents would meet the flight. OK, probably more information given to me than need be.

There were not many people on board, in fact first class was empty, so we decided to seat her there in the first row, where we could see her for takeoff and landing. Everything seemed to be fine until we started our taxi and she started yelling. My flying partner said, "Go back there now and sit with her for takeoff. I'm afraid she will get up and start running around the aircraft when we are taking off."

Obviously, this was a last-minute decision but probably a very good one since I sat there and held her hand, told her everything was OK, and I was not going to leave her, so she gradually calmed down. Thank goodness, there were no passengers in first class which made it possible for me to watch her for the entire flight and help her with her meal. I might add here that she had unbearable body odor and greasy hair. What kind of a place had she been living in? All I could think of was they should have been ashamed of themselves and her family too.

When we got to LAX an agent met the flight saying her grandparents were going to be late because they were driving up from Palm Springs and she would take her somewhere to wait. I knew she would not understand and she was used to me now, so I offered to stay with her. Well, it was close to three hours before they came to get her. What to do?

As I sat there with her, I thought she was a darling child because she was childlike, and really needed to have her hair brushed and combed out. Don't ask me why, but I got out my hair brush, and comb and proceeded to gently brush her hair. She seemed to really enjoy this, so I gave her my brush and comb and told her these were hers to keep. I only wish I could have washed her hair too.

Finally, the grandparents arrived and I gave my new friend a hug and she smiled a big smile back at me. Now off to the hotel for my long overdue layover. I checked into my room, changed my clothes, called my flying partner and said, "I'm ready for that Margarita now! I'll meet you in the lobby."

As I was walking out of my room to have my much-needed Margarita, who did I run into but our captain. He said, "Are you just getting to the hotel now?" I explained to him what had happened and he said, "That was really kind of you, you went the extra mile for that girl."

Much to my pleasant surprise he wrote a letter to the manager of flight attendants at ORD where I was based telling her about what I had done. She called me and told me she was giving me the Employee of the Month Award. It was a parking space right in front of the hangar. Kicker is, I only got to park there once because the air traffic controllers went out on strike and all the rest of my flights were cancelled. Wouldn't you know it?

Moon Over LA-LA Land

THIS WAS BACK in the era when TWA was experimenting with some really cheap fares to entice the public to fly with us. They had started flying a 707 "all" coach configuration (no first class) from Chicago to Los Angeles and back, only once a day. The flight attendants had nicknamed it "Roach Coach." I know it's not nice but we had to have some fun.

Unbelievably, we served a beautiful thick filet mignon, with twice stuffed baked potato, vegetables, salad with three large shrimp on top of it, dessert and roll with butter. And this was in the day and age when people actually had leg room. All for $79 one-way! Can you imagine today, getting legroom and a filet mignon dinner with all of the sides for only $79 in coach?

Well, this flight was always full. People were lined up to take advantage of this deal. Normally there would have only been four flight attendants working this plane, but with these loads they put on two more to work for a total of six. These two flight attendants were referred to as "extras." They had to sit in an aisle passenger seat, in the row where there was a window exit, for takeoff and landing. I was one of the extras along with a very "newbie" flight attendant. Shall we say short time at the job and a total rookie.

I was working the aft end of the aircraft along with two other flight attendants and we were very aware of a gentleman wearing a cowboy hat because he never took it off. An attractive woman was seated next to him and he was buying her nonstop drinks. They were both probably in their forties. Oh yes, the drinking, the batting of the eyelashes and the staring into each other's eyes, you could just about feel the heat.

Now we had started our descent into LA and were preparing the cabin for landing, when we noticed on this full flight that there were "those" two seats that were suddenly empty. Where were they? The lav possibly? You think?

Oh, you've got to be kidding us! One of the lav doors, in the rear of the plane on this 707, was suddenly moving, in rhythm ... consistently all by itself ... with the "Occupied" sign showing in the lock.

The three of us looked at each other and then one of us started knocking on the lav door, while yelling. "Please return to your seat for landing!" This was another eye rolling moment as I went to my window exit seat. The newbie was already in his seat and I whispered to him what was happening back there.

Remember, we are now on descent and only had minutes before we would be landing, as he jumped up and said, "They can't do that!" and he ran to the back of the plane, as all of the passengers were staring at him. He opens the lav door from the outside, to be greeted with a full view of a "moon" with its hat still on!

All three of them landed back there in various states of standing. Ouch! I seriously doubt if any of them were comfortable, if you get my drift. Fortunately, I didn't have to look.

Bite Off a Nose or an Ear

IN THE EARLY 1970s, TWA flew many charter flights. These were usually fun trips and gave us an opportunity to go to places that TWA might not fly to, or you might not be senior enough to hold a regular scheduled flight going to that destination.

Saudi Aramco, which was the Saudi Arabian Oil Company (formerly known as the Arabian-American Oil Company), was based in Dhahran, Saudi Arabia. We flew charters transporting US employees to these mid-east oil fields. These were great trips, usually with lots of flight time and layovers in Ireland, Paris, Rome and obviously Houston.

The plane we flew then was a Boeing 707 with an all-first class configuration. Meaning all of the seats from front to rear were first class seats not coach. There was a modified first class service, not all of the whistles and bells that you normally get in first class on an international flight but still great food, free movies and free liquor. Which I might add we loved because there was no hassling with money for these. We just had to be sure "not" to overserve liquor to the passengers who were mostly if not all oil rig workers.

Managers, supervisors and some Arabian oil sheiks were seated in the front of the plane and everyone else was seated next. The only women and children on board were Muslim and frankly, there were few of them.

My flying partner and I were working the aft galley and cabin while two other flight attendants were working the forward galley along with a purser. We worked from the back forward and they worked from the forward back with the five of us meeting in the center of the plane. During the meal service, a passenger came running into our galley saying someone was choking. We were serving steaks and one of my greatest fears came true. I ran up to the passenger, who was standing in the aisle, asked him if he could speak and he nodded his head NO. Immediately I tried to do the Heimlich maneuver. The man was huge and I couldn't get my arms around him. Another passenger seeing me struggle got up, whacked him on the back and out flew some of his New York strip steak into the next row of seats. Crisis averted!

After dinner, our oil riggers always wanted more drinks. We would mix them in the galley and watered them down on purpose. You'll understand why in a minute, who needs drunks on board when you have this to deal with.

Just as we sat down in our jump seat to take a break after the service, a commotion broke out in the cabin. Two of our oil riggers started brawling! It progressed from the aisle and into our galley area trapping us in our jump seats. Fortunately, we had our phone there to call the pilots. Out came the flight engineer with an axe that was in the cockpit, (scare tactic) but he quickly turned around and went back into the cockpit when our brawling oil riggers could have cared less.

The next thing we hear is the captain blasting on the PA system, "EVERYONE IN YOUR SEATS AND BUCKLE UP! We are approaching Bangor, Maine and I will land this bird and have the police meet the flight. You have 20 minutes!" It worked! They were quiet for the rest of the flight, probably the prospect of being arrested and losing their jobs finally came through. $$$$$

Note: The two guys were a little bloody but didn't require much bandaging. The goal was to bite off the other guy's nose or ear! Sure glad that didn't happen. Can you imagine trying to keep a nose or ear on ice to be sewn back on. Later the captain laughed about it and said not to write a flight report to the company about this incident. Something like this happened to him before. Really?

Ralph Lauren Uniform

ON ONE PARTICULAR flight I noticed a very cute man boarding and sitting in my cabin section. Being shy around men I am attracted to, I did not know how to go about getting him to notice me. Therefore, I decided to give the most flamboyant emergency demonstration of my life. All smiles, some direct eye contact with him, and a few of what probably looked like the Lakers cheerleader moves.

After what I thought was a FABULOUS demo, he actually motioned for me to come over. I leaned in to hear the words I wanted to hear ... "Hi, my name is—. Would you like to meet me for drinks later?" But what he actually said was, "Your fly is open." I bolted to the rear of the plane and never looked at him again for the rest of the flight. Thanks Ralph Lauren uniform!

Don't Call Me Peter Pan

I HAD ONLY been working as a TWA flight attendant for about four months, and was excited to be flying a trip from JFK to Amsterdam that TWA only flew in the summer. Little did I know how exciting this trip would be ...

Here is the back-story: In the working crew there were also four really brand-new flight attendants too. Having "newbies" and that many of them on one flight can be trying on the rest of the experienced flight attendants. Why? Because too many explanations had to be made to the newbies for the service to flow smoothly. Normally everyone just gets on the plane, knows what they are supposed to do and gets busy doing it. And they are very savvy about all of the safety issues we had to deal with. You will understand that comment later.

Back to the flight: We had just started the meal service in coach and had served four rows, when we entered into a weather system that caused severe turbulence. The plane was shaking and dropping so much that you could literally feel the pressure on the aircraft, as the pilots were trying to fly to a higher altitude to get above this awful weather.

As we were rocking and rolling in the sky, the captain came on the PA system, and said that all passengers should remain seated with their seat belts securely fastened, and for all flight attendants to immediately take their seats too. I was trying to walk down the aisle, holding onto the tops of seatbacks to steady myself, and at the same time to look like this is no big deal to give the passengers confidence as we bounced around.

When I finally got to my seat, I noticed one of the carts was not properly secured by the door. It was the liquor cart, which weighed about two hundred pounds. And on top of it there were passengers seated right next to it. Now the turbulence had gone from bad to really bad!

I could see the liquor cart moving on its own as we were dropping, shaking and trying to gain altitude. As a relatively new flight attendant, I have to admit it was all very scary since I had never been in that kind of turbulence. Nevertheless, the one thing I knew was, I had to secure that cart before it tipped over and fell on those passengers.

You would not know this, but there were locks at each door that were supposed to be used to attach those carts to during the service. We called them "mushrooms" (think of a mushroom now growing out the ground) because you pulled them up approximately four inches, and then slipped the cart over the top of them, the cart was then locked into the floor and could not move. Mega important detail especially in turbulence!

I pulled the cart forward to find the mushroom, which was difficult in this circumstance, remember I was dealing with two hundred pounds, and the plane was shaking and rolling. I spied it, bent over and pulled up the mushroom. With that done, I quickly went around to the front of the cart and started to push it toward the mushroom to lock it on. Precisely at this moment the plane just dropped out of the sky! The cart and my feet were suspended in midair, and I felt like I was frozen and could not move a muscle.

The look on the passengers' faces was one of fright and amazement all in one. I knew I was suspended in the air, and in that split second all I could think of was "please" don't let that liquor cart land on my feet, please, please!

Well, when the cart and I made contact with the floor, it was so gentle; it was like an out of body experience ...

How I was able to get that cart attached to the mushroom then, God only knows. But I did and finally made it to my jump seat, to ride out the rest of turbulence while contemplating what had just happened.

I never mentioned to anyone what I experienced, as I thought they would think I was crazy, but I have never forgotten that feeling of weightlessness to this day. One could only explain it as very strange, as well as terrifying! This was something I never wanted to experience again. And our passengers probably never wanted to experience that kind of turbulence again either, as they all clapped when we landed in Amsterdam.

By the way, I had some strong words for the "newbies" who did not attach that cart to the mushroom. As in, lock those carts on the damn mushrooms, I'm not Peter Pan!

I Can Hardly Wait to Get to the Pub Tonight

IRAQI LEADER SADDAM Hussein ordered the invasion and occupation of neighboring Kuwait in early August 1990. Alarmed by these actions, fellow Arab powers such as Saudi Arabia and Egypt called on the United States and other Western nations to intervene. Hussein defied the United Nations Security Council's demands to withdraw from Kuwait by mid-January 1991, and the Persian Gulf War began on Feb. 24, 1991 with a massive U.S. led air offensive known as Operation Desert Storm. After days of relentless attacks by the allied coalition in the air and on the ground, U.S. President George H.W. Bush declared a cease-fire on February 28th; by that time, most Iraqi forces in Kuwait had either surrendered or fled.

As explained above, Saddam Hussein had invaded Kuwait and the world was on edge as to what was going to happen. It was a major topic of discussion even down to the London cabbies. We were laying over in London and had our three-hour nap, after being up all night flying over from Kennedy, and were now off to Harrods for some R & R known as shopping therapy. As I got into a hackney with my BFF and flying partner, we told the cabbie to take us to Harrods.

Off we go through the crowded London traffic when the cabbie says, "Are you Americans?" I was sitting behind him and could see my face in his rear-view mirror and I said, "Yes," as I nodded to him in the mirror.

He then said, "What do you think President Bush is going to do with Saddam Hussein?" Now remember we are still in a slightly addled mind state having only had three hours of sleep. I had to ponder on this for a few seconds and then I heard myself saying, "I think he is going to clean his clock."

The cabbie sits up straighter, looks into the rear-view mirror at me, and says, "Clean his clock. Is that an American expression?" I turn to my BFF and say, "Is that an American expression?" She nods yes and I tell him, "Yes, it is an American expression."

By the smile on his face and his tone of voice, you could tell he thought this was great! Then he says, "I can hardly wait to get to the pub tonight to tell the blokes that one." I'm thinking, OK, glad you liked it.

Now flash forward and I am back in the states, at my hair salon. The woman who owned it was a Brit and I would take her British magazines for her shop or British candies that she loved instead of tipping her. We are chatting away, and I tell her about the cabbie and what I had said to him. My question to her was, "Why did he like my American expression so much?"

She proceeds to tell me that in Cockney Brit speak, clock means face. So an old American expression was now introduced to a Brit. Bush 41 cleaned Saddam's clock. Cheers mates!

Scuse Me

THIS STORY COMES from a friend of mine. He was working the meal cart and was chewing some much-needed "breath freshening" gum, after having eaten garlic and onions on a sandwich.

Working the cart, serving hot meals, he asked the passenger at the window seat, "Would you like chicken or beef?" At which point the gum flew out of his mouth, landing in between the legs of the sleeping passenger in the aisle seat.

After turning bright red, but maintaining his cool, he carefully reached between the sleeping passenger's legs to retrieve the gum ... don't you know the passenger woke just at that moment ... OMG! A man with his fingers down between another man's legs, and frankly it was a little too close to the crouch. Yikes!

My friend had a very deep southern accent and said to the startled passenger, "Scuse me, sir, but thars sum gum tween yur legs and I was tryin to git it before it messed up yur pants."

The professional, my friend was, he followed through! The passenger ended up thanking him for a "wonderful" flight upon deplaning.

Oh well ...

How it Began and Ended ... 1954–1959

BEFORE I STARTED flying for TWA, my mother and I thought that my sister should interview with the airlines for a stewardess position. At the time, she worked in a laboratory looking at mice all day long, and we thought she needed to get out into the real world. But after we phoned a number of them seeking information we gave up.

As fate would have it, I accompanied my best college friend on the train from Providence, Rhode Island to Boston, Massachusetts for her scheduled interview with TWA. The TWA interviewer was so excited to have two Brown University college grads in the room at the same time that he interviewed me too. Well, surprise, we both got accepted for the next level of interviews.

My friend had also interviewed with United and liked their uniforms better than TWA's, so she accepted a position with them. I know, pretty shallow but those were the times and this job was meant to be a lark! Only for a few years at best.

So, off to Kansas City I went for my first plane ride alone and my second interview. All I remember about it was that I was 5'9" tall and was worried about being too tall, so I wore a full skirt and "flexed" my knees to make sure when they measured me that I was a little shorter. Well, it worked and I was welcomed to training and the exciting world of TWA!

My first flight was on a Martin 404. Whoever came up with the idea of making you the only hostess on your first flight should have been fired. Thank God, I had a wonderful cockpit crew who told the passengers there would be no coffee service on the next leg, as we were expecting turbulence. They saw that I was totally too pooped to pop after two coffee services, and a meal on the previous three legs that were only twenty minutes long and forty passengers who wanted their money's worth!

As you probably know, we were not getting rich with this job. Therefore, it necessitated having a number of roommates. I remember my first apartment in Jackson Heights, NY that slept five but there were six of us. The rule was we slept in the first bed we came to when we got off a flight. The good news was there was not really that many times all of us were there together. My second home was a great three-story house in Forest Hills Gardens by the famous tennis courts there. We were actually able to pick up matches at the last minute because tennis was not the popular sport that it is today. They also had a wonderful piano bar there, which was known for Roger Williams before he was THE Roger Williams.

Note: For those of you who don't know him in 1955 Williams recorded *Autumn Leaves*, the only piano instrumental to reach #1 on Billboard. It sold over two million copies, and was awarded a gold record. Billboard magazine ranks him as the top-selling piano recording artist in history with twenty-one gold and platinum albums to his credit. Plus, Williams was known as the "Pianist to the Presidents", having played for nine US Presidential administrations, beginning with Truman. His last White House performance was in November 2008 for a luncheon hosted by First Lady Laura Bush. Plus, he played for us in that little piano bar. Probably not the highlight of his career.

But enough about Roger Williams; back to my third apartment, which was a sublet from a man who had three carpets on each floor, and yummies for the cockroaches who scattered noisily if you turned on the light at night. The good news, it was furnished. The other thing I remember about these abodes is the neighbors who expected wild airline parties but never got them. Fantasy can be so much more exciting than real life.

I know you are thinking, "What was the job really like in the '50s?" Well, you wore the proverbially girdle whether you needed one or not. There were no microphones/PA systems when I started, so we stood in the front of the cabin and projected our voices, i.e. YELLED. And yes, I would give cockpit tours when the cockpit doors were allowed to be open. I remember asking little girls to pass gum and they loved wearing my hat while they were doing this. We even had fan clubs where we could write to them. They were so cute!

Yes, as everyone knew, we were the "airline of the stars." Oh, the celebrities I had on flight, from Debbie Reynolds, Dennis Weaver, Cyd Charise, Eddie Fisher, Sammy Davis Jr., Walter Winchell, Joe DiMaggio, Walt Disney, Hal Holbrook of Mark Twain fame, and the NY Yankees with five Hall of Famers on the team then. But the one I will remember the most was former President Harry S. Truman who asked me to share a cup of coffee with him, so he could get away from the autograph seekers. Now how many people have coffee with a President of the United States? They all contributed to the life I look back on with joy and pride. But trust me, they didn't have to be famous to be nice.

The nicest passenger on one of my flights was a Navy officer who needed a band-aid for some bleeding on his neck. Of course, I spent some time talking with a number of passengers on purpose "so" I could really spend some time with him. By the time I worked my way back to this handsome man with the band-aid, the other hostess had brought him one. BUT, I sat down next to him, and we talked, and talked, and eventually made a date for the next day. I remember thinking … "Mrs. John Shields that sounds nice …" And as they say, "The rest is history." He was my one true love.

In parting when I left TWA on my final flight, I told the passengers they all represented my passengers over the last five and half years I flew. It was all I could do to choke out a thank you to them for giving me such a great life. If only I had had a crystal ball ...

Nine Carats and We Aren't Talking Carrots

I WAS WORKING a flight from Los Angeles to Boston when who got on? Mia Farrow! She had just been engaged to Frank Sinatra and it was all over the newspapers.

Mia had her short haircut then which I might add was adorable on her and she probably did not weigh more than a hundred pounds. Some in the newspapers had described her as waif-like, but I thought she was gorgeous and so very humble.

Don't ask me why, but before you knew it, she was showing me her engagement ring. To say it was a showstopper would be putting it mildly. The ring looked like a "huge" diamond Bumble Bee. Later I read in the paper that it was NINE carats and Frank Sinatra had paid $85,000 for it. Remember this was in the '60s too!

I have to admit it was great cocktail chatter on my part telling my friends that Mia Farrow had been showing me her engagement ring.

Now flash forward: who do I have on the flight from London to JFK but Mia again. Now she was married to Andre Previn and they had six children together, three of which were adopted. If someone asked me to describe her, I would say she was a real earth Mother, very down to earth, and always so sweet and loving to her children.

The children were all great too but I have to admit that one little girl by the name of Lark and I bonded. She became my little shadow on the plane and we hung out together the entire flight.

Lark and I would stroll from first class to coach a number of times that day and I thought to myself, as we were walking past the other passengers, "If you only knew that Mia Farrow and Andre Previn were in first class and this is one of their sweet little daughters."

Decades later, I read that Lark had died on Christmas Day. I'm sure Mia Farrow and Andre Previn were devastated. I too had tears in my eyes remembering that lovely child who I fell in love with many years earlier. Rest in peace sweet Lark ...

From the World Famous to the Infamous

NOW WHEN I look back on my flying days, I realize it was pure liberation and exhilaration, not to mention opening my eyes to an entirely new world with no comparison to the Harry Clever Airport in New Philadelphia, Ohio, the town in which I grew up. I know I can hear you now saying to yourself, "Where in the world is that?" Short geography lesson, it is seventy-one miles south of Cleveland, Ohio and 119 miles northeast of Columbus. Its claim to fame is, John Glenn did his initial flight training at the Harry Clever Field. Enough said.

Now this was back in the '70s and the world was truly opening up for me. I remember it like it was yesterday, the world famous opera singer, Luciano Pavarotti, came bounding on board, literally arms flung OPEN and in his beautiful operatic voice, as if he was singing just to me, I heard him saying, "HELLO." Upon arrival, it was the same except a bit more because he actually stopped at the door before deplaning, and in his micro enchanting performance again sang to me, "GOODBYE," in his effortless high C! I vowed at that point I would see him in concert someday.

But shortly thereafter, as I was still pretty much a flight attendant larva who had not yet gone through my metamorphosis into a world class sophisticated traveler, I was working a flight from ORD to Las Vegas. There was a first class passenger traveling with an "entourage around him." He had the diamond horseshoe ring, a very expensive looking suit replete with a dress shirt that had French cuffs, gold cufflinks and a silk tie. And lest we forget a pocket square too. His companions said very little and I knew even less!

At the time, I was a huge fan of Mario Puzo's novels, like *The Godfather*, and had grown up on the television series *The Untouchables* that was about

Eliot Ness and his federal agents fighting the mob, so you can understand now where I was coming from.

But back to this passenger, he truly did look like a glamorous crime character straight out of the Warner Brothers studio. I will add he was very polite! Upon deplaning, I told him that he looked like he just stepped out of a Mario Puzo novel. He kind of grinned, pinched my cheek with a little shake and then said, "Aren't you a cute little thing."

I likely wouldn't have remembered this but as I turned to the agent, who was greeting him, this agent was turning white. I later found out my polite passenger was one of Chicago's most notorious crime bosses. Ignorance is bliss! My metamorphosis was beginning now.

Should Have Waited

IT WAS JUST another flight from LAX to STL, except we did have on Rudolf Wanderone Jr. in first class. I can hear you now thinking, "Who is Rudolf Wanderone Jr.?" Ever heard of Minnesota Fats, an American professional pocket billiards player, who became quite famous. Anyway, Minnesota Fats with his custom billiard carrying case was in first class. He was nice, quiet and wasn't calling notice to himself. You could tell though that some of the passengers did recognize him as they boarded.

Boarding was normal, no problems and then the dreaded announcement from the cockpit came. "Ladies and gentlemen, we are having a problem and a mechanic will be boarding in a few minutes to see what the issue is. We will keep you posted." It was the usual look of frustration on most of the passengers' faces now. About ten minutes goes by and then the captain gets on the PA again and says, "Well, the mechanic has informed us that we have such and such a problem and it will take an hour to fix." Audible groans could be heard now from the passengers and then the familiar cry started from all of the businessmen, "I need the OAG!" OAG stands for *Official Airline Guide*. It was a "huge" paperback book and had all of the flights in the U.S. listed by origination, destination, airlines, and times. Remember this is before computers and cell phones.

Immediately it was like wild fire spreading through the cabin. There is an American flight leaving in forty-five minutes. Now, off go around twenty of them with their briefcases and garment bags, fleeing like people rushing away from a tsunami.

Minnesota Fats and probably forty-five people were left on the flight. But here is where it gets interesting. About fifteen minutes later the captain gets on the PA and says, "All is fixed, return to your seats, so that we can leave immediately." And off we went to St. Louis.

As we were starting our descent into STL, I went into the cockpit and asked the captain, "By the way, are we going to beat the American flight into St. Louis?" He said, "Yes, they're about twenty minutes behind us."

Ah, so now the fun begins! I told the other flight attendants that we were ahead of the AA flight. "Let's go over to the AA gate and meet 'our' former passengers as they deplane."

Oh, the plot thickened here. Not only did we go to the gate, but we just simply walked across the tarmac to where the AA flight was going to pull into. There weren't jetways then in STL, so we approached the AA agent who was going to push the stairs over to the front door for deplaning. We told him what we wanted to do and he started to laugh and said, "Go for it."

Now, as the AA passengers deplaned down the steps who was waiting to greet them to STL, but four TWA flight attendants in uniform, standing in a row like a welcoming committee.

The AA passengers looked a little surprised as we said, "Welcome to St. Louis." But then one by one our peeps who had to leave us like lemmings going to the sea, started to come down the stairs.

They were "stunned" to see us as we said, "You should have stayed on board, we've been here twenty minutes waiting on you," with our biggest TWA grins! Good times and loved Minnesota Fats. Oh, what about our former passengers, most of them laughed.

Thanks For the Memories

Photo of 1st class cabin on L-1011 with swivel seats and movie screen. The flight attendants pictured are <u>not</u> the authors of this story. Photo courtesy of the Jon Proctor Collection.

WORLD FAMOUS ENTERTAINER, comedian, dance and song man, TV and movie star, Bob Hope was on my flight from Chicago to Las Vegas.

Mr. Hope was traveling in first class and after we landed and parked, he was the first passenger to get off the aircraft and walk down the stairs to the tarmac. While the other passengers were deplaning, I saw him struggling to climb back up the stairs. This was no small feat, as he was going against the tide, and he was shaking hands with everyone who was walking down the stairs. You could see people saying, "Wow that was Bob Hope."

When he finally got to the top of the stairs, he told me that he had forgotten his beloved golf club and he couldn't go on without it. Now it was my turn to buck the tide of passengers in the cabin who were trying to deplane. I made it to his seat and checked out the overhead compartment and sure enough there was the golf club.

As I returned it to him, before he left again, he kissed my cheek and called me his life saver! I learned that day not to judge what is important to people. That golf club had probably seen many an USO military show and who knows maybe had been twirled by Mr. Hope on one of his TV specials too.

Thanks for the memory Mr. Hope, you were a fabulous entertainer!

Four Levels of Anxiety

I HAD RECENTLY taken up golf and was really into it! So much so that one month when I was flying with a friend of mine, who was a "three-handicap," yes you read right, who had offered to give me lessons on our two-hour ground stop in Las Vegas, I was immediately in! Note: It was springtime in Las Vegas, so it wasn't brutally hot yet, this is important.

Picture a flight attendant with her suitcase and her five-iron boarding the flight. Common sense had dictated that a driver or three metal wood was just too long to carry around, so it would be the five iron. For those of you who are golfers I'm sure this makes perfect sense.

We arrive in Las Vegas and the passengers deplane leaving us now to our own devices called golf lessons! Needless to say, one cannot swing a golf club on a plane, putt maybe? Kidding! Remember a jetway is not flat so where to go? Outside of course to the ramp.

Having anticipated my lesson, I had intentionally worn my uniform slacks and had tennis sneakers to wear. Can't take lessons in heels and golf shoes with metal cleats on the ramp, I don't think so. Off comes the jacket, on with the sneakers and down the jetway stairs we proceed to the ramp.

Now picture two flight attendants in uniform sans jackets, out on the ramp, under the wing of the plane to be in the shade, her instructing and me swinging away. I'm sure any of the passengers who were looking out the windows from the terminal couldn't believe their eyes. For whatever reason it didn't seem to faze the ground workers at all. And who knows what the control tower was thinking? Probably now we've seen it all.

After about a half hour lesson, we went back on the plane to freshen up before our next group of passengers boarded. Note: On this particular flight I was working the lower galley. On the L-1011 the galley for business class and coach was in the belly of the aircraft, and we had two lifts for flight attendants to use to move the serving carts up and down in and obviously ourselves.

So, I casually put my five iron in the lift and off I go to the lav for that needed freshening up. When I came back someone had used this lift and it was in the lower galley. I push the up button for that lift and a few seconds later I hear this awful grinding noise! AND the lift is not moving now. What the blank is racing through my mind! I then put two and two together, and realized that my five iron must have fallen sideways and now was keeping the lift from moving.

Instantly four levels of anxiety set in ...

MY FIVE IRON! Oh Geez—did I break my five iron? I can see it bent now!

THE LIFT! OMG is the lift broken?

EVEN MORE PANIC BIG TIME! How was I going to explain this one to the captain if the lift is broken?

MY JOB! Vulgarity whispered on my lips. I could lose my job if this lift is broken!

I push the down button now praying that the grinding noise will stop and the lift will move. There is a God, the noise stops and the lift starts moving down. Oh Lord, thank you!

I frantically jump into the other lift and take it down to the galley. I'm literally jet propelled, I know bad pun, jump out of that lift, and fling open the door to the other lift as my five iron falls out of the door towards me. There was the culprit who wouldn't let the lift move.

I pulled it out and looked it over. Didn't look bent? Totally amazing! Now does the lift still work? I hit the up button and YES it was smoothly operating. If I could have had a drink then I would have or maybe two.

Moral of the story: Buy Callaway clubs ...

P.S. I know you are thinking, did she have any more lessons from her friend on the ramp in Las Vegas? What do you think?

Jokester or Not

I WAS WORKING a full load on a flight from Paris to JFK. Everything seemed to be in order until ...

I was stopped by a passenger waving at me and he had something in his other hand. He said, "Look what I found in my salad." I looked down into the palm of his hand and there was the largest black bug, like a "super" large roach, on its back with its tiny legs stuck up in the air. It looked like it was plastic. I've never seen such a large black bug!

My first reaction because it was so large was this guy is pranking me, this has to be fake. I looked at him and started to laugh and said, "Good one." He looks at me like I'm the rudest person in the world and then says, "No, it was in my salad and I think it drowned in the salad dressing when I put it on the salad." I'm still thinking you've got to be kidding me, this is a rubber bug. Thank God I didn't come out with something smart as in, "Well, we just wanted you to have some more protein or I hope the bug didn't eat much of your salad."

At this point, I leaned down to take a closer look because I still thought he was kidding me and then I saw a few of the small legs still moving. YIKES! I have to admit I jumped back and let out a tiny squeal of shock.

Talk about embarrassing, needless to say, it was many free drinks for him the rest of the flight and a new salad.

Sorry if you are reading this, I really thought at first you were pranking me.

Just a Little Help From a Friend

WE WERE FLYING a Boeing 767 and had a light load of passengers and only one of note in first class, Al Unser Jr. who had just won the Indy 500. He was traveling with his race team manager and they both seemed very nice, unassuming and not demanding.

My flying partner and I knew one another very well and had even socialized with our husbands as a foursome where we resided, since we didn't live that far from one another. She had confided in me that her son, who was approximately 12 years old, was being bullied at school. Always hate to hear things like that because I think we all have been there at one point in our lives, whether as a child or an adult.

But back to our flight, all of a sudden, I thought, hey she should get an autograph from Al Unser Jr. for her son. He could take that to school and no one else would have one. Stop those bullies in their tracks. I made that suggestion to her and she said, "I never ask anyone for their autograph." I replied, "But this is different, it is for your son," and she said, "No, I just don't have the nerve to do that."

Well, I did! As Al Unser went to the lav I thought now is my chance. I approached his manager, and just explained to him about the bullying situation and wondered if Mr. Unser could give me an autograph for my flying partner's son to show off at school. He was so kind and said, "Of course. I know Al will do that and I even have some photos in my briefcase of Al standing next to his car that he just won the 'Indy 500' in. He can sign one of them for her son."

WOW this was great! Mr. Unser came back to his seat, and I could see him speaking with his manager, and then he looked in my direction and waved for me to come back. He had a picture on his drop-down table and said, "What is his name?" I gave it to him and he wrote a wonderful note with the boy's name in it. I was thrilled to give this to my friend now.

Since I hadn't told her what I was doing she was shocked. I said, "Better go back and thank Mr. Unser now." Of course, she did and was thrilled to have it for her son.

The following week we were flying together again and I asked her, "So, how did the picture go over at school?" She looked at me beaming and said, "He is the popular kid now. And what is really funny, they didn't know his mother was a flight attendant and flew all over the world. He didn't know if they were more impressed with that or Unser's autograph, but he is a total Rock Star now."

Celebs and flight attendants can't get much better than that. And good riddance to bullies!

My Father Is My Hero

IT WAS DECEMBER 22, 1975, and my family was traveling back from New York City to Milan, Italy where we were living at the time. We had been Christmas shopping in New York and taking in the sights and sounds of the holidays. My father was a purser for TWA and was actually working our flight back to Milan that evening.

One of the wonderful benefits of being a family member of an employee for TWA was that you could use company passes for travel. Moreover, not only that but you could travel in first class too if the seats were available. They were, so that night my mother, brother and I were seated in first class, but we even had our own row to ourselves. In addition, we had the ever-watchful eyes of my father, making sure that we were always on our best behavior. One of the stipulations of traveling on a company pass.

The flight had a festive air to it, and was filled with holiday travelers, their children, and the famous tenor, Luciano Pavarotti, no less. Pavarotti liked to travel in coach and sit over the wing section of the aircraft because he said that was the safest part of the plane to fly in.

Our flight 842, a Boeing 707, left approximately two hours late, with a passenger load of eight people in first class, 117 in coach and a crew of three in the cockpit and five cabin personnel. Even though we were two hours late, the flight had made up thirty minutes of that flight time for our arrival in Milan.

As we approached the Malpensa airport there was extremely heavy fog shrouding it and we could not see anything outside of the windows. Our captain attempted to land but then circled again, to finally set the Boeing 707 down on the runway, or so we thought. Within a matter of seconds, there was a very strong impact with the ground. We were NOT on the runway but actually had landed outside the runway, then struck a transistometer and a

CAT 11 television camera. We felt like we were skidding now on our wings. Little did we know in that nanosecond that the landing gear and all four engines had separated from the aircraft in that slide. People were screaming in fear and being tossed around like packages. Then came the final crash where the fuselage split between first class and coach, and the cabin filled with cold dense fog!

I was only turning eleven years old and still remember this as if it was yesterday. The aircraft split right behind me and my seat was thrown to the opposite side of the plane as the nose was also flipped to the side. I was actually trapped in my seat then.

I was knocked unconscious for some time, but I recall when I came to, trying to get out of the plane from a little crawl space, but I could not move. I did not realize that my seat belt was still fastened, and that my long hair was tangled and caught in the wreckage.

As I started to call for help, I heard a voice saying, "I hear someone." It was the captain and my father who were combing the wreckage to make sure everyone was off the aircraft. My father immediately recognized my voice, and we later learned from the captain, and a few other crew members that he instantaneously gained superhuman powers, and was single handedly lifting seats and pieces of wreckage to make his way towards me.

When my father and the captain found me, they quickly assessed the situation and I recall hearing the words, "We need a knife." I heard several voices calling out for one and was later told that a small pocketknife was thrown to them from someone outside the aircraft. The captain then proceeded to cut my seat belt to free me, but then they realized that my long hair was caught in the wreckage and I heard him saying, "We need to cut her hair."

I remember saying, "Noooo, not my hair," and then hearing my father saying with a very stern voice, "Do you want to get out of here?" He then took the pocketknife from the captain and proceeded to cut my long hair to free me from the rubble. The two of them lowered me into the waiting arms of a flight attendant, whose name was Linda, who then ran away from the plane, while carrying me to safety.

An aside: My father and the captain had already pulled the first officer out of the cockpit where he had sustained severe injuries to his back. They had used a piece of the fuselage as a makeshift stretcher to carry him away to a safe area.

As an adult now who survived this terrible crash in the dense fog, I know that the entire crew did an amazing job of evacuating the passengers. They kept everyone calm and away from that aircraft, which was covered in jet fuel and could possibly have ignited. We were definitely Traveling With Angels on that flight because it was truly a miracle that everyone survived.

My father continued his career with TWA where he retired as a flight service manager.

Daddy you will always be my hero ...

Tipping and We Aren't Talking Restaurants

OH, THOSE WONDERFUL layovers in Zurich. The hotel we stayed in was a Sheraton and was built at the base of some mountains with beautiful woods. It was summertime and the weather could not have been better. Note: there also was a corral behind this hotel where they kept "cows." This will become an integral part of my story.

We had a wonderful layover, but our flight service manager had disappeared the night before with another crew, another airline, and we did not see him until pick up the next morning, when we were going back to the airport for our flight home. He did not look very "perky" that particular morning and then told us about his unique experience the night before. He had gone "cow tipping," or as some like to pronounce it, "cow teeping."

Here is how that escapade started: We had all gone to the pool to get some sun and "debrief" after we got in from our flight, and that is where he met the other airline crew and ended up going out to dinner with them. Sometime during dinner, they exchanged stories of growing up. He was Portuguese; they were from the Midwest farm country in the U.S.

One of their pastimes (and maybe some of you have heard of this) was "cow teeping." Did you know that cows sleep standing up? I guess the idea is to walk up to a sleeping cow and push it over ... REALLY?

After dinner and much vino, they decided to try this with the cows behind the hotel. It was very dark and late, so they could not see very well. Our flight service manager made the grave mistake of picking the BULL to "teep over." I know, I can see your eyes now! This bull was NOT happy about being woken in the least and "charged" him.

The fence around the coral was not that high and made out of wood, BUT ... it also had a wire running across the top of it and YES FOLKS there was a small electrical current running through it. As he went to climb over the fence to escape the charging bull, he straddled the wire. Now, I don't care how small of a current it was, when it's in your crotch it AIN'T TOO PLEASANT! He made it out without being gored by the bull, but was walking funny for a while. Stop laughing. I doubt very much if he ever went COW TEEPING again.

Yee-haw ... git along little doggies ...

It Is True ... She Did Have Violet Eyes

IN 1956, I was based in Chicago flying out of Midway. I was working flight 88 which originated in Los Angeles, with a stop in Chicago and then on to LaGuardia. This particular Super G or Super Constellation (Connie) had sleeping berths. When the flight came into Chicago, I was informed by the hostess (we were not called stewardess or flight attendant then), who had worked the flight into Chicago from Los Angeles that Elizabeth Taylor was sleeping in one of the berths.

I was given a list of instructions that had been written by Ms. Taylor. One of them was that about forty minutes before arriving in NYC, I was to awaken her and give her a glass of orange juice. So, at the appointed time I woke Ms. Taylor and offered her a glass of orange juice.

Now you might not know this, but people actually slept in their lingerie or PJ's in those sleeping berths not like today in their clothes! Oh, Ms. Taylor looked divine in a beautiful pink silk robe, which she had on over her nightgown. She asked me if I could assist her to the bathroom with her garment bag while she carried a small overnight case. How do I remember this from so many years ago? This was Elizabeth Taylor! Some things you never forget even at my age. Twenty minutes later, she emerged from the lav, looking stunning and totally like a movie star!

After we landed, I helped her gather her things and handed them to the ramp agent who started to carry them down the steps for her. To my surprise she turned to me and said, "What a lovely way to travel," and then handed me what I thought was a $5 bill. I have to admit those beautiful "violet" eyes mesmerized me; I thanked her and told her we were not allowed to take money, but it had been my pleasure to have her fly with us.

When I handed the bill back to her, I saw that it was $50, which would have been a huge windfall for me at that time in 1956. I will always remember Ms. Taylor who was one of many "stars" who flew that particular flight and one of the nicest!

Open Mouth and Insert Foot

THE TIME WAS very early in my flying career, in the late '60s. After the inflight meal service was finished, I went into the cockpit to sit down and spend a few moments out of the cabin, which was already "blue" with cigarette smoke.

In the course of the conversation with the captain, he told me that he had a photo he would like me to see and pulled out his wallet. The photo was of a beautiful baby boy with his lovely young mother, both smiling for the camera. Oh, it must be his daughter and grandchild.

I'll preface the next part of this story by saying that the captain was probably around mid-fifties, but to a sweet young twenty-something he was OLD. So, I smiled and said the appropriate "aww-beautiful." Now, if I had just left it at that I would have escaped with no damage done. Nope I just had to complete my thought. Seeing the proud look on his (old) face I added, "Your first grandbaby?"

The proud look instantly disappeared while at the same time there was a distinct snort of laughter from the vicinity of the flight engineer's desk. The captain stonily informed me that NO it was his new son. Oops, time to exit!

I made some lame comment of congratulations and promptly got up to return to my "blue heaven." Once safely out the door and out of sight of the captain, I turned to look at the flight engineer, grimaced, and being young and limber pulled my right foot up to my open mouth. Another SNORT.

Major lesson learned!

You Light Up My Life … Or Maybe Not!

IN MY EARLY days of flying out of Chicago, I often flew the extra position, otherwise known as a "5th." Usually this was a series of flights that were known to be regularly full and involved a meal service that might not otherwise be completed without an additional flight attendant. These were not particularly popular positions because rarely did you fly with the same crew twice, therefore, the usual camaraderie of flying partners was missing. However, as a junior flight attendant, your seniority might be improved by flying these less popular flights. Also, these trips often included longer layovers in cities you might not otherwise be able to hold.

So it was that I found myself holding a series of flights this month with long layovers in Boston, one of my favorite cities for shopping and visiting historical sites. This particular flight landed in BOS in the evening and gave me the entire next day to putter around the city. The major drawback was on the third day, the departure was at the ungodly hour of 5:45 AM, which the crews referred to as o' dark-hundred. The hotel was the Sheraton at Copley Square, a pleasant, upscale facility and very centrally located, but for unknown reasons, this hotel turned out to be my arch nemesis.

The first trip I arrived on time and found my crew transportation into town, checked in and relaxed with room service before hitting the sack. The next day was great; up at a civilized hour, shopping in the cute boutiques, visiting select historic sites and clam chowder for lunch before returning for an early bedtime. I had no sooner fallen asleep than a commotion in the hallway and a reflection of lights on the ceiling of my room forced me to the full-length glass windows of the 24th floor, looking out on the street. The entire front of the hotel was lined with firetrucks! Like a well-trained flight attendant, I put my hand to the door of the room to test for heat and feeling none, I cautiously cracked the door open.

Many other guests were also peeking out and there was a vague smell of smoke. I knew better than to panic but I was now wide-awake. I wet a towel, stuffed it along the base of the door and tried to call the front desk, which was naturally busy. Knowing I had only hours before my wake up call, I went back to bed.

About ten minutes had passed when someone was pounding on my door. Again, with the chain still attached, I cracked the door and there stood a firefighter, in full regalia; hat, heavy jacket, pants, boots, gloves and he was carrying a nozzle. Just a nozzle. Didn't seem very functional but what did I know; HE was the fireman! And he told me to stay in my room. Now this seemed annoying to wake guests to tell them to do nothing but HE was the firefighter.

Unfortunately, I didn't get much sleep the rest of the short night, and spent several hours staring at the ceiling and pondering the nozzle/no hose situation. I found out later that someone had set off a "smoke bomb" on a lower floor and the smoke rose through the air ducts. So much for a good night's sleep.

The second trip was again routine, and I spent a day browsing through Faneuil Hall Marketplace and enjoying fresh seafood. I turned in early and hadn't been asleep for more than an hour when a door slammed, and an argument ensued in the adjoining room. A man and woman were in a heated debate over her implied behavior. Yes, I could hear every word and most of it was pretty ugly with each calling the other unpleasant names. After about twenty minutes of this "entertainment," the voices trailed off and I tried for another shot at sleep.

I had just drifted off when I heard the woman sobbing and the man uttering words of comfort. Sighing, I quietly listened until the sounds were again replaced by silence. I rolled over and closed my eyes. Suddenly the roles were reversed, and the man was sobbing! He promised he would never raise his voice to her again (I could only hope) if she would only forgive him. He carried on a bit less than she had and once more, there was quiet. Calculating how long before my wake-up call, I made another attempt at sleep. It was not to be.

Next came the familiar sounds of hotel living, the bed in the next room rhythmically rapping on the wall right behind my head accompanied by the usual moans and groans. Dear God, this finally has to be the last act in this drama! Maybe I will get an hour or two before my alarm goes off. I waited for the climax, (horrible pun!) and the blessed quiet that I hoped meant they had nodded off.

Just on the edge of drifting off, my eyes shot open. A horrible falsetto voice, I was never sure whose, began singing, "You light up my life, you give me hope to carry on ..." Three choruses and he/she knew all the damn words!

Needless to say, it was a VERY short night. The next morning as I was leaving around 4:45 AM, I slammed my door as loud as possible and slid a note under their door that read, "Bravo! What a performance!"

I traded out of my last Boston layover. The chowder wasn't worth it and I needed rest ...

It Was the '50s ... Fate ... One Inch to Tall

I WAS BORN and raised in Knoxville, Tennessee and graduated from the University of Tennessee in 1955. In the fifties you either got married, taught school, became a librarian, or worked in an office as a receptionist or secretary. I was going to be a teacher, but my secret dream was to become an "airline hostess."

I really wanted to do it in the worst way and had interviewed with American and Delta who were the big carriers in Knoxville then. Well, I'm sure you all know that there were certain standards we had to meet to be hired and one was height. I was tall, 5'8" but willowy and slim.

Guess what? I was one inch too tall for them! They flew Douglas equipment and didn't want the hostesses to be over 5'7". I'll explain this in more detail later.

Very disappointed and having my dream crushed I decided that I would teach, but then I saw an ad in the *Knoxville News Sentinel* that TWA was going to be in Knoxville at the Andrew Johnson Hotel, which I might add was the BEST in town then. I really didn't know anything about TWA. Why? Well, it was considered to be a Yankee airline. They just didn't fly into many southern states then.

Off I went in my best suit, heels, hat and gloves to the Andrew Johnson Hotel for my first interview. I made it through! The next thing I know I'm on several airlines to get to Kansas City for another and final interview. As I told you earlier, the other airlines used Douglas equipment, but TWA flew Lockheed aircraft and they could accommodate taller hostesses because the overhead racks were higher. To think that something as mundane as an overhead rack could keep you from getting a job.

Well, TWA wanted to expand and one of the questions I was asked during the interview was if I would like to be based in Knoxville or Atlanta. Would I? Silly question. I later found out that they hired a number of us from the south. And what did we get to do? Well, we were representatives with the company executives when they were being wined and dined, by those southern cities, to open bases there.

We just smiled a lot and cooed in our southern drawls about how much we loved those southern cities. And I might add we were not allowed to drink in our uniforms, but we did sneak a few alcoholic beverages when no one was looking. Possibly a little Southern Comfort? Wink ...

But I digress, I remember one of those dinners very well when TWA was being courted in Nashville. The Andrea Doria had collided with the MS Stockholm and forty-six people had died. I have to admit I had never heard of those ships then, but the influential Nashvillians that we were with knew all about the Andrea Doria and were despondent.

My days of being based in the south never materialized since TWA didn't open any hostess bases there, but my new world was opening up to me. Yes that Yankee airline that flew all over the world and flew so many celebrities, I was part of it now. Ah the memories, from Eddie Fisher who sang to us all the way from LAX to NYC, Lucille Ball who seemed to have taken over one of the bathrooms just for herself to everyone else's chagrin, Bob Hope, Steve Allen, Satchmo and President Truman after he was out of office. I even had an episode with a movie star whose name will go unmentioned, who wanted me to climb in one of the sleeper berths with him! Trust me I closed his curtain in a hurry! I was so young and naïve, if it had been today what I would have said.

And speaking of things changing. My granddaughter doesn't believe me when I tell her about how we had flight "checkers" who met us before we went out on a flight to check our grooming, but also would flick their fingers on our derrières to make sure we were wearing the required girdle! Can you imagine now someone flicking your derrière at work?

But my fondest memory was when I was working alone on a Lockheed L-049 Constellation. It was a night flight from SFO to NYC with a stop in Albuquerque. Who came on board in ABQ before the passengers but none other than Howard Hughes! As most of you know Mr. Hughes owned TWA then and was very famous in Hollywood as a director and producer of films. He strode into the cockpit, announced that he would be flying the plane, and told the captain to take the first officer's seat and the first officer could ride on the extra jump seat in the cockpit. I was so young at the time that I didn't realize it was a very historic thing that was happening. I'm sure others saw Mr. Hughes flying TWA planes, filled sometimes with his movie star friends too, for he was always near his beloved airline.

Many years later, my mother and I happened to be at the Princess Hotel in Mexico City when Mr. Hughes died there. It was so sad, this once powerful man, who was a handsome daredevil, died alone except for some caregivers he employed.

It all seems like so long ago when this young woman from Knoxville got teased by the flight crews, all the time, about her southern accent, and asked if my shoes were comfy as they would say, it was probably the first time I wore shoes. Yes, they were mostly Yankees but I grew to love them. Just think it was all because I was one inch too tall!

I know there must be a God for it was the dream job of a lifetime ...

Postscript ... I flew from 1955 to 1960. In those days, the airlines would fire a stewardess for a variety of reasons such as turning thirty-two, getting married, pregnancy and even weight. I quit in 1960, due to the fact, I was getting married and then I had two children.

Well, things started changing in the late '60s with the EEOC and Title VII. One day I went to my mailbox and there was a letter from TWA with the familiar red letters at the top. They offered me my job back and my choice of bases. Oh, I was so tempted! But with two young children, two dogs, and a husband who traveled on business a lot, let alone not having the money to hire a full-time nanny it was out of the question. Wish I had kept the letter to have shown it to my granddaughter who still can't believe that an employer could do those things.

JFK-FCO-CDG-ORD-JFK
or
Twilight Zone

I WAS AN international purser on what TWA called reserve because I was so junior in seniority that I couldn't hold what we referred to as a line of time. This meant I was basically at the company's mercy, and they could call me out for any flight, any time, at their discretion.

A call came from scheduling to cover a flight with a full cabin crew. I was told the first leg of the trip we were to ferry the plane (no passengers) to Rome. We thought our crew was covering a charter flight the next day. After our Rome layover, we returned to the airport as scheduled and asked what type of charter we would have now. TWA operations in Rome said we would not have any passengers and that we were ferrying this plane to Paris. OK, off we go to Paris with no passengers.

Upon arriving in Paris, catering came on with our crew meals and we asked what group we would be having on board, and they said, "No passengers, you're ferrying this plane to Chicago." Another "what" moment? Again, we had an empty flight.

After we were airborne, I decided why shouldn't we dine while watching a movie? I turned on the movie and we munched away while enjoying a movie on our way to Chicago. Upon arrival in Chicago, we asked what now? TWA scheduling said, you are laying over here and tomorrow the entire crew would be deadheading, which means riding as passengers, on a flight home to JFK.

Was this The Twilight Zone? On the other hand, maybe I would wake up and have dreamt this? No, it really happened, and we got paid for this too.

Just Another Day At the Office

I WAS A purser and hired in 1967. I first flew out of JFK, flying international flights, and then transferred to LAX in 1970. In LAX I also flew the purser position on our international flights to Honolulu, Guam, Hong Kong, Bangkok and back.

We were boarding passengers in Honolulu for Guam, when a very inebriated man came in the front cabin door of the Boeing 707. Why me, was all I could think of now? This called for a quick meeting with the captain about this passenger. I didn't want him on the plane because from past experiences I knew, problems on the ground always mean problems in the air.

The captain came out of the cockpit, spoke with him, and then said to me that everything was fine since he promised not to drink and he would be good. SURE! We've all heard that story before and I don't want the passenger on board. Well, he is the captain and that was his final decision, the passenger would stay.

Shortly thereafter, we left HNL for GUM, and after we were airborne this inebriated passenger came up to the 707 first class lounge area and sat in one of the seats. He was joining another passenger who was already sitting in this lounge area. You guessed it, it did not take too long before the two men got into a yelling match and it looked like a fight was starting to erupt. So much for being good.

I immediately went into the cockpit and told the captain what was happening, and it was probably time for someone to come out of the cockpit to handle this problem.

Now it was the flight engineer who appeared to quiet down this situation. One small problem was that it wasn't really quieting down. After he goes back into the cockpit and they have their powwow, they decide to restrain the inebriated passenger who was in the lounge. You guessed it again, who had to help him? Who do you think?

Those trusty seat belt extensions came in handy sometimes since this was before plastic handcuffs were provided for us. Praise the Lord, he is restrained and eventually falls asleep. Let us call it what it was, passed out.

All was quiet for quite a while, until later when the captain came out and spoke with him. Well, you guessed it, the captain decided to take the restraints off. You know where we are going again. At this point, the passenger hit him. A total sucker punch.

You know what the captain did then? He went back into the cockpit and sent out the flight engineer again to restrain the passenger. The flight engineer and moi! I don't think this was part of my job description when I was hired? Combat pay? Never saw that on a pay card. Surprise, surprise, guess who was met in Guam by the authorities. As they say, just another day at the office.

Moral of the story: Don't let drunks fly!

A World-Famous Clown Doing His Thing

RED SKELTON WAS seen frequently making airline connections in St. Louis. He was always by himself just walking the concourse to his next flight. People were very surprised to look up and see this world-famous actor, comedian and artist standing in the check in line with them. Note: Mr.

Skelton was famous for his clown comedy sketches, as well as many more characters on his television show. His artwork was also on display at the Sands Hotel in the '60s and was predominately drawings of clowns.

Here is a great memory: I was an agent in charge in St. Louis, otherwise known as a "Red Coat" for the red jackets that we wore. My most AMAZING encounter with Red Skelton was the time I saw a group of about twenty people huddled around two people, crouched down on the floor of Concourse C, in St. Louis. My airline "emergency mode" kicked in thinking it was a heart attack, or other medical emergency and I ran to see what it was.

When I got to the group, I looked down and there was a TWA flight attendant on her knees, leaning forward with her uniform jacket off, exposing the back of her white blouse to the person behind her. The person was none other than Red Skelton and he had an assortment of colored markers in his hand which he was using to draw a clown on the back of her blouse with.

I asked, "So, you travel with a box of markers?" The flight attendant said, "They're mine. I knew I'd run into Mr. Skelton one day and I asked him to draw a clown on my blouse." Mr. Skelton said in his comedic voice, "I never turn down a beautiful woman's request." Everyone laughed.

It was amazing to see the vibrant colors take shape and the final clown drawing appear with the famous Red Skelton signature on her back. I said aloud, "That drawing will be worth a lot of money someday!" And they are.

Thanks for all of the great memories and rest in peace Mr. Skelton. We know you are still entertaining and drawing in heaven!

Once You Have Tasted Flight

I WAS RAISED in Sedalia, MO and graduated from Central Missouri State College. As you might remember Kansas City, MO was a TWA town. In fact, the state was really TWA country too. It was something that the state was very proud of and to work for TWA, well you were also proud to tell people that. So not knowing what I really wanted to do with my life, and the call of adventure was ringing in my ears, I decided to apply for a hostess position.

In those years, we had not graduated to being called a stewardess, yet let alone a flight attendant.

I finished training in July of 1966 and my assigned base was in Chicago. My best memories there were getting to actually work as a hostess on the Constellation, and getting stuck in NYC at Christmas in a snowstorm that closed all the airports. Mere shades of adventures to come.

In January of 1967 I transferred to Kansas City, and flew domestic flights until May of 1968 when I became a hostess dining instructor, at the TWA training center in downtown Kansas City. During my first year of teaching, there was a new position that opened up. It was to create the in-flight dining service procedures for the about to be launched magnificent 747, and much to my delight I was chosen along with another instructor to do this. This became a full-time job and remember we did not have computers at the time. So, the dining service classes we were preparing to be taught to the flight attendants would be by slides and written instructions.

Our adventures with this project started at the Boeing facilities, in the Seattle area, where we made several trips. We got the grand tour and a group of us, about twenty, from various departments including the corporate offices were the first class that Boeing trained on the 747. We learned the aircraft from nose to tail and even did a slide jump from an elevated mock-up for the upper deck emergency slide. The thing I most remember about that jump was that at the top before jumping you could not see the bottom of the slide. Yes, it was intimidating.

The first view of the interior we saw was after we climbed a set of stairs that were rolled up to the far back right-hand side door. When we stepped inside everyone was awestruck at the size, even more so because there was nothing in it except the circular staircase all the way in the front of the plane that went up to the upper deck and cockpit. It looked like acres of space, and we all wondered how we would ever do a meal service for 400 passengers on this airplane. Hard to imagine now but all we had ever worked on were single aisle airplanes in those days.

Back at the training center the other instructor and I spent countless hours trying to work out a service on an airplane with two levels, two aisles, five zones and an upper deck. This was done using paper shells attached to a magnetic board and small round magnets we could move around. Quite a challenge but remember it was 1969. No computers, no cell phones, no texting. The stone ages!

In December of 1969 we (instructors from the training center and flight attendant supervisors from JFK) were excited to be a part of a promotion flight for TWA and Boeing. We were on TWA's airplane, but it was still owned by Boeing. The flight started in Seattle and there were about seventy-five passengers and crew on board; the crew was all from TWA and the passengers were Boeing officials including their CEO. We decided early on that there was an expert for every function of the airplane.

Our first stop was JFK where we stayed overnight to do two promo flights the next day. The first was quite unusual because a TWA board meeting was being held on the airplane while in flight. One of the areas on the plane had been outfitted with a beautiful board table and refreshments were served by the crew. The Boeing group was also on board. Can you imagine that happening now with all the security and restrictions?

The second flight was to introduce the NY Port Authority to the 747. This was supposed to be the end of the trip, however Air Canada had somehow learned that the 747 was in NY and made a request to Boeing to bring the plane to Montreal. Boeing asked that our TWA crew remain with the airplane, and we flew to Montreal the next day and did two more very similar promo flights. No board meeting this time. We had a great time since Air Canada sent a complete crew of flight attendants and pilots to join us on the adventure.

Afterwards we pre-cleared US customs and flew back to Seattle the same day. While on the flight to Seattle we had a reversal, where the Boeing PR crew served the TWA inflight crew their dinner at the board table, and the CEO of Boeing, at the time, came around and thanked us individually. As a souvenir, we were each sent a model of the 747 in Boeing's colors.

Now it was back to work with a lot more working knowledge of the airplane. Many more hours were spent at the magnetic board and now there was another huge problem to solve. The first delivery was in January of 1970 and it was "one" airplane. Everybody needed it. Pilots, ground crews, training, maintenance etc. Plus we needed pictures to show in the training classes. Only a few even knew what the airplane looked like on the inside. Thus, our next big adventure.

Our manager of in-flight training, arranged for a very unusual time slot for the other instructor, myself, some of our safety instructors and the audio-visual group to go on a four hour long pilot training flight. That wouldn't happen today either. The pilot in charge of the training gave us a small briefing. He would make an announcement at some point, and we were to sit with our seat belts fastened preferably by a wing if we wanted a really unusual experience. They took the airplane into a "practice stall" and you can't imagine how those wings flapped! It was amazing. At the end of the flight, he got on the PA and asked all of us, about seventeen, to crowd in the cockpit for landing, "another no-no," and we did. As we approached the runway, he lifted both hands from the yoke and said, "It is landing itself." Not a big deal now but then it was incredible!

We were supposed to do a practice service in Boeing's mockup, but our service equipment, i.e. food carts and liquor carts were not ready. So, the first time the service flow that we had created was actually performed would be on a commercial flight. Talk about trial by fire! As stories came back, we learned it was a bit chaotic and slight changes were made. However, the final service flow was nearly identical to what we had spent so many hours working out.

There was one last 747 experience. The 747 was scheduled to do what was called a "proving run," giving the stations that it would be flying into a chance to see it before commercial flights actually started. I really wanted to be a part of that and while I was unable to go on the domestic portion, I joined it at JFK and flew the European portion as a staff ground trainer. It was the time of airplanes being "blown up" in the desert by hijackers, and this flight had been targeted, so we were always on high alert. The security was very intense up to and including military tanks at some of the airports.

My favorite stop was Paris. We were still flying into Orly and a hanger had been specially designed for the 747. After it was pushed back into the hanger the wheels sat on metal plates that lowered the airplane, then scaffolding was rolled up around the plane, and I got to do something that those I worked with knew I always said I wanted to do. It was such a behemoth that I always wanted to pat it on the nose, and with the scaffolding I got to do just that. A French newspaper showed up and I was used as the model standing in the engine, a common picture everyone wanted at that time. This flight accomplished one more first for TWA. At JFK we were the first airline to have our own customs, in our terminal, instead of going through the International Arrivals Building. The proving run was the first flight to use it. At this point, our project was pretty much completed, and I was stepping into a new job in a new location. I was now going to be an analyst at our corporate headquarters in NYC.

But as fate later would have it, I would transition to doing the same work on the Lockheed-1011 as I had on the 747. The biggest difference was that we worked with other airlines purchasing the L-1011, to create the serving carts to be used on that aircraft. This meant many trips on the 747 between JFK and LAX to the Lockheed facilities. It also meant going through every nut and bolt on the carts and trying to get all to agree. We would come up with a plan and the U.S. Food and Drug Administration would nix it, so back to the drawing board.

An interesting fact: a feature that was offered by Lockheed for the windows, and was in the mockup, was a polarized window operated by a knob beneath the window instead of having a window shade. We had fun experimenting with it and I just recently read that some company is working with that technology again. I suspect that expense kept the airlines from using it at that time.

We did a practice service in their mock-up, and a funny story about that mock-up was that Lockheed was pushing the lower galley concept but had not originally included it in the mock-up that was in a hanger, to show what they were trying to sell. The airlines wanted to see the galley fully functioning, so they had to dig out a space under it and build the galley. This galley would also require having elevators on it to bring up the food to the cabin. A story related by those at Lockheed was that the "lifts" were originally called elevators, however by using that term the aircraft would have had to have the "elevators" licensed for each city it flew into, so they became lifts. A very good plan there!

The L-1011 was now ready, but could not fly because of too many problems with the Rolls Royce engines being built in the UK. So, the airplanes were built but sat in Palmdale with weights on the wings waiting for their engines.

My next project was on the airplane that never flew. I was set to go to Crowley in England to visit and learn about the Concorde since at that time Boeing was on track to build the SST. For a number of reasons, it got canceled. There is a YouTube video called the *Planes that Never Flew* and it goes into detail as to why the SST never became a reality. I was so excited about this project and it broke my heart when it was canceled.

But as time went by, I realized that I really wanted to do the job I had been hired for, and that it was to fly the line and see the world. I missed the freedom of changing my schedule every month, seeing new cities, exploring the world and meeting so many interesting people on the plane. The great thing about TWA was that if you went into management from the flight attendant ranks they would let you return to flying. We were all so lucky!

I recently ran across this quote; it is so true and why so many of us flew for so long:

"Once you have tasted flight, you will forever walk the earth with your eyes turned skyward, for there you have been and there you will always long to return."
LEONARDO DA VINCI

Thank you, TWA, for the ride of a lifetime from June of 1966 through July of 2003.

The City of Angeles
TWA's First Boeing 747

MOST OF OUR readers would not be familiar with a Boeing 747 aircraft, but in 1970 this was a momentous occasion when the "first" 747 took off for a domestic flight. Today new models of aircrafts come out with little to no fanfare but not in this case.

Why was there so much interest in this plane? Let us explain: First of all, the plane cost $25,000,000 in 1970. Then there was the space; passengers aboard TWA's 747 Super jets had more space than any other competitive airline would be offering. It had 342 seats, originally fifty-eight in two first class sections and 284 in the three coach sections.

Photo of City of Angeles 747.
Photo courtesy of the Jon Proctor Collection.

Between the first class sections there was a small conversation lounge and also first class passengers had the use of an upper deck lounge behind the cockpit that had fifteen seats. These would not be sold. The feeling of roominess that personified the 747 carried over into the size of the passenger seats. In coach, seats were about two inches wider than other jets, or eighteen inches. There was more leg room to stretch out. Shin room has been increased from eleven inches to sixteen inches. And those luxurious first class seats were now a bucket style.

For the benefit of those of you who have never been on a 747, perhaps the best description is for you to picture, if you will, the lost passenger on inaugural Flight One. No kidding. The seat belt sign went on, and there was a gentleman walking in the aisle, obviously confused. "I can't find my seat," he said. He was rescued by an alert hostess. Moral of the 747 story: memorize your seat number.

But back to that glorious first flight and day:

It was 8:54 AM, February 25, 1970 when the first ever domestic 747 was dispatched for its non-stop flight to New York from Los Angeles, opening a new era for TWA. To say that TWA employees were proud would be an understatement. This was the first domestic flight for a Boeing 747.

The inaugural flight had 254 passengers on it and had just been christened "The City of Los Angeles" with a bottle of champagne by Ms. Elizabeth Yorty, wife of Mayor Sam Yorty.

This beautiful gleaming Super jet pulled out of the gate after it had been saluted with air plumes shot into the air by two units of Engine Company 80, the fire unit based at Los Angeles International airport.

The overwhelming favorable passenger reaction to TWA's 747 service was echoed by the nation's press. Syndicated columnist Earl Wilson, who devoted most of his February 24th column to the TWA/Paramount movie premier on the plane, said, "The flight was handled so ably, with never a quiver of doubt, that the sophisticated travel editors and movie experts aboard let themselves go with applause both on take-off and landing ..."

Ned Hudson of the *New York Times*, commenting on the inaugural flight said, "Attending the TWA event had none of the operational difficulties that plagued the Pan Am 747 inaugural flight to London on January 21 ..."

In Los Angeles, the *Herald Examiner*, carried a five-column photo of Mrs. Sam Yorty christening the 747 inaugural flight, plus a full page of pictures and a story.

In a full-page story by John Hughes in the *New York Sunday News* (which had the nation's largest circulation) it was noted, "The 747 had entered domestic service and had passed the test of new equipment with seeming ease ... Captain J. E. Frankum brought the inaugural plane in so gently that a spontaneous roar of approval arose and everyone applauded for at least three minutes ... We were unloaded into TWA's brand-new Flight Wing One ... The service that should generate the greatest interest will be TWA's own Customs clearance facilities," he added.

Flight 100 touched down at JFK at 4:50 PM. But the fanfare was not over yet. It was dubbed the "CAKE-OFF" (as the Long Island press referred to it) with a specially designed sixty pound "supercake" shaped in the form of a TWA 747 for Captain Frankum and other dignitaries to cut at JFK.

Deplaning passengers, guests and passengers waiting to board Flight 1 back to Los Angeles were treated to a champagne reception replete with cake.

Joining Captain Frankum in the cockpit for the inaugural flight were captain Billy Tate and flight engineer John J. Hough. Cabin attendants included Dieter Ruf, service manager; pursers Jim Tighe and Fred Duss, and hostesses, Dana Boyle, Sharon Schreiner, Donna Pennoyer, Katherine Slicks, Pat Tighe, Mickey Wilson, Jan Zimolzak, Casy Linwick, Riki Wakeland, Suzanne Boohar, Carol Kahler, Nancy Ricioli and Bernie Gosey.

The west bound inaugural Flight 1, was commanded by Captain S. Gordon Granger, first officer Hugh Graff and flight engineer Jack Evans. The cabin crew included flight service manager Tom Mannino, purser Egon Ruf and hostesses Margo Whyte, Jona Caldwell, Dianne Reynolds, Mercedes Rivera, Linda Hickey, Virginia Etzold, Pamela Dillow, Caroilne Cullum, Sandra Johnson, Nancy Harbert, Joanne Capece, Marilyn Vezzosi and Judy Ziles.

And so dear readers a glorious age of flying was to begin now with TWA's Boeing 747. This information was collected from the March 9, 1970 company newspaper called the *Skyliner*.

P.S. We mentioned that the employees were very proud of their first 747. Here is more information from the *Skyliner* newspaper.

Preview at JFK Draws Thousands

New York - Nearly 5,000 TWA employees and their families from the tri-state area of New York, New Jersey and Connecticut celebrated Washington's Birthday holiday (Monday, February 23) with a preview inspection of the TWA 747 and Flight Wing One, the world's first operational terminal designed specifically for the 747 and future generation supersonic transport.

The 747 arrived at JFK shortly before dawn on the 23rd, and following an intensive ground training session was opened to employees at 9 AM.

Host Dan Reid, vice president-New York region, said, "It was one of the most gratifying days I've had since joining TWA, just looking at those excited smiles and hearing the enthusiastic remarks about the Flight Wing One and the 747 was enough to really convince you that this is just the beginning.

Here is a comparison of the Boeing 747 to a Boeing 707-331B:

Takeoff thrust for the 747 (per engine) 45,000 lbs. vs. 18,000 lbs.

Wing Span for a 747 was 195' 8" vs. 145' 9"

Overall length for a 747 was 231' 10" vs. 152' 11"

Height for a 747 was 63' 4" vs. 42' 6"

Maximum Takeoff weight for a 747 was 710,000 lbs. vs. 331,6000 lbs.

Passenger Capacity for a 747 was 342 vs. 142

Maximum Space Payload 747 was 112,500 lbs. vs. 41,900 lbs.

Yes, it was big!

The Perfectly Trained Little Pooch

THIS WAS IN the days when first class was really first class. From the passengers to the cuisine! One particular woman in first class stood out though. She had on a lovely outfit, great jewelry and had brought on a dog carrier with a Yorkie in it. The little beastie was totally adorable and very quiet. You wouldn't have even noticed there was a dog in the cabin.

We were serving chateaubriand in first class, carved at the passenger's seat. This lady had ordered it and I noticed at this point that she had her little Yorkie in her lap while I was carving her chateau. TWA had rules that all dogs or cats must be kept in a kennel under the seat at all times. But this little baby was being so good, and I just wasn't in the mood to tell her the dog had to go back in the little cardboard kennel that TWA provided. Why rock the boat or the plane? Besides, no one ever saw the dog out because she was sitting by herself in the last row.

Now I was pouring wine in first class and when I got back to her, I noted that she was feeding the little darling some chateau. Cute, all is well. About ten minutes later, after I had picked up dinner plates, we started our dessert service. As I got to her with the dessert cart I saw no "cute and adorable" in her lap. Hmmm, I guess she put the dog back in the carrier. Oh no ... you aren't going to believe this one.

She had placed one of those little towelettes that you can carry in your purse, on the floor. It was spread out and the little darling is doing his business on it. Yes, the tiniest little poop you could ever imagine. The dog is finished; then she wraps up the little poop. Puts it in a barf bag (we used to have them in the seat pockets), takes it to the lav and throws it out.

No one ever knew but her and me. I promise you it was done so quickly there wasn't even a smell in the cabin. As I said, "Perfectly trained little pooch."

Necessity Is the Mother of Invention

I WAS WORKING the galley position on a breakfast flight. The flight attendant who was working the cabin position came back to me on the ground and said, "Did you get any specials today? I need two Koshers." What is a special? At that time, we meant a meal that was ordered by the passenger when they booked their ticket. It could have been a vegetarian, low fat, Kosher etc. But it had to be ordered when they made their reservation, otherwise we did not have them.

One of the responsibilities of the flight attendant working the galley position was to count the meals to make sure our meal count corresponded with the passenger count. At that time, you would know if you had those "special" meals. Therefore, I knew there were no specials boarded.

Now getting back to the passengers who had requested the special meals on this flight. My flying partner, unfortunately, had to relate the bad news to them that she was sorry, but the kosher meals they had ordered had not been boarded. Note: very important we could not call the commissary and have them rush over specials. We weren't holding flights for that problem.

To her relief the passengers didn't throw a fit and asked her what was being served for breakfast? She told them for the entrée there was a cheese omelet with ham. They asked her if we could take the ham off the plate before we cooked it. She said, "Of course that is no problem."

Now TWA didn't board meals in a warming oven. We had convection ovens to actually heat food, and in first class to even cook many of the entrees. Now this is important, when working the galley position, you did not turn on all of the ovens at the same time because the food in the last couple of ovens would end up being over cooked, think rubber, by the time you wanted to serve it. This required that the ovens were staggered with their cooking times.

The passengers who ordered the kosher meals were one of the last passengers to be served. Well, you know where this is going. I had forgotten to take the ham off of two of the plates in my last oven. So, there were no ovens that hadn't been turned on where I could take ham off of the plates and cook the two omelets. Now the flight attendant working the cabin position says she needs the two without the ham on them. Oh no, just kill me now!

What to do? Sometimes necessity is the mother of invention. I went to the lav and got a handful of paper towels. Fortunately, I had extra clean plates in a drawer. I took out the two hot plates with the omelets and ham from the oven. Plop the omelets on the paper towels and pat off all of the ham juice. Viola, omelets on clean plates with no remnants of ham or ham juice. Problem solved, whew!

Later when my flying partner was picking up their trays they said, "This was the best omelet we ever had on a flight." She smiled sweetly and said, "Oh I'm so happy. I'll tell my flying partner that too."

And we know the secret why … think about it. OK you haven't figured it out, ham juice.

My First Flight ... A Night to Remember

IT WAS MY first flight, and I was greeted by a senior crew. When they learned I was brand new they immediately said, "Just hang out in the lounge and stay out of the way."

The producer, John Sturges, who produced some "no name" films such as *Bad Day at Black Rock*, *Gunfight at the O.K. Corral*, *The Magnificent Seven*, *The Great Escape*, *Ice Station Zebra* and *Hallelujah Trail* was on board in first class. He saw how young and naïve I was and asked if he could see Vegas for the "first time" again through my eyes.

No worries I thought since he would be my chaperone, so I said yes, but I also confided in him that I didn't think I had the appropriate dress to wear to see Vegas. He offered to meet me at the Flamingo Hotel shops and he would purchase a dress for me.

Next thing I know we are off to see the Sammy Davis Jr. show. Who were we sitting with? Mr. and Mrs. Charlton Heston. I could hardly talk! Surely, I do not need to tell you who Charlton Heston was?

After the show was over, we all went up to the penthouse in the hotel for an after party with the Rat Pack. For those of you who do not know that notorious group, it was Frank Sinatra, Dean Martin, Sammy Davis Jr., Peter Lawford and Joey Bishop. When Dean Martin found out I was a "stew" for TWA he laughed, and handed me his drink and said, "He wanted it shaken not stirred." I must have looked like the deer in headlights at this point, my hands were shaking and I could hear him laughing. The wonderful thing was Mr. Martin and in fact all of them were so nice to this shy young thing from Missouri. I was such a bumpkin! I remember Mrs. Heston saying that they were just lucky people, and I looked at her husband and replied, "But, he was Moses." I told you I was a country bumpkin then.

Who was at this party too? Joey Heatherton who said she wanted to adopt me. Joey Heatherton! She was gorgeous! Joey (we were on a first name basis now) had appeared a number of times on *The Tonight Show*, where she coached Johnny Carson on the finer points of dancing "The Frug." Plus of course she had been on *The Dean Martin Show* and I could go on and on, but you can see why she was running with the Rat Pack now.

Over the years I saw the Sammy Davis Jr. show many more times, and he always pointed me out and said, "Hey kid." He was so nice. Can you imagine this was my very first trip and layover? I was HOOKED being a stew. Wouldn't you be?

Postscript: Now I have to tell you something funny. You'll love this. The crew didn't know about Mr. Sturges offering to take me to see Las Vegas, and had told me to stay in my room as I wasn't old enough to go into the casinos. They had tickets to see the Sammy Davis Jr. show and their seats were way in the back, whereas I was up front with Mr. and Mrs. Heston and my important escort, Mr. Sturges. When Sammy saw the Heston's and Mr. Sturges at the beginning of the show, he had the spotlight put on our table and came over to say hello. Remember my crew is in the back of the room in shall we say the cheap seats. They ignored me all the way home the next day. Still makes me laugh! Thank you, Mr. Sturges, for introducing me to Las Vegas and all of those wonderful people.

Making New Friends

AS A REALLY junior flight attendant there was still the fascination, the passengers, the mere chaos of boarding, the actual flight, all in search of reaching our fabulous destinations.

For me going overseas especially to London was a treat, filling my soul with adrenaline and wanting to drink up the mystic of the unknown. There was Big Ben, Hard Rock Cafe, Hyde Park, the Changing of the Guard, Harrods and so much more to explore!

Now the flights from STL to LRH were held by super senior flight attendants, so to be able to pick up a trip, or be assigned this route was always a treat for us newbies. The downside was the senior flight attendants who typically dominated these international scheduled flights were known as the "slam clickers." What was a slam clicker? A crew member who went into their room, slammed the door and clicked it shut, with a see you later.

On this particular flight we actually had a fifty-four-hour layover in London! Woo who, right? I was ready to see the sights and wine and dine. Sadly, it had become routine for many of the senior flight attendants to bid these trips only to accumulate flight time and get paid international pay. Several went to the grocery store and then went to bed, got up later, took a walk, and then went back to their hotel room. I guess I couldn't blame them because it was old news for them, been there done that before. Well, this wasn't happening for me. I've got to see, smell, and check out lovely, charming, cool London.

Since I knew I was flying with some slam clickers, and had met some great passengers on my flight, I decided to meet and hang out with them on my layover. Yay, so now I have some new friends who want to meet me and go do some things in London. And best of all we were all staying at the same hotel, the Kensington Hilton.

I was so excited to actually have someone to do some things with in London; I promised to call them in the morning, once we had all gotten settled and decide on a time to meet in the lobby. Note: the crew had its own transportation for layovers and we didn't see the passengers after they deplaned.

I had "assumed" they were staying in my hotel, the Kensington Hilton. NOT! I called around unsuccessfully to other Kensington area hotels to locate them to no avail. So there go my plans and my new London layover buddies. I was so bummed with the thought of being alone and bored. Lesson learned there, never, never assume.

OK, get it together and get out of this room. Unfortunately, I was now fending for myself on this layover, in basically uncharted waters, sans any crew members. Senior crew did come in handy after all because they knew the ropes. This was going to be a solo adventure, heading to Harrods where else. Oh, another challenge to figure out the "tube." The underground train transportation can be a little confusing when you are first starting out, but I didn't want to pay for a cab. New experience once again! I even impressed myself for successfully making it to Harrods.

Oh Harrods, be still my heart. It was just prior to Christmas and the store was beautifully decorated. It was truly amazing! At the time I was thinking Lady Di loves Harrods and now I could see why. As I started shopping, I stumbled on a Santa scene like no other I've ever seen. It was a winter wonderland filled with not only holiday decorations galore, but ladies dressed up like fairies with Santa. Very different from anything I'd seen in the states.

Being alone and wanting to kill time and licking my wounds from losing my new buddies, I thought you might as well get a photo on Santa's lap, besides it would make a great souvenir.

Much to my total surprise as I am sitting on Santa's lap, I hear some girls yelling, "Hey there's our flight attendant." I could feel my face turning bright red, as I felt silly sitting on Santa's lap now. But they are all yelling at me, "Oh we're so glad to have found you. We had given up hope."

What are the odds that you would run into your new friends in Harrods? After a wobbly start to my day we ended up eating Shepherd's pie, drinking lagers and promising to meet the next morning. Then the best happened when I returned to the hotel. There was another TWA crew in the lobby where I knew some of the flight attendants, and we had a blast together for the remainder of the evening.

As only a flight attendant's life can be, I met my new friends the next day and then returned to the states, to fly another trip a few days later back to London, where again I hooked up with my new passenger buddies. We enjoyed one another's company so much that I'm still in contact with them.

Cheers to TWA, Harrods and good friends!

All Hail Our Pilots

I NEVER DID find out why the cockpit decided to fly through a huge hailstorm into Chicago while supposedly trailing a tornado. Did they have a bad case of "get home itis," or were they just three ex fighter pilots from the Vietnam days who looked at a hailstorm as nothing in comparison to the flak they avoided while flying in their fighter jets? I suspect the severe storm felt safer all things relative.

As I sat in my jump seat, with my seat belt tightly strapped around me, looking aft at some of my passengers, I noticed they were either looking at me or leaning slightly forward in their seats to try and look out the windows. They had grim looks on their faces. I know they were studying my reactions and I was trying not to look concerned. Something like smiling through a root canal!

The last half hour of the flight, the plane seemed to be slipping and sliding with abrupt steep banks and drops. I had never had such a wild ride and fortunately never one exactly like that again. As the plane finally landed at O'Hare, there was wild applause from the passengers and I knew I wanted to kiss the cold, wet ground outside too. I later learned that we were the last flight to land before they closed ORD due to weather.

When I saw the shattered cockpit windows, the tennis ball sized dents and peeled paint all along the nose and wing edges I truly then understood what an amazing job our pilots had done. We could have ended up on the *Smithsonian Channel* docudrama series in an episode on *Air Disasters*.

The really strange thing about being a flight attendant, we all had some type of experience like this but yet we all got on our next flight and forgot about it. Maybe it was sheer madness or the fact that we had total trust in our pilots and our mechanics. On the other hand, possibly it was a combination of the three.

*Flak, anti-aircraft fire.

Felix Unger Strikes

I HAVE BEEN very lucky in my TWA career to have met ALL my favorite celebrities. It was like I sent out a message to meet X and they would appear.

This also worked the opposite way when a neighbor, who had told me she was terrified to fly, walked on my flight and exclaimed as she grabbed me around my neck, "I knew you would be on my flight. I was so terrified to fly today. Thank God you are here!" Her frequent flyer husband was so shocked he didn't speak for half an hour after we were airborne, when finally, he took my offer of a Bloody Mary. Frankly, I think now to his great relief, probably a tranquilizer was kicking in for her. Even today, she tells me I was her Guardian Angel that day. Me thinks it was probably more like the Xanax but whatever ...

But getting back to my favorite celebs, who walks onto my flight with his wife but Tony Randall. Again, it was happening, yes, it was Felix Unger himself! For those of you who might not know this, Felix was a character played by Tony Randall, on the TV hit sitcom *The Odd Couple*. He was the fastidious, neurotic part of the odd couple to the Jack Klugman character Oscar who was the slob.

Anyway, I pulled out all the stops to impress Tony, offers of drinks before takeoff, newspapers, magazines, and super service were in order. That is, until I offered him and his wife a deck of cards.

Picture me holding three decks of cards to offer to my first class passengers when OMG, he grabbed all my cards and said, "I'm hiding these," and proceeded to shove them into the seat pocket. To say I was a little taken back at this would be putting it mildly, as this was not the reaction I was expecting.

Then he said, "I hate the sound of cards being shuffled and slapped around. I don't want them and I don't want anyone around me shuffling them either."

Alrighty then, no cards today. Not one. Felix shall be obeyed.

Maybe art does imitate life ...

Monkey Lamp Blues

I WAS FLYING a trip that was what most people would think, have you lost your mind? We left ORD (Chicago) at 7 AM and bounced around the countryside literally all day. Our layover was only nine hours in Columbus, Ohio. Yes you read right, but we only had one leg home the next morning from Columbus to Chicago and our trip was over. Why in heaven's name would a group of senior flight attendants bid something like that? It was the magic number. What was that? We got approximately nine hours of flight time, plus we were home the next morning at 9 AM. Even though it was hard we only had to do it eight times and we had all of our weekends off. That is called rationalization, but it worked for us.

Everything had been going just fine until one trip coming back from Columbus into Chicago, when the flight engineer opened up the cockpit door and said, "Are you two Jones and Smith?" I said, "Yes," and he said, "The agent meeting the flight has tickets for you to use on United. You're going someplace." And he slams the cockpit door shut.

We looked at one another with that deer in the headlight stare, when my friend said, "They can't do that. We are going back to our domicile. We are at the end of our trip!" I looked at her and said, "Guess what? We aren't on the crew bus going back to the hangar to get in our cars to go home. Those jerks can do it to us."

Well, we open the door on arrival and the agent says, "Are you Jones and Smith?" We nod in the affirmative and he says, "I've got tickets here on United for the two of you to go to Detroit." We're saying under our breath, "What the hell are we going to do in Detroit?" Meaning where are we going after Detroit. He shakes his head and says, "I don't know, you'll have to call scheduling and find out."

After the passengers deplane and our fellow flight attendants who were being spared this torture wished us luck, we slowly walked over to United. Why slowly? Because the flight left in thirty-five minutes, and we were hoping that it would take us thirty-six minutes to get there. Oh, "boo-who" the plane would be pulling out of the gate. Then we could tell scheduling that we were "soooo" sorry, but we missed the flight. Damn United! They were having a mechanical delay so our plan was foiled by ten minutes.

OK step number two. We didn't know what we were supposed to do when we got to Detroit, so our next plan was, we'll drive them nuts. Let's be the last people who get off this DC 10. And we were. There was a TWA gate agent standing on the jetway with this panicked look on his face, "Are you Jones and Smith?" We nodded yes and if our looks could have killed, well you get the picture. He said, "Come down the jetway stairs with me. I have a car parked down there and I'll drive you across the ramp to the plane." We did as we were asked and in the car we said, "Where is this plane going? And why did you need two flight attendants?" He said, "Two of the flight attendants out of the four got food poisoning on the layover and can't work the flight. And you are going to St. Louis." At this point I'm thinking forget the food poisoning, if I could get my hands on them, they would be dead right now! I look over at my friend, and she is rolling her eyes and making a face like she is gagging.

Up the jetway stairs we climbed with our bags, the engines were running, and the passengers had their heads stuck out in the aisle looking at us when we boarded. I looked at the two flight attendants standing there and immediately knew they were light years junior to us. I said, "Ladies, we are not having a good day. We are senior to you and we are using our seniority. We are working first class and you can handle coach." At that point I stuck my head into the cockpit, gave the flight engineer our pay card and said, "I'll talk to you later."

Now it was obvious that the passengers thought we were the reason they were leaving late. Time to clear that matter up. PA in hand I said, "Ladies and gentlemen for your information we are the reason you are leaving now not the reason you are late. We have just flown in from Chicago to work this flight." There were actually some people who clapped.

So off we go to St. Louis. What would happen after St. Louis? More fun, as in not. Then we had to go to Oklahoma City, then back to St Louis and then on to Washington D.C. Remember we had been up very early, had worked from Columbus to Chicago then flown to Detroit, plus we had worked like dogs the previous day and now this. And every leg was full!

The last leg into Reagan airport we had Barry Manilow on flight. Barry was up front with his manager or whoever and they had a lackey who was flying in coach. When we started our descent, the lackey said to me, "I have to get off of the plane before Mr. Manilow to make sure that his car and driver are there and get his luggage." Remember I said the flight was full. Plus, he was really talking to someone who didn't care at this point. I looked this kid in the eye and said, "I don't care if you run around buck naked on this plane, or if you push people out of your way to get off before Mr. Manilow. There is no empty seat that you can take in first class." I know, not nice, or professional but TWA had "broken" me that day.

But the story doesn't end there. Jones and Smith are now laying over in D.C.. We check into the hotel and I'm so exhausted that I have my head in my arms resting it on the check in counter. Jones is telling them we need to be on the same floor. The plan was to have room service together, wine with our meal and get some miniatures out of the mini bar in the room for cocktails before we ordered. Boy did we need a debrief. As in a drink!

We go up to our rooms, and I tell my friend I'll change my clothes, come over to your room, and we can have those badly needed cocktails and then figure out what we want to order from room service. I unlocked the door and walked into a room that smelled like someone had just been smoking a cigar. Gross! Oh, Lord help me. I go over to a window and have to forcibly push it up, so I can air out the room. I could have jumped out at this point, but I was hanging on for a cocktail. The wind blasts through the open window into the room and the drapes are literally flying backwards. Now I use all of what is left of my strength to force the window closed. At this point I look down at an armchair and what is behind it but a pair of men's used black socks. You've got to be kidding me. I went into the bathroom, and for whatever reason looked up and the paint was chipping on the ceiling. With my strength waning now I go over and sit down on the edge of the bed, and what do I see but a ceramic monkey with a lampshade on its head for my lamp. Now it starts, the sobbing ... I can't believe I'm in this room after the last two days of hell!

Fortunately, my friend is in the room across the hall from me and I go over and knock on her door in tears. She opens the door and says, "What is wrong?" All I can say is, "I can't stay in a room with a monkey lamp," through my sobbing. Well, after she examines and smells my room of torture she says, "I'll take care of this. Come over to my room." And off she goes to the lobby and front desk.

Oh Lord, I don't know what she said to them, but she returns with a key and says, "You are in the adjoining room next to me." Well, one would think that would have been better, but I was so out of it at this point that when we opened up the connecting doors to the two rooms, and I saw that I had twin beds, I had my next emotional crisis and said, "I can't sleep in a twin bed," through more sobbing. Yes, I was irrational at this point. My wonderful friend immediately says, "Oh, I slept in a single bed when I visited my grandmother, when I was a child. I'll sleep in that room and you can sleep in mine. Now we really need to have that drink." That was the understatement of the day.

Oh, it should be that easy. Wrong! There were no ice machines on the floor. We had to order ice through room service for $6. Yes, you read right, but at this point we probably would have paid $100!

Now a gentleman with a name badge that says, Jorge, appears fairly quickly with our bucket of $6 ice. He sees that we are looking at the room service menu and says, "Are you ladies going to order room service this evening?" "YES!" in unison was the answer. He said, "Well, I can take your orders right now if you like." Finally, something was going our way and I had calmed down, or so I thought.

We are going for it, the full dinner experience. We order a bottle of wine, and then my dear friend orders her salad and entrée plus a dessert. It is my turn now. "I'll have a salad and the sole almondine. I would like a large pot of tea please, not one of those little teapots, but a coffee carafe of tea and I would like a crème brûlée for dessert."

Jorge says, "Madam we do not have the crème brûlée tonight." Now remember I am still emotionally fragile. I find myself throwing my body prostrate onto the bed and wailing, "But all I wanted was the crème brûlée." Jorge must have seen it all, for he doesn't bat an eyelash, calmly picks up the phone and calls the kitchen. He then says, "We have apple pie. 'No,' I wailed. We have pecan pie. 'No,' I wailed. We have ice cream and sorbet. 'No,' I wailed. 'All I wanted was the crème brûlée.'" Finally, he says, "Madam, they just told me that they have banana crème pie this evening." I sniffled, and patted my eyes and said, "banana cream pie" while sitting up. "OK, if you promise me that it was made today." At this point, picture a woman with no makeup left on, swollen eyes and still sniveling. And what was my friend doing while I was having my nervous breakdown. Mixing our drinks with a smile on her face, like this was totally normal behavior.

Approximately forty-five minutes later our very patient Jorge returns with a wonderful huge table on wheels. It was covered in a white tablecloth with matching napkins, glasses of water, wine glasses, my huge pot of tea and teacups, the salads, the desserts and a wine cooler with our bottle of wine. He removes our entrees from a warming drawer under the table and places them in between the silverware. Then he pulls up two armchairs to the table for us to sit down in. "Would you ladies like me to open your wine now?" We nod, and smile and I control myself not to enthusiastically clap like a small child at a birthday party. As he is pouring our wine, my friend says, "Jorge, would you like to join us for a glass of wine?" Even in my addled state of mind I'm thinking, "Now she has lost it. She is inviting the waiter to join us for wine. Oh, what the hell!" What does he say? "Yes." She goes into the bathroom and gets a water glass and proceeds to pour him a glass of wine. He sits down on the edge of the bed, and now the three of us are engaged in some small talk. Yes, you are still reading right.

When Jorge finishes his wine, he asks if everything is to our liking, and we smiled and said it was lovely. He proceeds to the door, opens it, and then turns to us and says, "Ladies, if you need anything and I mean 'anything' (dramatic pause here) in Washington D.C., just ask for me and I can get it for you." He closes the door and leaves us speechless for a moment. Then we break out into gales of laughter. He must have thought we were crazy. And actually, I was for a few hours. Everyone deserves a break down occasionally! Even today as the two of us look at a dinner menu and it has crème brûlée on it we will laugh.

If you ever hear a woman saying, "All I want is my crème brûlée, you will know it is me."

Remember Karma

DURING MY FLYING career I had to deal with an epileptic seizure, insulin shock, miscarriage, hyperventilation, people fainting, what I thought was a stroke and yes, the good old getting sick to their stomachs and throwing up. Some of these required the paramedics while others a barf bag and club soda. It all came with the job.

I still remember this one incident vividly though. I was picking up meal trays in coach, when I saw a woman who appeared to be passed out in her seat. I had not been serving the trays since I was working the galley position, but remembered the other flight attendant saying, "There is a woman in the last row that has had too much to drink, she is slurring her words."

Now I was picking up trays at this woman's row and she was definitely passed out. I saw she had a Medic alert bracelet on her wrist, and I told the passenger seated next to her to get up, so I could get into her. Well, it said on the bracelet that she was a diabetic. My first reaction was that we needed to get some orange juice inside her. But no that wasn't going to work, how would she swallow? Maybe some sugar under the tongue. No, that would not work either. I made an announcement on the plane that we needed a doctor. Fortunately, we had one on board who diagnosed her with what he thought was insulin shock. In other words, she had taken too much insulin before she got on the plane. I immediately went into the cockpit, and told them we needed the paramedics as soon as we landed and what the doctor thought was the problem. The good news was we were only about twenty minutes out from landing at this point.

We were flying on a Boeing 727 that had steps that could be lowered out of the tail of the aircraft. As soon as we were parked at the gate, we lowered the steps for the paramedics to come on board since she was in the last row. They immediately started working on her and had a stretcher to take her off the plane and down those steps to a waiting ambulance.

Now you aren't going to believe the self-absorption of some people! Behind this last row of seats, where this woman and the paramedics are, there was a hanging area for garment bags. It is very apparent that we have paramedics on board working on a passenger when this man says to me, "I need my garment bag, can't you get back there and get it for me?"

Are you f-ing kidding me ricochets through my brain like an exploding bullet! As I'm then thinking sure, I'll climb over some rows of seats, climb over the paramedics and this woman, to get your overstuffed garment bag, climb back over the paramedics and this woman with it and then climb over some rows of seats.

As I'm biting my tongue, I looked at this person (I will not call him a gentleman) and said, "I'm so sorry sir, there is a passenger in insulin shock and the paramedics are working on her now to SAVE her life. I think your garment bag can wait."

How self-absorbed can one person be? Remember Karma can be a bitch, too!

Is This a Short Order Kitchen

I WAS FLYING a breakfast flight. Usually, we would get on the PA system and make an announcement about what we were serving, so that we didn't need to repeat it 120 times.

Here is the announcement: Ladies and gentlemen in the coach section of the aircraft. For breakfast this morning we will be serving a cheese omelet with ham and hash browns. Also, with your breakfast there is a bran muffin with butter, a fruit cup and orange juice. If you would like a second beverage please let us know when we are serving you. We hope that you will enjoy your breakfast this morning.

Sounds rather easy right? The flight is full of businessmen who know the game. They want coffee with their meal and they are happy. I get to this one row and I ask the lady seated in the aisle seat, "Would you like breakfast this morning?" She looks at me and says, "Oh, it sounds great. Yes, I would like breakfast, but I would prefer whole wheat toast." I'm thinking, oh really? And what pops out of my mouth but, "Oh, I'm so sorry our toaster is broken today, so I can't make toast." She smiles back at me and says, "Oh, no problem, the muffin will be fine."

I thought the male passenger sitting across the aisle from her was going to split a gut trying not to laugh, but the grin on his face said it all. No, this is not a short order kitchen and yes, we do "not" have a toaster!

It Might Be Very Expensive

WHY IS THERE always one person on most flights that just wants to see how far they can push you? Well, this was how my flight started ...

The passengers were boarding and we had a heavy load, not full but close. I was walking through the area where I would be working on a Lockheed 1011 when a passenger stopped me. He said he was traveling with his family and wanted to smoke after we were airborne. I told him that he was seated in a NO Smoking zone, but that the zone behind him was a smoking one and it was not full. He could just go back there any time to smoke.

Well, this was his response. "I want to smoke and be seated with my family here. I'll just smoke here." Hmm, oh really raced through my mind. So, I gave him his alternatives.

Sir if you smoke here it is very simple what I will do. I have a passenger manifest and I can get your name off it. Then I will send a report to the company that you had been informed that this was a no smoking zone, and that there were seats in the smoking area where you could go and smoke. You declined and insisted that you would smoke here in a nonsmoking zone. The CAB and the FAA will be informed, and you will be sent a fine for not complying with a crew member's request. I believe the fine is around $1,000 for this. So, it is your choice. Smoke here and it probably will be one of the more expensive cigarettes that you have smoked, or go to the smoking zone behind you.

I just walked away then because this topic was not up for further discussion. Yes, he did go to the smoking section for his nicotine addiction. As I said, there is always one who has to push the limits. My question is why?

Hey Little Mama

I FLEW QUITE a bit with my "best friend," and this was one of those flights that we both still remember.

Some of your passengers stand out for one reason or another, but this fellow was what one might describe as a "down-home-mountain man," type. He wore the overalls, had the accent, sported a long gray beard, the whole bit. Today he would probably have his own show on the *History Channel*.

Why did we get a kick out of him? Because every time he asked for something he would say, "Hey lil mama, ain't ya got no …? Hey lil mama ain't ya got no … milk? Hey lil mama ain't you got no … window seat?" You understand now.

So, as we were sitting on our 707 jump seat, across from the lavs, one of the lav doors flew open, our mountain man was sitting on the toilet and he said, "Hey lil mama, ain't ya got no toilet paper?" My BFF says, "No big Daddy," and slammed the door shut.

That was in the '70s and we still greet one another with, "Hey lil mama …" Hmm, I believe that might be a Rap song now? How times do change.

X Rated

SOME OF YOU might remember the wonderful meal services on our Lockheed 1011's. This meal service had a little extra something …

One evening from JFK to LAX, I was working the first class aisle position, which meant that I was responsible for serving all of our food to our first class passengers.

They had been enjoying appetizers and cocktails, the salad cart had been wheeled through first class and now it came time to serve a large beef roast. Some of you might also remember, for a short time, we served a roast instead of the chateaubriand. I can see you licking your lips now! Yes, we did have wonderful food years ago and this was one of those flights.

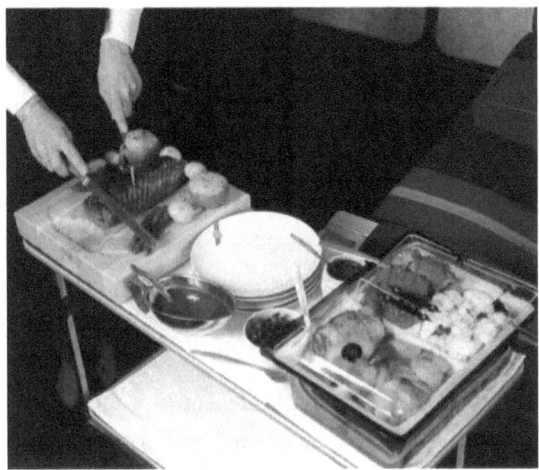

First class serving cart showing flight attendant carving a chateaubriand at a passenger's seat. Photo courtesy of the Jon Proctor Collection.

Back-story: The roast was not as tender and easy to carve as the chateaubriand was. Picture me now carving this roast from the serving cart, in the aisle, at the passengers' seats. Au jus gravy, vegetables and potatoes all served off this cart. It was quite the show!

I am carving the roast and what happens? I carved it right off the end of the cart and into the aisle passenger's lap. This was an OMG moment! I grabbed the roast off his lap whispering apologies. Then I snatched a cloth napkin, which I had hooked on the end of the cart and started rubbing like crazy to clean up the mess I had made.

Unfortunately, in my zeal to clean off his trousers I had not noticed that he started to enjoy it too much, if you get my drift. His wife unbeknownst to me had been watching this out of the corner of her eye, when all of a sudden, she took off her headset and socked him on the side of his face, while calling him a nasty name. I think there may still be an imprint of her diamond ring on his face! Just saying …

This was the day when I decided if possible, to never work the cabin position in first class again. I would be a galley girl for the rest of my flying career!

Do I Want to What

THE LAYOVER HOTEL in Lisbon had very interesting doors to the rooms. There were metal numbers on the side, a lighted doorbell and a big maid's call-light on top.

I had commuted from Denver and been up about twenty-four hours before getting to the hotel. Being exhausted and not thinking clearly, I let my crew talk me into taking a train trip on the layover. So, after two hours of sleep, I slapped myself awake and headed to the lobby. My eyes were so bloodshot, I could hardly see and I was just out of it.

For no particular reason I was walking close to the wall instead of the center of the hallway. Down at the far end of the hall a man was heading towards me to one of the first rooms. I was about ten feet from him when he got to his room. Instead of going to his door he decides to stop in the middle of the hall and to let me pass, remember I am hugging the wall. The man is facing a door—you guessed it—I think it is the elevator, so I go and stand next to him. Now, the two of us are standing there facing his room. He does not know what to do and I am just not getting it.

Quite a bit of time has passed now and he starts squirming around. I, on the other hand, am checking my nails, looking at the doorbell, thinking he has definitely pushed the button and actually wishing I didn't have to ride the elevator with this weirdo who is acting strange. And what's with the squirming?

Finally, he looks over at me and says, "Você quer entrar?" or, "Do you want to come inside?" It was like in the cartoons where the character suddenly realizes what they are seeing, and the item enlarges and jumps out at them! I look at the door, and then the bell and finally at him. I'm mortified, and start mumbling about the elevator and run away with a bright red face. I am sure he thought I was some forty-five-year-old hooker trying to get in his room.

By the time I finally got to the lobby I was laughing so hard I could hardly tell the crew what happened. Thank God we were heading out of town on that train trip now. He was the last person I didn't want to run into again in the hotel.

Toodles, tenha um bom dia!

Doodah Inspection ... As Only the British Can Do

IT WAS THE early sixties and I was flying with a good friend of mine who was British. We were working a MAC charter, hauling troops from Europe to McClellan AFB in New Jersey. The flight was unremarkable except for the thrill of fulfilling a small role for our nation, and the fun of meeting a sampling of our fine young service members.

The guys were understandably excited about returning home to their families, sweethearts and the US soil. When we arrived at McClellan, they impatiently stood, filling the aisle and slowly moving toward my Brit flying partner. She was bidding "adieu" to them as they left and welcoming them home, when one of the anxious young men called to her and said, "Is there anything in particular that we need to do when we de-plane?"

My ever so proper British flying partner, fumbling with her words, replied, "You need to show your—ah, ah,—your 'doodahs'." Without missing a beat, the fellow turned around, cupped his hands around his mouth and shouted mischievously, "Hey you guys, we've got to show our doodahs!"

Note: In Brit speak doodah is an informal word to refer to something the speaker can't name precisely. After that episode she refrained from using the word "doodah." It was funny!

Take My Nose Please ... Facelift and Nose Job

I WAS WORKING on a Lockheed 1011 in coach. During the flight, I learned that the legendary Phyllis Diller was in first class. For those of you who don't know her, she was an American stand-up comedian best known for her eccentric persona, her self-deprecating humor, "wild hair and clothes," and her exaggerated cackling laugh. My father loved her!

So, I decided that once the meal service was over, I was going up to first class and getting her autograph for my dad. I was told she was in the first row on the left-hand side sitting at the window.

What to get the autograph on? TWA stationary of course and now I headed up to first class. This was not in the flight attendant manual of proper behavior. You were not to ever approach a celebrity and ask for an autograph, but then I never did quite follow the rules. So here I go with my pad in hand, walk up to first class, turn around to face Phyllis, and tell her how much my dad loves her ... well, this is where all possibly could have gone wrong.

In the window seat, is a "normal" looking woman with a headscarf on, and the lady in the aisle is looking a lot like "Phyllis." My co-worker "definitely" said she was seated at the window. Not wanting to make a mistake, I look down for a minute and see that the "Phyllis" lady in the aisle has sneakers on and the "normal" looking lady at the window has skinny shiny pink low cut pointed boots on. Dead giveaway! Remember Phyliss was known for her outlandish clothes.

Well, now I know who the REAL Phyllis is. I give her my spiel about my father's infatuation with her and she signs her name to my pad with a loving message to my Dad. I walked back to my co-worker to find out what was going on. Apparently, Phyllis was on her way home with her "stand-in" after having facial surgery. A potentially embarrassing moment made right with a pair of pink shiny boots. Loved her!

P.S. Phyliss never kept her "work" silent. Allegedly she had seventeen different plastic surgery procedures done. Go Phyliss!

Fire They Shouted

I WAS WORKING a JFK flight departing for Madrid and continuing on to Barcelona on an L-1011. Boarding had been completed, the doors were shut and we were preparing for departure. While we were doing our final checks, and getting ready for the emergency demonstration there was a collective gasp, and shouting started from the passengers in coach as some of them rose out of their seats.

Then we heard someone shouting FIRE! This is one of those words that you never want to hear on an aircraft! What had happened was a torching of one of the engines which was not uncommon on a L-1011. We would tell the passengers that this was normal and not to worry everything was OK, which was precisely what we started to do.

But not so today when we heard the engines shutting down. Almost immediately, the front door was reopened, and a mechanic that happened to be the husband of one of my flying partners came on board, wanting to know why we had not evacuated the plane. Well, what we could not see was what he then described to us. The torching was not the usual small amount and then gone but completely circled around the entire wing! That is what some of the passengers saw, but we did not. The employees on the ramp were amazed that no evacuation had taken place.

Our captain praised us for our cool, and calm demeanors, and reassuring the passengers during and after this event. He said he was literally ten seconds from initiating an evacuation and as it turned out it was completely unnecessary. The plane was checked out, and we continued on to Madrid.

As fate would have it, our cheap thrills were not over yet. On final descent we all of sudden experienced a missed approach. Our L-1011 went from landing to going straight back up. All I could think was you've got to be kidding me! What was the problem now? A small plane had turned onto the runway that we were landing on. Not good is putting it mildly ...

We did a go around and landed with no more problems. There were probably some of our passengers, at this point, who were questioning flying TWA again. How was our next leg to Barcelona? Thankfully, uneventful!

How Sweet It Is to Out Fox Them

WORKING A NIGHT flight in first class, I noticed that someone had cleaned out the top drawer of the liquor cart. I mean it was completely empty! Interesting, now how could that be? I recalled a gentleman passenger had just been in the coat closet earlier, going through his gigantic garment bag. Maybe?

Later during the flight, this passenger fell asleep. I turned into Miss Marple. Agatha Christie would have been proud! I quietly went into the coat closet and felt the outside of his bag. My fingers were like laser gloves seeking out miniatures! Hmmm ... kind of lumpy, I thought.

I probably should not have, but now in character as Miss Marple, I unzipped the garment bag and there were the contents of the liquor drawer. Can you imagine his surprise when he opened his bag later on and found it full of empty liquor miniatures?

Hope you learned your lesson sir? Cheers!

Welcome Home

I WAS A flight attendant for TWA, from 1969 until 1977, and was based in Chicago and San Francisco. Here is one of my memories that I will never forget.

When I worked on a flight, I always tried to gauge the mood of the passengers I was serving. After all, some were on their way to a party, and some were returning from a funeral. The people I felt most sensitive to were soldiers who had been fighting in the Vietnam War.

On one particular flight, a young soldier was pre boarded to escort the body of someone who had been in his unit. When I found this out from the agent, I went to his seat row where he and I both looked out the window, staring intently and respectfully as the coffin was being loaded into the belly of the aircraft.

Throughout the flight, he refused all service. No beverages, no snacks, no meal. I checked on him several times to see if he would change his mind, but he would not. After we landed and as I was saying goodbye to departing passengers, he walked toward me, gently held me by the shoulders, and then kissed me on the mouth. For a few seconds, I was stunned into silence and then said, "Welcome home," as he strode down the jetway. I wondered what would become of him and hoped for something good.

Captain Bob, Do It Again

Photo of children's book distributed on flights.
Courtesy of Kylene Kulm.

IT WAS ONE of those flights that started out so nicely. The passengers all seemed to be in good moods and there was nothing exciting to speak about happening on the ground.

During boarding we had taken an adorable small boy up to the cockpit to meet the pilots and to get his Junior Crew member wings. He was thrilled and kept referring to our captain by his first name, Captain Bob, while he was in the cockpit.

So off we went with a full load of passengers who just wanted a drink and their snack. Nothing else but …

After we were airborne for about thirty minutes, we got a call from the cockpit alerting us to some turbulence that was reported ahead. The captain told us to put away the beverage cart immediately, and to stay in our seats buckled up until he told us it was safe to move around the cabin. Now remember people, if you hear the captain telling you to stay in your seat until he tells you to get up, and the flight attendants are to remain seated too, you know you are going to be rocking and rolling, so to speak.

The turbulence was really bad and when a flight attendant tells you the turbulence was bad it is really bad! Anything not tied down was flying around the cabin and some of the overhead compartments had even popped open with things starting to fall out of them too. I remember clutching the seat of my jump seat and holding on for dear life.

People were for the most part frozen in place with the occasional small squeals that come from fright. My flying partner was the color of his white shirt while I was trying desperately to look professional and calm, just in case anyone happened to turn to look back at us.

To say it was a totally discomforting experience for everyone would be putting it mildly, until suddenly that little boy, seated with his mother about five rows ahead of us, let out a high pitched "WHEEEE." And then we heard a small voice say, "Mommy, make Captain Bob do it again."

Out of the mouths of babes, it totally broke the tension and you couldn't help but laugh!

Paul Newman

I HAD PAUL Newman and one of his daughters on flight coming back from Rome to JFK. I was passing menus saying, "Hi, my name is Sandee," when he looked up and I stopped mid-sentence as those electric blue eyes met mine. He was the nicest, most casual and natural passenger ever.

After we were airborne, he asked if the two of them could go up to the upper deck lounge (it was closed because we were short staffed) to stretch, as they had had a long drive to the airport.

Of course, the flight service manager gave me permission to open it, and there I was with Paul Newman and his daughter watching them doing stretching exercises before the meal service began. Mr. Blue eyes himself!

During the meal, he was very interested in the salad cart and he said, "You know I make a mean salad dressing myself." He launched his Newman's Own line for charity right after that. Little did we know that this was in the works ...

Bomb Number Two

ON MARCH 7th, 1972, I bounded up the stairs in TWA's hangar at JFK International Airport, for check in, which was required an hour and a half before my scheduled flight. As usual, I was looking forward to the flight to Las Vegas where the crew got to stay at the Tropicana Hotel, one of the nicest layover accommodations for TWA flight crews.

When I got to the scheduling desk, the scheduler said that there was a situation going on at the airport and we would likely be delayed, so just go to the crew lounge and he would come update everyone shortly. Minutes later he came to the lounge to tell us about what had been unfolding at the terminal. The company had received an anonymous call from someone who said they had planted bombs on four of TWA's aircraft. They had demanded ransom money in exchange for divulging the placement of the bombs. Just to let the company know they were serious, they told them the "aircraft identification" number, not the flight number, with the first bomb on it. This was important because most likely only an insider could identify these visible numbers on the aircraft as a frame of reference.

When the company was given that info and raced to find the numbers tied to scheduled flights, they found a flight that had just departed JFK for LAX which had the corresponding numbers. So, faster than the fastest talking person in the world could say "circle back", the pilot of that flight was instructed to turn around and land back at JFK. By this time, we were told the ground crews that service the aircraft were refusing to go near the planes. Because of that, the FBI and security teams would be inspecting the aircraft, aided by K-9 bomb sniffing dogs. A bomb was found on that plane with only minutes left to go before it was timed to go off! Obviously, things were getting more real by the minute.

A plan was made to have the security teams inspect each plane, one by one, and if cleared, they would be released to take off. Later in the afternoon we were finally informed that our flight had been cleared to go. We only had ten passengers brave enough to still fly with us, after observing the chaos at the airport that day. We were to lay over in Las Vegas and then the next day fly back to JFK on the same aircraft, so it appeared that this would be the easiest leg of our entire trip with only ten passengers.

Fast forward: We had left New York now and about two hours into the flight the crew phone rang in the back cabin. My flying partner answered the phone and the captain requested that he come to the cockpit immediately. This was unusual because there were two flight attendants in the first-class cabin who normally would take care of requests from the cockpit. My flying partner returned after several minutes, looking a bit rattled and said, "I have something to tell you, but first I think I need a drink." Disclosure: Neither of us had a drink!

Uh oh … this was not sounding too good. He continued, "Our captain got a call from TWA headquarters, and was informed that they had received another call from the person who planted the first bomb, and that person had given them new aircraft identification numbers that corresponded to our plane. TWA told the captain that he could land in Denver and security could perform a second inspection of the plane, and if cleared, this would allow us to continue to Vegas, or he could elect to not stop and complete the flight." My flying partner said the crew was in the process of looking around in the cockpit, and the captain wanted us, as inconspicuously as possible, to look around the cabin for anything suspicious without letting the passengers know something might be amiss, as not to panic anyone. We quickly inspected the whole cabin and my partner then reported to the cockpit.

When he returned, he said the captain had decided that the cockpit crew did not find anything of concern in the cockpit and he had informed TWA headquarters that he was not going to stop, but would continue on to Las Vegas.

With great relief, we landed in Las Vegas a short time later in the early evening, but on a runway lined with fire trucks and police cars. Passengers were of course wondering "WHAT THE HELL!"

Our plane had to be left at the end of the runway, and not parked at the terminal building until a further inspection was completed. The crew and passengers, therefore, had to deplane down rolling stairs that had been brought out to our aircraft, and the poor passengers had to open their luggage for inspection right there on the tarmac, before proceeding to the terminal. We were told to just go get some much-needed rest and wait for our morning wake-up call, prior to our return trip to New York.

It was pretty hard to fall asleep, so I wasn't in that big of a stupor when the phone rang in my hotel room, and I noticed the wake-up call had come in an hour earlier than expected. The voice on the other end of the line brusquely said, "Get your clothes on, get to the airport, and do not talk to the PRESS!" So, now I am wide awake, putting two and two together, and knowing this had to be related to the previous night, I was pretty upset. Kind of feeling a little PTSD!

At this point, I thought, I am going to quit if they tried to make me get back on that same plane for another day of craziness! I decided to call my husband back in New York and tell him I would most likely return to New York via horseback and unemployed. He replied in an unemotional, flat voice, probably why he eventually became my ex-husband, "Oh, a plane blew up on the runway this morning in Las Vegas, which was probably your plane, so you don't have to worry about having to get back on that one." With New

York being three hours ahead of Las Vegas, he was already hearing the news that I hadn't heard yet.

I proceeded to the airport with my stomach in a knot! The entire crew from the night before was assembled in the crew operation/waiting room and we were told we would ferry back to New York on another plane. (Term ferry: plane would have only crew on it no passengers.) We were then escorted across the tarmac to our arranged flight.

As I was walking on the tarmac beside the flight engineer, what appeared right before our eyes but our plane from the night before, now parked at the terminal building, with the whole front end of the cockpit blown into twisted pieces of metal, with strewn pieces of toilet paper wrapped about the wreckage.

Then I hear the flight engineer saying to me, "The word is that it looks like the bomb was in the first aid kit and when we were looking for anything suspicious in the cockpit last night, I saw the kit and the wire lead seal was in place, which is a sign it had not been opened." Note: these kits are an assembly line product and must be replaced whenever the seal is broken, even if you only used one band-aid from it. He continued, "I considered opening it, but with the seal in place I decided it was OK. What if I had decided to open it, and it was a trigger bomb? My God, I wonder if we will ever know?" We continued to walk in silent contemplation.

It certainly was becoming clear now the extent of detail known to the bomber, access to the tarmac, plane, and interior items. It should also be noted here that the first bomb was found inside a black bag labeled CREW, inside the cockpit. Most of the time the cockpit crew has two bags each that they bring on board and keep in the cockpit. With three crew members, times two bags each, it was probably not noticed if there were seven bags instead of six, with each member assuming the extra bag belonged to one of the other crew members.

Now back to the plane we had brought in from JFK. It had stayed out on the end of the runway and was checked over by another security team. After being checked, the aircraft was towed to the terminal to prepare it for the return flight the next morning. That would have been our flight.

The story goes that the police officer assigned to stand guard overnight was on the tarmac, at the rear of plane, when the bomb went off saving his life. A supervisor assigned to sign off on the readiness of the interior for the morning flight had forgotten his pencil and had gone back into the terminal to get it, when the bomb went off, therefore saving his life too. Unreal!

I thank God that our captain made the decision to finish the flight rather than stop in Denver. We might have had yet another search that yielded nothing, and put us an hour or two behind schedule, or worse.

I ended up flying a few more "uneventful" years, and no one ever found two other bombs or the bomber.

I find in sharing this story, I am amazed at how vivid the recall can be of the times in your life that make their unforgettable marks. I am grateful to have a little less drama at this age, and glad I reached it! I will always cherish meeting the amazing gals and guys I flew with, and some of the most interesting passengers one could imagine!

I would advise those of you reading this story not to whine about life's little inconveniences, as your situation could be a lot worse than you could imagine ... a lot!

Here's Hoping You're Having a Wonderful Life

IN THE SUMMER of 1971, when I began my career as a flight attendant with TWA I was looking forward to seeing the world, meeting celebrities on my flights, having fun with co-workers on layovers, and a different schedule every month, so that I was never bored, all of which I did experience. There was also the fear of a medical, or mechanical emergency in flight, which I unfortunately had to undergo too. But nothing could have prepared me to be a child psychologist to a young boy whose mother had just told him she didn't want him anymore, and put him on my flight from St. Louis to Orlando to go live with his father.

It was April of 1992, and I was working on a Lockheed-1011 flight from St. Louis to Orlando. I was helping the flight service manager at the first class boarding door, when the gate agent came onto the plane and wanted us to come to the cockpit with her, so she could fill us in on what was about to transpire.

A woman had just brought her twelve-year-old son to the TWA airport ticket counter, to purchase a one-way ticket for him to Orlando. On the way to the airport she had told the boy that she didn't want him anymore and was sending him to his father. The boy was in tears at the ticket counter, and he had no suitcase, or belongings of any kind with him. He would be traveling as an unaccompanied minor, which required lots of paperwork and a phone call to the boy's father to make sure he would be there to pick him up. Because of all of these last-minute details we would be delaying our departure.

Our pilots were terrific and really stepped up. They insisted we bring him to the cockpit as soon as he boarded. The captain called for extra supplies, i.e., children's wings, a children's book on the L-1011 aircraft, *Sports Illustrated* magazines, car magazines and a meal for him because we were only originally scheduled to serve a snack.

I was put in charge of our distraught and frightened young passenger, probably, because my crew knew I had two boys who were about his age. As fate would have it, we had a lighter than normal load that day and an additional flight attendant in the crew, so the captain told me I could sit with him for takeoff and landing.

Because of our light passenger load, there were plenty of opportunities to sit and chat throughout the flight, and finally he started to cheer up a bit when we talked about baseball, and his hopes that his dad would take him to Disney World. But what really made his day was when the captain announced over the PA, on our approach into Orlando that he was dedicating the landing to him. Finally, I saw a big smile on that sweet young face.

Upon arriving in Orlando, I walked him out to the gate area to meet his dad and stepmother. There were lots of tears all around, but meeting his "new" parents I could tell he was going to be in good hands. We exchanged phone numbers and addresses, so I could mail him a photo we had taken of him in the cockpit.

I have replayed that particular day in my head, many times over the years, even though I had other sad moments during my flying career, which

I also didn't expect when I began, but this one was especially hard on me and my entire crew.

Chad would be in his late 30s now. Here's hoping that he is living a wonderful life!

The Magical Mystery Tour

IT WAS 1974 and TWA furloughed a large number of flight attendants. As penance they gave all of us a "round" the world pass to use during our furlough. Of course, we weren't making any money now, small details, but being young and naïve, who needs that! Another detail, this was before credit cards were available to everyone too, so I didn't have one of those. Again, details, details ... only a twenty something wouldn't be concerned about any of this. All I knew was that the Magical Mystery Tour was waiting to take me away and I didn't even need to pay for it. Or, so I thought.

So, off I went on an adventure with another furloughed flight attendant to see the world. Our magic carpet would drop us off, pick us back up and along the way, we made it to Hong Kong. What a ride, all on $600 worth of Travelers checks. Some of you might be old enough to remember that is what everyone used when they were traveling out of the U.S. since the American Express card killed you on the exchange rate when you got your bill. I know dinosaurs roamed the earth then too!

Anyway, long story made short, all of the "gold" and jewelry in Hong Kong mesmerized me, therefore when we arrived in Bangkok I was nearly broke. Yes, I spent it all on fool's gold as it turned out. Now, what to do? I got into one of those three wheeled Thai rickshaw taxis and went to Western Union to beg my folks for more money to finish my adventure. They were none too happy since it was 2 AM in Arizona, but my dollars were wired and my magic carpet continued with a stop in Tel Aviv. I remember those sexy Israel soldiers patrolling the aisles dead serious with machine guns. They obviously were more interested in terrorists than us. Finally, I got home two weeks later and yes, I will always remember my MAGICAL MYSTERY

TOUR adventure. It is stamped in my brain and every time I hear the Beatles song *Magical Mystery Tour* mine comes to mind. Oops, another dinosaur attack, The Beatles, google Paul McCartney!

Note: My cattle rancher father never wore the caftan I brought from Morocco as an apology gift. LOL! Still no magic for him!

The Parisian Way

I HESITATED SENDING this in for the book, in fear of someone getting offended, but it's all in fun and my apologies in advance if it does offend anyone.

I was the flight service manager on this particular flight from Paris. We all know that it is very common in Europe to snap your fingers when you need "service." A Frenchman sitting in the coach section, who I might add was proficient in English, kept snapping his fingers at one of my "female flight attendants." She was totally ignoring him trying to give him a quick lesson in "the American way," which is "do not" snap your fingers at the staff.

The flight attendant in the above situation had already told me about this rude man and that she would handle the situation. If you're reading this girl, I know you remember. The man kept snapping and snapping. Finally, she couldn't take it anymore and went up to the passenger "wobbling" her head side to side with both hands on her hips. She looked directly at the passenger's face and said, "Honey, it takes more than two fingers to make me come," and walked off.

Every passenger who understood the double meaning roared with laughter and the fingering passenger was left dumbfounded. A few minutes later he stops her and demands to speak to the head steward, which would be me. After she told me what she had said I have to admit I laughed out loud, but now had to go deal with this problem.

Trying to keep a straight face, I listened intently with lots of eye contact. He complained about the fingering comment, and when he was through there was that long pause for emphasis and I said, "Sir, please don't finger my girls on the aircraft." I pointed to the call bell and showed him how to operate the button. There were no further fingering incidents after that.

You Met Whom When You Were Getting a Massage

WHILE ON A layover in Tel Aviv at the Hilton Hotel, a very good friend of mine, who was another TWA flight attendant, was also on a layover with a different crew at the same hotel. I was happily surprised when she called me, and invited me to come along with her to a concert that evening.

Oh, the people you meet when you are having a massage. You aren't going to believe this one, but she had gotten into a conversation with none other than the well-known conductor Zubin Mehta. Yep! He invited her to attend a concert that evening in Tel Aviv, bring a friend and even offered to drive her to the concert building.

Well, I immediately said, "Sorry I'm busy tonight. NO, I'm just kidding! Of course, I want to go!" So, who picks us up in his rental car? Zubin Mehta …

Talk about a once in a lifetime experience. Just meeting him, then talking with him, being driven by him and most importantly attending the concert that evening he was conducting. Who gets to do this? And the cherry on top, we were seated behind the orchestra on the podium that faced him and the audience behind him. You can imagine how exciting this was, and a memory I'll never forget.

Justifiable Hamicide

I WAS WORKING a morning flight from Miami to St. Louis, on a Boeing 707, back in the days when we were still hand delivering the meal trays to our passengers. There were approximately thirty male passengers who got on together but were scattered in seats in the aft section of coach. I heard some Spanish being spoken between them and assumed they were probably Hispanic as we were leaving from Miami. As TWA was not only a domestic carrier but an international one too, this was not unusual.

Once the plane leveled off, we started our breakfast service, which was scrambled eggs and ham plus all of the goodies to accompany it. I was running out trays and had served the first two rows when things started going south immediately. As I was returning to the galley to get some more meal trays, one man in this group I had served stopped me and asked, "Is this ham?" To which I replied, "Yes." He then said in broken English, "I no eat meat ... I'm vegetarian!" What could I do? I apologized and said that we did have vegetarian meals, but they needed to be ordered when you purchased your ticket and made your reservation, so that the meal would be put on the plane by our commissary. I explained to him that we did not have a choice for breakfast and asked him if he wanted me to remove his entrée plate and he nodded yes.

I continued taking out the meal trays and each time I was in the cabin I would be stopped by one or more of these Hispanic gentlemen, each asking if that was ham on their plate, to which I said, "Yes," and then went into my spiel about vegetarian meals etc. Bottom line ... some of them would refuse the meal entirely; some would eat it if I took it back to the galley, and had the ham removed and some would eat around the ham. This insanity went on for at least 10 rows!

Now this was a short flight time with a full load of passengers, and here I was serving some of these people twice, stopping to explain the situation to them and trying to communicate with people who had limited English. To say that I was becoming irritated and frustrated would be an understatement. By the time I got to around the tenth row I had reached my patience limit. When I placed the next tray in front of another one of these men in this group, he immediately looked at the entrée and asked, "Is ham? No eat ham ... am vegetarian."

You know there are times in your life where there is no thought process, and you just react. It is like an out of body experience. Your brain is going to explode. What did I do? Are you ready? Picture this, I calmly reached over and with my hand, I picked up the piece of ham off of his plate, straightened up, and threw it to the back of the airplane, like it was a Frisbee, where it landed by our jump seat. I then asked him "sweetly" if this was now acceptable to eat. Needless to say, he was startled speechless, as I then calmly walked to the back of the plane as if throwing ham was totally normal. I reached down and picked up the offending piece of ham, turned and looked at my flying partner in the galley, who was now staring at me with incredulous eyes. She knew what I was going through in the cabin with these people, but certainly did not expect to see a piece of ham go flying past her!

Well, there must have been an airplane God on board that morning because not one person said another word to me about their breakfast, or the flying ham. I guess that I scared them into silence. Later that night at dinner, we were all rehashing my mental breakdown and the crew was having some good laughs at my expense, when I told them that it would have been "JUSTIFIABLE HAMICIDE."

End of story: I was convinced that this would be the end of my flying career because surely someone would write a complaint letter to the company. Nada, nothing! There was an airplane God who said she just lost her mind for a few minutes, let it be.

Where Are My Sunglasses and Cane

SOME OF MY favorite memories come from flying with great captains and the fun times we had on the plane.

One of our captains in particular had a crazy sense of humor. He came out of the cockpit wearing his jacket buttoned up askew, hat slightly placed at an angle and very dark sunglasses on. However, what made this even funnier was that he had a white cane that he was using to walk down the aisle of the cabin with.

Then he would stop, and start speaking to some of the passengers and ask them how they were enjoying the flight. The looks on their faces were priceless! It only took a few of them in first class to realize they were being pranked and then everyone started laughing.

The Music of the Night

SOME OF MY most memorable experiences in London were attending the theater and musical events. Upon arrival, we would check with Derek at the Kensington Hilton to see if tickets were available. He was in charge of hotel guests' excursions, tours, getting them tickets to plays and other events in the city. If you needed tickets, he was your man.

The Phantom of the Opera had only been open for a short time, so we asked about that and were told to check back at 5:00 PM when tickets were released. We didn't have much hope in getting seats for that evening, but somehow Derek had worked his magic and we were going.

Upon arrival, we were so excited and watched as the theater filled. An oddity was that the row we were in had seats that remained empty next to the aisle, which we thought a little strange. All of a sudden, my friend said, "Oh my God," and I said, "What is wrong?" Nothing was wrong, we just happened to have seats in the row that Andrew Lloyd Webber and his entourage were now arriving to be seated in. We were stunned!

Well, if this row was what Andrew Lloyd Weber liked to sit in, we decided they must really be choice seats. Bravo Derek!

And thank you Derek for getting us great seats too for *Starlight Express*, *Les Miserables*, *Miss Saigon*, *Chess*, *Cats* and many others. All of my wonderful memories are evoked when I play the CDs that I purchased in London for these London performances.

Ah yes, The Music of the Night …

What Happens In the Galley Stays In the Galley

IN THE EARLY days of the airline industry only men could be pilots, and only women could be "stews," or as they were called at TWA "hostesses." On our international flights where the crew also included a purser that position could only be held by a male too. Can you imagine a company trying to get away with that today? NOT!

Flight attendant in Valentino designer uniform, in L-1011 lower deck galley, standing in front of a lift door. She is not the author of this story, nor in this story. Photo courtesy of the TWA Museum.

Then in the early '70s all of that changed. Companies could no longer discriminate, using sex or age to determine who would be hired for a job. They also could not make you sign a form saying you would quit at age thirty-two, or that if you got married you would quit, or if God forbid you got pregnant you would quit. All of these factors changed the airline definition of who could be a flight attendant, purser or flight service manager. Look out people, it was going to be a new world and I was joining it!

In 1976, I was in one of the early groups of male flight attendants that TWA hired. This new oddity led to some gentle hazing by our more senior ladies. Here is my welcome aboard introduction. I was going out on an L-1011 to LAX, on what was called an "observational" flight. You were to observe and learn from the experienced flight attendants about how to put all of your new information from training into action. Trust me training was nothing like the "real world."

I appeared at the crew briefing and presented my letter of introduction to the flight service manager which also asked the crew to "show me the ropes," so to speak. I'll add here that I was the only male flight attendant on board this flight.

After helping out in various ways and learning some of the tricks of the trade that our instructors "never" taught us, the service was finished. The flight service manager then sent me to the lower galley which actually was in the belly of the aircraft for a tour. This position was particularly hard because you literally controlled all of the meal preparation for business class and coach. I was learning the pitfalls of the ovens, locations of equipment and yes, how those lifts worked that went up and down to the galley.

Picture me now, I thought I was so smart from all of this new training as I got into the lift and pushed the switches to go back up to the main deck. Little did I know how those lifts could be used! About halfway up, the galley lift stops. The door below me opened which stopped the lift. That was news to me. What the hell is happening now?

So, you can picture this, an elevator consists of a cab which can also be called a "cage," "carriage" or "car" mounted on a platform within an enclosed space called a "hoistway." If the cab is stopped about halfway up by the galley door being opened you can see someone's feet, and if you open the lift door on the main deck you can look right down on them too and see the entire person. Now you've got the picture?

Remember the galley flight attendant had opened the lift door in the galley below and the crew on the upper deck had opened the lift door there too, so that they could now look into the lift. I felt like a fish in a fishbowl and of course had NO idea of what was about to happen. Oh, all of those sweet "leering faces!"

The galley flight attendant has a can of whipped cream and she starts filling my socks and shoes with it. I'm dancing around like a maniac in the lift to no avail while I am listening to peals of laughter from my crew, who were peering down on me.

Initiation accomplished! Have to admit I did it to some poor unsuspecting newbies too. Good times and loved those senior flight attendants. In fact, so much so that I married one.

So, You Want To Go Where

YOU WOULD GET the most amazing view every time you flew into Cairo on a clear day. What was it? If you were seated on the left-hand side of the plane, as it banked over the Nile, you would spot the Giza Pyramids on approach before landing. Breathtaking to say the least!

It was indeed one of those beautiful clear days. We had just flown in from Paris and were on our approach into Cairo. The plane was making a big banking turn, over the pyramids, when all of a sudden, this elderly little French woman came up behind me and tugged on my shirt. I turn around, and look down and she has this confused look on her face, points out the window and says, "NEW YORK CITY?" I just mumbled under my breath, "Oh, SHIT."

To make a long story short, we arranged to keep the woman with us on our Cairo layover in spite of the fact she didn't have a visa. One of our female crewmembers graciously volunteered to share her hotel room with her on our layover. Then the crew took her out on the town and showed her Cairo. You haven't seen Cairo unless you do it with an airline crew! As another remembrance of her trip we introduced her to Said Gouzlan's jewelry shop, our favorite place to get our cartouches and he gave her a lovely silver chain as a remembrance.

The next day it was back to Paris with shall we say our "diverted" passenger. There were lots of hugs for us, as she deplaned, and I guarantee the gate agent made sure she got on the flight to JFK this time.

Just one of many stories from being a crewmember for an amazing airline that had amazing employees.

Going the Extra Mile

NOTE: THE AIRCRAFT I was flying was a 727-231 during the time when TWA had a huge carry-on luggage compartment that was located after the boarding door in first class that all the passengers could use when they boarded.

It was a rainy evening in Philadelphia and I was working the first class galley. The passengers hadn't started to board yet, when the gate agent came on to advise us that Zsa Zsa Gabor would be pre boarding. She was returning to LA via Chicago after being on the *Mike Douglas Show*.

Now for you youngsters who are reading this, Ms. Gabor was not only a striking blonde actress but had quite the personality. One could say she was not afraid to speak bluntly and she sure did love good jewelry. But then she got that from her mother who had owned jewelry stores throughout Europe.

Zsa Zsa was really a Hollywood celebrity and socialite who had come to epitomize what most people thought of as Hollywood! Zsa Zsa as she was simply called, was known for her nine marriages, many personal appearances on television shows, her Hungarian accent, a "dahlink" catchphrase she loved to use and advice about the opposite sex, versus her film career. And we might add she was beautiful!

But getting back to our celebrity passenger. The gate agent told me that Ms. Gabor had a companion that would be pre-boarding before her, to advise us of her special needs. Special needs, interesting?

The first class galley was being loaded by the commissary, as the companion of Ms. Gabor boarded the aircraft. He was rather blunt, and to the point, where one might consider him even rude, and he informed me that Ms. Gabor would arrive in ten minutes and she would like to have a hot cup of coffee.

The commissary agent who was loading my galley overheard this, immediately gave me a coffee pot, the coffee bags and a PLASTIC coffee cup, so I could start making Ms. Gabor a fresh pot of coffee. Her companion had other ideas! Upon seeing the horrors of a plastic coffee cup, I was immediately informed that only a china cup would do. Well, our commissary agent had none on his truck. I ran off the plane and went over to the aircraft parked next door ... nothing in china there! I then ran off that plane onto a third one parked next to it. NO china cups! I reluctantly went back to the plane because I knew Ms. Gabor was going to be boarding the aircraft, for what I thought might be an end of the world crisis because I couldn't find a china coffee cup. Guess what? She didn't care for any coffee.

Now when Ms. Gabor boarded, she had a small dog in a dog carrier, and proceeded to put the dog, and carrier, in our huge carryon luggage compartment that I told you about earlier and then she went to her seat which was at a bulkhead. NO, you can't put a live animal in that luggage compartment, and it can't be at a bulkhead either it has to be under a seat. Thank God, the first class passenger load was light, and I offered to put the dog, and its carrier at row two for takeoff and landing. I thought this was the perfect solution, but Ms. Gabor was not happy with my idea and just wanted the dog in the carryon luggage compartment. There is a God because she finally saw that my suggestion was a much better idea. So, one coffee cup and one little dog crisis are taken care of.

After we were airborne everything seemed to be going well. Our service was completed in first class, and I went to the coach cabin to help them finish theirs. As I was returning to first class some pretty severe turbulence started, and I heard the four-bell ring from the cockpit which meant sit down now. I sat down immediately in an empty seat, as we started some pretty serious up and down rockin' and rollin'.

Who stands up? Ms. Gabor looking terrified! I motioned to her to get her attention, and then told her to sit down and buckle up. She just stood there and in her heavy Hungarian accent said she wanted me to sit next to her. Then hanging onto the seat backs she moves herself to row two and announces that she wouldn't sit down until I was sitting next to her. Well, you won't believe this one, but I practically had to crawl to her, made it to the seat next to her and then held her hand until things smoothed out …

As I said, "Going the extra Mile."

April 8, 1937
HOSTESS INSTRUCTION LETTER NO. 177

IT HAS BEEN necessary within the past few months to furlough hostesses because of several flights ceasing operations. Effective immediately, if it becomes necessary to furlough hostesses, married hostesses will be furloughed first—based on seniority—since it is unfair to the single girls to have their means of support taken away.

It has been the policy of TWA to allow hostesses to remain in the employ of the company after they are married. Whether or not to continue this policy is being given consideration by the company.

Lately, it has been noticed that a few of the married hostesses have evidenced some indifference in their work. This may be because of the fact that more independence is felt. If the above conditions do not improve, it may be necessary to discontinue the policy of retaining the married hostesses in the company's employ.

Ruth K. Rhodus
Chief Air Hostess

Approved:
John B. Wolitor
Supt. of Passenger Service

Well, looks like they reconsidered; no more married hostesses until many, many years later!

He Who Laughs Last

WE WERE FLYING a 747 from Tel Aviv to Paris. Toward the end of the five-hour flight the word was "keep everyone in their seats after we land, we've had an incident and authorities will be boarding the flight."

Keep four hundred plus passengers in their seats after the engines are shut down—impossible! What do you know, the captain made an announcement that everyone was to remain in their seats until they were told they could deplane. After a few minutes, two timid TWA agents came on and asked the man sitting across from my jump seat to come with them.

Here is the story: This man had been smoking in the aft lav. The inflight service manager had repeatedly asked him to come out of the bathroom to no avail when all of a sudden, he opened the door and slugged her in the jaw with a ring that left a mark on her face! Needless to say, she went immediately to the cockpit to tell the captain that she had been assaulted.

Now inside the TWA office in the Paris airport this passenger said that the flight attendant slugged him and he was going to sue TWA. At that point I guess those two wimpy TWA agents got scared, offered him a first class seat to New York on United and the TWA plane continued to NY without him.

In those days the passenger was always right and the airlines were terrified of lawsuits. The flight attendant got the "last word" though; she took the man to court herself with the help of a FBI friend. As I said, "He who laughs last."

Can you imagine today with cell phones what would have happened. Handcuffs for him and definitely not a first class ticket home!

Thursday, May 25th, 1979

AH, THE END of May finally and a beautiful day to fly. Just a little turn around to finish the month off, then the weekend and the holiday to enjoy.

We left ORD for Hartford Connecticut. It was only about one hour and forty minutes of actual flight time. In Hartford, we would spend maybe ninety minutes on the ground. Just enough time for the pilots to get their flight plans made for our return to ORD, the flight engineer to do his walk around outside, and for us to straighten up the cabin, check out our supplies for the return trip and spend some time gossiping.

The agent got on and asked us if we had everything we needed for our service back to ORD and we told him we were ready to go. He said, "I'm going to start boarding now and you'll have a full load, have a good trip." Well, we only had to serve beverages, liquor and some peanuts, so it was no biggie.

I was working the first class aisle position that day, so was technically in charge and one of my responsibilities was to give the safety announcements. I also coordinated things that happened in the cabin with the captain. Again, usually not a big deal.

Everyone was on board now, we did our safety demo, checked seat belts, seat backs, that luggage was stowed correctly and then the aircraft started backing out of the gate. We took our seats and began our taxi. Yes, four hours from now I would be home, making plans to go out for dinner since I didn't like to cook when I got home from work. Probably some delicious pizza from our favorite pizzeria. Yum I could taste it now.

The plane taxied out to the beginning of the runway, and we found ourselves sitting there for what seemed like an unusually long period of time, when we heard the captain on the PA telling the passengers that there were weather delays at O'Hare and we would have to wait to take off.

What? Weather delays, we just left there around three hours ago and everything was fine. It was supposed to be a beautiful day. My flying partner and I exchanged looks like, "What the heck is he talking about." I told her, "I'm going into the cockpit and find out what is going on."

As I entered the cockpit it was totally silent and grim looks were on our pilots faces. I'm still in a quandary, thinking this is totally strange. So of course, I said, "Hey what's going on? There isn't a weather problem in Chicago."

The captain was turned at an angle in his seat looking toward the first officer, and he turned his head toward me and said, "American just lost a plane at O'Hare." My mind started to whirl and I was saying to myself, lost a plane, lost a plane? Then I heard myself saying, "Was anyone hurt?" And the next thing I hear is his voice saying, "We think everyone was killed."

KILLED! No that can't be raced through my mind. I felt like someone had punched me in the gut! My eyes started to fill with tears and I know I was speechless for a minute, when I heard the captain saying to me, "You may tell the other flight attendants but not the passengers. I don't want anyone panicking and saying they want to get off of the plane. Right now, we are just waiting to hear from air traffic control when we can leave here."

I pulled myself together, wiped my eyes and left the cockpit; while passing my flying partner I told her that I was going to go get the other two flight attendants from coach and we needed to have a meeting in the first class galley. She looked a little mystified now.

How do you tell your flying partners that over 200 people are probably dead now at O'Hare? As we all stood in the first class galley with the curtain closed, I quietly began, "I have some very sad news AND you may not make a sound after I tell you this. I don't want the passengers to hear us or see us upset. Do you all understand?" They nodded but looked so puzzled. I could feel myself sucking in some air to prepare myself now for what I had to say and my eyes started to tear up again. I whispered, "The captain just told me that American lost a plane at O'Hare and he believes all of the passengers and crew died. He doesn't want our passengers to know, and we have to carry on, as if there is just a weather delay as he told them. Do you all understand?"

I could see them standing there like frozen inanimate objects, and then all of the silent tears from each of us started. We cried quietly, and hugged one another for a few minutes, and then as the professionals we were, we returned to our jump seats to wait. It made no difference that it was an American flight and not a TWA one. In our large fraternity and sorority known as airline crews, we were all related and whenever there was a tragedy like this, we were all shaken to the core. It was like a member of your own family being killed. I know that might sound strange, but I believe it was true for 99.9% of us.

Time seemed to crawl, and then one call button went off, a second, a third and a few more. I could see the flight attendants answering them in coach, and of course, I had mine in first class to deal with. People were saying things like, "I don't understand this. I just talked to someone before I got on the plane, they told me the weather was fine in Chicago. What's going on here?" And of course, there were the ones who said, "I have a connection in Chicago, you are making me miss it!" I have to say, it took great self-control to not tell some of them, "Listen, 200 plus people just died at O'Hare. Trust me I don't care about your problems!" But I heard myself saying, "Sir, there is a weather delay at O'Hare, and all of the flights are being delayed, so I'm sure you will not miss your connection. TWA is well aware of everyone's connections and they will be able to help you once we get to the gate."

After about thirty minutes of holding at the top of the runway, I went back up into the cockpit and asked the captain if we could start a beverage service while we were sitting there; he said, "No, as soon as we get clearance to take off, I want you all in your seats not working out in the cabin. I want to get out of here as soon as we can. But after we are airborne give them complimentary drinks."

Tick tock, tick tock, tick tock. Would we ever leave? Finally, the captain comes over the PA system and says, "We have been cleared to take off. Will the flight attendants please return to their seats immediately." I made an announcement following the captain's reminding people to make sure their seat belts were fastened tight and low, all seat backs should be in their upright position, and all tray tables stowed now. The roar of our engines started, as we rolled down the runway gaining momentum and then we were airborne.

What would we be returning to? I had no idea how bad it really was. We didn't know that the plane went down on takeoff and flying debris from the crash had hit a trailer park near O'Hare. Or that a repair garage where four men were working had been hit too, and two men died on the scene and two had extremely bad burns. That flames from the crash scene could be seen as far away as eight miles, as thousands of pounds of jet fuel exploded. Yes, it was a picture of what hell might be like.

I only went into the cockpit twice to see if they wanted anything during the flight. I never asked for any more information and they offered none. Silence was golden for a while. The details would all unfold on TV after we were home, safe and sound.

On landing, the passengers could see the scorched field and debris, plus the engine lying by the side of runway 32R. A few passengers on deplaning asked what had happened and we just said quietly that American Airlines had a crash on takeoff. We knew they would find out everything about the tragedy once they entered the terminal.

TWO HUNDRED FIFTY-EIGHT PASSENGERS, THIRTEEN CREW MEMBERS AND TWO INDIVIDUALS ON THE GROUND PERISHED THAT DAY ...

But there was also this reminder of the hellish nightmare for weeks and weeks. What? Because the engine that had fallen off, landed next to a runway that we had to drive past to get to the employees parking lot and hangar for TWA, we were reminded of it all of the time. I would try not to look at it, as I drove down that road, but it was impossible not to. After what seemed like an eternity, it was finally removed ...

All these many years later I can still see that huge engine, lying next to the road. A reminder of the dangers of our job and how one should cherish every day. May they all be resting in peace.

Note: What had happened exactly? For a chilling read, google *The Ghosts of Flight 191* published in the *Chicago* magazine on May 7, 2019.

Where Has All the Glamour Gone

AH YES THOSE good 'ol morning flights from St. Louis to somewhere filled with business travelers who mostly just wanted something to eat, lots of coffee and to be left alone. Well, maybe not so much on this flight.

The agent had boarded an older gentleman who needed a wheelchair and a lot of assistance. He was seated by a window about two thirds back in the airplane. I thought it was strange that they would seat him there, but it wasn't my decision.

We are airborne now and started our morning beverage service, which was served from a cart starting in the front of coach and moving toward the back of the plane. I was working the tail end of the cart, which is airline lingo means the rear of it, so I'm going backwards. About five minutes into the service, a call bell was rung. I turned around and could see it was our wheelchair passenger. I walked back and asked him how I could help and he "demanded" a whiskey. I explained that we would get to him shortly and returned to the cart. About two minutes later, he rang again with another "demand" for a whiskey ... I told him just a few minutes more that there were passengers ahead of him still waiting to be served. I don't think I even got back to the cart when he punched his call bell again. I returned to him and once again, there was a demand for a whiskey. At that point, I decided to serve him just to shut him up and be done with it. When I gave him his drink and asked for $3 for the cocktail he went off! "$3 bucks?! $3 bucks?!" "Yes, that's the price of our cocktails," I replied, trying not to sound as aggravated, as I really was then. He grudgingly dug into his pants pocket and pulled out $1.80. When I tried to correct him on the change, he "yelled" that it was all he had. Sometimes it is just easier to forget about it, so I opted to take the $1.80 and write the rest off.

We finally finished our service when his bell went off again. This time he tells me, get ready for this one, that he has to pee. Well, there was no way I could move him and get him to a lav and I told him that. He gestured up to the overhead bin and said for me to retrieve his "pee bottle." Yep, his "pee" bottle! Learn something new every day.

I got it for him, and he asked where he could go? Of course, the answer was nowhere but there because we couldn't move him. I then made an executive decision. I got a blanket (yes, we did have those for our passengers then including pillows, I know amazing!) and requested that the passenger seated in that row with him, and another in the seat in the row in front of him, to please remove themselves for a few minutes. Picture me now holding up the blanket around him, so he could "pee in privacy."

Well, quite a few minutes passed when I asked him, "How was it going?" (Stop laughing!) To which he replied that "he was working on it." I was by now losing all feeling in my arms ... a passenger seated across the aisle from all of this looked at me and said, "You are NOT paid enough." I nodded my head and silently agreed with him. Don't ask what happened to the pee bottle. Let's put it this way, I washed and washed and washed my hands!

From Russia With Love

IT WAS THE early '80s on a Boeing 747. Just another trip from London to Chicago via a polar route. But then maybe not! We are to learn this is the captain's last flight. (Retirement age for the cockpit crew was 62 and mandatory.) His family of seven, his children, grandchildren and wife were to meet him at O'Hare for a grand celebration!

I was working the upstairs deck section behind the cockpit which was business class and also taking care of the pilots. This would be fun, our captain's last trip. Or would it? Something told me on my way onto that plane that this would not be a normal flight ... and it was his final one.

So, dinner and drinks are served, time for the movie and to feed the cockpit. All the window shades are pulled down to see the movie and I press the play button for the movie to start.

Just then the cockpit door flew open! "Kathy, get up here!" Wow, are they hungry or what? I hurried in and the captain proceeded to tell me to grab the flight service manager (FSM) and go to the aft left and right doors to see if we could see any Russian MiGs following us!? What? Yes, Russian fighter jets!

The U.S. military air frequency had contacted our plane. Our cockpit was told to take a sharp left, which they were doing, as I scrambled down the stairs from the upstairs business section to go find the FSM.

Now to put this in perspective: on September 1, 1983, a Korean Air Lines 747 passenger jet flying from JFK to Seoul, Korea via Anchorage, Alaska had been blown up by a Russian MiG fighter, for "veering into

Russian airspace" a week before. All 269 passengers and crew perished! This happened during the movie and when all of the window shades were down too. "We thought it was a spy plane," was the Russians' feeble excuse for an answer to this air disaster.

Fortunately, I found the FSM right away, grabbed his arm while mumbling to him, "I'll explain later, come with me now," as I charged down the aisle with him behind me to the back-left door. Note: The window shades in the cabin were down for the movie. All the doors on a 747 had a large covering for their window too that we manually placed there to block out the sun and shade the cabin for the movie.

I told the FSM to remove the shade in the window and start looking out to see if he could see any Russian MiGs following us, while I went to the other rear door to look. To say he looked stunned would be putting it mildly! Neither of us saw anything but blue skies. Then he called the cockpit from the aft door and told the captain, "We didn't see any MiGs." I'm sure the captain was probably yelling the command, "Keep Looking!" as the FSM told me, "He says keep looking!"

OK, I knew this flight was going to be interesting but really this. After the FSM and I returned back into the cockpit, I heard them talking to the U.S. military air frequency. If we veered south the Russians would have to turn around. Why? Because our military knew they would run out of fuel before they would be able to get back to their base. And you thought our country wasn't watching your back!?

We did head south as ordered and this new route added two hours to our flight time, as it was much longer. BUT no more signs of Russians, Thank God!

When we landed, there was a huge waiting reception for the captain at the foot of the stairs, with many TWA pilots, flight attendants, his wife and family, plus management, to meet him for his last flight. Before he kissed his wife he said, "Honey, sorry we are late, just turbulence, had to change course," and then he turned and winked at me.

What a trip! The movie could have been *Top Gun* with Tom Cruise.

007

IN THE 1960s I was an airline hostess. Yes, TWA liked to refer to us then as "hostesses" because we were to behave as if we were giving a party at home but instead it was on the plane. Well, this particular party, (hear me clearing my throat now), was from St. Louis to Cleveland and then on to JFK. I was working the first class position which we referred to as "A" on a Boeing 707. Therefore, I had the responsibility of being at the boarding door to meet and greet all, make the announcements and then to take care of the first class passengers.

In St. Louis a man boarded who shall we say, stood out. He was wearing a tall black hat, a long black coat and was carrying a large leather tote bag. He didn't want his coat hung in the first class coat compartment, and placed it and his hat in the overhead rack. He also seemed protective of this leather tote bag, and carefully placed it in front of where he was seated, under another first class seat. Now at this particular time you did not put your bag under the seat in front of yours like you do today but actually under your own seat. I did not bother to say anything since there was no passenger seated in front of him that would need the space for their bag. In reflection now, I know why he wanted the bag there because he wanted to be able to see it at all times.

Now having noted how he placed his carryon bag, the next thing he did was proceed to start reading a newspaper UPSIDE DOWN! It was obvious to anyone that observed him that he appeared to be nervous. OK, maybe he was a first-time traveler? However, this was really strange.

After I made our boarding and safety announcements, the plane took off, and then the fasten seat belt sign was turned off and what did he do? He got up immediately and took his bag into the forward lav. Hmmm, now this is getting concerning. This guy was just too odd! In addition, to put this really into perspective it was the era of "bomb" scares on planes.

We started our meal service, and I was taking out drinks, and then serving snacks, but still he was in the lav. Now this is really getting to be strange! What the heck was he doing in there anyway? I told my flying partner that I was going to go speak with the captain about this man. Well, the captain agreed with me that his persona, and actions were suspicious, and said, "I'll turn on the seat belt sign and you make an announcement to the passengers that we're going to have turbulence and everyone must stay seated. Tell them they have to immediately return to their seats."

I made the announcement, and emphasized that turbulence had been reported in the area, and the captain had requested that all passengers return to their seats and stay seated until the seat belt sign had been turned off. But no, he was still in the lav!

What to do? I pounded on the door and asked him to take a seat for his safety, but he still didn't open the door, so I told him if he didn't come out, I would open the door from the outside. For those of you who don't know this, a sharp object like the tip of one of our knives on your trays could be inserted into a slot in the door and we could open the door from the outside.

Just as I was getting ready to open the door from the outside he pops out, bag in hand, and looks at me with "knives" in his eyes as if I could kill you now! That was unnerving, to say the least and trust me another trip was made to tell the captain about this too.

Well, the captain had the plane do some bumps and kept the seat belt sign on for the rest of the flight. He also told me that he would have a passenger service agent meet the flight when we opened the door at the gate. This man was going to get a surprise! The agent told me to point him out when he was deplaning because he had notified authorities and they were going to detain him for questioning. After the passengers had deplaned, and before we had a new group get on to go to New York, another ground agent went into the lav, where I said this person had been forever, and proceeded to come out of it with bags of items. I had no idea what was in the bags, or even what he was looking for. It was only getting stranger and stranger.

Now the plot thickens. Remember we were in Cleveland and going on to JFK. After I arrived at JFK, I was met by the head of TWA security and two FBI agents. They wanted to know exactly what had gone on during that flight. In addition, I had to write down the story in long hand, sign it and put down my company payroll number. I could not resist, I put down my real company ID number followed by "007." Fortunately, the company and the FBI had a sense of humor because they did laugh. Remember all of those James Bond movies were out then.

So, what was this man up to? Why was he in the lav forever? Unbelievably he was part of a smuggling gang! His job was to put "watch parts" and other valuables into the back of compartments in the lav. I know, watch parts? The smuggling gang already knew what planes would be going on to Europe, actually to London and Frankfurt, where the items were to be picked up by other gang members out of the lavs. Hmm, seems like an inside job to me. Then the FBI agents told me that this gang was actually very dangerous, and if I had any unusual confrontations to call them immediately. Well, that made an impression and I carried around both of their identification cards for years. Really, I could have been on a hit list!

Just call me, *"On Her Majesty's Secret Service*, 007"

Unlimited Salad and Breadsticks

Photo salad cart in 1st class courtesy of the Jon Proctor Collection.

I WAS FLYING the polar from LAX to London and was serving the bread and breadsticks in first class. One passenger asked what the breadsticks were. I replied with a smile, "Italian chopsticks." I just thought I was being witty.

A few minutes later, I looked back into the cabin and saw her carefully eating her salad with the breadsticks.

Coffee, Tea or

IT WAS THE mid-sixties and I was twenty years old. I was working first class on a breakfast flight on a Boeing 707. We had a full load of first class passengers on board that morning and I was working the cabin position, which meant I would be serving the passengers. Normally the flight attendant who was working the galley position (preparing all of the food) would take the passengers' food orders for first class, but this morning she asked me if I would do it for her. I said, "Sure." She said, "The omelets go first, there is always a problem with the alternate entree. They don't like it."

As usual in those days, first class consisted of all businessmen. When I returned to the galley, I told her, I had no problems. I only needed ten of the omelets and all of the rest were quickies. She said, "WHAT!" I told her again I needed all the quickies. She looks at me as if I am straight off the farm and says, "Quickies that is pronounced quiche!" I looked out into the cabin where I saw ten pouting, grumpy faces waiting for their omelets and the other happy expectant faces waiting for much more. They were disappointed ... but then maybe they liked their quiche? Wink!

Only Socks

YOU CAN'T MAKE these things up. We had finished our service on a Boeing 747 which as some of you might remember was a huge aircraft. The movie was running when a passenger came into the galley area where we were all taking a break. What does he announce to us? "There is a man sleeping on the floor back by one of the doors. I think you better go take a look at him."

I'm thinking, "What the—," sorry but it was a long trip and someone sleeping on the floor was just one more irritation that I didn't want to deal with. So, off I go toward the back of the plane and what do I find? A man that is NUDE, except for his socks, lying on the floor! It is one of those out of body experiences and my first reaction was, "OMG is he dead, what is going on here?" I bent down and could see that he was breathing and get this one, he was snoring! Oh, have we handed out all of the blankets, raced through my mind now? I've got to cover him up before someone else walks by.

Fortunately, the container where we stored the blankets still had a few in it. I grabbed them up and threw them over the sleeping man. What next? Thank God there were male flight attendants on board that flight. I quickly rounded them up and said, "This is above my pay grade. You've got to get him into a seat and dressed. I think he is drunk? I'll go see if I can find his clothes." Well, guess what? His clothes were in an empty row along with his flask. He obviously had been enjoying too much Scotch, thought he was at home and removed his clothes for a good nap, woke up and had to go potty. He didn't make it to the lav which was only a few feet away from him.

I let the male flight attendants handle this one and trust me his flask was taken away!

That Wonderful Feeling of Safety

YOU WILL WONDER by the end of this story, why I would ever title it as I did. After all, this is a story about probably the only thing close to a real emergency that I ever had while flying.

I never had a ditching or evacuation. I never had a baby born onboard or someone suffering a heart attack. I never had a cockpit issue with one man down, or a malfunction in the galley ... OMG "No hot food!"

I may have run out of steaks, and only had lasagna left to offer passengers, or no more bananas for splits in first class, but always had enough

Galliano for Harvey Wallbangers, and pillows and blankets for those who wanted them for the night.

But NO real emergencies and for that I am eternally grateful. Having said that, this was the closest thing I would say that could have gone very wrong, and yet did not because we flew with the best in the industry.

I loved and flew London for the last eight years of my career and this morning, as we took off from Heathrow, I sat in my jump seat, making eye contact and chatting with the passengers in front of me as usual. But then, almost immediately I saw the "B" in British Airways, as big as life, out one of the passenger's windows. That's all I saw, just a big blue "B."

We banked hard to the right, to the point where anything that was not secured, began flying and all I remember was smiling. "No matter what", just keep smiling.

I don't know if that expression was frozen on my face, or part of the job that I might have been trained to do in order to keep calm in the cabin. After all, most of our training was to get people off the plane in an emergency. In this case, we would hopefully be staying "ON." But it was working, as all eyes looked my way, hoping for reassurance and that everything was going to be OK. Moreover, I'm sure that every other flight attendant on that 747 was doing the same.

When we leveled off, it was some time before the seatbelt sign went off and there was an announcement from the captain. I don't remember exactly what he said, but I'm sure it was also reassuring without saying, "Well that British Airways got a little too close, but not to worry folks. We got out of their way." Imagine a passenger sharing that announcement with friends and family on the ground?

So, this is why I've titled this story about feeling safe because that is what I always felt back in the '70s and '80s flying with a crew that was like family and going through an experience like this. I respected our pilots, and knew of the tremendous responsibility they took when transporting hundreds of people daily. As for being like family here are a few of my memories:

One time on a layover the captain took us all "gliding." That I will NEVER forget. He rented a glider and took us up one at a time. I had the opportunity to feel like a bird! He let me release the cord, and the towing line and at that moment there was no sound. Just sight and thrill. I rode the thermals and the captain let me soak it all in, without speaking. I will never forget the mountains and canyons that we glided over. I felt totally safe and relaxed.

And there was a time when one of the pilots took us all up in a helicopter. Now he may have just had a friend who owned one, but again this was on one of those "extra" long layovers. It was San Francisco and he took us at night over the city! It was breathtaking. I never wanted to land. I probably would have been afraid if I had known that helicopters have NO gliding properties, but then I was with one of our pilots who I trusted and put my life in his hands.

The days where we ferried the plane with no passengers was probably one of the best things, I always looked forward too. The cockpit door was secured open, and we were asked by the captain, "Who wants to ride up front?" The thrill of taking off over a major city or landing with that runway rushing up at you and the wheels touching down! Those days are maybe gone, but I do have the memory forever.

However, let me finish my story about our "near miss" with British Airlines. Once we were back to normal, it was time for me to go into the cockpit and get the crew's orders for lunch. It seemed like a long time but apparently not long enough.

I entered to find them all a bit pale and when I asked them what they wanted for lunch, the captain just turned graciously and said, "Hey is everything OK back there?" To which I replied, "Yes." Then he said, "We could use a little more time up here, so could you come back later?" And of course, I said, "Got it," because they were the guys that I always would do anything for and we were always made to feel part of their team.

Whore De Ovaries ... Delicious

SUMMER OF 1973 ... My new roommate and I were on what they called reserve. In other words, TWA crew scheduling could put you on any flight that was missing a flight attendant. So, this evening we were to work from JFK to Paris.

Photo of 1st class caviar and appetizer cart on International flights.
Photo courtesy of the Jon Proctor Collection.

Both new and junior, we were stuck working first class on a full Boeing 747. I did not know my new roomie well, except she was four years older than I, and had grown up all over the world as the daughter to someone in the diplomatic services, making her quite worldly in my eyes. Me, I was barely twenty-one and just out of the "ole" cactus patch, having had my first TWA interview in LAX. In addition, it was the first time I had ever been out of little Tucson, AZ.

But back to our flight, I am chicken to take on that first class galley, which really needed someone with lots of experience, so I opted to work the cabin position. My roomie, now flying partner, is working feverishly setting up the galley, which she had never done before either. I picked up the first class menu and studied it like a human anatomy textbook. Do you think this was a disaster in the making now?

After takeoff, we served cocktails and then I had the dreaded appetizer cart to deal with. I didn't have a clue about any of the food on that cart or what it was. Picture me asking the first class passengers if they would like some WHORE DE OVARIES, or I also have some PAAY-TEA, and I can put those little black eggy things on toast or B LIN NEES, more SHAM PAG KNEE, some smoked fishy thing, SALL MOON.

All the passengers are smiling up at me and in my naiveté, I thought I was doing a TERRIFIC job! After winging around first class, I get back to the galley and find my roomie/flying partner sitting on the spiral stairs that went up to the lounge and cockpit, holding her legs tightly together, with tears running down her cheeks.

I was so concerned if she was OK, when she asked me if that was an act or for real? I had no idea what she was talking about. She did finally explain. Needless to say, I was mortified to go out in the cabin again, so I made her switch positions with me. Who would have thought that down the road I would "love" those little black eggy things on blinis with some Sham Pag Knee?

P.S. TWA actually served Beluga caviar from Iran years ago. Those were days!

Translation: Whore De Ovaries—Beluga Caviar; Paay-tea—Goose Liver Pate; Sham Pag Nee—Champagne; B Lin knees—Blinis: Sall-moon—Smoked salmon.

Yo Ho Ho and a Bottle of Rum

A GOOD FRIEND of mine, who was a flight service manager with TWA, had the reputation of being a joker. Yes, one could say he was the "wild card" in the deck. Boy did he like to have fun.

We were working on a Boeing 747 to Madrid, Spain and what does he take out of his suitcase before boarding the passengers? A gorgeous life size fake parrot! He then puts it on his shoulder and proceeds to place a patch over his one eye. Now I hear him on boarding, "Aaaaaarhh, ahoy hearties."

He didn't stop there but proceeded to work the entire flight with his parrot and patch. There was a lot of pirate speech especially to the children, Yo Ho Ho, Shiver My Timbers, and Pieces of Eight.

You just couldn't help but laugh and the passengers loved him too. Those were the good old days of having fun on the plane with your passengers and crew.

Sadly, he is now in Fiddlers Green, heaven for pirates …

Club Soda

TWA HAD JUST worked out a deal with the Airfone company to install phones in the "center seat backs" on some of our 727s. This was really a big deal! Remember cell phones hadn't been invented yet and everyone would run to a pay phone in the airport to stand in line to make a call.

First issue with this new technology, it was expensive to use! Secondly, how would you like to be in the row with the person who wants to make a call when they aren't in the center seat and you are? Might want to wrap that phone cord around their neck after a while. Lastly, who wants to sit next to a chatterbox?

Note here: You all want to use your cell phones on the plane when you're airborne now. Think long and hard about that option. Sitting next to the incessant talker, finding out more about their personal lives than you need to or ever wanted to know? Why do I see some fist fights starting over that? Just saying …

But back to my flight: I was working the coach beverage cart and was somewhere around row ten, when I heard this man chatting away really loudly on the phone in his row.

Having never spoken to anyone about this new technology, when I got to him, I whispered because he was on the phone, "How's the reception?" Whereupon, he replied, "Great, until my brother-in-law threw up."

YUCK! I looked at the passengers to his left and right and they seemed to be fine. Then it hit me, he's talking with his brother-in-law now.

I'll never get this opportunity again! "Sir, may I have the phone please." He doesn't hesitate and hands me the receiver. Remember the cord is short, so I lean over the aisle passenger and speak to the brother-in-law on the phone, "Hey, heard you weren't feeling well. I would suggest you drink some club soda and remember it is great for taking stains out of clothes too."

I casually handed the phone back to my passenger while everyone within hearing distance started to laugh. Hope the guy didn't have the flu. Club soda can only help so much!

Is It a Bat, Is It a Squirrel, No It's What?

Movies in flight. In a typically forward-thinking move, TWA was first to contract with Inflight Motion Pictures, Inc., for film showings on coast-to-coast nonstop and transatlantic flights. It's still a TWA exclusive.

Photo of first class movie screen courtesy of the TWA Museum. Circa 1964.

WHEN WE FIRST hit LA as new hires, the wig salesperson was at our door. How that miraculously happened, who knows? Human hair wigs for $150, ugh, kind of high back in those days. Nevertheless, we went for it. Being on reserve which is called stand by, meat on a hook, or when TWA can call you morning, noon or night to go work a flight at any crazy hour it made sense to have one.

Those wigs had to be professionally cut and trimmed but they were allowed. So, we each wrote the check and now were the proud owners of wigs. I have to admit here it really looked better than my own hair.

As I said earlier, my roommate and I were on reserve and were called out to work a Boeing 707 flight from LA to JFK. This was exciting because we had never flown together before. OMG, it was the "Royal Ambassador" coast to coast service, which was a really big deal and everyone while they were in training, dreaded the thought of having to do it in real life! But you have to learn someday, so it was going to be trial by fire.

We put our wigs on, off to the airport and went for it. We were perfection! Just saying ... Everyone was wined, and dined and our dining instructor from training would have been proud! Now it was movie time. The movie screen was pulled down for the movie. It was a huge screen, located in the middle of the isle and you had to bend over to get under it.

We were finally taking a breather in our jump seats, totally exhausted from the stress and really all of the work that went into that service. Now what? A passenger call button went off. My roomie/flight attendant partner jumps up and starts to go down the aisle under the movie screen.

One small problem, she didn't lean far enough forward. You got it! There was her $150 wig dangling off the bottom of the movie screen now. The passengers went into hysterics as she tried to untangle it and get it released from the screen. I don't know if the wig looked more like a bat, or a flying squirrel as it dangled in the air, but the important thing here is no matter what she still looked beautiful and the passengers loved her! Making TWA proud again, wink!

I Go to Rio ... No ... You've Got a Friend

I WAS WORKING the upper deck lounge on a Boeing 747 nonstop flight from JFK to LAX, in 1978. A couple was pre-boarded by a TWA, PR agent. I had not received the passenger manifest list of names yet, and the PR agent was on and off the plane like a flash of light. Who was this couple? They didn't look familiar to me. Must be VIPs but who knows?

No worries ... I went over to them and asked if they would like a beverage before takeoff. They told me no, but she said they would love some pillows and blankets because they would like to sleep the entire flight.

I said, "I'll get you some and I won't wake you for the service, but if you need anything else just ring and I'll be happy to get it for you." I returned with the pillows and blankets, and I don't know why but I said to this woman, as I nodded in the direction of her traveling companion, "He looks like Peter Allen, the singer from Australia." And she replied nonchalantly, "Him, a singer? Naaaaah." He just smiled.

When the door closed, I was given the passenger manifest and saw that the couple upstairs was Carly Simon and James Taylor. Oops ... I didn't recognize either one. They slept almost the entire flight. Couldn't have asked for nicer passengers.

Napolis

TEL AVIV TO Paris on a Lockheed-1011. The entire crew is up in first class dining on our hummus and tahini before our flight, paying absolutely no attention to the agents, as they purposefully "pre-board" a unique, elderly woman, en route to Paris.

Fast forward, the plane is airborne: we are now in the aisle serving hot meals when I get to the "pre-boarded" elderly woman. I ask her what she would like to eat and she bursts out screaming at me in a language that was not Hebrew. I ask the passengers sitting next to her what she wants, and they respond with, "We have no idea who she is, she was seated when we boarded." UH-OH! Upon further inspection not only is this woman ranting in some other language, but we take notice that she is also "blind."

Moving on … one of the more caring flight attendants (not me) takes a meal to the galley, cuts up the food into tiny bites and begins to hand feed her. Guess grandma did not like our home cooking, as she began to spit the food all over the place, on passengers, the seatbacks and the caring flight attendant. OK Granny, so you don't like the meal.

And the story continues … as I am walking down the aisle, the flight service manager grabs me and says he needs help with this woman, she needs to use the lav. By this time, we had discovered she spoke Italian and so did the flight service manager. Whew.

I prayed all we would have to do is drag her to the back to the lav, despite all of her loud ranting and protests. Of course, the entire aircraft was well aware of "Princess Charming" now.

We get the woman back to the lav, and the flight service manager proceeds to describe the facilities and where everything is located to her. Our plan was to quickly close the lav door and pray some more. Not to be the case! As the flight service manager is doing his best to assist, he suddenly looks at me with very wide eyes and says, "Oh shit, we have a problem!" Huh? What kind of a problem could we have at this point? She is wearing something … wearing what … what is a "something?" Diapers! YIKES, as he looks at me hoping my motherly instincts will kick in.

In protest I banter back, "Oh no, not me … I have NEVER changed a real baby's diaper, let alone some eighty-five-year-old woman, who is now screaming and crying in Italian. Get one of the mothers on board back here, make an announcement to see if her family is hiding in a closet or something, get a nurse—DON'T GET ME!!!!!!"

To the rescue, another flight attendant shows up. Now four of us are trying to fit into the lav, all focused on diaper detail, and wouldn't you know it, just as we have dropped her "drawers" we hit an air pocket, and the plane starts hopping around like the Easter Bunny and Granny is grabbing at any body part she can find, our body parts to be exact.

But this adventure is not over yet …

Granny says she is going to "Napolis" which we hope is a side street in Paris. Digging through her bags to find her tickets, we discover that "Napolis" is actually INDIANAPOLIS and she has two plane changes once she reached New York, not to mention immigration and US Customs, escalators and a transfer to the domestic terminal. Piece of cake, NOT!

Can you just imagine the eager anticipation of some dear, loving relatives in "Napolis," as Granny is on the way for many weeks and months of warm lovely conversation? Talk about family "dumping" from Tel Aviv to Napolis.

So next, we notified the Paris operations that we had a problem, (this was after we got the cockpit to stop laughing,) and told them they needed to make a decision about what to do with "Granny." Paris was not too pleased with their role in our little drama. They thought we might offer to take her to our hotel rooms and then escort her to New York the following day. Nice try guys! And you should have seen the Paris outbound crew when they found out about having to take Granny to New York ... mutiny on the L-1011.

Not sure, whatever happened to Granny. We thought that Paris should send Granny back to Tel Aviv because she was not able to travel alone. Do you think some Tel Aviv agent got his pockets lined that day? So what else is new ...

The ideas began to flow about what they should do with Granny; call the family and hire a nurse in Paris to travel with her, make someone from the family come to Paris to escort her, find a taxi and make up some address ... anything!

To this day, I never did find out how Granny survived, or how the agents and other crews survived with Granny either. Hope Granny enjoyed Napolis ...

Sticky Notes Left Out Something

UPON BOARDING MY flight from Newark to LAX, I was getting ready to work in the first class cabin, when a young flight attendant boarded and asked where I wanted her to work. I said, "The first class galley position is open." Her eyes grew very large and I swear I thought I heard her gulp, as she told me this was her first working flight. I said, "No problem, everyone has their first flight. If you need any assistance, I will be happy to help you."

What does she do? She proceeds to post sticky notes with writing on them all over the galley. Well, this was something that I had never seen before, but I didn't question her. Each to their own. After takeoff, I asked her if she needed any help and she reassured me that she would be okay. Great, that was good news, so I started serving cocktails in first class.

Now she was in the galley working away and heating up food in the ovens that would be served shortly. No worries or so I thought.

Picture four businessmen in the lounge area, seated across from the first class galley that the newbie was working in, innocently playing cards, when all of a sudden there was an explosive sound that actually shook the aircraft. Instinctively, I swung around and started to run to the galley. The flight engineer came flying out of the cockpit running toward the galley at the same time. What awaited us in the galley? The oven door had been blown off! There was black bean soup covering not only the flight attendant, but the entire galley and lounge, including the men sitting there playing cards.

This flight attendant apparently put ALL the black bean soup cans in the oven without opening them and they exploded, blowing the oven door off. The passenger, in the lounge closest to the galley, had his cards fanned out and they were covered with black bean soup, as well as his glasses and suit. Initially he was in shock but suddenly realized the pain of hot soup all over him. Then all four men jumped out into the aisle with cards flying everywhere. I grabbed whatever I could to wipe the soup off their skin while the flight engineer attended to the flight attendant. It was a "total miracle" no one was seriously hurt!

TWA had quite a cleaning bill though. I guess none of those sticky notes explained how to heat the soup on the plane? The new flight attendant disappeared for the rest of the flight, and I never saw her again. I think she was hiding in coach ...

Mrs. Brisson

Actress Rosalind Russell.
Photo courtesy of Cara Ooi Collection.

I HAD BEEN flying for two months and was on call or "reserve" as they say, out of JFK. I was usually on a transatlantic or transcontinental flight. This time I was being sent to Los Angeles on a Boeing 747.

Before saying goodbye to my roommates at 30 East 68th, I would say in a slow east coast accent, "You may contact me at the Brisson residence," and they would all laugh. I know you are saying, "Who?" The Brisson residence in Beverly Hills was the home of Rosalind Russell, my favorite actress of all time, and she was married to Mr. Freddie Brisson.

Now fast forward to my return trip from LAX to JFK: I was awoken at 7 AM by a ringing phone call. It was TWA scheduling. "How fast can you get to the airport?" they asked. I said, "One hour," and they said, "You've got thirty minutes." So, I threw myself together and went directly to the airport for this flight. As I entered the first class door, it was literally shut behind me by the ground crew and off we departed.

The flight service manager was obviously relieved to see me and said, "You're working first class aisle. Rosalind Russell is in 1A." Time stopped as I stared at him. "This is a miracle!" I exclaimed. "A bloody miracle!"

I waited on Mrs. Brisson for the entire trip and was fortunate enough that she would engage me in small talk. We found out we shared a birthday on June 4th, and believe it or not I even told her what I would tell my roommates every time I left for a trip to LA. If she thought that was strange, she didn't let on and just smiled, and we continued to chat the entire flight.

She became so relaxed around me that she confided she was going to Sloane Kettering Hospital to be treated for breast cancer. I felt devastated for her. Unfortunately she died from breast cancer in November of 1976 and I remember it brought tears to my eyes. Later this same disease would enter my life and I thought of her during my treatments. A beautiful, vivacious and quick witted, strong woman! As she said in Auntie Mame, "Life is a banquet and most poor suckers are starving to death."

Life is strange but I believe I was on that plane to entertain Ms. Russell on one of her last flights. My pleasure, indeed.

Greetings

IT WAS GETTING close to the time for boarding the passengers now, and since I was working first class, I decided to make a quick run into the lav to check my makeup and hair. No need to close the door for this.

We were flying with a very shall we say, "playful" captain, who saw me in the lavatory, decided to jump in there with me and then he slammed the door shut. Well, we somehow got locked in there. Picture two adults in one small lav. It can happen. After some banging on the door, he was finally able to get it open. But it gets worse ...

Who was standing there to greet us, as the captain and I popped out of the lav together? Some of my first class passengers! Nothing was said, but I could hear some folks giggling. Trust me I was not.

He could go back up into the cockpit, I on the other hand had to see these same people for the next two hours. Wonder what they told their friends and family later?

Give Me Your Cash

Photo Howard Hughes piloting the plane courtesy of the TWA Museum.

ONE OF THE stories I heard about our infamous and famous owner Howard Hughes was this one. He had commandeered one of TWA's planes, and while in flight called the tower at Newark, NJ, to report that he needed to land due to some engine problems. After landing he taxied to the TWA gate area, went inside, and told a TWA ticket agent that he was out of money and to give him all of the cash he had. He signed a receipt for the cash and flew away.

Considering that he would take TWA planes at his discretion, fly them himself as the captain, with of course a TWA cock-pit crew to work as his first officer and flight engineer it really isn't that farfetched.

Galley Disaster Turns to Buffet Style

I FLEW FROM 1957 through1960 and was based out of Newark, NJ. I'm sure some of you think of it as the stone age but it was the beginning of the glamour years of TWA. And yes, we did serve food then! But all was not glamorous sometimes and we had to cover others' mistakes with some humor. We'll just call this "Galley Disaster."

Our flight commissary personnel always did their best to load those galleys as quickly as possible. Their last question to us was usually, do you need anything else and then if the answer was no, they were gone in a flash! Unfortunately, on this particular flight the commissary personnel had forgotten to secure everything properly. You are beginning to get the picture now.

We were serving Hungarian goulash for dinner. Well, when we took off all of the goulash fell out of the carrier and like slow moving lava started flowing down the aisle. Food, broken plates and all! What is a girl to do? I picked up the PA mike and made an announcement, "Ladies and gentlemen, we are trying something new tonight. We decided to serve a buffet. So, if you see something you like going by, just help yourself." The laughter was wonderful and broke the tension of the moment. Needless to say, we had to turn around and go back for a little clean up and some more food. Well, maybe more of a major clean up.

And yes, they all loved the goulash ...

Be Still My Heart

ONE OF THE most glamorous aspects of an airline hostess's job was the opportunity to entertain celebrities as if they were in your flying home. It was extra good fortune to fly for TWA, which as Howard Hughes's baby, was "the airline of the stars" and afforded its employees plenty of up close and personal interaction. It wasn't often that I personally caught sight of the great ones, but I was lucky enough to meet one who was most important to me. My idols of the era were Cary Grant, Michael Douglas and Rod Taylor.

No one would question my fascination with Cary Grant, but why might you ask, "Michael and Rod," when I could be serving cocktails and talking with Clarke Gable, Gregory Peck or Gary Cooper?

Let me explain: In the early '70s, Michael Douglas had not yet achieved his phenomenal fame and was mostly noted for being Kirk Douglas's son. EXCEPT BY ME! I was crazy about his character in *Streets of San Francisco*, a weekly detective series on TV. To this day, Karl Malden, who was the lead detective on the series, whose "buddy boy" was called "Steve," is the Michael Douglas I dreamt over. And I still think he is sexy.

Now as for Rod Taylor, he played a foreign correspondent in a 1960s serial called *Hong Kong*. He later went on to star in *Young Cassidy*, *The Birds*, *The Time Machine*, *The VIPs* and *Sunday in New York*, setting my aching heart pounding in each. But I always boasted that I knew him WHEN ... when he was simply sexy, handsome and a relative unknown. I drooled over the prospect of ever laying eyes on the guy.

So when my roommate, who was a reservationist at Western Airlines, reported that he had booked a ticket on them, and would be flying into San Francisco on a certain day and time, I was set to rearrange my flights so that I could be around his gate area to ogle my idol. I know it sounds crazy, but this is what young crazy girls did.

Little did I know that luck was coming my way. I was on the last leg of my flight schedule that would take me home to Rod. My final stopover was in Los Angeles. I was the first class hostess who stood at the front door to welcome everyone on board. As I repeated over and over again, "Welcome aboard," I heard a familiar Australian accent saying, "Well, we have a freckled-faced one today." I was face to face with the man of my dreams and managed not to faint. He DIDN'T choose Western, he was on MY TWA AIRPLANE and I was in heaven.

He did not disappoint me. Mr. Taylor was every bit as handsome, and as charming, as I expected. It didn't even matter that he was traveling with a gorgeous wife who had not one freckle on her fair skin.

For one hour, between LA and San Francisco, he chatted, joked, and cemented my love. If he or the freckle-less one only knew what was in my heart.

Today I laugh about my crushes from yester years, but fondly remember being able to spend time with one of them. Only as a "hostess" now called a flight attendant does one get to do this. Such good times and memories.

Plop, Plop ... Fizz, Fizz and We Aren't Talking Alka Seltzer

I HAD ONLY been flying a short time and was still a "newbie" at my job. The gate agent came on the aircraft, and said we were going to have a basketball team coming on board and he was going to start boarding the passengers.

Well, as fate would have it, I was working in the first class cabin and I thought oh how much fun we are going to have with these little kids. Surprise, surprise! The first passenger to board was so tall my eyes were almost level with his belt buckle. I found myself stammering, and finally stuttered out, "Welcome aboard sir." Then who starts coming on? The rest of the Milwaukee Bucks. Little kids, I know, what was I thinking?

Not being a basketball aficionado, I whispered to my flying partner, "Who are these guys?" She was obviously trying not to laugh at my naiveté and said, "That's your basketball team."

It was then that I realized these men were "professional" basketball players. I have to admit I was pretty nervous being around all of these famous athletes, even though I didn't know anything about basketball. All seemed to be going well until I was serving drinks. One of the players asked for another can of soda. Again, what was I thinking? I brought out a can of soda and proceeded to open it in front of the player instead of in the galley area.

You guessed it. The can exploded like a bottle of champagne. Fizz flowing everywhere including his lap! This was one of those OMG moments, as I ran to get some towels and bolted back to apologize profusely. Well, he couldn't have been more gracious and even refused the cleaning voucher I offered him. Bet you are wondering who this nice man was? None other than Mr. Kareem Abdul-Jabbar.

Thank you, sir, for your kindness, and needless to say I became a big fan and started to follow your illustrious career.

Batshit Crazy

LET ME TELL you about a flight to JFK from LAX. We used to say they opened the asylum doors when there was a "full moon" and put all of them on night flights for therapy. This flight proved that theory to be true.

The overhead lights were turned down to dim after the service, so our passengers could either watch the movie or sleep. My flying partner had gone up to first class to have a late snack from left-over first class goodies, so I was by myself in coach. I was being a good stew and checking on my passengers to make sure no one needed anything, was dying, or burning the place down with a cigarette. Yes, it was in those smoking days on a plane. I know, ICK!

As I said, I am out in the aisle when what do I hear? Screaming coming from the back of the plane. I charged back there to find a guy straddling a woman who was half in and half out of one of the aft lavs. He was violently shaking and choking her while she screamed for help.

My passengers, being mostly New Yorkers, were just standing around like they were at a prize fight. I jumped into the fracas, otherwise called assault, and started yelling at him to stop! Before I knew it, I was perched halfway on his back pulling at his arms, much to no avail. This was looking like a bad mixed martial arts fight at this point.

I frantically got off him and went to the interphone to call the cockpit. The flight engineer answers and I'm yelling into the phone, "I've got a guy back here who is batshit crazy, beating the living daylights out of a woman. He has her on the floor, with his hands around her throat, shaking her and she's screaming for help. Other passengers are just watching and NO ONE IS DOING ANYTHING to stop it. I need your help." To which the flight engineer says, "Can you repeat that? I can't hear you over some screaming." Can I repeat it? I'm in La-La land now! Then I hear myself yelling at the top of my lungs, "I've got a guy back here who is trying to kill a woman. I need your help. Did you hear me now?" And I slammed the phone back into its cradle.

All I could think was help me Lord, I'm on my own back here, when I finally convinced some passengers to help me. As we were pulling the guy off of this woman the flight engineer appeared with some seat belt extensions. With the help of the passengers, he was able to subdue this batshit crazo by strapping the seat belt extensions around his arms and chest. Fortunately, we were not a full flight, and they forced him into a seat in an empty row and fastened the seat belt around him. Picture a hogtied calf at this point. Let me rephrase that, a hogtied PIG!

When I finally got an opportunity to sit down on my jump seat to gain my composure, what do I see? My expensive panty hoses shredded and ruined from the two of them kicking me. If I could have only gotten my hands around his neck then, I would have choked him with those panty hoses. In our next contract, I wanted the union to get us combat pay. No more night flights for me with a full moon!

Oh, you're probably wondering who the woman was. She was his wife. And yes, the police did meet the flight and he was arrested. Plus, I never got the combat pay or even a new pair of stockings from the company.

Close Call

IT WAS 1955 and we were flying east at night, from St. Louis to New York, on a TWA twin propeller engine aircraft called a Martin 404. Flying at an altitude of approximately 10,000 feet we could see the ground below very well. There was literally a sea of unending lights, as we neared the populous eastern seaboard. Always breathtaking!

I was in the galley when I was attracted to a rosy glow in the cabin. What is that? As I walked forward and looked out of the window, I could see that one of the engines was on fire! My training kicked in immediately, and I calmly told the passengers to fasten their seatbelts and there would be no further smoking. I immediately then went back to my jump seat and buckled in. I felt sure that the pilots were aware of this and the last thing they needed was for me to be interrupting them, wanting to know what was happening.

Patience can be a virtue but in this circumstance the wait seemed to be an eternity, whereas in actuality it was only a few minutes until I could see that the glow had disappeared. Then shortly thereafter, the captain announced that we had had an engine fire but it was out now. He explained that they had shut off the fuel flow to that engine to prevent the fire from spreading, and had also "feathered the engine" which meant the propellers had been disabled on that engine too. Therefore, we only had one working engine and we would be landing at a closer airport in Newark rather than LaGuardia. His remarks were met by total silence.

We landed as if there wasn't anything wrong, and the passengers deplaned in a quiet and orderly fashion, as I bid them a restrained and brief goodbye. Little did we know until we were leaving the terminal that the poor passenger agent at the ticket counter was having a "wild time" handling the now irate passengers. All of their pent-up anxiety had burst forth, as they were forced to change planes and realized that they had just had a brush with death.

Never a dull moment!

Wig or No Wig

WHEN THE LOCKHEED-1011 first came online, there were many delays mostly because mechanics were in a learning stage regarding the aircraft's particular glitches. The answer to most delays in those days was always "free drinks" for the passengers and this particular situation was no different.

We were on our way to LAX from ORD and experiencing a terribly long delay on the ground. So long, in fact, we showed a free movie, news shorts, gave out plenty of peanuts and of course those "free drinks." Unfortunately, we could not serve food because we just did not know if we would leave any minute or continue to wait.

Finally, after three plus hours and still unable to figure out the problem, the captain decided we would switch to another 1011 that just landed. Hallelujah! However, this was no small undertaking either.

It meant that all of the luggage and service items had to be transferred to the other aircraft, besides getting the passengers off and over to the new gate. Finally, it seemed that everyone was off the plane and we started gathering our belongings.

However, "au contraire mon ami," as we prepared to leave, I spotted something in the back of the plane which looked odd. What? It looked like a wig on top of one of the seatbacks. Yes, either a wig or a small dead animal!

You are not going to believe this one! There was a middle-aged woman slouched over in her seat, clearly passed out from the free cocktails. Her blouse looked like it had been carefully draped across the seat back in front of her, with her disheveled wig gingerly balanced on top. Oh please, you must be kidding! The question, "why me, kept ringing in my ears." At least she still had on her bra, panties and skirt.

After I recruited two more female flight attendants to help me "redress" the limp passenger and rearrange her wig on her head, are you getting a visual here because trust me it wasn't easy. The agent ordered a wheelchair to whisk her over to the new aircraft. Talk about first class service. I bet you a hundred dollars right now this would never happen today.

Anyway, she peacefully slept fully clothed, with wig on, all the way to La-La land. My next career should have been a Hollywood stylist.

1956 Grand Canyon Crash a Game Changer

I WAS A flight attendant in 1964 and was flying out of MKC, Kansas City. I was married twice, my first husband predeceased me and later I remarried. My second husband when he was sixteen years old was supposed to be on a TWA flight that later crashed over the Grand Canyon. Literally right before the plane was leaving, the gate agent got on the plane and told him that his family called, he was needed at home and had to get off the plane. There were no stand-by passengers who were put on in his place because the agent had told them the entire plane was full and no one could get on. They had all left. So, the plane went out with one seat empty.

Years later, during my second marriage, we moved into a neighborhood where my neighbor behind me was a former TWA employee. He had been a scheduler on the ramp in LAX, who called out the flights, and we would stand at the back fence talking TWA for hours. One day I asked him if he had heard the story about the TWA flight going out one seat empty that had crashed over the Grand Canyon. He said he had but didn't know if it was just a rumor. I told him, "No, it's not a rumor you're living behind him. It was my husband who got off the flight before it left." He was totally surprised.

Later that day I went to my part time library job, and happened to tell the story about my neighbor and our conversation to one of the ladies I worked with. She got an almost sick look on her face, and said she and another couple were at the downtown airport in MKC that night, waiting for the flight as the other couple had a set of parents on it. I have to say I was stunned!

I learned that Mike Nelson was writing a book about the disaster called, *The Story of the Grand Canyon Disaster*. It was to be published for the 50th anniversary of this air disaster. Unfortunately, by the time I contacted him the book had already gone to print. He said I answered the fifty-year question of why the one seat was empty when there were stand-bys.

For those of you who are not familiar with this crash in 1956 it was between two aircraft, a TWA Lockheed Constellation and a United Airlines Douglas DC-7. It was June 30, 1956, and both had left California to eventually be cruising at the same altitude. Shortly after 10 AM both pilots reported to different communication stations that they would be crossing the canyon at the same position at 10:31 AM.

The Salt Lake City controller who had this information was not obligated to tell either pilot that they would be on a crash course. WHY? Because it was the sole responsibility of the pilots, at this time in aviation, to avoid other aircraft in uncontrolled airspace.

It was determined by the Civil Aeronautics Board that the pilots simply didn't see one another, after they pieced together what happened based on the wreckage because no one saw the planes collide. The TWA plane was found first and then the United aircraft in a very remote area of the Grand Canyon. It was so remote that Swiss mountain rescue groups, the Colorado Mountain Club, and military personnel were called in to find the bodies and respectfully remove them from the site.

Today this crash site is closed off to the public and the park service manages it as the resting place for 128 souls. There is a commemorative landmark plate at the canyon site overlooking the east end of the Grand Canyon where this terrible tragedy occurred.

Because of this air disaster and the deaths of 128 people the American public demanded that President Eisenhower do something. The Airways Modernization Act was passed by Congress and then the FAA, Federal Aviation Administration, began operating later in 1957. Thankfully, we now have many regulations that keep us safe and their deaths were not in vain. May they all be resting in peace ...

Charade ... I Heard That Voice

ON A FLIGHT from JFK to London I had my back to the jetway boarding door when I heard THAT VOICE ... Cary Grant! I know you are all asking now, "Was he as gorgeous as he looked in all of those movies?" The answer is, "YES!"

My head swirled around on my shoulders to see my flying partner greeting Gary Grant and telling him where his seat was located in first class. Oh, be still my heart! I had many stars on flight over the years but I was totally starstruck.

But here was the bad news, my flying partner was working the cabin position and I was working the galley. This meant I would have literally no contact with him. Now we were airborne and I'm asking her, "How is Mr. Grant? Is he nice? Have you been able to chat with him?" Of course, all of the answers were YES and I'm green with envy!

Later that night when the movie was on, and everyone was sleeping including Mr. Grant, I went out into the cabin to check on the passengers, and to obviously check on Mr. Grant to see if possibly he needed anything, when what do I see? Two flight attendants from coach squeezed into an empty seat in the center of the aircraft across from where Mr. Grant was sleeping. They were just sitting in silence watching him.

What's a girl to do? I squeezed in with them. I have no idea what we would have said if he woke up, and saw the three of us all sitting there watching him. Possibly, "Oh, Mr. Grant we were just waiting for you to wake up, so if you needed anything we could get it for you." That probably wouldn't have worked...

Welcome Aboard

AFTER I HAD been flying for around five years, it was really easy to spot male passengers you could kid with. It was late in the afternoon around five to six and your businessmen would be getting on in first class after a long day. You could tell by their body language that they were tired.

We would ask them if we could hang their coats and then we were to ask them if they wanted something to drink. I had usually picked out the ones I could playfully harass at this point. As they handed me their jacket I would say, "OK, sit down, shut up, keep your feet off the furniture and what would you like to drink? Bourbon, scotch, vodka or gin?" As they looked at me, startled by my request, I would then add, "I just wanted you to feel like you were at home," and give them a big grin.

They would always laugh and the ice had been broken. They could relax now, have a nice dinner, a few drinks and enjoy their flight. Their day was over, welcome aboard.

P.S. I'm sure you are thinking she must have gotten some negative comments back. Can honestly say, never. You can say most anything as long as it is done with a smile. Loved our business travelers!

How Many Dead Bodies Can One Flight Attendant Have On Flights

IT WAS IN the early '70s in my career and I was flying the purser position on a Boeing 707 to London. I was newly married to a Brit and each trip to England I would bring home a British newspaper for him.

After I returned home from this one particular trip, when he was reading his paper, he asked me, "Wasn't this your flight number?" There was an article about a dead man being found in customs who had been smuggled into the UK in a garment bag. Yes, a garment bag! Someone apparently wanted to avoid the red tape of shipping a loved one back for burial, all the way to Pakistan, or maybe it was just the expense? No idea how this ended. But it did make me think when I was kidding a businessman about his overpacked bulging garment bag and would say, "Hey, do you have your mother-in law in there," that it just might be true!

Later in my career, I was now a flight service manager on another trip to London and we were transporting a stretcher case. A family had reserved the whole right-hand side of first class for the stretcher and also had hired a nurse to accompany the man. All seemed in order. Little did we know the man on the stretcher was deceased when he was boarded, and his family was again trying to circumvent the red tape of transporting a body. We found this out the next day when we were leaving London.

Some people used to say that TWA meant Traveling With Angels. This put a new take on that theme.

Did I Really Hear Him Correctly

MANY OF YOU might remember the nightmares in Chicago when it came to taking off and landing. What do I mean? If you were coming into O'Hare, you might find yourself circling out over Aurora, IL, for an extra hour just to land. And then when you were on a flight trying to leave ORD you could be in a horrendous long line of planes all wanting to do the same thing, just get out of Dodge!

Years ago, TWA had a flight every hour on the hour to LGA out of ORD. They were all Boeing 727 regulars. What is a regular? It is the shorter version of a 727, galley in the center of the plane, first class held twelve passengers and coach sat sixty-nine. These planes had a three-man cockpit, three flight attendants and they had boarding steps that came out of the tail section of the aircraft. Plus, the flight attendants could lower them from inside the plane to the ground for passengers to board through. This is important to my story.

We had a full load of passengers and were leaving at 4 PM. We left the gate on time, made our safety announcement, and checked our passengers for seat belts and seat backs. I sit down in my seat across from the galley and buckle up. Everything is seemingly in order when what do I hear? "Ladies and gentlemen, we are number one hundred in line to take off. So, we will be going to a penalty box where we can shut down our engines to save fuel, until we are called out to get back in line for takeoff."

I got out of my seat and went up to the first class flight attendant's jump seat and asked her, "Did he just say we are number ONE HUNDRED for takeoff?" She replies, "I think so. That can't be right?" I'm thinking he had to have misspoken and I tell her I'm going to the cockpit to see if this is true. Well, guess what? It was! This was mind boggling to say the least.

I asked the other two flight attendants to join me in the galley for a pow-wow. Since I was senior, I took control. Let's get out the liquor cart ladies. Here's what I'm going to tell the passengers, "Ladies and gentlemen in the coach section of the aircraft. We will be coming through with the liquor cart and all liquor today is complimentary. We will be happy to serve you two miniatures of your choice, or another beverage. We will be coming through with the cart in forty-five minutes again to serve you another beverage of your choice. This flight was scheduled for a snack service and if any of you would like your snack, we will be happy to serve you now also. Please remember we only have one snack per passenger, so we will have to keep track of who's eaten and who hasn't."

So off we go into coach, everyone seems happy that we are serving them something to drink and eat if they want. We go out the second time with the liquor cart and also pick up glasses etc. that they are finished with. Then I made another announcement and told them if they wanted to have anything else to drink or their snack, just to ring their call button, or come up to the galley and we would be happy to serve them. Obviously, we had hours and hours to wait.

Remember this was in the day and age when we had plenty of magazines on board, pillows and blankets, and people had some leg room. Yes, real leg room!

To keep the airplane from getting stuffy we lowered those stairs in the rear, opened the galley door in the center of the aircraft, and put the straps across it to warn people not to step out and of course there was always one of us in the galley too.

Hours go by, supplies are getting low. I went to the cockpit and asked the captain if he would call our ramp and ask the commissary to bring us more ice, glasses, soft drinks, napkins, beer, wine and a new liquor kit. Oh, thank God we had those back stairs, so they could board the aircraft with our needed supplies.

Our passengers were milling around, and we were talking with them, collecting magazines and repassing them. I end up in the galley playing Liar's poker, with one-dollar bills, with three of our passengers. Yes, we needed some diversions too.

We are now into the fourth hour of sitting in the penalty box! Surprisingly no one was throwing a hissy fit over this. I decided to go up to the cockpit to take a much-needed break. When I entered the cockpit, the captain turned around and said, "Well, I've been waiting for you." I'm thinking WHAT? "Are they getting rowdy? Two of the flights ahead of us and one behind us have already gone back to the gates. The passengers were ready to riot and one even had close to a fist fight on it. I just said to the guys she'll be up here soon telling us we have to go back to the gate."

I kinda laughed at this point and said, "Well, actually no I'm just here to take a break. Everyone is fine." The captain looks a little stunned and says, "What are you doing back there that they are all just fine with?"

I said, "Well, we've been wining and dining them like they are in a restaurant. Eat when you want, drink when you want, booze is free, here's a magazine, would you like a pillow or blanket. And yes, I'm even playing Liar's poker in the galley with some of the passengers." He starts laughing and says, "Well, it must be the Liar's poker."

Five hours after leaving the gate we finally took off for LGA. It is night time now, our passengers are sound asleep, the lights are on dim and two hours later we land in NY. They cheered and clapped on landing! And guess what? We did too! Here's to free booze and Liar's poker. P.S. The captain wrote up a glowing report back to the company commending us on our professionalism and how well we represented TWA during a very trying situation. And we also got a number of accommodation letters from our passengers too. I know what you are thinking now, "Like that would happen today. Try getting a can of coke on a plane that would be a miracle, let alone a snack during a delay like that." We know how times have changed.

I Can't Get This to Work

A LOVELY ELDERLY lady was brought aboard by one of the ground agents and escorted to her seat in first class. She was very pleasant and chatty, wearing a bright royal blue pantsuit (how do I remember this stuff?), and her silver hair was beautifully coiffed. She was quite tiny and I remember her little feet didn't touch the floor.

At some point, she dozed off for her afternoon nap. A short time later, I looked back at her from the galley and could see that she had a perplexed look on her face and seemed to be struggling with something in front of her.

Walking back through the cabin, I stopped and asked if I could be of help. She continued to twist the tray table lock back and forth, back and forth, looked up at me and said, "I can't get this picture to come in. The screen is all white." So, I twisted the lever back and forth, back and forth, shook my head, and told her that her TV must be broken and I'd let the flight engineer know.

It was at this point she gave me a big smile and informed me that she still had all of her own teeth. There must be a connection in there, somewhere, but it still beats me.

Feeding the Multitude

I WAS WORKING a flight out of Philadelphia on a Friday night. Years ago, we always had a fish entrée besides meat for people to choose from on a Friday. It almost went without saying that we ran out of the fish because it was delicious and it was only served on Fridays.

You guessed it, I ran out of fish. This man got so upset with me as I offered him the filet of beef and began ranting, "I am a devout Roman Catholic, and I am going to report you." Note: As if I had any control over how many fish entrees TWA boarded. As in none.

It must have been my lucky day because there were a few priests on board. Hmm, possibly there was a ray of hope here? I explained the situation to one of them and he was so kind, "Not to worry, I'll help you. What is his seat number?"

I hear him saying to this man, "What is wrong my son?" This man in a loud and exasperated tone of voice then started telling the priest about how we did not have any fish for him to eat and he was really upset because it was a Friday.

The priest calmly blessed the filet of beef and said, "It is fish now. You can enjoy my son."

Sometimes the Lord works in mysterious fashion ...

Bobble Head

IT WAS 1995 and I was working a flight from JFK to San Francisco on a Lockheed 1011. All of the passengers had been boarded, luggage stowed and the doors closed for departure but the jetway was still in place. The flight engineer comes out of the cockpit and tells the flight service manager that an agent was bringing down another passenger. Evidently, he had been on an international inbound flight on TWA and it was late.

The agent knocked on the outside of the boarding door and the flight service manager opened it, so we could board this passenger. The flight was nearly full but there was a seat on the left-hand side of the aircraft for him. At the time, he was very pleasant and appreciative that we had delayed the flight for him, which you know is highly unusual. In today's world, this would not happen, period.

We pushed back out of the gate, started our taxi and the safety video was playing. I was standing near a door where this passenger was seated, when I saw his head moving all over the place. It was like a bobble head doll. His eyes were closed and he started shouting in a foreign language at the top of his lungs.

I thought initially that he was having a seizure or some sort of medical issue. As I walked very quickly to where he was sitting, another male passenger stopped me and said he understood what the passenger was saying. He told me the passenger said, the "Devil" was on the aircraft, we were all working for the Devil, and Allah said we needed to be wiped out and he was here to do Allah's work. OMG! This made the hair on the back of my neck stand up!

I turned in my tracks and got two other flight attendants to watch him while I went up to first class to find the flight service manager. She immediately went into the cockpit when I told her what was happening back in coach while I returned to this passenger. By the time I got back to him the other flight attendants were trying to calm him down because he was even more agitated!

Evidently, they told him if he did not calm down, he would be removed from the aircraft. All to no avail. The flight service manager appears now and tells him that the captain was coming back to speak with him. Thankfully, he calmed down a little now.

The captain appeared and told him, due to his behavior, he left him with no choice but to return to the gate, where the airport police would be meeting our flight and he would be removed from the plane. This was not what he wanted to hear, and got very upset again with the byproduct being more shouting and screaming at the captain.

Our captain was trying his best to diffuse the situation, and continued to talk to him in a calm way while repeating multiple times to him to stop yelling and calm down. I could hear him advising this man to go quietly, when the airport police boarded the aircraft because he was in a lot of trouble now. He reminded him a number of times that if he continued acting and behaving like this, it would only make matters worse for himself, with the police, when we returned to the gate. Then the captain got out the big gun, and also told him it would be a federal crime if he caused any trouble for the crew when we taxied back to the gate. As he was leaving, he turned to us and said, "If you have any problems call me right away."

Well, it is like watching water come to a boil, it always seems to take forever and our return taxi to the gate was no different. It felt like an eternity in our minds while the two of us continued to watch him. Finally, we heard the engines shutting down and we breathed a sigh of relief, but wondered how he would behave when the police got onboard.

What? It was as if someone turned on a light switch. All of a sudden, he was very calm and departed the aircraft with the police as if this was totally normal! Have you ever been in a bad car crash and are just thankful you survived? Well, I think that was how the crew felt after he left.

But here was the next problem. Now all of the bags in the belly of the aircraft had to be matched to the passengers on board for security reasons. No small task and hours later we finally left JFK.

I guess if there was any good news here, it was that we were lucky this passenger was removed while we were still on the ground. It would have been a very scary incident if we had been at our cruising altitude. I bet those passengers seated near him had a story to tell their family and friends later. I know I did ...

Fire In Pants

MOST OF THE sports teams and individual stars were very nice when we had them on flight BUT having said that there is always an exception to that rule.

I had an NBA basketball team, who will remain nameless, on board flying to LAX for a game with the Lakers. They nearly filled the Lockheed 1011 first class and when we say fill you can imagine all of those tall, massive men.

Unfortunately, they were behaving badly. Approximately half of them decided it was just fine to sleep on the floor! Yuck I know, sleep on an airplane floor. Now I know the legroom probably wasn't that good for them, but this was in the years when we actually had a lot of legroom, especially in first class. And I guess the seat belt sign didn't apply to them either since it was on. Oh, excuse us, we know you were so special and the hell with a seat belt sign, especially when you can sleep on the floor.

Anyway, they wouldn't listen to the flight attendants' pleas, this isn't safe for you, someone is going to get hurt, if there is an FAA inspector on board we could get fired. Nothing moved them! Even the flight engineer came out and tried to reason with them. Talk about the stereotype of spoiled, over indulged athletes!

OK boys, you don't want to follow the rules, well listen to this on the PA. The captain announced we had to make an unscheduled landing to offload uncooperative passengers for safety violations. That of course, meant they would miss their game the next day. Cha-ching!

Guess who got fire in their pants returning to their respective seats and shut up the rest of the flight. They lost their game the next day. Karma can be a bitch!

One Stormy Flight

THE YEAR WAS 1954 and I had just started flying. It was a night flight on a TWA Martin 404, twin-engine propeller aircraft. We were flying from Newark to Pittsburgh when we flew into a violent rain and hailstorm. To put it mildly there was no "coffee, tea or me" because we were all buckled into our seats, as the plane pitched and tossed, like a toy in the sky, at the caprice of Mother Nature. Finally, after what seemed like hours and hours, we landed at the Pittsburgh airport.

As I, the only hostess, and the two pilots walked to the crew lounge, we talked about the effects of the storm on the plane. Me in my naive way being new to the job said, "But the planes can take it." "No, they can't," snapped the captain. He was visibly edgy and who could blame him after that ordeal. Indeed, there was no using that plane now. The wings had to be checked to make sure the spars holding them had not cracked. The leading edges of the wings were dented, and the landing lights were broken.

Another aircraft was being flown in so that we could return to Newark. As I sat in the crew lounge, I thought about the dozen or so passengers who had been on that flight that I had a chance to talk with briefly. One woman told me this was her first flight. I wondered if she would ever fly again.

Me, well it was trial by fire and it wasn't stopping me. I flew for three more years and loved every minute of it!

Removal of a Violent Passenger

YEARS AGO, BEFORE cell phones, you didn't know about episodes like these on the plane. Here is the actual flight report that the captain submitted followed by two letters from passengers that were on board who were witnesses. The names of the crew and passengers involved have been redacted:

I was the Captain on Flight 269 on the 25th of June, 1979. We were en route from STL to LAX, at 39,000 feet. Approximately, over Farmington, New Mexico, I received a call over the interphone from the aft of the aircraft. The flight attendant asked for help from the cockpit to control an unruly passenger.

At about the same time another flight attendant knocked and entered the cockpit. She also asked for help. She was very upset. She said the passenger was demanding more beer and was using foul language, he could be heard in most of the cabin. One female passenger in the cabin was crying from fright. I sent the flight engineer back to see what he could do.

The coach cabin was full except for two seats. There were about 15 children, several of which were unescorted.

The flight engineer returned to the cockpit in three or four minutes. He said the passenger was demanding more beer and was using foul language. I asked him if he thought the passenger could be calmed down. He said, "No." At this moment, the flight attendant in the aft called again and asked for help. The passenger was in the galley demanding more beer in the same abusive manner and pushing the flight attendant.

I then sent the first officer back to tell the passenger he could not have more to drink and that if he caused any more trouble we would land.

In about two minutes, I got another call from the aft cabin. This time the flight attendant said, "You had better send the flight engineer back here because he is choking the first officer."

I told the flight engineer to get the handcuffs and subdue him anyway, you can. I was not there, but it seems that when the flight engineer got back there, five or six male passengers had the abusive passenger down. At this time, the handcuffs were put on and the passenger was placed in a seat with two male passengers next to him.

Back in time—when I sent the first officer back, I called L.A. dispatch to tell them of the problem. I wanted to land at either LAS (Las Vegas) or PHX (Phoenix). I received a release to land at LAS and dispatch said they would have the police there.

After the passenger was subdued, I went back to see if the flight could go on to LAX.

The flight attendants were very upset, the passengers were upset. We moved as many female passengers away as we could.

At this point, I talked to the passenger. He said, "I want a fucking beer." I said, "No." Then he asked if I could take the cuffs off, they were cutting into his wrists. I wasn't about to turn him loose after all that trouble.

It was my decision that the safety of the flight was in grave danger. When it takes two of the cockpit crew and five male passengers to subdue one violent male passenger—the flight is in danger and it was time to land.

In this report, I have tried to give only the facts that I had to work with at the time.

I would also like to make my commendation for the rest of the crew a part of this report. (Names were redacted here.) They were courteous and professional at all times; I am sure the passengers' comments will bear me out.

There were also several passengers that were of great help and should get a thank you from TWA. I believe flight attendant, (name redacted), has their names. A passenger who is a M.D., (name redacted), was with us all of the way. His report is included.

Now here is an "amazing part of this story" from the flight attendant on board who sent us the captain's flight report and the two passengers' letters: We made an unscheduled landing in LAS and the authorities hauled him away. This was 1979. He was represented by the NV Federal Defenders office, then headed by my future husband, who I didn't meet for another five years. When I asked him whatever happened to this guy, he said he was a real creep and got four years in Federal prison. The reports speak to the incident best.

Now the old adage of "it's a small world" really shows you how small it is! Here are two letters from passengers on board that flight:

I am writing this letter concerning the outstanding and courteous crew of TWA flight 269, on June 25, 1979, on the flight from St. Louis to Los Angeles. Approximately two hours into the flight an intoxicated passenger became very loud and aggressive, ranting and shouting obscenities in the cabin. The flight attendants answered his calls quickly and courteously. They followed the regulations and instructions of the captain not to serve the gentleman any more liquor. The flight engineer and the first officer both responded to aid the cabin attendants and attempted to calm him down. No amount of talk would soothe him. About 15 minutes later, he became violent and attempted to attack one of the other passengers. At this time, several other passengers restrained him, and the flight crew comforted him. An additional stop in Las Vegas became necessary to turn the passenger over to the authorities. Never have I seen a crew pull together so and attempt in every way to provide for the safety of their passengers. Again, the crew was at all times courteous and executed their duties perfectly. I commend them all in such a delicate situation!

I am a frequent air traveler and would definitely fly TWA again. Your personnel are excellently trained and very nice people. Thank you, (name redacted)

2nd letter from a passenger:

To Whom It May Concern,

We are writing in regard to the disturbance on the TWA flight 269, on June 25, 1979, from St Louis to Los Angeles.

After we had been served dinner, one of the male passengers started harassing one of the flight attendants, asking for a beer in an unnecessarily loud and abusive voice and using obscenities. The flight attendant tried soothing him, but he only became more aggressive and obnoxious, still yelling obscenities. In spite of the efforts of many of the flight attendants and in spite of other persons higher in authority also attempting to calm him down, he continued to grow louder.

The pilot was called and decided to stop at Las Vegas to put the passenger off and so informed the passengers. Shortly after that, the passenger causing the trouble stalked up the aisle toward the front of the plane. Some other male passengers stopped him, and he got extremely violent. The crew had to restrain him for the safety of the other passengers.

At all times, the flight crew reasoned and answered the man politely and in low tones. The man appeared to be quite intoxicated. The crew explained their reasons for refusing him a drink calmly and politely as well.

Sincerely, (name redacted)

Sir Richard Starkey

IT WAS THE '80s and I was working the upper deck on a Boeing 747 from LAX to JFK. I hadn't seen the passenger manifest, so I got a really pleasant surprise when I saw who came up the spiral staircase but Sir Richard Starkey, known to his fans as Ringo Starr, and his wife Barbara Bach. And I might add they were lovely.

The service went very smoothly, dinner was finished and it was time for the movie now. So, I asked people to close their window shades and I turned out the overhead lights. When what did I hear? Ringo in his booming English accent saying, "Night all!"

I'm sure those passengers repeated that story because everyone chuckled.

Night-night ...

Barf Bags Can Be Used For All Kinds of Reasons

MOST OF YOU wouldn't know that planes used to fly all of the time with less than full loads. (Airline jargon for number of passengers on board.) Yes, they would leave the gate with maybe 20–30% of the seats full. And you had no seat assignment. There were no calling out rows by the gate agent for boarding, first class passengers were called to board and then the coach crowd got on next when the agent announced their boarding was available. And those of us who were with the company traveling on passes (that is called a benefit and free), the agents would let us board with the passengers in those circumstances. Normally we boarded last.

What does this have to do with "barf bags?" Well, I had a friend who was also a TWA flight attendant and she told me this was a great way to make sure someone didn't sit next to you. So, I decided to try it out, here's the story:

I knew that the load was going to be light that day and the gate agent had already given me my boarding card. I wasn't in the mood to sit next to anyone and possibly be put in the situation of having to chat them up. What to do? I sat down in a coach row for three, in the aisle seat, then pulled out a barf bag from the seat pocket. The barf bag was then placed on a drop-down table in the middle seat. Wide open of course. Then I put my head back with my eyes semi closed and tried to have a look of total pain and discomfort. As anyone walked past and looked, I'm sure they were thinking, "Oh, there is a row with only one person," they then saw that barf bag and guess what? They kept on moving, mission accomplished. I had the whole row to myself. Thank you to my BFF who taught me the barf bag trick.

Don't try that today. You would probably be asked to take another flight by the flight attendant after they reported this to the cockpit.

Buh-bye

MOST OF YOU do not know that there are a minimum number of flight attendants that can work a specific airplane. This has to do with passenger loads and the doors being covered by a flight attendant in an emergency situation. And other times TWA, knowing that the flight loads were always full, would actually have these flights set up to have what we called an "extra" flight attendant working the flight, in addition to the rest of the scheduled crew. This was to make sure the meals were served and trays picked up before landing. I had some flights where we would literally take the trays away from passengers on descent, leaving them with their fork poised to their mouths, throwing the trays into the back lav for landing, and then sitting down to buckle up on our jump seats, as the plane was touching down on the runway for landing. All because it was impossible to finish the service without that extra flight attendant. No, I'm not kidding about the forks poised in the air and trays in the lavs.

But back to my flight: I boarded a plane in STL that was going to Las Vegas where I was the "extra" flight attendant to help during the meal service. This flight had started in Columbus, Ohio and a few passengers were already "lit," if you get my drift, when they got to St. Louis. To say the inbound crew aggravated me for over serving some of these folks would be putting it mildly. We could now be looking forward to a full load, short flight time and drunks already on board. A sure-fire concoction for trouble.

One man in particular in the overserved group was not only intoxicated but obnoxious too. He thought he was funny. NOT! Why does every drunk in the world think they are funny? Another topic for another day. I tried to just ignore him on this ground stop but when he decided to hang his long underwear from the overhead rack to dry (from a previously spilled drink) I yanked them down, tossed them at him and went straight up to the cockpit to tell them about this obnoxious drunk passenger.

The captain jumped up out of his seat when I told him what was going on, put on his jacket and hat, came out and walked right back to this man. Note: the passenger was easy to find, just look for the one sitting there with their long underwear in their lap. Stop laughing! I know you are.

Picture the captain at well over six feet tall, so he certainly had that commanding look of authority. He took one look at our "lit" passenger, and his long underwear, and told him to get his belongings and get off the plane. When he returned to first class, he looked at me and said, "Get the agent and get him now!" I saw a future flight on this man's itinerary, after he sobered up.

Later when we were airborne, another passenger seated a couple of rows in front of where this man had been seated asked me if I'd mind telling him just what the man had said to me ... I asked why and he said, "because I don't EVER want to say it to a flight attendant."

I smiled and said, "Just remember this. Don't hang your underwear, out to dry, from the overhead rack." Should have seen the look on his face as I walked away.

Lotus Position

I WAS NOT a flight attendant, only a TWA employee traveling on a company pass. I was flying from JFK to London and remember it vividly.

It was April 1968 and I boarded Flight 700 at JFK, a flight that left at 7:00 PM. As a company employee on a pass, you took whatever seat was available and thanked the agent when you got your boarding card. Then you got on board, made no waves and tried your very best to be the perfect passenger.

I was seated in an aisle seat in coach, next to a couple who were wearing traditional Indian garb and were both sitting in the lotus position. The gentleman was seated in the middle seat and his sitar was on the floor in front of us stretching in front of all three seats. He had refused the flight attendants' pleas to let them move the sitar. Of course, this left me having no legroom for fear of doing damage to this large instrument. Then there was the lotus position with his leg, knee and the bottom of his foot protruding into my seat area too. Picture me now sitting sideways with my feet, parts of my legs and kneecaps in the aisle. Every time someone wanted to go up or down the aisle, I was trying my best to squeeze my lower extremities back into my seat area.

But it only gets better ... Shortly after the doors were closed, but the plane had not yet moved, our purser got on the PA system and announced, and I am NOT kidding or exaggerating, "A bomb has been found in a British European Airlines flight bag. Will the passenger holding baggage check # ____, please claim your flight bag?" SERIOUSLY!!! Of course, no one claimed the bag, so we sat on the aircraft for hours. Finally, everyone had to de-plane, claim their luggage, have it inspected and re-checked before being allowed back on the aircraft.

The flight finally took off at 1:00 AM, the time we were due to land in London. To be honest I don't know how the crews did it. Putting up with the passengers, little to no sleep and still remaining professional. TWA did hire the best! It was just one more example of what you guys had to deal with.

P.S. Shiva took pity on me. They couldn't keep the Lotus position up and finally sat in their seats with feet on the floor and fell asleep for most of the flight. And the sitar was moved too.

We Didn't Like It

THERE WAS A small wine store across from the hotel where we stayed on our Milan layover. I had purchased two bottles of Chianti there, which I took home, and was very eager to try with my husband at dinner later that week.

My husband and I drank one of them and thought it was delicious but the other not so. In fact, we only took a few sips and both unanimously agreed, this bottle is not good. So, I put the cork back in the bottle (which by the way was almost full) and took it back on my next trip the following week to Milan, something only a flight attendant would do. I know you are thinking, what is she crazy? But this is before the TSA screening of liquids and it was so simple just to put it in my tote bag and bring it on the trip.

Now the important fact here is that our flight service manager on our trip spoke fluent Italian. I asked him to go to the shop with me and tell them I wasn't happy with this wine and I wanted my money back. Nessum problema as they say in Italian. (No problem) What happened? The store owner kept apologizing many times over and suggested another Chianti for me. Plus, he gave it to me gratis. People can't believe that I took a bottle of wine back to Italy and returned it. That is what flight attendants could do. The world was our Costco.

Lunch or What

BEING BASED IN Kansas City, we had a lot of "milk runs." Those were short hops where you had to produce the product, a "quick meal", in the least amount of time. I was only 20 years old and had not been flying that long. I was working the coach-cabin position, which meant that I was hand carrying all of the trays out to the coach passengers. Yes, it was done this way before food carts.

As usual, we were in a big hurry to get the meals out. The choice was lunch or a snack in coach, and of course, I had to ask each passenger for his or her particular request. Toward the end of the cabin, I got tongue-tied. I mean really tongue-tied! My next passenger was male and with true sincerity I asked, "Sir, would you care for lunch or a snatch?"

Oh, my Lord, I was so embarrassed, I didn't wait for his answer. Just the look on his face said it all. I ran back to the galley, and told my flying partner what I had just said and then said, "I need to switch positions with you. I can't ever go out there again."

Fortunately, she took pity on the newbie here and finished serving the meals for me. I can read that guy's mind now, "What did she just say? Nah, she couldn't have said that? But then ... maybe she did?"

Plenary Indulgences

I LOVED FLYING to Rome and often brought a friend along to share in my travels. This being another flight attendant who could share my hotel room with me on the layover and travel free on a company pass. Double win for both of us.

Such was a trip with my good friend and TWA flight attendant Gael. We started our adventure together by flying on the same flight from Chicago to JFK as passengers, and then while she passed the time in our crew lounge, I went to my briefing for our nonstop flight to Rome.

All went brilliantly and Gael had no problem getting on the flight as the passenger load was light. Now she was a "newbie" and believe it or not was a bit nervous about flying over the ocean since she had only flown domestic trips. I know it doesn't make much sense being a flight attendant and afraid of flying over water, but then as I said she was a newbie.

I repeatedly told her what land mass we were traveling over. For instance, Nova Scotia, Greenland, Iceland, Ireland, Europe ... you get it. No ocean travel at all, at least that I told her about, except for that minor part about leaving JFK and that water below. Here is where I immediately shoved a cocktail in front of her, as she was sitting in first class. Bingo, she didn't notice anything. Note: cocktails can cure most everything, and she quickly got over this fear so much that the next thing you know she had put in her transfer to fly international with me. So much for that water thing.

But back to our trip together. After our flight to Rome we took the proverbial short nap in my hotel room and were off to the races in the Eternal City, where we took a tour of Rome and the Vatican. As an aside, Gael is Catholic, and well versed in Vatican history and tradition.

Well, we hit the JACKPOT in terms of plenary indulgences! On approaching St. Peter's, Gael noticed that the "Twenty-Five Year Door" which is normally bricked off had been opened. This was HUGE for two catholic girls from Chicago.

We simply walked through the door, said the appropriate prayers, and just like that all our sins and past offenses were forgiven. Well, we walked back and forth through that door multiple times. No judging please.

To say that two young Catholic flight attendants from Chicago were not overwhelmed with the art, the history and the Swiss Guards would be putting it mildly. Needless to say, we also purchased as many religious items and souvenirs for our families as we could afford. Having something blessed by the Pope to give to our grandparents and parents, well it was the ultimate. But I have to admit, the piece de resistance of our first trip to the Vatican was a group of diminutive African nuns touring with us. They were simply lovely! It was literally like walking in a sea of black robes surrounding us. One could say we almost felt like our feet were floating over the ground.

So, there you have it; no sin, great rosary shopping and meeting the most wonderful group of nuns from Africa. It was a perfect day in Rome! One I will never forget with my good friend Gael.

From Pinball to Trashing

IT WAS BACK in the early '70s and I had been flying for a few years. International flights were still exciting to me and there was always something fun to do on a layover. Little did I know what Paree, or Paris as the bourgeoisie would call it, had in store for me on this trip.

Background: the purser on our flight had been flying around ten years. He lived in Florida with his wife and commuted up to Kennedy. He had lived in Paris for a number of years before he started his flying career and spoke three different languages fluently. Plus, he had a locker at the LaGuardia airport where he kept things that he had gotten on layovers. Why did he need the locker? Because he accumulated so many things from his overseas layovers that he couldn't take them all back on his flights home to Florida. What was he accumulating? Things that he would sell to antique shops in Florida.

Now back to my flight. The flight over to Paris was not exceptional. No celebrities, no crazies, just nice people going on vacation or business. When we arrived at the hotel the purser asked if anyone wanted to go to dinner that night with him. Three of us said yes and we made a time to meet in the hotel lobby.

As I said, he had lived in Paris for a number of years and when we met in the lobby, he suggested dinner in a part of town that none of us were familiar with. We got on the underground and the next thing you know we were getting off in the most picturesque area, with cobblestone streets, shops, restaurants and old apartment buildings. It was charming to say the least. We followed our "leader" now to a restaurant and when we entered you would have thought we were royalty. Oh, the "la bise" known as air kissing that went on between him and the staff, who he obviously knew quite well, and then of course we were quickly greeted with the same lovely French custom.

For those of you who are not familiar with the art form of "la bise" here is an explanation. You are to lean in and touch the other person's cheek with your cheek while puckering your lips and making a light kissing sound with your lips. Never and we repeat never touch your lips to their cheek and very important, you must make that kissing sound with your lips. Think of the kissing sound from your lips, not your voice. Comprendre?

But back to our evening, after a fabulous dinner that only the French can prepare, we left to go back to the hotel, and on the underground the purser suggested that we all stop at a bar and play some "pinball." The other two flight attendants begged off and said they were too tired but me, "Oh sure, sounds like fun."

As the two of us walked into this bar I was flabbergasted to see a huge square room, with pinball machines lining all four walls. There must have been a total of probably a minimum of seventy-five machines. In the center of this room was a four-sided bar with stools surrounding it. The place was brightly lit and all of the machines were in use making for a din of noise, but after a few minutes it all blended together. What to do? Obviously get two glasses of wine from the bar and wait for a machine to open up. Finally, one did and we jumped on it immediately and started playing.

After about thirty minutes my new companion, the purser, says, "I'm going to go to the les toilettes and then stop and get us another glass of wine. Guard our machine because someone will want it. If you have any problems, see those three men standing over there talking together, I recognize them.

They are a TWA cockpit crew. Just go over to them and tell them you are TWA." And off he goes.

So, I put my empty wine glass down on top of the pinball machine to show that I was claiming it and just started to do some people watching. Remember I said, there was a bar in the middle of the room. No one was sitting on the side of it closest to me, except one woman. She had dyed black hair, black eyeliner with wings at least a half an inch long coming out from the corners of her eyes (you ladies know what I mean) and lots of eyeshadow. She was wearing a low-cut sweater showing plenty of cleavage, with a skin tight skirt and a pair of stiletto heels. A cigarette dangled from her fingers and occasionally a smoke circle would be blown through her ruby red lips. But when she looked in my direction, she was staring daggers into me. I'm thinking, what is your problem lady?

Within a few minutes my escort aka purser arrives back with two glasses of red wine and says, "Did you have any problems?" Still puzzled with this problems issue, I sipped my wine and said, "Why would I have any problems?" To which he replies, "Well, you're the only woman in here who isn't a prostitute." After I almost spit out my red wine on him, I laughed and said, "Oh, my God that woman over at the bar has been staring daggers at me." To which he replied, "Oh she is the madam. She probably is wondering what you are doing in here." Me too? This is another adventure.

After some more pinball, as we were walking back to the hotel, the purser said to me, "Do you want to go trashing tonight?" Trashing? What is trashing? He explains to me that he knows all of the best areas of Paris, their trash pickup days and goes on to say, "You can't believe what these people throw out. They just leave it on the curb. It's amazing. I have a locker in La Guardia because sometimes I can't bring everything home. I just put it in the locker and take it home little by little. And I sell this stuff to antique dealers in Florida. They love me."

As offbeat and possibly fun as that sounded, my better judgement and tired body both said, "No," to which he replied, "If I find something too heavy for me to carry, I'm coming back to the hotel and waking you up, so that you can help me carry it back." To which I simply said, "Don't do that because I will have to hurt you then." I laughed but he knew I meant it.

Flash forward now: We had boarded the plane, and I had stowed my crew kit and was getting organized for the flight, when I turned around and who was standing in front of me but the purser. He was wearing a vintage '30s or '40s leather cap with a chin strap and a pair of matching leather goggles with red lenses. Snoopy would have been jealous! I have to admit I was stunned for a few seconds and then started laughing and said, "Where did you find those?" With a slightly wicked smile he replied, "Last night when I was trashing, you should have come."

I have to admit there was a split second when I thought maybe he was right, but then my better judgement did click in again.

But that was not the end of the story. He boarded the passengers through the first class door with his Snoopy hat and goggles on. The passengers loved it! And after they were all on board I put on the hat and goggles, and went out to our first-class passengers to take their drink and dinner orders. I told them, "Just call me Lucy."

So many good times ... little did I know that many years later TWA's flight 800 to Paris would have a tragic ending.

Put It Where

THE THREE FASTEST forms of communications: telephone, text and tell a flight attendant. Well, this one went through the ranks like wildfire! Here's the story ...

Years ago, we actually had huge carry-on closets or more like bins, with doors on them that locked for takeoff and landing. They were located in first class but were used by all of the passengers, first and coach. Needless to say, they would be totally full and most of the time it took two flight attendants pushing into the doors, so that they could get them to lock. In other words, they were bulging.

The flight was full and at the last minute a passenger came running down the jetway with his bag in hand. It was too large to fit under a seat and definitely could not be put in the overhead since they didn't have doors on them like they do today. And now those luggage closets were full too.

The flight attendant says, "Sir, I'm sorry there is no room for your bag. I'm going to have to give it to the agent and let him check it." The passenger is furious and says, "Oh, just stick up your ass." Really! Now we're going to let you wait for it because this one is good ...

"Sir, if you had done that in the gate area before you were boarding, we wouldn't have this problem now."

Touché

Remembrances

MY FATHER, RAYMOND Edward Anderson, following his service in the U.S. Army and a brief career in banking, then went to work for Eastern Airlines. He started as a ticket agent, then became a supervisor of agents, and lastly was promoted to station manager with Eastern Airlines from the early 1960s until the airline's demise and liquidation in 1991. His friendship with a younger ramp worker for EAL, Winston Gary Goodin sparked a meeting with Gary's older sister, Clara, who my father married.

Their friendship started a ripple of meetings and events that in large measure directed the course of my own young life and career. I grew up with uncles and cousins, along with my father, who worked together and played together at the Jacksonville airport in Florida.

As a child I was fascinated by the airport and even more so with the flight attendants. I recently ran across a paper that I wrote while in grade school that jolted many memories. It was written on March 30, 1973:

"What I Want Most to do When I Grow Up"

The thing I want most to do when I grow up is to become a stewardess. Stewardesses always seem to be kind; have a good appearance and they help you when you need help. They get to travel all over the world. I think the best thing for me to be is to be a stewardess. I'll have a lot of fun and I don't think anything else will fit me.

Note: Had to giggle when I read this, my teacher gave me 100 A and of course I was very proud of that too.

So, as destiny would have it from a young child to college, I was determined to join the aviation family for myself. Fresh out of college I interviewed with an executive for Delta Airlines in 1983 when I was barely twenty-one, but at the time did not receive a job offer. But I was not about to say no to my dream about joining the airline industry.

Who would I interview with next? It was Trans World Airlines. I interviewed at the end of 1984 and was hired in early 1985 after a round of five grueling interviews. Following eight intensive weeks of safety and in-flight instruction in Kansas City, MO, I was flown to NYC, provided with hotel accommodations for one week, until I, along with fellow classmates could find an apartment and begin our lives as flight attendants living in Queens, taking the Q-10 to JFK to embark on our domestic flights.

To say that I have many personal and wonderful memories from my days with TWA would be an understatement, but one of the most interesting involved the return of the TWA Flight 847 hostages.

Now for those of you who are either too young to remember this or have forgotten about all of the hijackings that were going on in the airline industry at that time, I'll give you a little history. TWA had been operating a flight from Cairo, to Athens and on to Rome, TWA Flight 847. This flight number would continue on to the states out of Rome and most of the legs were always full. Remember TWA was the major American carrier in the area and because of this we were always concerned about hijackings. Especially because Athens was a hotbed of extremists at the time too.

On June 14, 1985, it happened. Our flight 847 was hijacked with 153 passengers on board, five flight attendants and three cockpit crew members. Captain John Testrake was forced to crisscross the Mediterranean from Beirut to Algiers and back again, landing in Beirut three times.

Captain John Testrake answering questions from reporters in
Beirut while one of the terrorists looks on.
Photo from now defunct *TWA Skyliner* magazine
and used by permission of Jon Proctor and Jeff Kriendler.

As the world watched in horror, Captain Testrake was pictured in the cockpit window with a hijacker holding a gun to his head. Little did we know what was happening inside the aircraft, the terror, the beatings, what the flight attendants and passengers were having to deal with.

Then the unthinkable happened. On June 15th during the first stop in Beirut a twenty-three-year-old U.S. Navy diver, Robert Stethen, was severely beaten by the hijackers, shot point blank in the head and killed, to have his body thrown from the forward cabin door onto the tarmac of the Beirut airport. It was horrifying!

All of us at TWA were extremely worried about our crew members and our passengers on that flight. During those seventeen days we were always asking one another, have you heard anything yet. What have you seen on TV? What will President Reagan do? Our passengers were quizzing us during this time too. It was a subject that the company had asked us not to talk about on the plane with them. And as the consummate professionals we did as asked. When would it end?

The nightmare was not over until July 1st, when the last freed Americans departed aboard a U.S. military plane from Damascus to Frankfurt, Germany, where after going to a military hospital in Wiesbaden they were met by friends, relatives and Vice President Bush. They were later flown back to the states to Andrews Air Force base on a TWA 1011 aircraft by a TWA crew.

Now this is where I became involved. On July 2, 1985, I received a phone call in the wee hours of the morning. Both my roommate David and I were on call, and we were given instructions to report to our domicile at JFK at the crew scheduling desk. After the crew assembled our flight service manager began to brief us. The company had ordered limos to take us over to LaGuardia, where we would transfer to a private bus that would take us to Andrews Air Force Base outside of Washington D.C. Once we arrived, we were to relieve the international crew which was airborne bringing our hostages back home, and then we would fly them back to JFK. To say I was stunned to be doing this would be an understatement and I wondered what the day had in store for us.

After we arrived at Andrews, my roommate and I, along with the rest of the crew, were given red carnations to pin on our uniforms and then we waited outside with a crowd, near to where the press was also assembled. There were going to be ceremonies on the tarmac replete with a military band playing and a color guard there to meet the plane. I have to say it was very moving when that beautiful red and white TWA L-1011, carrying the former hostages, touched down at 3:26 PM to cheering relatives and friends along with the press. There were so many carrying signs, and flowers and waving American flags furiously! Moments later family members were allowed to board the aircraft. I can only imagine the relief and happiness that all were feeling inside that plane.

Then the Presidential helicopter arrived carrying President and Nancy Reagan. We were told they had just flown over from Arlington Cemetery where they had laid a wreath on navy diver Robert Dean Stethem's grave. A solemn reminder in all of this happiness that everyone did not come home.

The President and Nancy Reagan then boarded the aircraft, and spent a few minutes of private time with the hostages and their families. They returned outside and came down the red carpeted stairs, stood at the bottom of them where they welcomed and shook hands with each individual person disembarking the plane.

I have to say it was inspiring to watch Captain Testrake being the first hostage walking down those stairs, followed by the other passengers and crew, as they each finally stepped on American soil for the first time since their ordeal began at the Athens airport on June 14th. After everyone was deplaned President Reagan and Captain Testrake spoke to the crowd. President Reagan said at the start of his remarks, "I'll have to wait for a second until I swallow the lump in my throat." Then he went on, "there's only one thing to say and I say it from the bottom of my heart, welcome home. We're so happy you're back safe and sound." He also said it was Nancy's birthday that Saturday and that "she's declared that you are the greatest birthday present she's ever had." At the close of the ceremony Reagan waved toward the group and said, "Go home." He had decided that a gala reception at the White House was not in order to speed the former hostages and their families home.

My memories have faded over the past thirty-five years, but I do know that at some time surrounding the boarding and disembarking, reunions and celebrations, our incoming crew had the honor of shaking hands with both President Reagan and First Lady Nancy, who bid our flight a safe passage home to New York.

Many of the returning hostages left for their homes with their families from Andrews Air Force Base, but our crew was deeply honored to accompany this plane and the remaining passengers back to JFK.

As an aside, my mother had recorded on VHS some of the newscasts that aired from that day's events, serving as video proof that her daughter had been a witness to this historical event. In the mid '90s when I went to re-watch the tapes with my husband, much to our dismay, we discovered that it had accidentally been erased by another recording of the Masters Golf tournament. So much for recording history. Most importantly though my memories of the day can never be erased, nor my wonderful days of being a TWA flight attendant.

We All Need a Hug

I WAS WORKING a flight from JFK to LAX in December of 1985. In my suitcase was a copy of Dr. Leo Buscaglia's book of lectures, *Living, Loving and Learning*. Now for those of you who are not familiar with his books, Felice Leonardo Buscaglia, also known as "Dr. Love," was an American author, motivational speaker and a professor in the Department of Special Education at the University of Southern California.

Hugging was his trademark! It happened by accident when an attendee wanted to give him a congratulatory hug after a presentation. Seeing this, hundreds of others began lining up to hug him as well. Eventually, the hugging sessions lasted longer than some of the presentations, but he was known to stay until he embraced the last person.

I recognized Dr. Buscaglia immediately as he boarded the plane, and I checked the names on my passenger list just to make sure it was him. It was! Now overcoming a lifetime of timidity, which one would never know since I was a flight attendant, I decided to greet him and tell him how much I appreciated his books, *Love*, *The Fall of Freddie the Leaf*, *Loving Each Other* and the current one in my crew kit.

His eyes sparkled and his smile was one of the kindest I'd ever seen. In hindsight I wished I had asked him to autograph his book, but as it turned out he gave me a much more special gift. Dr. Buscaglia rose from his seat and gave me one of his infamous hugs on a TWA L-1011.

I'll leave you with this thought, he was the first to state and promote the concept of hugs as needing five to survive, eight to maintain and twelve to thrive.

As he said, "It is not enough to have lived. We should be determined to live for something. May I suggest that it be creating joy for others, sharing what we have for the betterment of person kind, bringing hope to the lost and love to the lonely." Leo Buscaglia, March 31, 1924—June 12, 1998, a life well lived.

July 17, 1996
A TWA Jetliner Bound for Paris
EXPLODES

IT IS A date of infamy for TWA.

It is a date that we can remember exactly where we were when we heard the tragic news that one of our 747 aircraft exploded shortly after takeoff from Kennedy airport.

It is a date when we all say another prayer for those who perished.

It is a date we still shed a tear when we remember it.

It is a date when many of us still make the pilgrimage to visit the memorial site outside of Mastic Beach, NY, to say another farewell to our friends, family members and passengers aboard that doomed flight.

It is a date that we who worked for TWA will always sadly remember.

May all on board always be resting in eternal peace ...

***

For those of you who are not familiar with this tragic event, it was the evening of July 17, 1996, when a TWA Boeing 747-100 took off for Rome with a stopover in Paris. There were 230 people on board that evening. The plane climbed to an altitude of 13,800 feet on a clear night when the federal aviation officials lost radar contact with it at 8:45 PM. Many witnesses on a beautiful clear summer evening reported seeing a flashing streak of light going up in the air toward the plane. Then there was an explosion turning it into a flaming ball of wreckage, which fell into the water approximately nine and half miles south of Suffolk shore, followed by a massive search of approximately five miles of debris in the ocean for survivors. None were found. A full four years passed before the National Transportation Safety Board, NTSB, released its official report. It was found that the probable cause was that a spark in the center fuel tank led to the explosion. Many ask why the world's 747 aircraft weren't grounded and checked for this problem. This leads to many questions since they were not. Unfortunately, in all likelihood all of the questions and documentaries made about this tragedy will never be answered. At least in our lifetime.

We would like to share four individual stories with you about that tragic day. The first story is written by a flight attendant who either by fate or a higher power was kept from working that flight on 7/17/1996. The second story is from one of our senior flight attendants who also questions her fate. The third story is written by a very junior flight attendant who explains how he and his crew reacted to the news when they heard what had happened, as they were the crew who was to work that aircraft back from Europe to JFK. The fourth and last story is from one of our TWA pilots whose fiancée was aboard that flight and how he deals with his grief.

We hope that if you are on Long Island that you will visit the TWA Flight 800 International Memorial. It is a beautiful site for reflection and remembrance which is located next to the water, with wonderful gardens and a Memorial wall listing all of the names of each who perished that night. Please look at their website for more information. The memorial is located off of the William Floyd Parkway, Mastic Beach, NY, at the Smith County Park.

That Fateful Day

I NEVER WANT to give "it" the title of anniversary because that is too much of a sugar coated term. What is it? It is the horrific day, when TWA Flight 800, a Boeing 747-100, exploded and crashed into the Atlantic Ocean near East Moriches, New York, on July 17, 1996, at approximately 8:31 PM EDT, 12 minutes after takeoff. All on board perished.

I am going to tell my story about this fateful day ...

It has always seemed odd that I can remember everything about that day even before this tragedy happened. I woke up in the morning, it was one of those hot bright summer mornings in NYC, and the air-conditioning was going full bore to keep my apartment cool at 37th and Lexington Ave.

My routine when I woke up was to roll over and boot up my little laptop. Recently TWA had enabled us to go online and look at open flights for that day. These were flights that you could trade into that needed flight attendants. Now remember this was back in the day of dial up internet. The laptop booted up and I tried to go on-line but the computer crashed hard!

On this day, I was scheduled to work a flight late in the afternoon to San Francisco on a Lockheed 1011. It was a great flight or trip as we called them, but I wanted to look at the open trips for that evening "just in case" there was something better. No dice today because of my computer crash, so I got out of bed and went about my usual day to get ready for my trip later in the afternoon.

My mode of transportation was the Cary Bus from Grand Central to JFK, and after arriving at the airport, I went downstairs to the TWA computer room to pull up all the pertinent info for the flight. As soon as I opened the door, I saw Lonnie Ingenhuett, a flight attendant, staring back at me in a reflection from a mirror. We smiled and waved at one another. A little note here: people used to get Lonnie and I mixed up all the time because we looked alike, and there was usually the question that we would ask one another, "So, will I have to apologize for you again." Then we would laugh.

I went to a computer, and Lonnie came over and got on one next to me, while his girlfriend Barbara Kwan, also a TWA flight attendant, stood next to him. We were all exchanging pleasantries, talking about our trips, when he told me that in the morning there were eight cabin crew positions open on this particular trip and that they had traded into it. He explained that they were to deadhead (that means ride as passengers) to Paris, and then the crew would catch a commuter flight down to Rome where they would layover. Evidently, the company had a broken 747 in Rome that had been down on maintenance and they needed a crew to work it back to JFK the following day.

Ah what a bummer, I would have loved to be with this group, especially when I saw the names of everybody on that crew. Actually, now there would be two crews on that 747, one working the flight and another one just deadheading on that aircraft. They were all such special people and I knew they would be having a great time together.

Lonnie, Barbara and I all finished our check in duties and let the company know we were there, then said our goodbyes and the obligatory "Hope to see you soon, have a safe trip." And off we went to our respected aircrafts.

Fast forward now, my plane had taken off en route to San Francisco and I was working the first class cabin. It was a few hours into the flight when I was called to the cockpit. As soon as I opened the door, I could immediately tell by the looks on the pilots faces that something was up. They had just gotten word that TWA flight 800 had gone down off the coast of Long Island.

I think for a moment that my brain started swimming with this information when they told me and I could not take it in. It was like being frozen in time, as the mountains in Vail Colorado floated underneath us.

Lonnie and Barbara's smiling faces immediately jumped into my mind. Then I started remembering all of the other crew members on that flight that I knew too. This can't be happening! I hear myself asking, "Do you know if there are survivors? I don't understand how a 747 just falls out of the sky?" The cockpit really did not have any good answers.

After some more conversation about what they knew and didn't know, the captain decided that I should take the crew, a few at a time to the lower galley (the L-1011 had a galley in the belly of the plane where passengers could not go) and inform them about this terrible accident in private. He felt it would be better for them not to be seen by the public for a while, when they learned about this, and they really needed to know before our arrival in San Francisco.

Down in the galley when they learned the news about flight 800, some stood there in a stupor for a few minutes looking like they had just been punched in the gut, while others shed tears and immediately came to me for an embrace. It was even more upsetting when I shared the names of people that I thought were crewmembers on that ill-fated plane. I heard over and over again from each one of them, "No, it can't be! This is not happening. I just flew with this person. My God they have children."

There was not one of us that did not know someone on that flight. Some were our personal friends; some were former roommates and some we knew had family members that were traveling that night on flight 800. You see, even though we were a large group of employees this job was not like going to the office each day. You flew with so many different people over the years. And many of the flight attendants on board had been with the company twenty, thirty years or more. We would find ourselves going to Rome one day with one another and then London or Los Angeles or Oklahoma City a few months later together. We were all vagabonds with suitcases, flying to wonderful places, coming home to our families or friends to leave shortly thereafter to fly with another group of flight attendants. It was like a huge brother or sisterhood where we were all interconnected.

We knew about each other's families, socialized at home together, where we all lived, who was pregnant, who just had a baby or a grandchild, and where they were planning on going on vacation. Yes, there were thousands of us but we were all connected together in so many ways, from all of those many years of knowing one another. Sharing our lives on the plane and layovers. Those intimate conversations on the jump seats after the meal service, or during the movie. This was not like sitting in a cubicle, or a private office in a building getting to know a handful of people over lunch, or at the yearly office Christmas party. We were one huge family.

After telling each crewmember about this awful news and really the little I knew then, I went back up to the cockpit and told the captain that the entire crew had been briefed. He asked how everyone was doing, and I told him they were all total professionals and were working as usual as a team now. The passengers had no idea. Thank God, people did not have their own laptops to use on board the aircrafts yet. In time, they would find out about it when they deplaned.

While I was in the lower galley, I had thought about what it would be like when we got to San Francisco, probably there would be television crews and reporters there trying to interview TWA personnel. This was really the last thing we needed! I asked the captain, if he could speak with our operations department, when we got close enough to SFO, to see if it was possible for them to arrange to have our transportation van that picked up us in front of the terminal, instead come back onto the tarmac to pick us up and take us to the hotel. How they were able to do that I still do not know, but they did. Moreover, it was a Godsend not to have to walk through that terminal.

To this day, I am still so proud of my crew being the professionals that we were, even in our shock and grief, we continued working as if nothing had happened. A full plane of passengers never had an inkling or clue as to what they were going to learn once they landed.

Now, if you go back to the start of my story and remember that little laptop that I was talking about, well that little laptop never was able to boot up or work again. If you do not believe in "guardian angels," or the hand of God having an influence over our daily lives, this true story and my reflection of this "fateful day" just might make you think twice. I would have traded into that trip in a heartbeat but for an unseen hand.

See all you guys on the other side when I am called.

Was It Fate

I BEGAN MY flying career with TWA in 1961 in the winter, and was based out of New York's Idlewild Airport. At that time TWA had what we referred to as Super Connies, which were those propeller aircraft that you only see in movies now. I loved working in the galley but those planes did not love me.

As I said, it was winter and usually the weather was bad. All of that bouncing around in the skies from one airport to the next in the states, with cigarette and cigar smoke in the air, resulted in plenty of airsickness for me. My passengers even handed me their airsick bags.

I was actually thinking of quitting because of this airsickness problem. Then as fate would have it, one day my roommate came home and said, I PASSED THE BERLITZ LANGUAGE TEST! TWA had a policy then that to be able to fly international flights the hostesses, today called flight attendants, had to pass a language test. Maybe flying an international flight without all of those many legs bouncing around in the states would be the answer to me keeping my job. She said the test was easy; just answer twenty questions in any language. I knew that four years of Latin would not help me, so I memorized twenty answers in French from the Berlitz course. They went something like this. Please do not worry, I will get your food. Please do not worry, I will get you a blanket, etc. etc. etc.

Note: At that time, one could pass the Spanish language test but that didn't mean you had to spend the rest of your life flying to Madrid, you could change it up with Paris, or some other exotic city. The same for every language. Why? Because there was always a purser (and they were all men, women could not be hired to be pursers then, yes you read right) on the flight who spoke the language of destination. As TWA was desperately in need of language qualified hostesses, Berlitz helped pass me with my pathetic French language skills.

I was in heaven now flying flight 800 to Paris. Out on Wednesdays, back on Fridays, the rest of the week off. We could sign for our meals at one of three small hotels in Paris and order most anything on the menu. Yes, just sign the bill and they sent it to the company to be paid. It was flaming this, and gourmet that, and then we continued on to another one of the hotels and finished with a fantastic French dessert. Now just don't think we went crazy here, liquor was not paid for by the company and we did have a cap per person on how much we could spend but it never seemed to be a problem. I know it's fabulous, but they did this for the international crews then. Domestic layovers, well you were on your own to pay for your food. Domestic crews were treated like the stepchildren. I know double standards!

Anyway, the good news was I also got over the problems with airsickness. I loved Paris so much that I flew nothing but that flight for over six months. Then I finally broke down and started flying other flights to amazing cities that TWA went to, but Paris was always my first love. What a life!

Sadly, many years later TWA's flight 800 exploded over Long Island shortly after takeoff in July of 1996. The exact cause is still debated. Many believe it was shot down by a missile. TWA retired flight number 800 after that. My heart still grieves for all who perished that day, some I had known for many, many years.

The question will always be, was it fate that gave me Berlitz to keep my job, and send me to Paris at the beginning of my flying career and then kept me from flying to my beloved Paris on July 17, 1996? Only fate knows ...

Flight 800 and Her Lessons of Love

AT 8:02 PM ON July 17, 1996, TWA flight 800, a Boeing 747, pushed back from gate 27 at the TWA Flight Center at New York's John F. Kennedy International Airport, destined for Paris' Charles de Gaulle Airport and Rome Fiumicino. At 8:19 PM the majestic red and white airliner lifted gracefully into the twilight of the warm summer night and made a gentle, sweeping turn out over the Atlantic, beginning what was to have been its long overnight crossing. At 8:31 PM, nearly the exact same moment the sun hid her last light behind the horizon, an explosion of controversial origin brought the 747 and all those aboard down into the sea approximately seven miles east of Center Moriches on Long Island's Fire Island. Within minutes, hundreds of small craft responded in a heroic effort that lit the night as the people of maritime Long Island displayed a humanity and generosity of spirit that touched the world.

Half a world away, blissfully unaware of the horrors that had befallen our inbound equipment, my crew and I were resting peacefully on the second of two beautiful nights in the Eternal City, enjoying one of the most coveted layovers in the TWA system. I was a new-hire reserve TWA flight attendant and had gotten the call for the trip from crew scheduling just after my reserve duty had ended. The scheduler had informed me that I was under no obligation to take the trip but thought that once I heard what the assignment was, a 747 trip with a fifty-hour Rome layover, I might be interested, provided I could get myself to the airport in an hour, which I most certainly made happen. And so, it came to be that I found myself ensconced with wide-eyed wonder in the city, that quickly captured my heart and holds it tightly to this day.

On the morning of July 18th, I awoke casually, made strong espresso in my room, and sat down to enjoy some fresh bread and prosciutto that I had purchased the night before. Suddenly there was a furious pounding on the wall from the room of my flying partner, a fellow reserve and neighbor in Kew Gardens, next door. I threw on a shirt and looked into the hallway and saw that his door was open. He motioned me in, his face ashen, where he sat glued to the television, mesmerized and unable to speak. The image on the screen was one of blackness. A field of darkness, dotted with occasional orange flames. Within a few seconds of glancing at the image, the phone rang and my friend answered the call. It was from the front desk informing us that our flight was "indefinitely delayed." When my friend asked for particulars, the response was, "We haven't further information, but you may want to look at the CNN channel."

Hanging up the receiver, he relayed the conversation to me, and I put together what I thought made perfect sense given the images flashing across the screen. In 1986, I had been booked on a Pan Am flight to Rome that had been cancelled when Mediterranean airspace had been closed due to the U.S bombing of Libya. Certainly, the images we were seeing must be those of burning oil fields in the night, images made familiar during the Gulf War. Clearly, we must have gone back into Libya in the night and were now unable to overfly the area as had been the case in years past. "Oh," I said with a sigh of relief, "It's just more Desert Storm stuff. We'll be stuck here for a while. We may as well just head down and get a cappuccino," feeling somewhat excited by the prospect of staying another day in this beautiful city, and in no hurry to get back to the Q10 bus and an apartment shared with seven other new hires in New York. "No, no that's not it at all," then my flying partner said, "Look!" as at just that moment, the words "TWA 800" rolled across the bottom of the screen. My stomach lurched and a deafening pounding began to throb in my temples, as all went dark, and my head spun in confusion while I tried to figure out what this all meant. "*Timetable*!" We both screamed nearly in unison, as he began rummaging wildly through his tote bag looking for a schedule, and he then began frantically flipping through a dog-eared copy he found inside. It was a summer 1996 *System Timetable* with a painting of a Constellation, a 747, and the words "Celebrating fifty years of Transatlantic Service" proudly splashed across it. "Paris!" he shouted out next and a heavy sorrow descended upon the room as the implications of this information became clear: a 747, lots of fuel, a big crew and a heavy load.

After a moment, we began discussing our own dilemma. This news was terrible but we couldn't quite connect how this tragedy in New York was the cause of our "indefinite delay" out of Rome. We were scheduled to operate flight 849 home, which flew from Rome to New York and then on to Los Angeles. As we sat in his room for about an hour, glued to the television and awaiting further word from operations, a note slid under the door informing us of a gathering of the crew, in one of the hotel function rooms in an hour. We found ourselves joining three other 747 crews who were all staying in the hotel. Now some forty TWA pilots and flight attendants had come together to seek and exchange information, to comfort and console one another, and in many instances, to begin the process of mourning the lives of those lost.

It was here, in this expansive meeting room that the agonizing answers to our many questions were provided, and we came to learn of the perfect storm that had caused our flight out of Rome to be cancelled. It was the night of July 17th and a mechanical problem had grounded the late New York to Rome flight # 848, causing it to be combined with the Paris flight # 800. Thus came to be the unique routing of flight 800's New York to Paris, and then on to Rome journey, instead of two separate non-stop flights. This now meant that the crew originally assigned to operate the Rome flight would now deadhead (ride as passengers) on the Paris sector, and then continue on to Rome as working crew. Flight 800 now carried a total of thirty-five JFK based pilots and flight attendants instead of the standard seventeen. And to make matters worse, TWA's flight 810, Boston to Paris, had cancelled that night also, and those passengers had been routed through JFK as well.

In that meeting room, we sat in a wide circle, all forty, some of us, in various states of shock and grief. Perhaps one of the most heart-wrenching experiences I have ever been a part of was that of passing the flight manifest around that circle. Watching the hearts of my colleagues break open, as their tear-filled eyes scanned the list, was more than I could do and I had to look away often. Of course, it came into my own hands soon enough and I, as did we all, knew several of the names on the computer printout. I closed my eyes and saw Flight Engineer Richard Campbell standing on the spiral staircase smiling down, and laughing heartily with me in the first class galley, as we exchanged witty banter on my last trip just a week earlier. I could feel radiant, twenty-four-year-old Jill Ziemkiewicz, in step beside me, as we walked down the concourse in St. Louis a few weeks earlier, our wheeled suitcases in tow, gushing on about the perfect gown she had just found for her upcoming wedding that summer. And I could see Flight Service Manager Lani Warren, standing proudly in her timeless Ralph Lauren uniform, at the boarding door of the 767 that had taken me back to Boston after I had just been hired at company headquarters in St. Louis that summer. I remembered how she had come back after the service to welcome us as new hires to TWA, share her experiences and pride in a TWA career that had spanned decades.

As I began to shudder reading the list, a strong and solid arm reached out and around me seemingly from nowhere, and a 747 captain I had not met before took me under his wing for the rest of the morning, lending me some much-needed strength. Before long, the mourning turned toward celebration, and we started to share stories and remembrances of our friends. Little groups broke off and eventually laughter began to ease the pain a bit as well, and I got the privilege of watching my TWA family do what they did best, loving one another. Yet I felt that as a new hire, I had no right to my pain, and I feared that I had no place among people who had just lost loved ones of twenty or thirty years, so I tried to sneak back to my room, feeling ashamed and something of an accidental voyeur. But one senior flight attendant saw me make my clandestine move for the elevator, and intercepted me, and would not allow me to run from the moment. She gently guided me to a quiet corner, and we had a beautiful and loving talk. She told me that we were one TWA family and reminded me that this loss affected us all no matter how long we had been with the company. She went on to say that certainly our beloved airline would never be the same again, and no one knew what the future would now bring, but that we were all on equal footing in our confusion and fear. She told me that this loss would affect us all deeply but differently, and to expect many different reactions and to take nothing personally, and to just give every one time and space to go through whatever they must. Then another senior flight attendant came up and hugged me tearfully, wanting to know how I was doing and then another. Here were these beautiful, elegant women who had just lost lifelong friends reaching out to this new hire to nurture and soothe my pain, and soon I found that I was able to do the same in kind for still others. This was the real lesson of that day, what those wonderful women taught me in Rome in the aftermath of flight 800 was that the more we give of ourselves to care for one another, the more profound the healing we experienced for ourselves. Today, I no longer shy away from someone else's pain; instead, I now offer to sit quietly alongside them in it. When we sit and hold someone's hand, our own hand is held as well, and when we love another wholeheartedly, we love our own hearts back to wholeness.

After some time, a few of us wandered down to the hotel restaurant and had a somber meal with some other company employees that we had just met there. I had little appetite and only nibbled on some hard rolls but the company did me good. Afterwards, I felt myself needing a still more profound sustenance. Only a higher power could provide comfort in the midst of such an emotional storm and I longed for a place of spiritual refuge. A quick walk through the lobby and hallways turned up a few others who felt the same. I remembered that Pope John Paul II had long traveled on TWA aircraft and had called TWA "Traveling With Angels." Although not Catholic, I hoped the nearby Sistine Chapel could provide some spiritual consolation that had thus far proved elusive that day, and soon five or six of us headed out for the Vatican. Once atop of the long ramp at the entrance to the walled city, we simply flashed our yellow and red TWA I.D. badges to the guard, whose face immediately softened into a look of compassionate understanding and we were immediately shepherded inside the museum. We wandered through the beautiful artifacts of the Vatican Museum collection which provided a welcome distraction, but it was the Sistine Chapel that beckoned ahead, promising solace, serenity, and some blessed relief from the sorrow of the last several hours. As one enters the Sistine Chapel, the silence is enveloping and insular, and there is a serenity that quiets the soul. It is as if time ceases to exist and instead one finds an eternal, impermeable stillness. It was, as hoped, the one place I felt out of sorrow's reach. And there I found comfort, as I lifted my heart in prayer for my colleagues and their passengers lost at sea, for my broken-hearted co-workers, and for my company which now faced unprecedented challenges.

When the first TWA aircraft arrived in Rome a day later, we boarded with great trepidation, not knowing what had brought the mighty and venerable 747 down to earth two days earlier. Suspecting terrorism, we braced ourselves for any number of unpleasant scenarios on our return flight to JFK. Yet we steeled ourselves, not only because we now had a job to do in honor of our fallen colleagues, but because on board with us now were several family members of those lost in the crash. One such passenger was an elderly Italian grandmother who had lost both her daughter and granddaughter in the crash. Seeing me struggle with my own emotions, and shaking as I tried to pour coffee in the aisle, she rose up from her seat and put her arms around me, whispering "bambino, bambino" and stroked my hair, as we just stood there in the aisle together, comforting one another. This is how it was all the way back to New York, the passengers and crew connecting in such a loving and a human way, and getting through the ordeal together. Our arrival in New York was both somber and celebratory at once. We were met by both the base manager and our union representatives, who escorted us to Hanger 12, where we received a tear filled and hearty welcome from most everyone we came across. The sight of Air Force One parked inside the hanger and black-clad snipers positioned on the roof and scattered throughout the employee parking lot, however, was not lost on any of us, and ratcheted up the already high anxiety to even loftier levels.

A few days later, I was assigned a bittersweet trip on which I am very proud to have served; it was on a Douglas MD-80 aircraft from New York to Denver and then continuing on to Salt Lake City, carrying the human remains of four of flight 800's victims, including one of our pilots. First class had been emptied except for the families and I was assigned the front cabin. The families were pre-boarded at JFK by TWA Care Team volunteers and we were introduced to one another before general boarding commenced. In 1990, I had been working as a gate agent with SkyWest Airlines at LAX, when a tragic air traffic control error led to the runway collision between a USAir 737 and a SkyWest Metroliner with the loss of all aboard the SkyWest aircraft. I had escorted a family in much the same way in the aftermath and I was more than happy to help in this instance as well.

We took off from JFK around sunset and headed west for Denver. As I served the first round of drinks, I found that most everyone was more interested in meeting and talking with one another, and surprisingly with me as well, than eating, so we decided to hold off on dinner while everyone visited. The families got to know one another, shared stories about their loved ones, and even included me in these conversations where I learned about all of their beautiful memories. Everyone wanted me to know how wonderful TWA and its volunteers had been to them despite the negative publicity we had received in the press. The criticism had been that the airline had been slow to release the passenger list, but the truth was that the FBI had seized the manifest, nearly immediately, after the accident and the airline was prohibited from commenting on it.

On our flight to Denver it was a beautiful, clear night and we chased the sunset into the inky twilight and deep violet night sky, as dinner was finally served. I kept the drinks flowing and laughter and a few tears filled the forward cabin. Upon landing in Denver however, things took a reverent tone, and we bid a teary and formal farewell to our new family, and handed them over to more TWA volunteers and a phalanx of TWA staff, who lined the jetway to pay their respects, before we headed on to Salt Lake City where the scene was repeated as well. I found the honor of working this flight was not only life changing and humbling but I was forever grateful for it.

In retrospect, flight 800 was lost at sea, and the resplendent colors of our glorious TWA no longer grace the skies, but who will ever forget where they were the night of July 17, 1996, a night which marked a moment in time that resoundingly delineated a before and an irreversible after. What flight 800 taught me is what it meant to come together with indefatigable love in the face of unfathomable tragedy, to transcend darkness, and to soar to new heights never before imagined. What we woke up to in Rome that day, and around the TWA world was unprecedented and incomprehensible. Yet that morning crews the world over donned their navy uniforms, and rose to the challenge of delivering the gold standard of quality service and unparalleled safety, even as we grappled with staggering personal loss that took our breath away. Despite the uncertainty and confusion of those first days, the people of TWA held their heads high, and performed their jobs with admirable pride and professionalism that became the envy of an industry. Our passengers came aboard and expressed their continued confidence in our airline, our maintenance and our crews. Moreover, we worked diligently to show our gratitude and to prove to the world that its trust was well placed. In addition, we did it with a sense of renewed pride that morning and in the days to come, for we did it in honor of our dear departed colleagues, the crew of TWA flight 800, forever in our hearts, the true legacy of TWA.

Sunglasses for the Sea
First published in *Airways Magazine*
Written by, author Mark L. Berry

13,760 Feet—My Personal Hole in the Sky,
by Mark L. Berry, his personal memoir about TWA FL. 800

July 17, 2016
by Mark L. Berry
NEW YORK—It has been 20 years since Susanne kissed me goodbye on her way to work that included a business trip to Paris. 20 years since TWA Flight 800 took off out of JFK, and that red and white Boeing 747 rained back down in pieces.

Last year on July 17th, the press was there camped out in the sand. The ambitious crews were shuffling at the water's edge—cameras and microphones in hand, pants legs rolled-up above bare feet. I carried a pair of carnations to the ocean's edge, just like I did the first time 19 years before, at the first memorial service for Susanne and the rest of the 230 victims.

And like before, various media outlets were trying to capture my grief along with the other mourners for the passengers and crew whose lives ended in a fireball offshore Smith Point, Long Island.

I had mixed feelings about the press attendance. Grief is a difficult-enough emotion without a potentially unlimited audience peering at me through up-close camera lenses. But the news crews were also there to do some good.

The memorial site needs additional funding to maintain it, so the exposure would be good for soliciting donations. Also, I feel strongly that the truth behind TWA 800's demise still needs to be revealed—so I allowed them to capture my raw moment, and accepted the resulting lack of privacy.

Like the evening it happened, the sky was mostly clear and the sun was setting. The cameramen were taking advantage of the magic hour when the daytime glare was gone, and there was still enough ambient illumination so that artificial lighting wasn't necessary. My polarized Maui Jim sunglasses were hooked on the collar of my T-shirt since they were no longer needed to defend the day's strong rays.

Those sunglasses are mentionable because they were my late fiancée Susanne's—or at least the initial replacement for the pair she carried with her to her premature end. She'd bought them shortly before her final-flight demise, and they'd caused quite a discussion between us.

Me: *Could I wear them?*

Her: *No, you break or lose every pair you own.*

Me: *They're rather expensive, can we afford them right now?*

She looked at me unsure. All of our combined finances were out in the open as we attempted to qualify for the Connecticut house we were trying to buy together.

I worried those sunglasses were an extravagance at the time, but Susanne loved wearing them. They shielded her Danish blue eyes, and the stems disappeared into her long Scandinavian blonde hair. Ultimately those sunglasses came to me, mangled in an all-too-real representation of her final fatal moments, sealed in a clear FBI evidence bag along with the rest of her onboard belongings. Imagine opening the personal effects of your most loved one after they have spent a week in 140 feet of salt water, and then been sealed in a plastic 'evidence' bag.

I once tried talking out loud to her post-mortem, during a grief-releasing moment of levity: *And you think **I** don't take care of **my** sunglasses?* She didn't answer, even inside my head.

The store that sold those sunglasses to her refused to replace them when I visited. *The damage wasn't a result of their workmanship.* When I subsequently discarded them, that simple act unraveled me. It became my unexpected moment of truly letting go of her.

Years later I described that sudden grieving experience, and Maui Jim corporate relations eventually responded with a more favorable outcome than my retail store experience: they replaced her sunglasses along with a sincere note of sympathy. The new pair became a part of Susanne that I could once again hold onto, and then I wore them for her for many years.

Perhaps Susanne didn't want me to have the last laugh. Perhaps there is still some poetry to her life beyond her living years. Or, perhaps my ability to care for eyewear simply has never improved beyond the days when she accused me of breaking or losing every pair I owned. Those Maui Jim sunglasses were still hooked to the neck of my T-shirt when I waded into the surf with carnations in hand and the press in tow.

The flowers split apart as I threw them into the waves as hard as I could, once again symbolizing the release of my grief as I let go of my offering into the ocean; but I did not yet fully grasp the scope of what was really happening, as much as I thought I did.

As I waded back out of the foam from the breaking waves, a *Newsday* reporter asked me how I felt. I tried explaining that sending flowers into the surf was like letting go all over again—a symbolic act of honoring a burial at sea, much like shoveling dirt into a grave on land. But only then I realized this was also how I once felt while discarding Susanne's original mangled Maui Jim sunglasses into a trash can, and I reached for their replacement pair that should have been at my neck.

They were gone. They had flown free into the waves during the exertion of my floral goodbye. Either Susanne, or the sea, had once again reclaimed them.

Note: Author, Mark L. Berry, was a pilot for Trans World Airlines when that fateful night happened and TWA Fl. 800 was lost. His beautiful fiancée, Susanne, was a passenger on board. He shares his life in his memoir, 13,760 Feet—My Personal Hole in the Sky, which can be purchased at Amazon and is available for free in Amazon's lending library if you are a Prime Member. 13,760 feet is how high the TWA 747 was flying when it exploded into thousands of pieces and fell into the ocean. Mark is now a captain for American Airlines and you just might see him wearing his TWA baseball cap in the cockpit. Thank you Mark for letting us share your story.

Remembering TWA's employees, family members and passengers who perished in the crash of Flight 800, July 17, 1996

TWA Flight 800 International Memorial and Gardens, William Floyd Pkwy, Mastic Beach, NY 11951. Open to the public.
Photo courtesy of Linda Chabraja.

Flight 800 Crew

Captain Ralph Kevorkian
Captain flying First Officer Steven E. Snyder

Flight Engineer Richard G. Campbell
Flight Engineer Oliver Krick—in training
Flight Service Manager Jac Charbonnier
Flight Attendant Constance Charbonnier, wife of Jac
Flight Attendant Dan Callas
Flight Attendant Janet Christopher
Flight Attendant Debra Collins DiLuccio
Flight Attendant Arlene Johnson
Flight Attendant Raymond Lang
Flight Attendant Maureen Lockhart
Flight Attendant Sandra Meade
Flight Attendant Grace Melotin
Flight Attendant Marit Rhoads
Flight Attendant Michael Schuldt
Flight Attendant Melinda Torche
Flight Attendant Jill Ziemkiewiez

Earlier that evening the Rome flight had been canceled and the entire crew was deadheading on Flight 800 to Paris to work the aircraft to Rome.

Captain Gideon Miller
First Officer Rick Verhaeghe
Flight Engineer Douglas Eshleman
Flight Service Manager Lani Warren
Flight Attendant Sandra Aikens-Bellamy
Flight Attendant Rosemary Braman-Mosberg
Flight Attendant Warren Dodge
Flight Attendant Daryl Edwards
Flight Attendant Joanne Griffith
Flight Attendant Eric Harkness
Flight Attendant James Hull
Flight Attendant Lonnie Ingenhuett
Flight Attendant Barbara Kwan
Flight Attendant Elaine Loffredo

True Tales of TWA Flight Attendants 393

Flight Attendant Elias Luevano
Flight Attendant Pamela Cobb McPherson
Flight Attendant Olivia Simmons

TWA employees and family members on board that evening traveling as passengers:

Patricia Anderson, former TWA flight attendant and her husband Jay Anderson

Alecia Carlos-Nelson, former TWA flight attendant

Paula Carven, TWA flight attendant and son Joseph Von Hedrich

Vera Feeney, wife of TWA JFK ramp agent and daughter Deirdre Feeney

Francis Gasq, former TWA flight service manager and his mother Claire Gasq

Donald Gough, TWA captain and his wife, TWA flight attendant Analei Ralli Gough

Elsie Ostachiwicz, TWA JFK customer service agent and daughter Chelsea Harris

Pamela Lychner, former TWA flight attendant and daughters Katherine and Pamela Lychner

Twyla Nelson, daughter of former TWA flight attendant

Scott Rhoads, husband of TWA flight attendant Marit Rhoads

Susanne Jensen, fiancée of TWA Flight Engineer Mark L. Berry

And to all of the families, who lost their loved ones that were passengers on TWA flight 800, July 17, 1996, we offer our most heartfelt condolences. They will always be remembered in our thoughts and prayers.

> May all be resting in eternal peace …

In Conclusion

Photo of Howard Hughes and Jack Frye
courtesy of the TWA Museum.

FOR THOSE OF you who are old enough to remember TWA and for those of you who aren't, we just wanted to give you a little background of what was one of the greatest names in airline history.

Three men nicknamed "The Three Musketeers of Aviation," Walt Hamilton, Jack Frye and Paul Richter formed a partnership that would change the history of aviation starting in the 1920s. They founded America's first airlines, flying schools and maintenance facilities. They developed the first DC-1, the Stratoliner, the first pressurized airplane and the Constellation which was considered the jewel of the skies. Paul and Jack even did extensive Hollywood movie stunt flying which led them to meeting Howard Hughes during the filming of *Hell's Angels*.

In 1931, TWA moved to Kansas City where it established its central location and maintenance base, and inaugurated the first air cargo service in the U.S. with a shipment of livestock from St. Louis to Newark.

History was in the making now in 1932 because TWA wanted a tri-motor airliner that had very stringent requirements. Douglas submitted instead a design for a very modern twin-engine which was much more advanced than the Boeing 247. What resulted was the DC-1 and actually, only one was ever manufactured and was sold to Howard Hughes in January of 1936. But in 1934 the DC-2 followed, and it was longer and even greatly improved over the DC-1. Its inaugural flight was May 14,1934 and within two weeks it broke its own speed record four times, there was nothing in the skies that could match it for speed and comfort. On August 1, 1934, three transcontinental round trips per day were scheduled. The new service was advertised as "The Sky Chief." The coast to coast luxury liner took sixteen hours at 200 mph to make the trip but the passenger load factors skyrocketed. With the stretched fuselage, the DC-2 had room for berths and held from fourteen to twenty-one passengers. Passengers could now fly coast to coast at night in Pullman berths.

In 1939 Howard Hughes invested money into TWA and in 1940 under heavy secrecy construction of the Lockheed Constellation began. It was to have a range of 3,000 miles at over 280 mph. Each engine was able to propel the plane at an elevation of up to 20,000 feet. The passenger load was fifty-four, with non-stop hops coast to coast in about eight and half hours cruising above all inclement weather. This was the first plane in the world that could support transatlantic service.

WWII had other plans for the Constellation's first flight on January 9, 1943. The United States government, under war time requisitions, was to take possession of this Constellation and all others produced for the duration of the war. Thus, the plane was to be painted in wartime camouflage.

When the plane saw the light of day in Burbank, CA, TWA, along with Lockheed had succeeded in creating a masterpiece of aircraft design. On April 17th at 3:56 AM, the plane lifted off from the Burbank airport on its way to Washington, D.C. as the world's fastest commercial airliner.

The 2,400-mile flight was flown in 6 hours and 58 minutes, with the plane arriving at Washington National Airport, with a picture perfect touchdown in front of waiting crowds of military leaders, reporters and proud citizens. But military leaders got a big surprise when this plane landed, for it was not painted in Army green, but dressed out in blatant TWA colors and flown by Jack Frye and Howard Hughes. The brass were not pleased, but it was great advertising for TWA and the ever marketing Howard Hughes. The plane was then turned over to the military for the war effort and even fighter planes at the time couldn't match Connie's "top speed" of 340 miles per hour.

After the war, TWA's Constellation airplanes, known as the Connies, went into commercial passenger service, with routes in the United States, and then on to Europe and points further. They were off to France, Switzerland, Italy, England, Germany, Ireland, Greece, Spain, Egypt, Palestine, Jordan, Iraq, Saudi Arabia, Yemen, Oman, India, Ceylon, Portugal, Algeria, Tunisia, Hong Kong and Libya. Years later TWA, Trans World Airlines, a fitting name, was known by all.

The rest is history as TWA flew the world in Lockheed Constellations, Convair 880s, Douglas DC-9s, Boeing 707s, 727s, 747s, 767s, 757s and the Lockheed 1011s.

It truly was a great ride …

Photo courtesy of the TWA Museum.
TWA Museum, 10 Richards Rd. #110, Kansas City, MO.
Open to the public.

TWA History provided by Kaye Chandler Productions, from the private collections of Paul Ernest Richter, Jr., co-founder of TWA. The collection is now owned by his daughter, Ruth Richter Holden, former flight attendant for TWA.

Up, Up and Away
TWA

THE NEW YORK International Airport, also known as Idlewild Airport began construction in 1943 and started operations in 1948. By 1954, Idlewild, later renamed John F. Kennedy, had the highest volume of international air traffic of any global airport. In 1955, the Terminal City master plan was conceived for the Idlewild airport and it was decided that all major airlines would build their own terminals.

TWA always being a trend setter went to the renowned architect Eero Saarinen to discuss plans for building their new terminal. Who was to meet with him? None other than the director of public relations for the company. Why? Because TWA wanted their terminal to be a symbol of the airline when they were advertising.

TWA's terminal became not only a concrete symbol of technology but it truly captured the sensation of flight. How was that possible? Saarinen's design was a symmetrical arrangement of four curved, concrete shell roof segments. They flowed seamlessly from the piers that supported them. Each of the four was separated by narrow skylights, with a circular pendant clock at the center point where they all met.

You would not be alone to note the resemblance to a bird or plane in flight. Saarinen described it as an abstraction of the idea of flight itself. Not only was this free flowing look on the exterior of the building but it was carried through to the interior as well. With curved staircases, columns which disappeared into the ground and the ceilings, but there was also a sunken waiting area for the passengers. Through massive windows, viewing the operations of the airport was truly a magical way to start your trip. Then as if you were going on a space adventure there were two tubular corridors with TWA's famous red carpeting, which took you to the boarding gates. You would also see hundreds of thousands of custom white ceramic floor tiles and believe it not 486 variously shaped window panels. Remember TWA's livery was painted in crimson and white. Therefore, the interior mirrored those colors.

This genuine masterpiece of architecture did not happen in a short period of time. The plans were started in February 1956, and Saarinen's office created 130 possibilities. The drawings took approximately 5,500-man hours to complete. Finally, in November 1957, TWA announced that they had a design for their renown, never to be copied terminal.

It was not to be until 1960 that the terminal's bird like roof was poured as a single form. It took 120 hours and at the end of 1960 it was supported by four "Y" shaped piers, when all of the scaffolding was removed. This iconic master piece was dedicated on May 28, 1962.

By 1992 because of financial issues with TWA, the building was beginning to deteriorate. There was talk of the building being demolished. Fortunately, the New York City Landmarks Preservation Committee (LPC) had public hearings in 1993 and the terminal was designated a landmark in 1994, ensuring its preservation. The building was added to the National Register of Historic Places in 2005.

Flash forward to December of 2016 now. Hotel developer, Tyler Morse chief executive of MCR and Morse Development steps into TWA's history. The beautiful TWA building would be soaring again. Mr. Morse's attention to detail and passion for this project left nothing out, not even the smallest thing. As he said, "We wanted it to be historically authentic."

This time the most unique and beautiful building would be a hotel. Original details such as the custom white tiles floors had to be recreated, 486 various shaped window panels were all replaced with replicas of the originals. And speaking of originals, the departure board was restored. It was an iconic Solari board which took Mr. Morse to Udine, Italy where the original board was made over fifty years earlier. You can hear those distinctive sounds that flip signs made at one time, in all the train stations and airports worldwide again. Believe it or not, there are 34,000 flaps that had to be created by hand to preserve the departure board.

Remember we spoke about the signature clock in the center atrium, the chili pepper red sunken lounge and the two tubes with the chili red pepper carpeting. Well, they are there in all of their glory again, those red and white colors that everyone still thinks of as TWA livery. And just to make sure you don't forget those livery colors, there is a fully restored 1958 Lockheed Constellation, parked on the ramp outside of the sunken lounge, where you can even sit in the pilot's seat, look at all of the controls and enjoy an adult beverage. Memories of a golden age of flying.

TWA as an airline might be gone but she will never be forgotten. As we always said, "UP, UP AND AWAY. TWA."

Photos courtesy of the TWA Hotel

TWA'S ICONIC TERMINAL was designed by world renowned architect, Eero Saarinen. Designated a landmark in 1994, Mr. Tyler Morse of Morse Development restored the terminal to all of its "Golden Age of Flying" iconic stature. For more information go to: www.twahotel.com.

Note: Stephanie Johnson and Kathy Kompare, who collected the stories for True Tales of TWA Flight Attendants, have had the pleasure of staying at the TWA Hotel. Besides being beautifully restored you can enjoy their many amenities. Who would have thought that you could swim in a heated, roof top pool year-round, replete with "runway" views and a cocktail in hand? We did! We also enjoyed the huge gym that included a Peloton room, yoga studio and much more. Need more views of the JFK runway, just try laying in your bed in your room! No, we do not kid here. We loved it! Thank you, Mr. Morse, for a wonderful stroll down memory lane.

www.ingramcontent.com/pod-product-compliance
Lightning Source LLC
Chambersburg PA
CBHW030243010526
44107CB00030B/1316/J